JEROME'S WORLD

R. Danube

Black Sea

THRACE

Constantinople
Bosphorus

Adrianople

PONTUS

Sea of Marmara

Nicaea

BITHYNIA

GALATIA

Ancyra

MESOPOTAMIA

Nyssa

CAPPADOCIA

PHRYGIA

Nazianzus

Caesarea

Edessa

Iconium

Taurus Mts.

CILICIA

Beroea

thens

Seleuceia

Antioch

Chalcis

Salamis

Laodicea

Palmyra

Malea Pr.
Cythera

CYPRUS

PHOENICIA

Tyre

PALESTINE
See
←Inset

Sea

Pelusium

Alexandria

←Road to
Jerusalem

YA

Nitria
Scetis

E G Y P T

R. Nile

Red Sea

Tabennisi

Thebes

M.E.P.

JEROME

His Life, Writings, and Controversies

JEROME

His Life, Writings, and Controversies

J.N.D. Kelly

1817

HARPER & ROW, PUBLISHERS
New York, Hagerstown, San Francisco, London

FIRST U.S. EDITION

ISBN: 0-06-064333-1

LIBRARY OF CONGRESS CATALOG CARD NUMBER: 75-36732

76 77 78 79 10 9 8 7 6 5 4 3 2 1

For Minos and Katingo Colocotronis,
Yangos Colocotronis,
and Alec and Tony Georgiadis

Preface

It is surprising that Jerome, unlike his contemporaries Ambrose, Augustine, and Rufinus, has never been made the subject of a comprehensive study in English. He has fared better on the Continent, but none of the excellent, though now somewhat outdated, German, French, and Italian biographies that are available (J. Steinmann's is too light-weight to count as an exception) has been translated. It is my hope, therefore, that this book, as well as indulging a strong interest I have had over many years, will do something to fill the gap. Professional students will, of course, wish to explore certain issues more thoroughly than has been possible in a single volume; in most cases the notes should indicate where fuller discussions can be found. At the same time, since Jerome is one of the most human and fascinating figures of his epoch, I have tried to make the book accessible to the growing number of 'intelligent general readers' who are attracted by the early Christian centuries.

As those familiar with them will at once recognise, I am greatly indebted to the classic biographies of G. Grützmacher and F. Cavallera, the one particularly useful for its analyses of Jerome's commentaries and other writings, the other for its balanced (though in the case of the hero too reverential) assessment of the characters in the story. The footnotes testify to the army of contemporary scholars on whose specialist research I have freely and gratefully drawn. To single out individuals might seem invidious, but I cannot refrain from saying how useful I have found H. Hagendahl for the light he has thrown on Jerome's reading, P. Courcelle for his insight into this and other problems, P. Nautin for his solution of chronological difficulties and for opening up hitherto undiscovered mysteries, P. Hamblenne for his massive confirmation of my surmises about the date of Jerome's birth, and H. F. D. Sparks for his acute survey of Jerome's work on the Bible. This is indeed a period of intense and fruitful activity in Jerome studies; but even so the amount of work still to be done, most urgently perhaps in the provision of properly annotated editions of Jerome's works (even the letters have never received adequate treatment) is daunting.

PREFACE

The book was originally planned, as long ago as the summer of 1970, at the Villa Serbelloni, Bellagio, Lake Como. Certain sections of it in draft formed the substance of the Birkbeck Lectures which I delivered in April–May 1973. I am deeply grateful to the Rockefeller Foundation, New York, and to the Master, Fellows, and Scholars of Trinity College, Cambridge, both for affording me these opportunities and for their splendid hospitality.

On a more personal level there are two friends to whom I should like to express gratitude. The first is Henry Chadwick, who unselfishly let me keep his precious copy of Grützmacher, the Bodleian Library's set being incomplete, for several months. The second is my publisher, Colin Haycraft, who not only invited me to write the book and patiently put up with my (enforced) delays, but when it had been completed made suggestions for several changes and additions which I adopted with alacrity.

J.N.D.K.

Feast of St. Jerome

Contents

Abbreviations

ACO	E. Schwartz, *Acta conciliorum oecumenicorum*.
Anal. Boll.	*Analecta Bollandiana*.
Bull. litt. eccl.	*Bulletin de littérature ecclésiastique*.
Cavallera	F. Cavallera, *Saint Jérôme: sa vie et son oeuvre* (Louvain, 1922), 2 vols.
CCL	*Corpus Christianorum, Series Latina*.
CIL	*Corpus inscriptionum Latinarum*.
Codex Theod.	Theodosian Code.
CSEL	*Corpus scriptorum ecclesiasticorum Latinorum*.
DACL	*Dictionnaire d'archéologie chrétienne et de liturgie*.
DHGE	*Dictionnaire d'histoire et de géographie ecclésiastique*.
ET	English translation.
GCS	*Die Griechische Christliche Schriftsteller*.
Grützmacher	G. Grützmacher, *Hieronymus: Eine biographische Studie* (Berlin, 1901, 1906, and 1908), 3 vols.
JTS	*Journal of Theological Studies*.
LXX	Septuagint.
Mansi	J. D. Mansi, *Sacrorum conciliorum nova et amplissima collectio*.
MGH	*Monumenta Germaniae historica*.
Penna	A. Penna, *S. Gerolamo* (Turin-Rome, 1949).
PG	Migne's *Patrologia Graeca*.
PL	Migne's *Patrologia Latina*.
PLRE	*The Prosopography of the Later Roman Empire* (Cambridge, 1971).
PW	Pauly-Wissowa-Kroll, *Realencyclopädie der classischen Wissenschaft*.
RAC	*Reallexikon für Antike und Christentum*.
RB	*Revue Bénédictine*.
RHE	*Revue d'histoire ecclésiastique*.
TU	*Texte und Untersuchungen*.
VC	*Vigiliae Christianae*.
ZKG	*Zeitschrift für Kirchengeschichte*.
ZNTW	*Zeitschrift für die neutestamentliche Wissenschaft*.

The works of ancient writers other than Jerome are referred to in the conventional way by Latin titles, usually abbreviated (e.g. Eusebius, *Hist. eccl.*). For the convenience of general readers, however, Jerome's works are referred to throughout by English titles (e.g. *Comm. on Zephaniah*, not *Comm. in Sophoniam*). Where these references are to volumes of *PL* or *CCL*, the column indicated is normally (in view of the discrepancy between the editions of *PL*) that of Vallarsi (noted in both *PL* and *CCL* margin), printed after a colon (e.g. *PL* 25 :447); where the volume number is followed by a comma (e.g. *PL* 28, 1200), it denotes the column or page of that volume.

I

Birth and Childhood

(i)

Jerome was born at Stridon, in Dalmatia, almost certainly in the year 331. We have this date from Prosper of Aquitaine, lay theologian and chronicler, whose life (*c.* 390–*c.* 455) overlapped with his. Because of certain difficulties it has been thought to raise, most recent biographers have postulated a rather later date, usually in the middle forties of the fourth century. On inspection, however, most, if not all, of these supposed difficulties disappear, and there seem no solid grounds for discarding Prosper's testimony.[1]

Jerome's birth thus fell at a time when a momentous revolution in the Roman empire, particularly in its relations with the Christian Church, was well under way. The terrible crisis, caused by barbarian invasions, civil wars, and economic breakdown, which had shaken it to the foundations in the third century (235–84) had been overcome. An all-powerful, ruthlessly totalitarian administration now controlled every department of life; and for the first time supreme authority was concentrated in Christian hands. From 324 Constantine the Great, a Christian from at least 312, had been (after a protracted power-struggle) sole emperor of east and west, and was pushing through policies which increasingly favoured Christianity. Only a year before Jerome's birth he had solemnly dedicated Constantinople, the 'New Rome' on the Bosphorus which, equipped with splendid churches, was to be the administrative capital of the east. When he died in 337, he was succeeded by his younger sons, Constantius II (337–61) in the east and Constans (337–50) in the west, and both were keen Christians like himself. The accession in 361 of his half-brother's son Julian, called 'the Apostate' because, although brought up as a Christian, he sought to down-grade the faith and restore a reorganised paganism, meant only a momentary set-back to the new trend. After his death in 363 all the emperors, in east and west alike, were to be Christians.

The impact of this revolution on the Church was dramatic. At the beginning of the century it had been reeling under a violent persecution unleashed by the emperor Diocletian. Now it found itself showered with

[1] For a summary discussion see Appendix below.

benefactions and privileges, invited to undertake responsibilities, and progressively given a directive role in society. When Constantine ascended the throne, Christians had been a minority in the empire—a tiny minority in most of the west and in the countryside—and paganism retained an undisputed hold on all but an insignificant number of the governing class. Now people of all ranks, quick to notice that Christianity had become respectable and indeed fashionable, were streaming into the Church. For generations serious-minded conservatives, notably among the senatorial aristocracy of the west, were to cling steadfastly, often at considerable cost to themselves, to the traditional paganism; there was even to be a pagan revival at the end of the fourth century in the west. But with the great mass of ordinary people taking their cue from their rulers, the movement of steady permeation of society by Christianity could not be reversed.

The full triumph of Christianity was to come towards the end of the century, but the practical effects of the christianisation of the government were visible from the start. One of the most striking of these was the positive role which the Christian emperor was taking, and was expected to take, in the internal affairs of the Church, even in its decisions on doctrine. The controversy which raged over the divine status of Christ and his relation to God the Father provides an instructive example. In 325, just six years before Jerome's birth, Constantine had convoked a great synod at Nicaea (now Iznik, in western Turkey), later to be reckoned the first ecumenical council, with the object (among other things) of settling it once for all. As a result of his personal intervention a creed had been promulgated affirming that the Son was 'of one substance with the Father'. Contrary to Constantine's hopes, this did not dispose of the issue, for while the west generally supported the Nicene definition, the east tended to prefer interpretations which brought out the personal distinctions in the Trinity. So the debate was to rumble on throughout Jerome's childhood and earlier manhood (he himself, as we shall see, was to be challenged to take sides in it),[2] with the emperors summoning councils and proposing formulae designed to secure as large a measure of agreement as possible. These should not be seen as unwarranted intrusions on the part of the state. There was as yet no clear dividing line between the spiritual and the temporal; as a Christian the emperor thought of himself, and, provided he was orthodox (this was the point at which the theory soon broke down in practice), was accepted by the Church as being, the natural leader of the Christian people.

(ii)

Such was the world into which Jerome was born in 331, a world in which

[2] See below pp. 52 f.

the new religion was rapidly consolidating its ascendancy, but in which Christians were becoming more and more divided into those whose commitment was deep-rooted and the much greater number whose Christianity was conventional, superficial, sometimes opportunist. But if we can be reasonably sure of the date of his birth, his birthplace remains an unsolved mystery. The reason for this is that, while he tells us its name, the evidence he provides for its whereabouts is far from precise. We know its name from the brief, tantalising note which, when compiling his catalogue of distinguished Christian authors in 392/3, he inserted about his own origins. His father, he recorded,[3] was called Eusebius, and he himself was born 'in the town of Stridon, which was overthrown by the Goths and was once close to the border ("confinium") of Dalmatia and Pannonia'. Side by side with this should be set the reference by Palladius, the monastic historian (d. *c.* 430), to 'one Jerome, from Dalmatia'.[4] Dalmatia corresponded roughly with present-day Yugoslavia minus Slovenija and the Istrian peninsula, Pannonia with Hungary. The destruction of the town may have been carried out by the Goths in 379 when, after shattering the imperial army at Adrianople (Edirne), they swept through the Balkans to 'the roots of the Julian Alps'.[5] Before long Stridon had disappeared without trace, and neither archaeology nor subsequent literature retains any record of it. Indeed, but for Jerome we should never have heard of it.[6]

Persistent, if unavailing, efforts have nevertheless been made to discover it, practically all the suggestions advanced being in fact little more than guesses. For the first quarter and more of this century most scholars were satisfied that it must have been situated in the neighbourhood of Grahovo-polje, in Bosnia, where as it happens the pre-Augustan border between the Dalmatae and the Pannonii ran. Here a fragmentary inscription was said to have been found attesting a late-third-century boundary agreement between 'the inhabitants of Salvium and of Stridon'.[7] Their confidence, however, evaporated when it was gradually realised that the inscription,

---

[3] *Famous Men* (i.e. *De vir. ill.*) 135. The text runs, ' ... oppido Stridonis quod a Gothis eversum Dalmatiae quondam Pannoniaeque confinium fuit.'

[4] *Hist. Laus.* 41.

[5] So Ammianus Marcellinus, *Res. gestae* 31, 16, 7. A. Mócsy (PW suppl. IX, 1962, col. 578) accepts that this was the date of Stridon's destruction, as did Cavallera (II, 67).

[6] The sole independent mention of Stridon is in Jerome's autobiographical note just cited. The tradition that 'Domnus of Stridon, in Pannonia', was one of the bishops attending the council of Nicaea (325), preserved by Mansi (*Sac. concil. nov. et ampl. coll.* II, col. 696), is a mistake. The true texts of the surviving lists give simply 'Domnus, from Pannonia', without any reference to Stridon. See Gelzer-Hilgenfeld-Cuntz, *Patrum Nicaenorum nomina* (Leipzig, 1898); E. Honigmann, 'Une liste inédite des pères de Nicée' (*Byzantion* 20, 1950, 63–71).

[7] *CIL* III, 9860. For this theory see esp. Fr. Bulič, *Festschrift Otto Benndorf* (Vienna, 1898), 276–80: also *Miscellanea Geronimiana* (Rome, 1920), 253–330. Not only was the restoration of the missing letters extremely conjectural, but the inscription was further suspect because it represented the provincial governor Constantius (later Augustus; the father of Constantine the Great) as already bearing the name Valerius which, so far as was known, he only assumed later.

which had in any case certain suspicious features, was a forgery.[8] More recently opinion generally has rallied round F. Cavallera's thesis[9] that Stridon should be located somewhere between and a little to the south of Aquileia, the huge city (as it then was) at the head of the Adriatic, and Emona (Ljubiljana), the fortress town lying at the foot of the Julian and the Karavanke Alps to the west and north respectively. Today the area in question lies in north-western Yugoslavia, but in the fourth century it was Italian, an outlying part of the province of Venetia-Istria. The pressing need to defend Italy against barbarian inroads had caused its frontier to be pushed eastwards towards the end of the second century, a strip of Dalmatia and a larger segment of Pannonia (including Emona) being brought within the defensive zone and eventually annexed to Italy.[10]

The facts which, according to Cavallera, point decisively to Stridon's being in this north-western region are a number of personal references in Jerome's earlier correspondence. These make it plain (as we shall later see) that the big towns with which he and other members of his family had intimate contacts in the early 370s were Aquileia, with Concordia and Altinum still farther to the west, and Emona. To give but one example, it was a deacon of Aquileia who was to win over his sister, resident at Stridon, to the religious life, and to the clergy there that he was to entrust her because of the manifest unfitness of the clergy of Stridon.[11] Wherever Stridon was, it must have been within easy reach of Aquileia and the other towns mentioned. Cavallera sought to reinforce, and give precision to, his proposal by arguing that Jerome's description of his birthplace as 'close to the border of Dalmatia and Pannonia' cannot mean 'on the border' of the two provinces. He must have intended to pinpoint its position for his readers, but the frontier extended for several hundred kilometres. Cavallera pointed out that, while the key-word 'confinium' can signify 'frontier' or 'border' in Jerome's usage, it can also denote a region which separates two territories without falling within either.[12] If Jerome was using it with this sense here, he was giving a fairly exact idea of Stridon's location, in that eastern bulge of Venetia-Istria which lay between the adjusted frontiers of Dalmatia and Pannonia.

In spite of its wide acceptance, Cavallera's thesis is exposed to serious objections. It seems certain, for the reasons he stressed, that Stridon must have had reasonably good access to Aquileia and Emona. What is much

[8] Cf. G. Morin, 'La patrie de saint Jérôme' (*RB* 38, 1926, 217 f.). N. Vulić, *Festschrift A. Belić* (Belgrade, 1921), 30–2, had already divined that the inscription was a fabrication (I owe this reference to J. J. Wilkes).

[9] Set out in Cavallera II, 68–70: also in *Bull. litt. eccl.* 47, 1946, 60–3. In substance it goes back to Jerome's eighteenth-century editor and biographer Domenico Vallarsi (*PL* 22, 7 f.).

[10] On this see A. Degrassi, *Il confine nord-orientale dell' Italia Romana* (Bern, 1954), chap. vii.

[11] *Letters* 6, 2; 7, 4.

[12] Cf. Cavallera's examination of Jerome's use of the word (II, 69 n.1).

more doubtful is his placing it in close proximity to these towns. There is nothing to show that the Goths penetrated this heavily defended zone in the period in question. It is also curious that, if Stridon once existed there, no trace of it should have survived. Further, the area envisaged lay well outside ancient Dalmatia (except possibly the small slice of it annexed to Italy at the end of the second century), but Palladius states unequivocally that Jerome was 'from Dalmatia'. Cavallera was inclined to brush this testimony aside, but this was a mistake; Palladius had known Jerome personally. Besides, there are some scraps of evidence that Dalmatia was known to be his homeland.[13] If it was, the argument based on the meaning of 'confinium' falls to the ground. The word can have the sense which Cavallera suggested, but it more commonly denotes a common boundary between two (or more) territories, and this seems its natural meaning in Jerome's note about his origins. There is no reason to assume, as Cavallera did, that he was concerned to indicate Stridon's position precisely for his readers. It is more likely that he was speaking quite generally, as when we say (for example) that Strasbourg is on the Franco-German border.

In the light of the foregoing discussion it is evident that we cannot, with the information at present available, identify Stridon even approximately on the map. The most we can say is that it was in the province of Dalmatia, not too far from the Pannonian border, and that its inhabitants must have been able to travel comfortably between it and the important towns in the north and north-west. Even this latter datum does not supply much of a clue, for the road system connecting Aquileia and Emona with Dalmatia was good; indeed the former had close commercial ties with Istria, and through it with Dalmatia. The range of possibilities is wide, and it is profitless to attempt to adjudicate between them.[14]

(iii)

The glimpses we can catch of Jerome as a boy at Stridon are sparse but illuminating. His father, as we have seen, was called Eusebius, a name which he himself used occasionally in addition to Jerome,[15] and which was a favourite everywhere, especially among Christians in north Italy.[16] Like

[13] Cf., e.g., the very curious fact that, according to Jerome (*Apology* 3, 3; 7), Rufinus distributed copies of his pamphlet against his erstwhile friend in Rome, Italy, and Dalmatia. The references of the chronicler Marcellinus, an Illyrian, to Jerome as 'noster' (*Chron.*: *MGH auct. ant.* xi, 60; 63) may point in the same direction.

[14] On roads see N. Vulić, *Le strade Romane in Jugoslavia* (1938); on the commercial and ecclesiastical 'rayonnement' of Aquileia, M. Tadin, *Recherches de science religieuse* 37 (1950), 457–68; in general, J. J. Wilkes (to whom I am indebted for a personal communication on the location of Stridon), *Dalmatia* (London, 1969).

[15] *Chronicle* pref. (*GCS* 47, 1). This is the sole place where he names himself 'Eusebius Hieronymus'.

[16] G. Alföldy, *Die Personennamen in der römischen Provinz Dalmatia* (Heidelberg, 1969), 197.

his own (Hieronymus, i.e. 'of sacred name'), it was Greek (= 'devout'), suggesting that the family may have originally immigrated from the Greek-speaking eastern Mediterranean. From early times, but particularly from the middle of the second century, there had been a massive stream of such immigrants into Dalmatia and the neighbouring provinces.[17] But if so, it had become thoroughly Latinised by the time he was born. We are ignorant of his mother's name; indeed, he tells us practically nothing about his parents, and the very few references he makes to them, while not disrespectful, are perfunctory.[18] It is possible that their opposition, or at least his father's, to his monastic aspirations in his early forties caused him to clash with them,[19] and (since all his writings date from after this clash) this may explain his reticence about them. Yet it is worth noting that, many years later, he could dwell touchingly, and with down-to-earth realism, on the debt of love owed by a son or daughter to a mother.[20]

An unnamed grandmother lived at his home; as a child, he was to recall, there was a tender bond between them.[21] We also hear of a maternal aunt, Castorina, who was probably a member of the household.[22] In addition he was to have a sister, whose name is unrecorded, and a brother with the soundly Latin name Paulinianus. His relations with these two were in later life to be affectionate, and his influence on them strong. But both were very much younger than himself. Paulinianus was to be born in the middle 360s; of his sister all we can say is that he could refer to her as 'a girl' or 'a young woman', both bafflingly elastic terms, in 375/6.[23] He cannot have known either as a lad at Stridon.

Jerome's family was comfortably off, indeed wealthy. The property they owned around Stridon must have been extensive. Even after the devastation wrought by the Goths, he reckoned it worth his while in 398 to send Paulinianus all the way from Bethlehem (where he was then settled) in order to 'sell up the half-ruined farmsteads which had escaped the barbarians' hands'. The sum realised must have been substantial, for he planned to use it to refurbish his monastery with its hospice.[24] The

[17] G. Alföldy, *Bevölkerung und Gesellschaft der römischen Provinz Dalmatien* (Budapest, 1965), 187–9.

[18] *Letters* 22, 30 ('When many years ago I had left my home, my parents, my sister, my relatives . . . '); 66, 14 ('I was obliged to send my brother to my homeland to sell up the half-ruined farmsteads . . . and the ashes of the parents we shared . . . ').

[19] See below pp. 31; 34.

[20] *Letter* 117, 4 ('She carried you in her womb, she suckled you, she put up with your trying ways in childhood . . . She washed your filthy linen and was often befouled with dirty excrement . . . She sat by you when sick . . . She taught you to love Christ'). Cf. *Letter* 125, 6.

[21] *Apology* 1, 30.

[22] *Letter* 13.

[23] In *Letter* 82, 8 (early 397) he states that Paulinian has now reached thirty years of age. In *Letter* 7, 4 (375/6) he uses the terms 'adulescentia' and 'puellares' with reference to his sister.

[24] *Letter* 66, 14.

impression of affluence is borne out by his vivid recollection of racing as a child through the slave quarters of his home, and of being looked after first by foster-nurses and later, like other well-to-do boys, by a personal attendant.[25] As a child, adolescent, and young man he had as his bosom friend a lad called Bonosus, of similar position and upbringing as himself, whom he was to describe as having 'plenty of money' as well as a first-class social standing.[26] His father, as we shall see, could afford to give him an expensive education; and, unlike Augustine, he seems to have had no pressing need to take a job immediately his student days were over.

His parents, as his father's name hints and as he expressly states,[27] were Christians: 'as a baby' he had been 'nourished on Catholic milk'. They did not have him baptised, but were content (we must assume) to have him enrolled as a catechumen, the technical term for someone under instruction for church membership, which would make him count for most purposes as a Christian.[28] There was nothing singular or significant about this. Although Jerome himself was in later life to be an ardent advocate of infant baptism,[29] it was very common in the fourth century, even in devoutly Christian families, to postpone baptism until the storms of adolescence and early manhood were subsiding, or even until death seemed near. There could be a number of reasons for this, the chief being the almost intolerable burden imposed by the penitential system, as it had been then developed, on those guilty of serious sin after baptism. Jerome's personal friends Heliodorus and Rufinus, both from Christian homes, are parallel cases,[30] as is such a notable figure as Augustine, who was baptised at thirty-two.[31] His parents' deferment of Jerome's baptism cannot therefore be cited as evidence of their religious lukewarmness, but it nevertheless remains likely, in the light of subsequent events, that their Christianity was not of the fervid kind that their son was later to admire.

It was at Stridon, naturally, that he attended his elementary school ('ludus litterarius'), the normal age for which was 6/7 to 11/12 years. Some have conjectured, without any solid grounds, that at this stage he must have been taught by a tutor at home, but this is on balance improbable. Private instruction of that kind was in the fourth century

---

[25] *Letter* 3, 5 ('... nutricum sinus ... amplexus baiulorum ... ').

[26] *Letter* 3, 4 ('Ecce puer honestis saeculo nobiscum artibus institutus, cui opes adfatim, dignitas adprime inter aequales ... ').

[27] *Preface to Job* (PL 28, 1082B); *Letter* 82, 2.

[28] Cf. Augustine's revealing remarks in *Tract. in Ioh.* 44, 2.

[29] *Letter* 107, 6; *Dialogue against the Pelagians* 3, 18 f. When he wrote the latter passage, his attitude had sharpened under the influence of Augustine's teaching that infants urgently need cleansing from original sin.

[30] *Letters* 14, 2; 4, 2. Writing *c.* 400 (*Apol. c. Hier.* 1, 4), Rufinus himself places his baptism 'almost thirty years previously'.

[31] At Easter 387, along with his natural son Adeodatus ('born from me carnally as the result of my sin') and his friend Alypius: see *Conf.* 9, 6, 14.

restricted to extremely rich, aristocratic families.[32] In any case Jerome recalls having been dragged from his grandmother's arms to his 'enraged Orbilius'—the proverbial name, derived from a well-known line of Horace's about his own exacting preceptor, for a professional school-master with a reputation for beating.[33] In the western empire these elementary schools existed everywhere, in small places and big alike; they consisted generally of a modest room, often opening on the porticoes of the town forum and sheltered from the weather, the din of the streets, and prying eyes by a heavy curtain. Jerome's curriculum must have consisted largely of reading and writing, with the memorising and recitation of short texts. There was also, of course, elementary arithmetic; Augustine was to recall with a groan what a 'detestable jingle' he had found 'one and one make two, two and two make four'.[34] It is possible, too, that he picked up the rudiments of Greek, as Augustine was to do at his primary school at Thagaste. At any rate as an old man he was to describe the way 'we are accustomed' to teach the Greek alphabet to little boys (learning the letters first in the correct order, then inverting it), as if it were accepted practice.[35]

What was the young Jerome like at this stage? His character and personality almost wholly elude us; no companion of his boyhood has left the slightest sketch of him, and even the earliest of his very few, fragmentary reminiscences of his childhood date from his early forties. All his life he was to be a man of warm affections, as well as of ferocious dislikes and enmities. We can perhaps detect this trait coming to birth in his friendship, intense to the point of hero-worship, with his playmate and fellow-pupil Bonosus. While the speech of his family was Latin, he could probably get along in the Illyrian tongue with peasants and slaves. This would explain his recollection in old age of the word used in that 'barbarous native language' for the local beer brewed 'in the provinces of Dalmatia and Pannonia'.[36] He drops the remark somewhere that as a small boy he enjoyed playing games on holidays;[37] but this scarcely distinguishes him from any other small boy. More revealingly, he frankly confesses in a letter of 382 that years before, when he lived at home with his parents and relatives, he had been a glutton for luxurious food. When he had made his

[32] Cf. H. I. Marrou, *Histoire de l'éducation dans l'antiquité* (6 ed., Paris, 1965), 390.
[33] *Apology* 1, 30. Cf. Horace, *Epist.* 2, 1, 70 f. For Lucius Orbilius Pupillus, of Beneventum, see Suetonius's gossipy, informative note: *De gramm. et rhet.* 9.
[34] *Conf.* 1, 13, 22 ('odiosa cantio').
[35] *Comm. on Jeremiah* 25, 26 (*CCL* 74: 1019). For Augustine see *Conf.* 1, 13, 20, where he describes how much he hated the 'graecas litteras . . . quibus puerulus imbuebar'.
[36] *Comm. on Isaiah* 19, 5–11 (*CCL* 73: 292): the word was 'sabatum'. This may be a piece of miscellaneous information he had picked up; but if he was Dalmatian in origin, as seems certain, the most natural explanation would be that he knew something of the language as a child.
[37] *Apology* 1, 30.

decision to adopt the ascetic life, he had found this much harder than anything else to give up.[38]

In Roman schools great store was set by the cultivation of an efficient memory, which educationists regarded as the surest indication of talent in a child.[39] We may be sure that it was at his primary school at Stridon that Jerome began training his own astonishingly retentive memory, which in after life was to be the chief prop of his multifarious scholarship. It is likely, too, that he proved a quick-witted, eager pupil, for this would explain his father's ambitious plans for his further education.

[38] *Letter* 22, 30: it was the 'consuetudo lautioris cibi' that he found most difficult to give up when he adopted the ascetic life.

[39] So the famous first-century professor and writer Quintilian, *Inst. or.* 1, 3, 1.

II

Education at Rome

(i)

Eusebius sent his son to Rome for his secondary education. The normal age for starting this was eleven or twelve; if this was adhered to, and if our chronology is correct, the date must have been the early 340s. Bonosus accompanied Jerome, and the two probably boarded together. More likely than not, there was no grammar school at Stridon, at any rate none suitable for boys of their position and ability; so their parents sent them further afield. But why to the capital? There must have been a good school at not too distant Emona (Ljubljana), a prosperous military and commercial centre, and certainly at Aquileia, then one of the greatest cities of the world[1] and often chosen by emperors from Augustus to Theodosius I for their residence. There were of course first-class schools at even larger and grander Milan, also frequented by the imperial court and since 300 the seat of the vicar, or governor, of Italy. The most natural explanation is that the two fathers wished their talented children to have the best education available, and as a result of deliberate government policy Rome, like Constantinople, had peculiar advantages in this respect.[2] Secondary and higher education enjoyed enormous prestige in the late Roman empire, and any parent ambitious for his son's future was aware that a glittering, sometimes vastly lucrative, career in the all-embracing government service lay open to students who combined academic success with practical and political shrewdness.[3]

This is borne out by their choice of school. It was no ordinary grammar school that Jerome and Bonosus attended, but the one conducted by Aelius Donatus, the most celebrated schoolmaster of his time. Minutely learned in the pedantic fourth-century manner, he published an elementary grammar dealing with the parts of speech, and a more advanced handbook

[1] A great military, commercial, and industrial stronghold, it was often called 'second Rome'. The poet-professor Ausonius (d. *c.* 395), in his *Ordo urbium nobilium* ix, rates it the ninth greatest city in the world but fourth in Italy (after Rome, Milan, and Capua).

[2] See, e.g., A. H. M. Jones, *The Later Roman Empire* (Oxford, 1964), 707 f., with the notes in vol. 3.

[3] Cf. the line which Ennodius (*fl.* 500), rhetorician and bishop of Pavia, hammered out when recommending the study of liberal arts to young people, 'Put your back into these studies, and the world's at your feet' (*Opuscula* 6: *CSEL* 6, 408).

covering the same ground again but including an exposition of the faults
and excellences of style. He was also the author of elaborate commentaries on Terence's comedies and the poems of Vergil. Although greatly
admired and widely studied (his grammars continued in use throughout
the Middle Ages), these works drew lavishly on the writings of earlier
scholars and had little originality. Criticism of this, or just amused awareness of it, may have provoked him, when he was once expounding to his
class Terence's dictum, 'There's naught been said that's not been said
before', into the outburst recorded by Jerome, 'So to hell with those
who've said what I say before me'.[4] Jerome remained immensely proud of
having once been his pupil, and in later life was to flaunt the complacent
phrase, 'Donatus, my instructor', like an old school tie.[5]

It is not difficult to reconstruct, in broad outline, the curriculum Jerome
and Bonosus followed during their four or five years under Donatus. The
Roman programme of instruction, ultimately Hellenistic in inspiration,
remained remarkably stable for centuries, and even when society became
predominantly Christian generations had to pass before Christians in
general dreamed of altering it. Although there was some pretence of a
'general education',[6] including subjects like mathematics, science, and
music, the staple diet was in practice grammar, more precisely the analysis
and correct use of language, and classical literature. With the aid of
Donatus's own manuals,[7] which summarise his lessons in a highly con-
densed form, we can hear his class repeating by rote their declensions and
conjugations, the elements of syntax in the rudimentary shape to which it
had then evolved, and the catalogue of 'barbarisms', 'solecisms', and other
'vices of speech' to be resolutely shunned. Characteristically, the standard
held up for imitation was not the living language as practised by the best
contemporary masters (such an idea would have been greeted with
incredulity in the Latin-speaking, as also in the Greek-speaking, sector of
the empire), but the fossilised perfection of the past.

The same backward-looking reverence for the classical ideal dictated the
choice of authors to be closely studied as literature; without exception
they were the ancients. The favourites were Vergil, the foundation of all
Latin liberal culture, the poet *par excellence* (like Homer in countries where
Greek predominated); the comic playwright Terence, who had lived away
back in the earlier half of the second century B.C.; the historian Sallust, of
the first century B.C., admired for his moral aphorisms and epigrammatic
brilliance; and of course Cicero, valued equally as orator, philosopher, and

---

[4] *Comm. on Ecclesiastes* 1, 9 f. (*CCL* 72: 390). For the dictum see Terence, *Eunuchus*, prol. 41.
[5] Cf., in addition to the text cited above, *Apology* 1, 16; *Chronicle* A.D. 354 (*GCS* 47, 239).
[6] Quintilian, the late-first-century rhetorician and educational theorist, gives an idealised
description of this in *Inst. orat.* 1, 10.
[7] Edited by H. Keil, *Grammatici Latini*, vol. 4, 356; 359-62; 392-4.

rhetorical and stylistic theorist. But these do not exhaust the writers on whom Jerome must have worked. As an old man he was to reel off a string of poets and prose-authors, and commentators on them, whom he condescendingly assumes Rufinus to have read at school.[8] In addition to the chosen four just mentioned, this includes the playwright Plautus, the Epicurean poet Lucretius, Horace, the post-Augustan satirist Persius, and Lucan, early-first-century master of historical epic. Clearly he must have studied them himself 'as a boy'; otherwise he was exposing himself to a shattering riposte from Rufinus, who before their quarrel had been a close friend and had known him particularly well in youth. And no doubt there were others too. His writings are soaked in echoes of, or borrowings from, not only all the writers named so far (in very different degrees, of course), but also Ovid, the mordant first-century epigrammatist Martial, the renowned rhetorician Quintilian, the Stoic moralist and tragedian Seneca.[9] Curiously enough, he does not seem to have read Juvenal, a satirist who could have supplied him with much devastating ammunition.[10]

It would be unrealistic to suggest that Jerome acquired a thorough mastery of all these classical writers while at Donatus's school. The day would come when he was to have agonising qualms about their suitability for Christian eyes; but some thirty years were to elapse before that crisis, and in the interval he was continually reading them. Nevertheless, in view of his taunting remark to Rufinus he must at least have dipped into most of them at Rome, and we may be sure that Donatus gave him an exhaustive grounding in the principal four at any rate. The teaching method adopted in Roman schools strikes us as dry and pedantic in the extreme. After a preliminary explanation by the master, selected passages were read out, perhaps recited from memory, by the pupil. Then followed a systematic, word-by-word, line-by-line 'explication', in which the words and word-forms, any grammatical peculiarities, and the rhetorical or poetical tropes of the passage were minutely analysed and historical, mythological, or other allusions cleared up. The system employed involved a considerable use of question and answer, and, as Donatus's commentary on Terence's plays is extant (not, however, in its original form), we can observe how the process which he doubtless applied to Jerome and his class-mates operated. A knowledge of history, geography, general subjects, and indeed of moral behaviour, was not imparted directly, but was picked up incident-

---

[8] *Apology* 1, 16.

[9] For Jerome's non-Christian reading see H. Hagendahl's very thorough, reliable study, *Latin Fathers and the Classics* (Göteborg, 1958), esp. 269–97. For Jerome's knowledge of Seneca see Hagendahl, 118; 150–2; 297.

[10] He quotes *Sat.* 1, 15 ('et nos saepe manum ferulae subtraximus') three times (*Apology* 1, 17; *Letters* 50, 5; 57, 12), but this is his only citation from Juvenal, and the phrase is almost proverbial. Actually interest in Juvenal in the third and fourth centuries was pretty patchy: see G. Highet, *Juvenal the Satirist* (Oxford, 1954), 184.

ally, as the texts under examination suggested topics to be developed.[11]

Many, perhaps most, Roman boys must have found this routine a tedious grind. Not so Jerome. His attitude and practice in adult life strongly suggest that he revelled in the niggling minutiae of the schoolroom. So lasting was the impression that Donatus's lessons made on him that decades later we find him reproducing his master's definitions of technical terms like 'pleonasm' and 'antiphrase', along with the very illustrations of their use which can still be read in his advanced grammar.[12] Equally remarkable are the echoes we come across in his writings of Donatus's commentary on Terence,[13] and the much more numerous ones of his Vergil commentary (on the assumption that much of this is embodied in Servius's famous compilation).[14] Till his dying day he was to be a stickler for grammatical correctness, adroit himself in manipulating all the ploys of rhetoric and ready to tear apart any adversary whose diction struck him as sloppy or uncouth.[15] Though a schoolboy, he was a great stylist in the making, destined to be the finest of Latin Christian writers. Here at any rate he could not have got much help from his master, for Donatus's prose-style was shuffling and colourless,[16] at the opposite pole to the brilliant command of language he was to achieve. He could introduce Jerome to the techniques of literary craftsmanship, but for models his pupil looked to the great classical authors themselves, especially Cicero and Vergil, whom he was expounding.

Did Jerome's curriculum at this stage include Greek, of which he may have picked up a smattering at Stridon? Years later, when the two were locked in pamphlet warfare, Rufinus was by implication to deny it: 'Before his conversion [to the ascetic life] he was, like me, completely ignorant of Greek language and literature.'[17] Having been a fellow-student at Rome, Rufinus should have known the facts. But he was making a controversial point, and his words should not be taken literally. We know that Augustine, to his pain and grief, had to struggle with Homer at his

[11] For this summary, as for other summaries of Roman educational practice, I am indebted to H. I. Marrou, *Histoire de l'éducation dans l'antiquité* (6 ed., Paris, 1965), pt. III, chaps. iv, v, and vi.
[12] See *Comm. on Daniel* 11, 17 (*CCL* 75A: 710); *Letter* 78, 33: compare with these Donatus, *Ars. gramm.* iii, 6 (Keil, IV, 395; 402). For these and other points of contact see F. Lammert, *De Hieronymo Donati discipulo* (Leipzig, 1912). But for a warning against exaggerating these echoes see G. Brugnoli, 'Donato e Girolamo', *Vetera christianorum* 2 (1965), 139–49.
[13] For a good example cf. his criticism of Terence's epigram (*Andria* 68), 'Flattery begets friends, truthfulness enemies', in *Comm. on Galatians* 4, 15–6 (*PL* 26: 462) and Donatus's comment on the line.
[14] See Lammert, op. cit., 27 ff. Donatus's commentary is lost, but Servius (*fl.* 400), whose work Jerome did not know, used it extensively in compiling his own commentary on Vergil.
[15] For examples of attacks on supposed uncouthness of style or lack of education see *Against Helvidus* 16; *Against Jovinian* 1, 1; *Apology* 1, 17.
[16] See the remarks of G. Brugnoli, art. cit., 144 f. We can form an estimate of Donatus's style from, e.g., his biographies of Terence and Vergil.
[17] *Apol. c. Hier.* 2, 9.

relatively modest grammar school in north Africa;[18] it is hard to believe that the smartest academy in the capital offered poorer facilities. It is true, the study of Greek in the west had declined sharply since the days of Cicero, or even Quintilian, when education was virtually bilingual; but it had not died out.[19] What is certain is that Jerome did not acquire at school (indeed, in spite of his numerous references to it, was never to acquire) a first-hand knowledge of Greek classical literature.[20] This is not really surprising, for in the fourth century instruction in Greek usually remained elementary and did not continue beyond the grammar school. It is agreed that it was not until almost thirty years later, when he was residing at Antioch in Syria, that Jerome was to get down to the systematic study of the language. Even so, he must have been able to follow spoken Greek when he got there, for (as we shall see) he attended lectures by Apollinarius of Laodicea. He was, we have every reason to suppose, a first-class linguist, but the most natural explanation is that he had obtained a sufficient working knowledge of Greek while at school. This surmise gains support from the facts that Donatus interspersed his commentaries with Greek words and phrases, clearly assuming that his pupils would understand them, and that the rhetorical studies which followed also required some basic grasp of Greek technical terms.[21]

(ii)

Probably when they were fifteen or sixteen, like other lucky youths with affluent parents or well-off friends prepared to help them with the expensive fees, Jerome and Bonosus graduated from Donatus's grammar school to a Roman school of rhetoric, the nearest equivalent in the society of their day to an undergraduate university course. Professors of rhetoric occupied a higher social position than secondary schoolmasters, drew rather better (sometimes vastly better) stipends, and had more dignified premises placed at their disposal by the state or municipality. At Rome, for example, archaeological evidence makes it likely that in the fourth century the splendid *exedrae*, or semicircular halls, behind the porticoes of the Forum of Augustus and the Forum of Trajan were used for their lectures.[22] We have no means of identifying Jerome's professor. It has sometimes been

[18] *Conf.* I, 14, 23.

[19] For this see H. I. Marrou, op. cit., 379–85; A. H. M. Jones, op. cit., 986–91. Marrou perhaps exaggerates the decline, and Jones presents a more balanced picture.

[20] This conclusion, which is broadly that of A. Lübeck, *Hieronymus quos noverit scriptores et ex quibus hauserit* (Leipzig, 1872, 6 f.), is demonstrated in detail by P. Courcelle, *Late Latin Writers and their Greek Sources* (ET, Cambridge, Mass., 1969), 58–89.

[21] For the much discussed question of Jerome's knowledge of Greek see especially P. Courcelle, op. cit., chap. 2.

[22] See H. I. Marrou, 'La vie intellectuelle au Forum de Trajan et au Forum d'Auguste', *Mélanges d'archéologie et d'histoire* 49 (1932), 93–110.

conjectured that he may have been Marius Victorinus, the Neoplatonist thinker whose conversion to Christianity about 355 was to cause a sensation in the capital,[23] but there can be no question of this being correct. Jerome mentions him twice in the same context as Donatus, but while describing the latter as 'my instructor', significantly attributes no such role to Victorinus.[24] Similarly he breathes no hint that Victorinus had been his teacher either in a passage recording that the professor had taught boys rhetoric at Rome or in the compressed note he devoted to him in his *Famous Men*.[25]

Again it is not difficult to visualise the kind of training Jerome received at his rhetorical school. As the name implies, the courses conducted there were basically in the art of public speaking, the end in view being nowadays no longer political oratory (as in far-off republican times), but rather the career of an advocate or civil servant. Jerome would have to undergo 'preliminary exercises', learning to distinguish and handle the various forms (fable, narrative, moral anecdote, encomium, etc.) into which discourse was conventionally divided. Then he would be introduced to declamation itself. Sometimes he would be expected to compose and deliver 'persuasive speeches', advising some historical or mythological character how to behave in a specified situation. Sometimes the *mise-en-scène* was an imaginary law-court, and he would have to display his adroitness and eloquence, as well as his knowledge of jurisprudence, arguing for or against some controverted legal issue as fictitious as the court itself. Clearly he enjoyed this stage of his education, looking back on it in after life as the time 'when my enthusiasm for rhetorical study and erudition was white-hot'.[26] As an old man he was to recall with obvious satisfaction how frequently he had 'declaimed artfully veiled attacks' in the lecture-hall, while in his monastery at Bethlehem he was to be assailed by dreams of himself as a boy, 'with hair sleekly combed and wearing the specially donned toga, spouting petty forensic exercises before the professor'.[27] He writes as if these dreams were nightmares, congratulating himself on being now delivered from 'the perils of public speaking'; but he hardly succeeds in hiding his pride in his student-day triumphs.

Jerome's later writings illustrate how brilliantly he had mastered all the ploys of ancient rhetoric—its recognised genres and stylised procedures, its stock emotional appeals, its tendency to exaggeration whether in eulogy or in invective. But one or two of his reminiscences strongly suggest that

---

[23] For the date see P. Monceaux, *Histoire littéraire de l'Afrique chrétienne* (Paris, 1905) iii, 400 ff.

[24] *Apology* 1, 16; *Chronicle* A.D. 354 (*GCS* 47, 239).

[25] *Comm. on Galatians* prol. (*PL* 26: 369–70); *Famous Men* 101. For the reading in the former passage adopted above see P. Hamblenne, *Latomus* 28 (1969), 1098 (the usual reading is 'who taught rhetoric at Rome when I was a boy').

[26] *Letter* 52, 1.

[27] *Apology* 1, 30.

his curriculum at this period included some serious study of the law, no doubt as preparation for a possible career at the bar. Thus we have his graphic account of how, as a student at Rome, he would take part in fictitious legal actions in order to equip himself for real lawsuits, and would frequently rush off to the courts to observe barristers in action.[28] Rome was an important centre of legal studies,[29] and if Jerome (as seems likely) attended the formal courses provided there, this would explain the thousands of accurate references to Roman law and legal practice that decorate the pages he was to pen in middle and old age.[30]

(iii)

It has often been assumed that his rhetorical studies proper were followed by some formal training, however superficial, in philosophy, although there is general agreement that he had little aptitude for it and never became, like Augustine, a profound philosophical thinker. Admittedly there are passages in his later writings in which he seems to imply that he had been thoroughly indoctrinated with formal logic and even 'instructed in the learning of the pagan philosophers' during his schooldays.[31] From time to time he rattles off, with characteristic showmanship, whole catalogues of Greek philosophers with either the suggestion or the plain assertion that he had studied their works.[32] Sometimes, we should note, he had to beat an ignominious retreat after one of these brash sallies. When Rufinus jeered at his claim to have read Pythagoras, whose writings (if they ever existed) educated people knew were not extant,[33] he was obliged to confess that what he had intended was, not that he had read the actual texts of the Greek philosophers, but that he had learned their teachings as reproduced by Cicero, Brutus, and Seneca.[34] More relevant and specific, however, is a remark of his recalling that he had translated the commentaries of Alexander of Aphrodisias (the third-century commentator on Aristotle), and that 'a learned master had introduced' him 'to logic by way of the *Isagogê*, or *Introduction*, of Porphyry' (disciple of Plotinus and critic of

[28] *Comm. on Galatians* 2, 11 (PL 26: 408).

[29] See A. H. M. Jones, op. cit., 512 and 999. He recalls (III, 147, n. 99) that Augustine's friend Alypius, after studying rhetoric at Carthage, went on to Rome for law (*Conf.* 6, 8, 13); Germanus of Auxerre also went to Rome for the same purpose (*Vita Germ.* 1).

[30] G. Violardo collected these in his *Il pensiero giuridico di san Girolamo* (Milan, 1937), and went on to argue (p. 28) that they show that Jerome must have been 'a great jurist'. In a review (*Zeitschrift der Savigny-Stiftung für Rechtsgeschichte*, Roman. Abtheilung, lviii, 1938, 373–5) A. Steinwenter demolished this extravagant claim, but went too far in the opposite direction, contending that they do not go beyond what one would expect to find in a well educated Roman writer or what could be picked up in the rhetorical school.

[31] *Apology* 1, 30; *Letter* 84, 6: cf. *Letter* 50, 1.

[32] E.g. *Letter* 60, 5; *Homily on John* (CCL 78, 519: ' . . . legimus Platonem, legimus ceteros philosophos').

[33] Rufinus, *Apol. c. Hier.* 2, 7.

[34] *Apology* 3, 39.

Christianity). Modern biographers have tended to place these more serious philosophical exercises in his student period at Rome.[35]

This whole theory, however, bristles with difficulties. There is really no authority for the statement that 'the liberal arts course was crowned by philosophy, and notably by dialectic'.[36] Rome, like Antioch, witnessed a vigorous philosophical revival in the middle of the fourth century and[37] professors like Marius Victorinus, himself a highly original thinker as well as the translator of works by Plato, Aristotle, and Porphyry, lectured on philosophical subjects. But their lectures were for specialists, not for the general run of rhetorical students.[38] A second point is that it is highly questionable whether Jerome ever read the majority of the philosophers whose names he recites with such assurance.[39] Thirdly, we cannot assign his translation of Alexander of Aphrodisias to this period, if only for the reason that, whatever our estimate of Jerome's proficiency in Greek at this stage, it is hard to believe that he had enough of the language to tackle such a difficult work. It is practically certain that it was at Antioch, in Syria, in the middle 370s, when he had become expert in Greek, that he underwent his initiation into Aristotle's logic in the traditional order, with the help of Porphyry's *Isagogē* and Alexander's well-known commentaries.[40]

All in all, the irresistible conclusion is that while at Rome Jerome did not engage in any formal study of philosophy. This is not to say that he did not pick up a smattering of logical and philosophical jargon, along with a superficial acquaintance with the distinctive ideas of the main philosophical traditions. This he could hardly fail to do, since the text-books currently used in both grammar and rhetorical schools included numerous works (e.g., by Cicero) which were primarily philosophical in orientation. Even studying these with literary or rhetorical ends in view, he was bound to acquire that amateur familiarity with philosophical parlance and notions which, in fact, is the sum-total of which his writings give evidence.[41]

[35] *Letter* 50, 1. Cf. Grützmacher I, 124; Cavallera I, 10; G. Bardy, 'La culture grecque dans l'Occident chrétien au ivme siècle', *Rech. de science rel.* 29 (1939), 32.

[36] So Cavallera I, 10.

[37] Cf., e.g., Augustine's statement (*Ep.* 118, 33) that at that time 'the school of Plotinus [i.e. Neoplatonism] flourished and had a numerous group of acute-minded disciples and highly articulate students'.

[38] Apuleius charmingly confirms (*Florida* 20) that even in the second century philosophy was a highly postgraduate discipline, reserved for the very few and very lucky (like himself). After retailing the story that there are four cups at the banquet-table (one for thirst, one for gaiety, one for pleasure, one for madness), he states that for the great majority of students education offers only three: elementary school, grammar school, rhetorical school; philosophy is an exceptional draught for the privileged and specially interested.

[39] See P. Courcelle's careful discussion, op. cit., 64–72.

[40] P. Courcelle, op. cit., 49.

[41] Cf. H. Hagendahl's acute comment (op. cit., 319), ' . . . in reality his interest in philosophy was as slight as his knowledge of it was superficial.'

III

Life at Rome

(i)

At a first glance the rough outline sketch we are able to construct of Jerome's life and personality as a student at Rome might seem to be almost as devoid of concrete incidents and identifying traits as our blurred picture of his childhood at Stridon. In fact we are slightly better off. There are a few further items of information available which are both interesting in themselves and help us to understand the importance of this phase in his development.

First, we know something about the young men, or some of them, who were his close associates. One was Bonosus, the playmate of his Dalmatian boyhood, of whom he speaks in consistently glowing terms of admiration and affection.[1] Markedly different in character, the one apparently a model youth of undeviating rectitude and Jerome clever, sharp-tongued, and arrogant, the two were to exercise a profound influence on each other for many years to come. There was also the future writer, translator, and ascetic, Turranius Rufinus, a lad of exemplary bearing, scholarly, serious-minded, perhaps already over-solemn.[2] Of good family, at the very least comfortably off, he had been born at Concordia, a small town west of Aquileia, had probably attended the elementary school there, but had come to Rome for his secondary and higher education.[3] In later life Jerome was to be tragically, irreconcilably divided from him, but in a letter written about 375, when he still loved him wholeheartedly, he suggests that Bonosus, Rufinus, and himself had studied liberal arts together in the capital and been bosom friends.[4] He also hints that Rufinus

[1] *Letter* 3, 4 and 5 (it specifically mentions 'our studies at Rome').

[2] For Rufinus see F. X. Murphy, *Rufinus of Aquileia* (345–411): *His Life and Works* (Washington, D.C., 1945). 'Turranius', which was an ancient Roman family name and which is given by Apollinaris Sidonius (*Ep.* 2, 9, 5), seems the correct form. Jerome was frequently to caricature his serious demeanour (e.g. *Apology* 1, 30).

[3] Palladius (*Hist. Laus.* 46) describes him as 'very well born'. For his comfortable background see F. X. Murphy, op. cit., 3 f., although he is unduly cautious in assessing Jerome's references to his wealth. Murphy also (op. cit., 2) collects the evidence for his birth at Concordia. The date 345 given for his birth depends on the correct assumption that he and Jerome were roughly contemporaries and the erroneous one that the latter was born *c.* 347.

[4] *Letter* 3, 4 ('Bonosus tuus, immo meus et, ut verius dicam, noster . . .': addressed to Rufinus).

and he had 'sometimes erred, sometimes shown good sense' in each other's company.

It seems likely that a third member of Jerome's circle was Heliodorus, whose friendship with him was to remain unbroken throughout their lives.[5] Born at Altinum, then an important city on the marshy shores of the gulf of Venice, he may have met at any rate Rufinus, from nearby Concordia, in early youth. On completing his education he was to serve as a soldier for a time, but was to abandon that calling in his enthusiasm for the ascetic life. He was to become bishop of his native town at some date before 381, for he attended the council held at Aquileia in that year. Much later we shall find him encouraging Jerome in his literary projects and providing money to pay for stenographers and copyists.[6]

These three, like Jerome himself, were all well-off bourgeois boys from north-east Italy or Dalmatia. The fourth friend who calls for mention, Pammachius, came from an altogether different background and lineage.[7] A scion of the ancient *gens Furia*, he belonged to one of the noblest and richest Roman families. He was to possess vast estates in Numidia, to be a leading senator, and to hold proconsular rank. He was also (a rare phenomenon among male members of the Roman aristocracy at that time) a Christian, one moreover whose theological and religious concern, and involvement in Christian causes, were to become progressively more intense. Although their paths were inevitably to diverge for a great many years, Jerome was in later life to find him a staunch ally and defender in the capital. The fact that the two were already friends during these early student days emerges clearly from two letters which Jerome was to write to him in 393. In these he speaks of their 'friendship of long standing', and salutes him as his 'sometime fellow-pupil, comrade, friend'.[8] It is confirmed by a further letter in which Jerome reminds him how as young men they had both, along with the other students present, been convulsed with laughter in a Roman lecture-hall when the lecturer repeated a pithy saying of Cato's.[9] It is a guess, but a reasonable one, that they had met at Donatus's grammar school, which must have been a magnet to the affluent and well-born.

(ii)

In addition we have some information, woefully fragmentary but

---

[5] Cavallera was probably right in arguing (I, 14 n. 1) that Jerome's language in *Comm. on Obadiah* prol. (*CCL* 76A: 361–2) implies that Heliodorus was a fellow-student with himself and Pammachius at the rhetor's school. For Heliodorus's career as a soldier see *Letter* 14, 2 and 6.

[6] See below p. 284. For his presence at the council see Mansi, *Sacr. concil. ampl. coll.* III, 600.

[7] See his notice in *The Prosopography of the Later Roman Empire* (Cambridge, 1971), 663, with the references there given.

[8] *Letters* 48, 1; 49, 1.

[9] *Letter* 66, 9.

illuminating, about one or two of Jerome's activities at Rome, where he seems to have had (as we should expect) a full and absorbing time.

One of his most enthusiastic extra-curricular pursuits, and one which was to remain with him throughout his life, was the building up of a library. This was to become his most precious possession, and he was later to confess that, when he abandoned everything else for the religious life, he could not bring himself to surrender 'the library which I had collected at Rome with immense zeal and labour'.[10] He doubtless purchased a number of volumes, but he probably either had the majority transcribed by professional copyists or transcribed them himself; this would be the 'immense labour' to which he refers. As regards its contents, the passage quoted specifically mentions the works of Cicero and Plautus, but we may reasonably conjecture that it included other favourite writers like Vergil, Sallust, and Terence. At this stage it was almost certainly confined to the pagan classics. The library was to accompany him on the lengthy journeys he was to undertake in Europe and the Near East, and was to be finally installed in his monastery at Bethlehem. Continually growing in size and variety, it must eventually have become the most important private collection of the period.[11]

But we should not picture the young Jerome exclusively as a scholar and bibliophile. We may discount his references later in life to the scabrous songs chanted by schoolboys in every classroom or by smart worldlings at their banquets.[12] It is unlikely that he held aloof from the boisterous fun of his teenage companions, but these are not necessarily reminiscences of his own youthful experiences. What is more to the point, his later writings reveal that he was a man of strong passions which he had difficulty in controlling, and he seems to have found an outlet for them, both as a student and for years after, in the uninhibited society of the day. A time would come when he would be filled with revulsion for the disorders of his adolescence and early manhood, and it is from his later confessions of corruption, extravagantly worded and vague, that we have to estimate how real these disorders were.

Thus in a series of letters, most of them written some thirty years after this period, we find him bitterly lamenting that he is the prodigal son who has squandered the whole of the portion entrusted to him by his father, who has been 'befouled with the squalor of every kind of sin', and who lies like Lazarus in the sepulchre bound fast by the shackles of his misdeeds and desperately awaiting his Lord's summons to come forth.[13]

[10] *Letter* 22, 30.

[11] So C. Wendel in F. Milkau-G. Leyth, *Handbuch der Bibliothekswissenschaft* (2nd ed., Wiesbaden, 1955) III, 62.

[12] E.g. *Apology* 1, 17; *Comm. on Isaiah* xii, pref. (*CCL* 73A: 493–4), where he speaks of 'Milesian fables' and *The Testament of Corocotta*.

[13] *Letters* 2; 4, 2; 7, 3.

More precisely, he reproaches himself with having stumbled and fallen on 'the slippery path of youth', and recalls how he and Rufinus had on occasion gone astray together.[14] Later still (in 384) he was to confess that, when he was living alone in the desert, he would imagine himself immersed once again in the sensual pleasures of Rome. However chill his body, his mind would be surging with carnal desires and the flames of lust would burn up his half-dead limbs; meanwhile his fantasy would be haunted with visions of himself mingling with bands of girls.[15] And we have his frank admission in 393 to Pammachius, who as his fellow-student was in a position to know the truth, that if he exalted virginity to the skies, it was not because he possessed it himself but because he admired what he had lost.[16]

Scholars have extracted very different conclusions from these avowals, and some have attempted to play them down. They have argued on the one hand that the highly coloured language reflects Jerome's penchant for exaggeration and the rhetorical flourishes in which he delighted, on the other that it is the misleading but understandable habit of deeply religious people to magnify their pre-conversion peccadillos and represent them as enormities. Yet while allowance must clearly be made for these factors, enough that is concrete remains to convince us that Jerome's student days were marked by sexual adventures to which he was afterwards to look back with loathing. There is nothing improbable in this conclusion, and the denial of it makes nonsense of his obviously sincere professions of penitence and revulsion. It is further evident from the letters mentioned that, notwithstanding his baptism (which, as we shall see, took place at some point during his stay in Rome), Jerome was to continue for several years in the grip of passions which filled him with shame, and to be tortured with remorse for his enslavement to them.[17] The lack of detailed information is disappointing, but the realisation that in youth and early manhood Jerome was strongly sexed should assist us to understand his character and behaviour in middle and later life.

(iii)

Meanwhile, absorbed though he might be in his studies on the one hand and in the pleasurable excitements of the capital on the other, Jerome had not forgotten that he was a Christian. Bonosus and the others of his set

---

[14] *Letters* 7, 4; 3, 1 ('illud os quod mecum vel erravit aliquando vel sapuit . . .').

[15] *Letter* 22, 7.

[16] *Letter* 49, 20. Cf. *Letter* 22, 5, where his declaration that even almighty God cannot restore a virgin after her fall has a note of personal regret about it. See also *Letter* 130, 9.

[17] Cf. *Letter* 14, 6 (date 376/7), which seems to imply some recent sexual lapse. He was later to claim (*Letters* 15, 2; 52, 1; *Against John* 41) that his retreat to the desert had been motivated, in part at any rate, by the desire to discipline himself and make amends for his excesses.

were probably Christians too. The fact that they shared this common faith may have helped to draw them together, just as it may have prompted the young aristocrat Pammachius to join the group. We further get the impression that Jerome's Christianity was now less lukewarm than we earlier suggested the attitude of his family probably was when he was a child at Stridon. This at any rate seems implied by a striking reminiscence which his efforts as an old man to expound Ezekiel's description of the Temple instigated him to set down. 'When I was a youth at Rome,' he wrote,[18] 'studying liberal arts, it was my custom on Sundays, along with companions of the same age and the same conviction, to make tours of the tombs of the Apostles and the martyrs. Often we would enter those crypts which have been hollowed out of the depths of the earth and which, along the walls on either side of the passages, contain the bodies of buried people. Everything was so dark that the prophet's saying, "Let them go down living to hell",[19] seemed almost to have been fulfilled. Here and there a ray of light admitted from above relieved the horror of blackness, yet in such a way that you imagined it was not so much a window as a funnel pierced by the light itself as it descended. Then we would walk back with gingerly steps, wrapped in unseeing night, with Vergil's line recurring to us, "Everywhere dread fills the heart; the very silence dismays".'[20]

This narrative evidently refers to Jerome's visits to the catacombs, the vast network of underground corridors, at several levels, outside Rome in which Christians had buried their dead from the second century onwards. In the first half of the fourth century, with the cessation of persecution and the growing acceptance of the Church, the practice of paying honour to the martyrs became increasingly popular,[21] and these subterranean cemeteries, which had been confiscated and closed at the outbreak of Diocletian's persecution in 303,[22] began to be the setting of pilgrimages and cult services. In the popular imagination the deceased buried there, who in the vast majority of cases had in fact died in the ordinary way, were identified as martyrs for the faith. We know that Damasus, who was to become pope in autumn 366 and whom Jerome was later to serve in a secretarial capacity, took in hand the work of clearing, restoring, and embellishing the catacombs. Jerome's graphic account reveals that well before this

---

[18] *Comm. on Ezekiel* 40, 5–13 (*CCL* 75 : 468).

[19] Psalm 55, 15.

[20] *Aeneid* 2, 755 ('Horror ubique animos, simul ipsa silentia terrent').

[21] For an accurate popular account of the cult of martyrs see J. A. Jungmann, *The Early Liturgy* (ET, London, 1959), chap. xiv. Julian the Apostate denounced it as contemptible and contrary to Christ's instructions (*Against the Galilaeans* 335B–D).

[22] Cf. the statement in the *Depositio episcoporum* (*MGH auct. antiq.* ix, 75) that the Roman see was officially vacant for 7 years, 6 months, and 25 days from 304 onwards. We have indirect evidence for the restitution of the 'loca ecclesiastica' to the authorities of the Roman church in 311 in Augustine, *Brevic. coll. cum Don.* 3, 34–36 (*PL* 43, 645 f.).

refurbishing they were being visited by Christians, and provides valuable evidence of their state at the time. But it is even more instructive for the light it throws on his own mental and spiritual attitude. He expressly states that he and his companions were 'of the same . . . conviction ("propositi")'. This means that theirs was already a positively oriented Christianity, and their practice of visiting the catacombs discloses the form their piety was taking. The description itself in the original, it may be remarked, is a splendid example of Jerome's mastery of prose style, and while it dates from more than half a century later, it illustrates in its interweaving of classical and scriptural motifs the ever-present tension in his mind between the two cultures on which it had been nourished.

These Sunday walks in the catacombs are clear proof of Jerome's deepened interest in the Christian faith, and their impact on his impressionable mind is likely to have been profound. At all events it was during his residence in Rome that he took the decision to offer himself for baptism. He himself provides the evidence, recalling twice over in later letters to Pope Damasus that it was at Rome, from the see of Peter, that he had received 'the vesture of Christ' (the reference being to the white garment in which the newly baptised person was clothed on coming up from the font).[23] The date of his baptism is unknown, and all we can say is that it must have taken place before the accession of Pope Damasus in autumn 366. The bishop normally administered baptism, and even if Jerome was still in Rome in 366, it is inconceivable that he should not have mentioned the fact when he proudly reminded the pope that he had been baptised in Rome.

More interesting than the date of his baptism is the fact that, for all the awakened earnestness of his Christian faith, Jerome apparently did not immediately feel called upon to make a dramatic gesture of renunciation. In the fourth century it was common for really serious Christians, at their baptism or when they experienced a deeper conversion, to break with the world, abandoning career, marriage, and material possessions in order (in the expressive phrase of Cyprian of Carthage) 'to hold themselves free for God and for Christ'.[24] The ascetic strain which had been present in Christianity from the start, and which in the west tended to set a premium on virginity,[25] inevitably received a powerful practical impulse with the disappearance of persecution and the emergence of a predominantly Christian society where much of the Christian colouring was skin-deep. Monasticism of an organised kind was at this time just beginning to make a tentative, hesitant appearance in the west, but the withdrawal of

[23] *Letters* 15, 1; 16, 2.
[24] *De hab. virg.* 24.
[25] Cf. R. Lorenz, 'Die Anfänge des abendländischen Mönchtums im 4. Jahrhundert', *ZKG* 77 (1966), 28 f.

committed Christians, or 'servants of God', could take various forms according to their circumstances. Many years were to pass, however, before the challenge of renunciation was to present itself to Jerome.

(iv)

How long did Jerome's student days last? The general assumption has been that he must have attended his rhetorical school for three, or at most four, years, but this is no more than a guess based on the normal practice. A serious, ambitious student, such as we may reasonably presume Jerome to have been, might prolong this stage of his education for several years.[26] True, steps were to be taken at Rome to clamp down on this, and a law of 12 March 370 was to prohibit students from the provinces from remaining in the capital after their twentieth year.[27] But its enactment strongly suggests that the authorities were concerned about the number who exceeded the stipulated age-limit.

We have no means of ascertaining whether or not Jerome was one of these, but the possibility cannot be dismissed out of hand. In any case the obscurity which envelops his youth and early manhood becomes a blackout in the 350s. A whole decade and more of his life is lost to us, and while we can speculate about his doings we cannot hope for answers to our questions.

---

[26] See A. Müller, 'Studentenleben im 4. Jahrhundert nach Chr.', *Philologus* 69—NF 23 (1910), 298 f.; P. Petit, *Les étudiants de Libanius* (Paris, 1956), 63–6.
[27] *Codex Theod.* xiv, 9, 1.

IV

Trier and Aquileia

(i)

The black-out begins, slowly and patchily, to clear in 367 or 368, when Jerome was in his later thirties; he was to leave Europe for the Near East in 372. These dates are of course approximate, but they cannot be far out.[1] The half dozen years separating them he spent partly at Trier, in Gaul, partly in Dalmatia and north-east Italy. His movements and activities at this time are extremely obscure, with only a few isolated shafts of light piercing the darkness. But it is apparent from these that this was a period of crucial importance for his personal development and for the shaping of his career.

The actual evidence for his sojourn at Trier is much sparser, and less free from ambiguity, than we could wish.[2] For example, we have his note-worthy statement, set down in 374, that after concluding their studies at Rome Bonosus and he had settled 'by the half-barbarous banks of the Rhine', where they had 'shared the same food and lodging'.[3] Taken strictly, these words might suggest that they had resided much nearer the Rhine itself than Trier, which lies on the Moselle almost a hundred kilometres west of Bingen. There is another letter, however, written a year or two later, which can only refer to this phase in his career, and in which he specifically mentions certain books 'which I copied out with my own hand at Trier'.[4] This not only establishes the fact that he spent at any rate some time at Trier, but makes it likely that the rhetorical expression 'half-barbarous banks of the Rhine' denotes that city or its environs. This conclusion is supported by the fact that in late Roman usage 'bank', 'banks', or the related adjective ('ripensis') could embrace the whole region of which the river concerned was a prominent feature. Further,

---

[1] The former may be suggested (see below) by Valentinian's transference of the seat of government to Trier in 367. Jerome's presence there in 369–70 is confirmed by his reminiscence of the Attacotti (see below); perhaps also by the curious fact that Q. Aurelius Symmachus used exactly the same expression 'Rheni semibarbaras ripas' in a panegyric he delivered there on 25 Feb. 369 (*MGH auct. antiq.* vi, 1, 46). For the latter see below p. 36.

[2] For this section I am much indebted to J. Steinhausen's full and learned discussion, 'Hieronymus und Laktanz in Trier', *Trierer Zeitschrift* 20 (1951), 126–54.

[3] *Letter* 3, 5.

[4] *Letter* 5, 2.

there are examples of fourth century and later writers speaking of Trier as 'near the Rhine'.[5] As a matter of fact, it would have been difficult for Jerome and Bonosus to reside much closer to the Rhine at this juncture, for in 368 the Alamanni had surprised Moguntiacum (Mainz) and almost at once the emperor Valentinian I, accompanied by his son Gratian, launched a formidable campaign of reprisal across the river.

Two curious passages in much later writings also link Jerome with Trier. One is his often discussed remark that the native speech of the Galatians of Asia Minor was practically identical with that of the people of Trier.[6] He was to travel through Galatia in 372/3, not very long after his stay in Gaul, and this comment has generally been taken as evidence of his acute scholarly observation, as well as confirming his presence in Trier. It is much more likely, however, that in making it he was reproducing, as his wont was, an earlier source, in this case Lactantius, the distinguished professor of rhetoric and Christian apologist, who had lectured first at Nicomedia, in Bithynia, i.e. close to Galatian territory, but whom Constantine the Great summoned to Trier in 314 or thereabouts to act as tutor to his eldest son, Crispus.[7] Not only was Jerome's stay in Galatia probably too fleeting to allow him to dabble in comparative philology, but he had earlier quoted Lactantius as an authority on the Galatians, and an analysis of the context suggests that his borrowings went further.[8] If we accept that Lactantius was his source, however, the impression remains that Jerome had some knowledge of the speech of the Treveri; indeed, if his remarks were to carry conviction, he must have expected his readers to have grounds for assuming that he was personally acquainted with Trier and its inhabitants.

The other passage is a graphic note in which, after dwelling on the extraordinary food eaten by Sarmatians, Vandals, and others, he describes how as 'a young man in Gaul' he had seen 'a British tribe', the Attacotti, who regaled themselves with human flesh and, when they found swine, sheep, or cattle in the woods, cut off the buttocks of the males and the teats of the females, treating them as rare delicacies.[9] The Attacotti were in fact natives of Ireland,[10] and there is no evidence of their having ever invaded, much less settled, in Gaul. But in 367, along with Picts, Scots, and others, they carried out havoc-wreaking raids in Britain.

[5] So, e.g., Ausonius, *Ord. urb. nobil.* vi ('Trevericaeque urbis solium, quae proxima Rheno . . . '). For further passages see J. Steinhausen, art. cit., 150 f.

[6] *Comm. on Galatians* ii pref. (PL 26: 429–30).

[7] For Lactantius's relations with Trier see J. Steinhausen, art. cit., 127–34. Jerome reports (*Famous Men* 43: cf. *Chronicle* A.D. 317—GCS 47, 230) that Lactantius 'in advanced age was tutor to Constantine's son, Crispus Caesar, in Gaul'.

[8] For a good discussion see F. Müller, *Hermes* 74 (1939), 67–74.

[9] *Against Jovinian* 2, 7 (written 393).

[10] Cf. R. G. Collingwood and J. N. L. Myres, *Roman Britain and the English Settlements* (2nd ed., Oxford, 1937), 284 n. 1.

Theodosius, the father of the future emperor of that name, was despatched to the island with an expeditionary force, and ruthlessly crushed the wild hordes, returning triumphantly to the imperial residence at Trier in 369/70.[11] It is probable that he brought in his train some of the vanquished barbarians to exhibit to Valentinian I and the citizens. Jerome's reminiscence thus confirms his stay in the city, for it must have been there that he set eyes on groups of Attacotti and heard blood-curdling stories of their inhuman hunting and dietary customs.

(ii)

It is an intriguing question what object Jerome and Bonosus had in crossing the Alps with north-east Gaul as their destination. Since neither Jerome nor anyone else has left us any clues, we are never likely to know for certain; but some conjectures are likely to be nearer the truth than others. For example, we can discard the suggestion that they planned to continue their rhetorical education at Trier. Not only were they a bit over-age for that, but there was at this time nothing exceptional about the schools there.[12] Even more untenable is the theory of his eighteenth-century biographer, Vallarsi, that he wished to make Trier his base for a wide-ranging tour of the cities and, in particular, the libraries of Gaul.[13] The evidence Vallarsi appealed to was a letter written some forty years later in which, deploring the disasters of the barbarian invasions, Jerome recited the roll-call of the cities and regions of Gaul which had especially suffered.[14] But this is clearly a rhetorical flourish which in no way implies personal acquaintance with the places enumerated.

Much the most plausible proposal, although in the nature of the case it cannot be demonstrated, is that the two travelled to Trier in order to advance their careers.[15] Christians though they were, it has been argued, they may have decided that an appointment in the public service was the appropriate next step. Trier, we should remember, was the effective capital of the west for much of the fourth century. Between 306 and 315 it had been the favourite western residence of Constantine the Great, and after that the administrative seat of his eldest son Crispus, Constantine II, and Constans until his murder in 350. For a spell Trier suffered a decline,

---

[11] For the expedition see Ammianus Marcellinus, *Res gestae* 27, 8, 5–10. Jerome seems to speak as if he actually saw the Attacotti eating human flesh, but if the text is not corrupt we can dismiss this as characteristic exaggeration.

[12] It was only in 376 that the emperor Gratian, at the instigation perhaps of his tutor Ausonius, decreed that the teachers of Trier should receive higher-than-average salaries, thus in effect upgrading their schools (*Cod. Theod.* xiii, 3, 11).

[13] *Vita Hier.* 4, 3 (PL 22, 19): so too Grützmacher (I, 136 f.).

[14] *Letter* 123, 15.

[15] So Cavallera I, 17 (followed by most modern scholars).

but from 365 to 383 Valentinian I and his son Gratian resided mainly there. With its walls and gates, its magnificent public buildings (the impressive remains of which can still be seen), and its re-activated mint, it had once again become 'the splendid residence of princes'.[16] Not only was it the seat of the Prefecture of the Gauls, with its swarming staff of officials, but the network of ministries attached to the emperor's person was concentrated there. It was natural for talented, ambitious young men to move to Trier to find their fortune.[17]

It is certainly possible that Valentinian's establishment of his court at Trier may have given Jerome a motive for going there. Whatever the truth of this speculation, however, we have two fascinating items of information which reveal that his interests soon turned in an altogether different direction. First, the two books which (as we noted) he transcribed at Trier were important works by Hilary of Poitiers[18] (c. 315–67), next to Augustine (who had of course not yet started writing) the ablest and most original of Latin theologians. One of these, On the Synods (date 359), is an acute, fully documented survey of the creeds published in the east between 341 and 358, with the eirenic object of bringing together the western upholders of the Nicene dogma that the Son is 'of the same substance as the Father', and the strongly anti-Arian group which had recently emerged in the east and which preferred the formula 'of like substance' as doing justice to the distinctness of the persons in the Trinity. The other, Tractates on the Psalms (c. 365), shows Hilary reproducing, though with modifications and original contributions of his own, the highly allegorical exegesis of the great third-century Biblical scholar and theologian Origen.[18a]

We can only speculate whether Jerome found the originals which he transcribed in the houses of friends, in some public library, or perhaps in the library attached to the episcopal residence; Trier had had bishops since the latter half of the third century at any rate, and in the middle of the fourth century some of them were imposing figures. For our purposes the interesting corollary which emerges from this disclosure is that Jerome was now assiduously concerning himself with very recent, in part controversial Christian literature. These two particular treatises, he reports, he copied out for Rufinus, who was not apparently at Trier. As he mentions

---

[16] So Ammianus Marcellinus, Res gestae 15, 11, 9. Much useful information about Trier in the fourth century is collected in E. M. Wightman's Roman Trier and the Treveri (London, 1970).

[17] See the valuable section 'Les écoles et le recrutement des fonctionnaires' in H. Marrou, Histoire de l'éducation dans l'antiquité, 446–8.

[18] For Jerome's copying of these books see above p. 25, and Letter 5, 2. He himself reports (Famous Men 100) that in his work on the Psalms Hilary had 'imitated Origen, adding some matter of his own'.

[18a] See E. Goffinet, L'utilisation dans le commentaire des psaumes de S. Hilaire de Poitiers.

the fact quite by the way, we may reasonably infer that he was also devouring, probably copying out for himself, other Christian works too.[19] We thus get the picture of him not only enlarging and giving a Christian slant to his private library, but immersing himself, along with his friends, in the close study of the Bible message and the discussion of current theological issues.

This leads to the second concrete fact which we know for certain concerning Jerome's stay at Trier. It was there that he came to recognise the call to a much more dedicated form of Christian life than he had so far accepted. We have his assurance of this in his panegyric of Bonosus which has already been quoted several times, and which reaches its climax in an impassioned prayer to Jesus containing the sentence, 'You yourself know . . . how, when after our Roman studies he and I were sharing the same food and like lodging by the half-barbarous banks of the Rhine, I began, even before him, to desire to devote myself to You.'[20] This whole section of the letter is packed with emotional references to Bonosus's recent heroic withdrawal to an island off the Dalmatian coast to live the life of a hermit, and in the light of these there can be no doubt that by 'devote myself to You' ('te colere') Jerome means abandonment of the world and the adoption of the strict ascetic ideal. If Bonosus was to outstrip him in translating this programme of renunciation into action, thus ceasing to be a mere 'recruit' and becoming a 'warrior', Jerome here claims that he had been the first of the two to entertain it.

Our information is so fragmentary that we cannot tell whether this new resolve stimulated or was itself the fruit of the two friends' interest in Scripture and Christian theology. Quite possibly, however, it had received an impetus from influences which they came across at Trier. The new monasticism, which had been in full swing in the east for half a century, was now beginning to make tentative headway in Gaul and the west generally.[21] Trier was one of the centres where it caught on. Athanasius, always an eloquent propagandist of it, had been exiled there in 336/7, and may have sown some seeds; but the stirring was too widespread to be attributed to any single personality. What we know for certain, from a dramatic story told to Augustine about 385 by an official named Ponticianus, is that about a decade after Jerome's stay at Trier a group of servants of God, 'of the kind to whom the kingdom of heaven belongs,' were living in a hut close to the city walls. Two imperial couriers, going for an afternoon stroll while the emperor was at the circus, stumbled upon

---

[19] So Cavallera I, 17.

[20] *Letter* 3, 5.

[21] For particulars see R. Lorenz, 'Die Anfänge des abendländischen Mönchtums im 4. Jahrhundert', *ZKG* 77 (1966), esp. 12–18. Hilary had been one of the pioneers, but the key-figure was Martin of Tours after his discharge from the army in 356.

them, finding also a copy of Athanasius's *Life of Antony*, the Egyptian hermit (*c.* 250–356) who was reckoned to be the founder of monasticism. With its attractive presentation of the monastic ideal, this famous book proved an extremely effective instrument for its dissemination. When they read it, the two couriers were so affected by it that they decided to forsake their professional careers and serve God alone.[22]

It is tempting to read too much out of this story. It has been conjectured, for example, that Jerome and Bonosus may have had an identical experience, or even that they were the two imperial agents[23] (a possibility belied by Augustine's description of them as 'uneducated men'). But the incident does suggest that the religious milieu at Trier may have been well equipped to fire the imagination of eager Christians with the attractions of a more ascetic, committed form of life. It is likely that the ideals of renunciation and monastic withdrawal were being canvassed, perhaps put into practice, by earnest Christians in the city when Jerome and Bonosus were there. If so, it is not surprising that, with their awakened interest in Christianity, they should respond to their challenge. At all events it was there that Jerome underwent what has been called his first conversion,[24] and that he and Bonosus resolved, not indeed to make a clean break with the world as hermits or monks (they were not ready for that yet), but to renounce secular ambitions and live a life of detachment, contemplation, and discussion of higher things.

(iii)

We have no means of knowing how long Jerome's stay at Trier lasted. When it was over, he recrossed the Alps, probably accompanied by Bonosus, and spent a further period, equally indeterminate, in north-east Italy and Dalmatia. No direct contemporary evidence for this survives, but several letters which he was to write a few years later strongly suggest that he now resided at both Aquileia and Stridon, possibly also at Emona.[25] It is impossible to reconstruct, even in roughest outline, his moves at this stage or the order in which he visited these centres, much less the time he

---

[22] Augustine, *Conf.* 8, 6, 15. Jerome's friend Evagrius translated the *Life of Antony* into Latin in 371 or shortly thereafter, but a crudely literal version was in circulation some years earlier. See A. Wilmart, 'Une version latine inédite de la Vie de Saint Antoine', *RB* 31 (1914), 163–73; G. Garitte, 'Le texte Grec et les versions anciennes de la Vie de saint Antoine', *Studia Anselmiana* 38 (1956), 6.

[23] For this brilliant but implausible guess see P. Courcelle, *Recherches sur les Confessions de saint Augustin* (Paris, 1950), 181–5. For Augustine's reference to the couriers as 'indocti', see *Conf.* 8, 8, 19. Had Jerome been one of them, it would be odd if Augustine had not known the fact.

[24] H. v. Campenhausen, *The Fathers of the Latin Church* (ET, London, 1964), 131.

[25] *Letters* 1; 3; 5–14 imply close relations with people in these regions, some of them recently acquired friends.

spent at each. We may suspect, however, that while he would naturally wish to see his relatives after his prolonged absence, the real magnet was Aquileia. With his new and exciting sense of vocation he would want to think out his position and test his ascetic aspirations in a congenial environment. His old school-friend Rufinus, for whom he had transcribed Hilary's treatises at Trier, was at Aquileia, and may well have painted a glowing picture of the favourable conditions he might expect to find there.

At Stridon he would find, in addition to his parents, his sister, now a girl in her early teens, and his much younger brother Paulinian, still a child of five or six. He was setting eyes on both of them for the first time. His sister's behaviour seems to have been far from satisfactory, for he was to describe her at this time as wounded by the devil, spiritually dead[26]— or do these enigmatic phrases simply mean that she was not so serious-minded as her earnest older brother would have wished? Whatever the truth, he soon established a salutary influence over her. Paulinian, too, to judge by his subsequent conduct, fell under his brother's spell. Otherwise he does not seem to have derived much satisfaction from his home district. We know he got embroiled with his aunt Castorina in a fierce quarrel which dragged on.[27] Relations with his parents seem to have been cool. Were they disappointed, as well they might have been, by his radical, and to them meaningless, change of plan after the high hopes they had cherished for his future? Above all, the boorish rusticity of Stridon, and the material outlook of its Christian community, filled the eager ascetic (as he now was) with disillusionment. According to his blistering description,[28] people there made their belly their god and lived for the day, calculating a man's sanctity solely in terms of his wealth. The local bishop, Lupicinus, was a fitting lid for such a pot, guiding his flock like a blind man leading his blind companions into a pit.

The atmosphere at Aquileia, from the religious and personal points of view, presented a complete contrast, and one entirely congenial to Jerome. Here he found old friends who were also kindred spirits, like Rufinus and Heliodorus, and through them made new friends who encouraged his ascetic interests. Aquileia was no rural backwater like Stridon, but the capital of the province of Venetia-Istria, and a great military, industrial, and commercial stronghold. Its bishop, Valerian (d. 388), a champion of Nicene orthodoxy,[29] was a man Jerome could

---

[26] *Letter* 6, 4. *Pace* Cavallera (1, 23 n. 2), the mention of 'the slippery path of youth on which' Jerome had himself fallen clearly points to a moral lapse.

[27] *Letter* 13.

[28] *Letter* 7, 5.

[29] Basil of Caesarea, replying (*Ep.* 91) in 372 to a friendly communication, expresses satisfaction at his devotion to Nicene orthodoxy. He was to preside in 381 over the council of Aquileia (Ambrose of Milan played the leading role) which marked the victory of that teaching over Arianism so far as the west was concerned.

wholeheartedly admire; and he had grouped around him keen, like-minded clergy and laity. Prominent among these was the priest Chromatius, destined to be his successor and to remain Jerome's lifelong friend, his brother Eusebius (a deacon), and an archdeacon, Jovinus. Rufinus mentions all three respectfully, recalling that Eusebius had instructed him for baptism.[30] Jerome was to write to them in terms of intimacy and affection, congratulating them on cleansing the city of 'the poison of the Arian dogma'[31] (allowed an inlet, presumably, by the compromises of Valerian's predecessor, Fortunatianus). Among other friends we hear of a deacon, Julian, who became his sister's spiritual director, a sub-deacon called Niceas whom he was to get to know more intimately in the east, and a monk Chrysocomas whose conversations he was to remember with pleasure.[32]

What particularly thrilled Jerome about this Aquileian coterie was that all its members were devoted Christians who were also enthusiasts for the higher religious life. Like Trier, Aquileia was one of those western centres where monastic practices had early taken root and were now flourishing. The original impulse may have come from Athanasius, who had resided there in 345, but it is more likely to have spread from other localities in north Italy, such as Vercelli, in Piedmont, and Milan.[33] Even before Jerome and Bonosus arrived, Chromatius's household was organised as an informal religious community—a monastery, as Rufinus was later anachronistically to describe it.[34] Chromatius and his brother Eusebius were trying out the ascetic life, and they had been joined by the others mentioned above; perhaps they were taking their cue from Eusebius, the famous bishop of Vercelli, who had introduced to the west the eastern custom of the clergy of a district living together.[35] Chromatius's mother, too, as Jerome notes with ecstatic approval, as well as his sisters, had embraced the same austere commitment, the widowed mother forswearing any thought of second marriage, the sisters vowing themselves to virginity.[36] Little wonder that, surrounded by such heroic models, Jerome joined with Julian in planting a similar resolve in his own sister too, thereby restoring the wayward girl to the right path.[37] To live in such a

---

[30] *Apol. c. Hier.* 1, 4.

[31] *Letter* 7: for the congratulations see para. 6.

[32] *Letters* 6 (Julian); 8 (Niceas); 9 (Chrysocomas).

[33] For the emergence of monasticism in these centres in the fifties of the fourth century and shortly thereafter, see R. Lorenz, art. cit., 9 f.

[34] *Apol. c. Hier.* 1, 4.

[35] So Ambrose, *Ep.* 63, 66 and 71; *Serm.* 56, 4. It is an intriguing question whether he did this before his exile to the east in 355 or after his return *c.* 363. If the latter, he was probably drawing on his experiences in the Thebaid.

[36] *Letter* 7, 6.

[37] *Letters* 6, 2; 7, 4. These passages make it plain that Julian took the initiative, but Jerome's reference to 'the common glory in Christ' which they both share suggests that (as we should expect) he played his part as well.

society was heaven itself for him, and something of his excitement still lingers in the incongruously personal note which, when he wrote his *Chronicle* in 380, he inserted against the year 374, 'The clergy of Aquileia are accounted a company of blessed ones.'[38]

There were others too with whom Jerome forged links in the neighbourhood. At Concordia, to the west of Aquileia, lived an elderly ascetic named Paul, almost a hundred years old but belying his age by his vigorous health and tenacious memory.[39] He was a collector and ready lender of books, an admirer too of Tertullian (*c.* 160–*c.* 240), the famous African theologian and controversialist. Perhaps he communicated this admiration to Jerome, who was to make Tertullian's polemical treatises a quarry for his own.[40] Again, some distance to the east, at Emona (Ljubiljana), he was in touch with a 'monk' called Antony, and a group of women living in community as 'handmaids of the Lord' (further proof of the spread of monasticism in the region).[41] Finally, it was probably at Aquileia, in the circle of Chromatius, that he made the acquaintance of Evagrius of Antioch, shortly to be his host and patron in Syria, and his friend Innocentius. Evagrius was a man of noble birth and great wealth whom Eusebius of Vercelli, returning from exile in the east in 362, had brought to Italy and ordained priest. Apparently he wielded considerable influence with the imperial court, and had used this, at a critical juncture in the disputed papal elections, to assist Damasus (whose firm friend he became), and also to frustrate the policies of Auxentius, the astute Arian bishop of Milan (d. 374).[42] For a Greek speaker he had a rare command of Latin style, and about this time produced an elegant and widely read free translation of Athanasius's *Life of Antony*.[43]

(iv)

Suddenly and without any warning, as if a stone had been flung into a limpid pool, this sympathetic atmosphere was brutally shattered. Writing to Rufinus two or three years later, Jerome speaks bitterly of 'the unexpected whirlwind' which had torn him from his side, the 'impious rending apart' which had severed him from his beloved friend.[44] Because of it he

[38] *Chronicle* A.D. 374 (*GCS* 47, 247).
[39] *Letter* 10.
[40] See, e.g., Y. M. Duval, 'Tertullien contre Origène sur la résurrection de la chair dans le *Contra Ioh. Hieros.* 23–36 de saint Jérôme', *Revue des études Augustiniennes* 17 (1971), 227–78, esp. 278.
[41] *Letters* 12; 11.
[42] *Letters* 1, 15; 15, 5 (to Damasus: '. . . Evagrium presbyterum, quem optime nosti').
[43] Evagrius dedicated his book to Innocentius, mutual friend of Jerome and himself; and as Innocentius died in 374, it must precede that date. He seems likely to have written it during his stay in Italy, which he left in 372/3 on a mission from Pope Damasus to Basil of Caesarea.
[44] *Letter* 3, 3: 'Postquam me a tuo latere subitus turbo convolvit, postquam glutino caritatis haerentem inpia distraxit avulsio . . .'.

33

found himself obliged to leave his home and north Italy, where things were evidently getting too hot for him. Like many others of that generation, he resolved to go as a pilgrim for Christ to the east and to Jerusalem.[45]

What had happened? Part of the trouble, it seems clear, was that he had broken with his family. We have a side-light on this in his irreconcilable estrangement (as we noticed) from his aunt Castorina. More to the point, perhaps, we have a letter of his, dispatched from Syria to Aquileia about 375, thanking the deacon Julian for the news that his sister is holding fast to her religious vows. If Julian had not informed him, he complains, he would never have heard this, for 'here where I am now, I am completely in the dark not only about what is happening in my homeland, but even whether my homeland continues to exist'. Reading between the lines, we may conjecture that, coming on top of his own, to them disappointing, conversion to asceticism, his support of Julian's pressure on his sister to follow suit had been regarded by his family as the last straw. We can imagine the reproaches and recriminations, and Jerome's angry realisation that he had as little in common with his family as with the other material-minded Christians of Stridon.[46]

But much more than rupture with his relatives was involved. This would explain his decision to leave Stridon, but not Aquileia. It is apparent that ugly rumours about Jerome were being passed around and were being believed, and that his reputation had been blasted in the very circles where he might have looked for support. He himself protests to Julian that, however much 'the Iberian viper tears' him 'in pieces with injurious insinuations', he will not fear the judgment of mere men. As late as 376 he was to complain to Pope Damasus of 'an enemy who never gives up' but pursues him wherever he goes.[47] We cannot identify these darkly hinted at adversaries, but the whispering campaign against him was so effective that doors which had once been open were now being slammed in his face. At Emona, for example, the monk Antony and the community of virgins were deeply, irreparably shocked and offended by him. A letter of his to the virgins, written a few years later with the object of breaking down their stony silence, is particularly revealing. While protesting against slanderous gossip and begging them not to judge him hastily, he freely admits that he has done wrong and asks for their pardon.[48]

So far as we know, it was only Jerome who was attacked. Other members of the Aquileian group left Italy about the same time. Rufinus

[45] Letter 22, 30: 'Cum . . . propter caelorum me regna castrassem et Hierosolymam militaturus pergerem . . .'.

[46] Letter 6, 2. For this interpretation see Cavallera II, 75.

[47] Letter 16, 2.

[48] Letters 12 (to Antony: he had written to him ten times without getting an answer); 11 (to the virgins: he admits that God's handmaids have no fellowship with a sinner, but points to the harlot who was permitted to wash the Lord's feet with her hair).

sailed off to Egypt, Bonosus was to settle as a hermit on a rocky island in the Adriatic, Heliodorus went on pilgrimage to Jerusalem quite separately, Evagrius accompanied by Innocentius returned home to Antioch. But each of these had his own distinct, perfectly understandable motive for leaving; there is no reason for connecting their departure with Jerome's, much less for regarding them and him as victims of a common onslaught.[49] We cannot now unearth what Jerome had done to feed the scandal-mongers and occasion distress and indignation to good Christian people like the religious of Emona. We may suspect, however, that, not for the last time, his passionate temperament, his tactlessness, or his uncontrollable tongue, or some combination of these, had landed him in some major imprudence, some disastrous indiscretion. Whatever it was, faced with misunderstanding and resentment, and with defamers redoubling their accusations, he felt himself compelled to bid farewell to his family and turn his back not only on his home district, but even on Aquileia, where he had been so happy. He was never to set eyes on either again.

[49] For this view see P. Monceaux, *St Jerome: the Early Years* (ET, London, 1933), 76–8.

V

Interlude at Antioch

(i)

It was probably in the latter part of 372, when he was just over forty, that Jerome set out for the east. That it cannot have been much later is implied by the fact that Rufinus, whom we know he had left behind, was in Alexandria in early summer 373 and witnessed the brutal persecution which the government instigated there following the death of Athanasius (2 May 373) and the election of the orthodox Peter as bishop in his place.[1] Although his mood was disillusioned and bitter, Jerome did not rush off (as has been mistakenly inferred from a remark in a letter to Rufinus)[2] without any idea of his destination. He was dedicating himself to the kingdom of heaven, i.e. to the ascetic life, and his immediate plan (a plan to be fulfilled only after many years) was to go to Jerusalem,[3] which as well as being a mecca for devout pilgrims was beginning to attract monastic aspirants. None of the Aquileian coterie accompanied him, except possibly the sub-deacon Niceas, to whom he was to write recalling 'the journey we made together'.[4] But his baggage must have been inordinately bulky, for he insisted on taking his library with him. Whatever other sacrifices the enthusiast for asceticism made, he could not bear to be parted from this.[5] His expenses, both for travelling and for maintaining himself, must have been heavy. It seems that, however stormy his relations with his family, they were prepared to help him out financially.

We have a few clues to the route which he took. Reminding Rufinus two or three years later of their painful separation, he remarks, with characteristic echoes of Vergil,[6] 'Then "the murky rain-storm threatened above my head", while "sea compassed me on every side, on every side sky".' Both quotations conjure up Aeneas in the open sea with his fleet;

---

[1] Rufinus, *Hist. eccl.* 2, 2–4. In 2, 4 (cf. also *Apol. ad Anast.* 2) he claims to have been himself a victim of the persecution—a claim Jerome (*Apology* 2, 3) was to ridicule and dismiss as 'a barefaced lie'.

[2] *Letter* 3, 3, where 'in incerto peregrinationis erranti' does not mean 'wandering uncertain of my destination', but 'wandering exposed to the uncertainties of travel'.

[3] So he was to explain in *Letter* 22, 30, written at Rome in 384.

[4] *Letter* 8.

[5] *Letter* 22, 30.

[6] *Letter* 3, 3: cf. Vergil, *Aeneid* 3, 194; 5, 9.

their use in such a context makes sense only if, instead of travelling over-
land through the Balkans, Jerome made the first part of his journey by
ship down the Adriatic—probably to Dyrrachium (Dürres, on the
Albanian coast), where the Via Egnatia to the east began.[7] But whatever
route he followed, he must have passed through or made a diversion to
Athens. Years later he was to refer casually to having visited it,[8] and this
is the only point in his known career where such a visit can be plausibly
fitted in. The reference has the additional interest of incidentally confirming the impression we get of his never very robust physique. On the
Acropolis, he records, near the statue of Athena, he was shown a great
bronze sphere which was used by athletes as a weight-lifting test. He
himself, 'because of the weakness of my wretched body', was quite unable
to move it.

For his journey after Athens we have his own rapid summary in the
letter to Rufinus already quoted. It took him by land through Thrace;
then across to Pontus and Bithynia in Asia Minor; then through Galatia,
where we know from another source[9] that he visited Ancyra (Ankara);
then south-east through Cappadocia across the Taurus range to Cilicia and
the Mediterranean coast. Although he does not mention Constantinople,
it is likely that he passed through it, for the Via Egnatia terminated there.
In any case he was now following the great imperial highway south
through Anatolia. This was the route which pilgrims from Europe to
Jerusalem generally took; indeed there survives an itinerary, composed in
333 by an anonymous traveller from Bordeaux, which lists all the stages
for changing horses and for stopping the night, and the exact distances
between them.[10]

Jerome's progress seems to have been unhurried, and what with sight-
seeing in Athens and Ancyra and stops elsewhere (we hear of his spending
some time with a community of anchorites presided over by one Theodosius)[11] the journey probably occupied several months. This is confirmed by his reference to 'the scorching heat'[12] of Cilicia, south of the
Taurus mountains, which may point to the summer of 373. At any rate,
when he reached the coast, this heat and the long trek across the Anatolian
plateau had taken their toll of him. He was a broken man, exhausted and
ill, when at last 'Syria presented itself to me, as a secure haven to a ship-

---

[7] First constructed *c*. 130 B.C. (according to more recent opinion, *c*. 110–100 B.C.), the main
branch ran from Dyrrachium across the Balkan range down to Thessalonica, and then along
the Thracian coast to Constantinople. For a popular account (marred by whimsicalness and
numerous small inaccuracies) see F. O'Sullivan, *The Egnatian Way* (Newton Abbot, 1972).

[8] *Comm. on Zechariah* 12, 3 (*CCL* 76A: 896).

[9] *Comm. on Galatians* ii prol. (*PL* 26: 429–30).

[10] The *Itinerarium Burdigalense* (*CSEL* 39, 3–33; *CCL* 175, 1–26).

[11] *Letter* 2.

[12] *Letter* 3,3.

wrecked sailor'.[13] Like most travellers along the road to Jerusalem, he made his way to Antioch on the Orontes (Antakya, in southern Turkey), one of the greatest cities of the empire, a renowned cultural centre, and at this time the residence of the eastern emperor, Valens. Here his rich and influential friend, the priest Evagrius, welcomed him and gave him hospitality.

(ii)

Evagrius had reached his home in Antioch only shortly before Jerome's arrival, having travelled through Anatolia and called on Basil, the great bishop of Caesarea in Cappadocia (Kayseri), on a diplomatic mission from Pope Damasus. This was a time when relations between the eastern and western churches were under strain because of divergent approaches to the doctrine of the Trinity, divergences which were painfully reflected in the Christian community at Antioch. Briefly, while both east and west (Arianisers apart) accepted the Nicene teaching of the divinity of Father, Son, and Holy Spirit, most easterners had come to deem it desirable, in order to avoid confusing the persons with one another (the heresy known as Sabellianism), to describe them as 'three hypostases'. Since Latins regarded 'hypostasis' as the Greek equivalent of 'substance', and in the Nicene Creed 'hypostasis' and 'essence' or 'substance' had been treated as synonymous, to speak of 'three hypostases' seemed to verge on tritheism, or at least on Arian subordinationism. Thus at Antioch, where there was an Arian bishop, Euzoius, recognised by the government, the orthodox-minded were split into two discordant factions. The bulk of them, led by Bishop Meletius (now in exile), adhered to the new 'three hypostases' theology, while a small, fanatical group under Bishop Paulinus repudiated is as contrary to their interpretation of Nicaea. To make the schism worse, there was soon to be a third bishop, Vitalis, orthodox as regards the Trinity, but sharing the heretical opinion of Apollinarius (who had consecrated him) that Jesus had had no human soul, its place being taken by the divine Logos.[13a]

During these years, since his appointment in 370, Basil of Caesarea was patiently striving on the one hand to form a united anti-Arian front in the east on the basis of the formula 'one substance, three hypostases', and on the other to persuade Damasus of Rome both to acknowledge this as orthodox and to recognise Meletius as the true Catholic bishop of Antioch. So far he had met with rebuff after rebuff; and not only was the com-

---

[13] *Letter* 3, 3.

[13a] For Vitalis (Bitalios) and his consecration by Apollinarius, probably during a stay in Antioch in 373–5, see Sozomen, *Hist. eccl.* 6, 25, 1–3; Theodoret, *Hist. eccl.* 5, 4, 1.

munication which Evagrius had recently brought him from the pope a further cold douche,[14] but he now learned to his intense disappointment that, having finally returned to his native city, Evagrius was refusing to hold communion with the Meletian church.[15]

Evagrius can scarcely have refrained from discussing these great matters with his guest, and before long (as we shall see) Jerome himself was to be caught up in the doctrinal controversy. For the moment, however, his mind was occupied with other things. His original idea had doubtless been to make a brief stay with Evagrius before resuming his journey, but the broken state of his health obliged him to extend it to a full year; in the event the planned pilgrimage to Jerusalem was to be postponed indefinitely. One letter written a year or two later speaks of the 'repeated illnesses' which have shattered his 'poor body, weakly even when it is well', and of his having 'experienced every sort of sickness' in Syria;[16] another records the mental and physical prostration as a result of which he had been brought to the verge of death and had almost lost consciousness.[17] In Evagrius's comfortable mansion he would have every care and attention, as well as enjoying the affectionate company of Evagrius himself, his friend Innocentius, and others who turned up from time to time. There were books to read, perhaps also to transcribe; there were no doubt earnest talks about the ascetic ideals all these friends were bent on pursuing.

Here too, living for the first time in a Greek-speaking household and city, Jerome must have taken steps to improve his knowledge of written and spoken Greek. It was probably now[18] that, with a 'skilled tutor' to guide him, he studied Aristotle's treatises on logic, using Porphyry's *Introduction* and the famous commentaries of Alexander of Aphrodisias (early third century), and making his own translation, perhaps as a linguistic exercise, of the latter. In addition, at the earnest entreaty of Innocentius, he tried out his hand as an original writer, throwing off a piece of brilliant if artificial prose as (we may suppose) a graceful compliment to his host. Cast in the form of a letter to Innocentius,[19] it recounts the story, macabre but edifying, of a poor Christian woman of Vercelli who a year or two previously had been wrongfully condemned to death

[14] Cf. Basil, *Ep.* 138, 2. On the whole question see M. Richard, 'S. Basile et la mission du diacre Sabinus', *Analecta Boll.* 67 (1949), 197–201; E. A. de Mendieta, 'Basile de Césarée et Damase de Rome', *Biblical and Patristic Studies in Memory of R. P. Casey* (Freiburg etc., 1963: ed. J. N. Birdsall and R. W. Thomas), esp. 127 f.

[15] Cf. Basil, *Ep.* 156, 3.

[16] *Letter* 3, 1 and 3.

[17] *Letter* 6, 1.

[18] *Letter* 50, 1: see above pp. 16 f.

[19] *Letter* 1. According to some (e.g. Grützmacher 1, 53 ff.), Jerome wrote it while still at Aquileia; but para. 15 seems to imply that Auxentius, the Arian bishop of Milan, who died in 374, was dead at the time of writing.

for adultery, had survived excruciating tortures and no fewer than seven strokes of the executioner's sword, and had eventually been pardoned by the emperor as a result of Evagrius's chivalrous intervention. The earliest of Jerome's surviving compositions, it betrays the beginner in its turgidity, exaggerated pathos, and extravagant use of rhetorical tricks. But it already reveals his uncritical credulity and Jesus-centred devotion as well as his flair for brutally realistic description.

One or two other incidents stand out from this obscure phase of Jerome's life, although their relative dating is bound to be conjectural. One happy day, for example, his old friend Heliodorus arrived, on his way back to Italy from a pilgrimage to Jerusalem which he had found trying and upsetting.[20] He brought the wonderful news, which Jerome dared not at first believe because he had it only at second hand, that Rufinus was in Egypt visiting the monks in the desert. Soon corroborative reports poured in, and he could at last be sure that Rufinus was at Nitria, some 80 km. south of Alexandria, the famous centre of Egyptian monasticism.[21] Jerome was overjoyed; at least two others of the Aquileian circle had followed his example. But a third, an even more precious friend, had done so too, making a far more decisive break with the world. Either from Heliodorus or from some other visitor Jerome learned that Bonosus had abandoned family, home, indeed everything, and had settled all alone as a God-dedicated hermit on a rocky, deserted islet of the Adriatic.[22] Jerome's ecstatic account of his heroic self-sacrifice still exhales his passionate affection and admiration, as well as his chagrin at not being able to emulate him.

There were tragedies, however, to offset these joys. A malignant fever suddenly struck his friend Innocentius, and he died. In his grief Jerome speaks of him, in images borrowed from Horace and Plautus, as 'one part of my soul', 'one of my two eyes'.[23] His other 'eye', the only one now left him, is Evagrius, to whom he feels he is becoming an increasing burden because of his illnesses. But hardly had the wound inflicted by Innocentius's death begun to heal when another death reopened it, that of Hylas, a slave of the aristocratic and immensely wealthy Melania, Rufinus's patron, who, as it happened, was now with him in Egypt. Hylas had been living in Evagrius's household, and had won Jerome's warm regard: 'his upright behaviour' (the comment is eloquent of contemporary Christian social attitudes) 'had washed away the taint of his servile condition'.[24]

Meanwhile poor Jerome was in a mental and spiritual turmoil, torn by

[20] *Letters* 3, 2; 4, 1; 14, 1.
[21] *Letter* 3, 2: cf. *Letter* 4, 2.
[22] *Letter* 3, 4–6. Many others did the like. For a summary of the evidence see R. Lorenz, 'Die Anfänge des abendländischen Mönchtums im 4. Jahrhundert', *ZKG* 77 (1966), 11 n. 77.
[23] *Letter* 3, 3. For the images see Horace, *Carm.* 2, 17, 5 (cf. 1, 3, 8); Plautus, *Pseud.* 179.
[24] *Letter* 3, 3.

conflicting desires and racked by agonies of vacillation and remorse. He had come to the east full of dreams of throwing up everything for the ascetic life, but now that the hour of decision had struck he could not brace himself to take the plunge. His illnesses, intermittent but taxing, gave him something of an excuse, but he was also uneasily aware of the fascination pagan literature, his beloved library, and the intellectual delights of Antioch had for him. Even more shattering to his ideals, in spite of good resolutions he still found himself the prey to sensual longings which, he was sure, made him utterly unfit for the higher life. His letters written at this time or a few months later lay bare his morbid, guilt-ridden state of mind.[25] The most poignant is the short note he sent to Theodosius, the leader of the anchorites with whom he had lodged on his journey south.[26] His recent visit, he explains, has filled him with a yearning to join just such a community, which seems to him the nearest thing on earth to paradise; but, crushed down by every kind of sinfulness, he feels completely unworthy. He is like the diseased sheep which has strayed from the flock, like the prodigal son who has squandered his portion and cannot yet thrust carnal temptation from him. His only hope is that the prayers of the good monks will assist him to reach his goal.

(iii)

Although certainty is impossible, it was probably during this first stay at Antioch, in mid-Lent 374 if our chronology is correct, that Jerome had the frightening dream, or rather nightmare, which can fairly be said to have effected his second conversion.[27] Many prefer to place the episode a year or two later, when he had retired to the desert of Chalcis,[28] but against this is his own statement that it occurred when he was still making his way to Jerusalem[29]—a project he must have put off when he withdrew to the desert. Our information about his extraordinary experience comes from

[25] *Letters* 4, 2 (written at Antioch); 7, 3; 11 (written in the desert).

[26] *Letter* 2. Theodosius is perhaps to be identified with the remarkable founder of the monastery at Rhôsos (now Asruz), on the coast at the entrance to the Cilician Gulf, whom Theodoret describes (*Hist. relig.* 10: *PG* 82, 1388–93). For the site of his monastery, probably the modern Turkish village of Kale, some 20 km. south of Asruz, see P. Canivet, 'L'emplacement du monastère de S. Théodose de Rhôsos au Skopelos', *Byzantion* 38 (1968), 5–17. The monastery took particular pains over the entertainment of guests, and Jerome may well have turned aside and stayed there before moving on to Antioch.

[27] Supporters of this view include Grützmacher (1, 154), Cavallera (1, 29: cf. esp. n. 3), and A. Penna (*S. Gerolamo*, 26–8).

[28] For able recent statements of this case see C. A. Rapisarda, 'Ciceronianus es, non Christianus. Dove e quando avvenne il sogno di S. Girolamo?', *Miscellanea di studi di letteratura cristiana antica* 4 (1954), 1–18; J. J. Thierry, 'The Date of the Dream of Jerome', *VC* 17 (1963), 28–40. P. Antin. now supports it: see *Revue des études latines* 41 (1963), 376 f.

[29] *Letter* 22, 30. For his abandonment of the project see *Letter* 5, 1 (written from the desert), which speaks of his desire to go to Jerusalem as having been extinguished.

the letter he wrote ten years later to his spiritual protégée, Julia Eusto-chium, to confirm her in her resolve to embrace virginity. In the preceding section he has been cautioning the young girl against rhetoric, lyric poems, the clipped pronunciation affected by fashionable ladies, above all against reading Horace, Vergil, and Cicero, authors incompatible with Christianity. This leads him to tell his own 'unhappy story' as an object-lesson.

According to this,[30] when he made his decision to break with the world, he just could not bring himself to give up his laboriously acquired collection of classical books. However much he fasted, watched through the night, or wept over his sins, it was always to Cicero or Plautus that he came back. Even if he recovered his senses and opened the Bible, he was immediately put off by its uncouth style. Then in mid-Lent a wasting fever seized him, he was reduced to a bundle of bones, and people actually despaired of his life. Once while he was in this state, he felt himself all of a sudden caught up in the spirit and dragged before the tribunal of a Judge, before whom he lay grovelling and blinded by dazzling light. When the Judge inquired what he was, he replied, 'A Christian'; but the Judge retorted, 'You are lying. You are a disciple of Cicero, not of Christ; for your heart is where your treasure is.' The Judge then ordered him to be flogged, but he was much more tormented by his guilty conscience than by the blows, and cried out for mercy. The bystanders also interceded, asking that he should be given a chance to amend his ways. He himself swore a great oath, 'Lord, if ever again I possess worldly books, if ever I read them, I shall have denied You'. At once he was released, and returning to this world convinced the most incredulous by his tears. Jerome concludes his narrative by protesting that this was no idle dream. The reality of his experience was attested by the tribunal and the judgment, by his shoulders swollen black and blue, and by the fact that from that date he had studied Christian literature even more zealously than he had previously studied pagan books.

In the original Jerome's report is a magnificent piece of rhetorical description: so magnificent that many have questioned its veracity.[31] The whole incident, they have maintained, is a fiction which he deliberately contrived so as to impress on his readers as forcibly as possible the impropriety of a Christian's reading pagan authors. But such scepticism is unwarranted. Its best refutation is his own reaction when Rufinus, in 400, taunted him with having violated the solemn oath he had taken to the Judge.[32] Not for one moment did he deny the experience. His tactic was to

---

[30] *Letter* 22, 30.

[31] E.g. A. Schöne, *Die Weltchronik des Eusebius in ihrer Bearbeitung durch Hieronymus* (Berlin, 1900); E. Bickel, 'Das asketische Ideal bei Ambrosius, Hieronymus und Augustin', *Neue Jahrbücher für das Klassische Altertum, Geschichte und deutsche Literatur* 19 (1916), 456; P. Labriolle, 'Le songe de St Jérôme', *Miscellanea Geronimiana* (Rome, 1920), 227–35.

[32] *Apol. c. Hier.* 2, 6–7.

protest that it was only a dream, and that he could not be bound for life by a promise made in a dream.[33] But it is also refuted by the appeal he made to Eustochium and her mother Paula, around 389, to bear witness that for more than fifteen years he had never turned the pages of Cicero, Vergil, or any pagan writer.[34] He was clearly referring to the dream and the promise which he had so eloquently described in his earlier letter to Eustochium.

Jerome's experience, then, actually took place, even though he has elaborated his account of it for dramatic effect (ironically enough, incorporating snatches of imagery and phrases from Vergil).[35] We are not, of course, obliged to believe in the objective reality of the persons and events that figured in the dream. What seems evident is that, surging up from his uneasy subconscious, they accurately reflected the deep psychological tensions by which he was racked. There was, after all, an irreconcilable conflict, of which he himself was all too painfully aware, between his enthusiastic world-renouncing aspirations on the one hand, and his wholehearted delight in the classical, humanist culture, to which everything he wrote at the time bears witness, on the other.[36] There was nothing new in this conflict. Christians had been involved in it at least from the time of Tertullian, with his abrupt, 'What has Athens to do with Jerusalem, or the university with the Church?',[37] and it was to haunt successive generations of Christians after him. It is not surprising that in his case, delirious as he was with illness and excessive mortifications, his pangs of conscience found an outlet in the fantastic shapes of his nightmare.

Its impact was apparently immediate and effective. For a decade at least after that day Jerome seems to have striven to observe his promise strictly, shunning the study of the pagan classics and, so far as he still quoted from them, relying on his retentive memory.[38] The time was to come when he was, step by step, first to modify and then drastically to reinterpret this self-denying ordinance. His revised, more liberal literary theory is eloquently set out in Letter 70, written more than twenty years later, in which he first recalls that Moses, the prophets, and St Paul had all used pagan literature, and then argues that, just as God allowed the Israelites to take into their houses beautiful non-Jewish female captives provided their heads were shaven and their nails pared (so Deuteronomy 21,

---

[33] *Apology* 1, 30 f.

[34] *Comm. on Galatians* iii prol. (*PL* 26: 485–6).

[35] J. J. Thierry has listed some of these in *VC* 17 (1963), 33 f.

[36] See the sensible remarks of H. I. Marrou, *Revue belge de philologie et d'histoire* 38 (1960), 420.

[37] *De praescr. haer.* 7, 9. Jerome echoes the outburst with his own 'What has Horace to do with the psalter, Vergil with the evangelists, Cicero with the Apostle?' (*Letter* 22, 29).

[38] Thus he assures Paula and Eustochium (cf. *Comm. on Galatians* iii prol. cited above) that, if any snatches of the pagan classics have crept into his writings, he had remembered them 'as through the mists of an ancient dream'. Cf. also his protest to Rufinus (*Apology* 1, 30) that a promise concerns future conduct, and does not involve the elimination of a man's memory.

10–13), so Christians might safely adapt the splendours of secular literature to their purposes so long as the noxious elements were first excised. It was this change of attitude, of course, which was to cause him to be so embarrassed by Rufinus's taunt and to play down the importance of the dream. But there seems little doubt that in the years immediately following its occurrence he took it very seriously[39].

(iv)

Probably when he was regaining his health and spirits, in the spring or early summer of 374, Jerome began to feel once more the urge to fulfil his ascetic aims. Now it was no longer a question of going to Jerusalem; he would join the famous hermits in the Syrian desert, within reasonable reach of Antioch. His eagerness may have been whetted by conversations he had with a saintly old monk, Malchus, whom he had met on Evagrius's estate at Maronia, some thirty Roman miles from Antioch, and whose remarkable adventures he was to set down many years later in an edifying tract.[40] But, always gregarious by nature, he wished for a comrade, and so put the strongest possible pressure on Heliodorus to accompany him.[41] Heliodorus, who was sincerely seized with the monastic vocation, was momentarily attracted, but hesitated, unable to make up his mind. His painful memories of his recent journey to Jerusalem made the east repugnant, and he yearned to be back with his family at Altinum. Asceticism might take many forms, and surely he could equally well devote himself to it in the circle of his kinsfolk and retainers. There were long discussions and arguments, with Jerome vehemently insistent and Heliodorus 'softening his refusal with flattering words'. At last he made the great decision and, amid the tears and expostulations of his friend, set out for Italy—'driven away', as Jerome was to comment morbidly, 'by my wickednesses'.[42] Yet he made the parting easier by insisting that, once he had first-hand experience of the desert, Jerome should write inviting him to join him there.

Meanwhile, as if to prove to himself and others that he had abandoned his former repugnance for the language of the Bible, Jerome was preparing his first essay in scriptural interpretation. It was a commentary (now

---

[39] For a close analysis of Jerome's practice, and gradual return to a judicious reading of the classics, see H. Hagendahl, *Latin Fathers and the Classics* (Göteborg, 1958), 312–28. Like H. I. Marrou in his review cited in n. 36 above, I in general accept Hagendahl's conclusions. For the completely contrary view that Jerome kept his promise till the end see R. Eiswirth, *Hieronymus' Stellung zur Literatur und Kunst* (Wiesbaden, 1955), esp. 28 f.

[40] *Life of Malchus* 2.

[41] *Letter* 14, 1–3. In *Comm. on Obadiah* prol. (*CCL* 76: 59–60) he recalls the efforts he and Heliodorus had together made to settle in the Syrian desert.

[42] *Letter* 6, 2.

lost irretrievably) on Obadiah, the briefest of the prophets. We can date this relatively exactly, for more than twenty years later, when dedicating a more mature commentary on the same book to Pammachius, he was to recall that he had composed the earlier one 'when my dear Heliodorus and I were intent on settling together in the solitude of Syrian Chalcis'.[43] His exegesis, he added, had been wholly allegorical and mystical, for he had been ignorant of the historical setting. In later years, when he had developed his skill as an exegete, he became thoroughly ashamed of 'this brash initial effort of my youthful talent', and had privately vowed it to the bonfire. Imagine then his embarrassment and shame when a young man arrived from Italy (the meeting took place at Bethlehem) who actually possessed a copy and began praising it to the skies. Poor Jerome could only hang his head and attempt to disguise his blushes, consoling himself with the reflection that renowned authors like Cicero, Tertullian, Origen, and Quintilian had all in their day produced juvenilia which they later deprecated as amateurish.

In a more personal strain Jerome wrote at this time, probably in the summer of 374 after Heliodorus's departure, one of the most beautiful and emotionally uninhibited of his letters.[44] It was intended for Rufinus, but because he did not know his address but heard he was expected in Jerusalem, he directed it with a covering note to Florentinus, a western monk residing there who had been unstintingly helpful, among many others in distress, to Heliodorus.[45] Its object was to tell Rufinus how overjoyed he was to learn that he was in Egypt and how bitterly he regretted that his illnesses prevented their meeting, and also to bring him up to date about Bonosus's noble act of renunciation (its climax is the panegyric of Bonosus which has been already mentioned more than once). But what is most remarkable is the passionate admiration and love for Rufinus with which the letter overflows. The student familiar with the sneers and abuse with which Jerome was in later years to heap his one-time friend can only rub his eyes with astonishment as he reads these expressions of tender intimacy—for example, how eagerly he longs to embrace Rufinus, and to press with his lips 'that mouth which has some-times gone astray with me, sometimes shown good sense'. As he remarks to Florentinus, Rufinus was 'inseparably tied to' him 'by brotherly love'.[46] The letter ends with the exultant protest (how cruelly to be belied!) that nothing, however rich and gorgeous, can bear comparison with love: 'affection is beyond price, and friendship which can cease can never have been genuine'.

[43] *Comm. on Obadiah* prol. (CCL 76: 59–60).

[44] *Letter* 3.

[45] *Letter* 4.

[46] *Letter* 4, 2. For the praise of affection see *Letter* 3, 6: 'dilectio pretium non habet; amicitia quae desinere potest vera nunquam fuit.'

VI

The Desert: Joys and Trials

(i)

Full of ecstatic praise for Bonosus, Jerome's Letter 3 to Rufinus is also shot through with envy for his friend's heroic renunciation and with remorse for not having been able, like him, to break completely with the world. Clearly the time had come for him to fulfil the ascetic dreams he had glimpsed at Trier and Aquileia, had spoken of so wistfully to Theodosius the anchorite, and had canvassed, unsuccessfully but with passionate conviction, with Heliodorus. At last, after his many vacillations and excuses, Jerome made up his mind and went off, not to Jerusalem, but to the Syrian desert. It was the late summer or early autumn of 374, perhaps early 375, he was in his early forties, and in the euphoria of decision he no doubt imagined that he was abandoning the world and the conventional society of his fellow-men for good.

While we cannot precisely pin-point his retreat, his own notes provide a rough idea of its location. It was in the neighbourhood of Chalcis, more exactly Chalcis ad Belum, on the confines between northern Syria and the region west of the Euphrates overrun by semi-nomad tribes of Saracens.[1] Today the ruins of Chalcis, with its acropolis, lower town, and cemetery, in part surround and are in part covered by the mud-coloured, sugar-loaf huts of the hamlet named Qinnesrîn ('eagle's nest'), 88 km. east-south-east of Antakya (Antioch) and 27 km. south-west of Aleppo or Haleb (Beroea). In Jerome's time it was a bustling centre of agriculture and commerce, important caravan routes from Antioch and Beroea passed through it, and it was also a strategic point in the Roman 'limes' (he uses the term more than once), or elaborate zone of defence in depth designed to protect the province of Syria and its capital, Antioch. The town itself stood in a rolling plain, considered the most fertile part of Syria,[2] but a few kilometres to the south-east the vast desert began and, dotted with occasional oases and criss-crossed by military roads, stretched to Palmyra and beyond. It was a menacing desert, varied in aspect but everywhere exposed to the scorching sun, and cut across by sterile valleys

[1] *Letters* 5, 1; 7, 1; 15, 2: cf. *Life of Malchus* 3.
[2] Pliny, *Hist. nat.* 5, 81.

46

between rocky cliffs in which generations of cave-dwellers must have lived.[3]

When Jerome came here to find God, we must not picture him as living in total isolation. The desert (more correctly, semi-desert) in the vicinity of Chalcis was no solitude. Apart from scattered peasants scratching an existence wherever there was a patch of earth, it had become peopled with colonies of hermits who, while technically solitaries, maintained in different degrees some minimum of relations with each other. In Egypt, the classic home of anchoritism, the custom had sprung up in the first half of the fourth century of whole groups of hermits settling in some deserted region, each occupying a cell or cave out of sight or hearing of the others, but meeting together on Saturdays and Sundays for worship.[4] This practice had spread to Syria, where the hermits, for the most part simple, unlettered people speaking only Syriac, were renowned for their austerities and eccentric devotions. Squalid and clad in garments made of hair, they sometimes lived like beasts on raw herbs or loaded their bodies with heavy chains.[5] Jerome records having seen with his own eyes one who had lived for thirty years enclosed, feeding on barley bread and muddy water, and another who kept himself alive in an abandoned cistern on a diet of five dates a day.[6]

The object behind these extraordinary practices was twofold. Negatively, these monks wished to subdue the body, which on their interpretation of Christianity was evil in itself, and so to crush every carnal impulse. To this end even such seemingly innocent activities as eating and drinking were reduced to a minimum, while sleep was made as difficult as possible. But, positively, they were contemplatives; bewailing their sins, they above all desired to draw close to God and maintain uninterrupted communion with him. This was indeed the motive for the most spectacular of all the Syrian extravagances, the habit of living (St Simeon Stylites was the most famous example) on a pillar which, as often as not, was gradually increased in height so as to be farther from earth and nearer to heaven.

These were the ideas which inspired Jerome when he installed himself in his cell, probably a natural cave in the rocks. Like the other monks, like Malchus whose life he was later to describe, he supported himself 'by the daily labour of my hands and by my own sweat',[7] presumably tilling a

[3] For the geographical details in this paragraph I am indebted to P. Monceaux and L. Brossé, 'Chalcis ad Belum: Notes sur l'histoire et les ruines de la ville', *Syria* 6 (1925), 341–50; R. Dussaud, *Topographie historique de la Syrie antique et mediévale* (Paris, 1927), 476 f.; R. Monterde and A. Poidebard, *Le Limes de Chalcis* (2 vols., Paris, 1945); also to the British Admiralty Geographical Handbook *Syria* (Naval Intelligence Division, 1943).

[4] Cf. Palladius, *Hist. Laus.* 7, 3.

[5] For the hermits of Syria see A. Festugière, *Antioche païenne et chrétienne* (Paris, 1959), 245–356 (esp. 291–310: 'Traits charactéristiques de l'anchorétisme Syrien').

[6] *Life of Paul* 6.

[7] So *Letter* 17, 2.

plot of sparse soil and weaving mats or baskets. He himself was to depict in retrospect the lonely landscape burned up by the sun, the miserable diet with which (gourmet though he had been) he kept his skeleton-like body alive, and the bare earth that formed his bed.[8] One or two of his letters from this time distil his deep sense of sinfulness and penitence; while years later he was to recall, with romanticised exaggeration, the bitter tears he had shed as he strove to discipline his rebellious body.[9] Yet from time to time he had his reward: 'After my copious weeping, after fixing my eyes on heaven, I sometimes felt myself mingling with the ranks of angels, and I would cry with joyful exultation, "I run after You in the fragrance of Your perfumes".' Or, as he confided to Heliodorus, 'Believe me, here I see a strangely brighter light; here I rejoice to throw off the burden of flesh and soar to the pure radiance of heaven.'[10]

(ii)

Whatever Jerome's original plans or expectations, his sojourn in the desert was to last only two or three years, if that. The chronology of this period of his life is extremely obscure, but while their exact order cannot be determined we catch glimpses of some at any rate of his activities and states of mind. One impression that the modern student cannot help forming is that, for all the reality and severity of his mortifications, his self-imposed seclusion must have had some highly unusual features. For one thing, his friend Evagrius kept in close touch with him all the time, driving out frequently from Antioch to visit him and taking charge of his mail.[11] Jerome laments that his depression at his patron's periodical departures fully equalled the joy excited by his arrival. For another, while we have ample evidence of his penitence, prayers, and spiritual exercises, he had brought his ever growing library with him (his cave must have been roomier than most), and evidently spent a great deal of time reading books (Christian ones now, of course), and also having them copied. As always, he believed that a Christian should 'meditate on the law of the Lord day and night'.

All this comes out in a revealing letter in which he requests Florentinus, the Latin monk settled at Jerusalem with whom he had corresponded from Antioch, to get Rufinus to send him the eloquent commentaries of Reticius, bishop of Augustodunum (Autun), on Song of Songs, as well as to return the copies of Hilary's exposition of the Psalms and treatise *On the Synods* which he had transcribed for him at Trier. He also encloses a

[8] *Letter* 22, 7.
[9] *Letter* 22, 7.
[10] *Letters* 22, 7 (echoing Song of Songs 1, 3); 14, 10.
[11] *Letters* 7, 1; 15, 5.

list of other works he does not possess (the list is unfortunately lost) with the request that Florentinus should get them copied and despatched to him. In return Jerome offers to supply him with any books, especially on Scripture, he wishes; a mutual friend has told him of his needs in this respect. Florentinus need not fear that this commission will be troublesome, for Jerome's library is extensive and (this detail makes one rub one's eyes) he has young protégés, or assistants, in his service who are expert in the copyist's art.[12] We can only speculate who these 'alumni' were. The term was technical for an exposed child whom people had taken into their family as a slave or adopted son, and some have conjectured that they may have been foundlings like this, perhaps put in his way by Evagrius, whom Jerome had taught to read and write.[13] Others, with more plausibility, have identified them as young monks from the vicinity whom he had trained for the purpose.[14] But whoever they were, their presence adds an intriguing touch to our picture of Jerome's desert solitude.

Reading, biblical studies, and book production apart, Jerome was busily employed learning or improving his knowledge of languages. Writing to friends at Aquileia, he remarks that the only Latin conversations he can now have are with them through the medium of letters. Inevitably the native speech of the great majority of monks and others in the neighbourhood was Syriac: 'Either I must learn the barbarous gibberish or I must keep my mouth shut.'[15] Since this latter alternative was scarcely compatible with Jerome's temperament, we may conjecture that he picked up at least a smattering of Syriac. He must have done so if he was to maintain necessary day-to-day relations with other monks, or with peasants or nomads; and his later writings confirm this with their frequent citations or explanations of Syriac terms. It is fairly clear, too, that he greatly improved his understanding of spoken Greek, which was the language used by the better educated. It is true that there is an ironical remark in a letter to the local priest Mark (to which we shall come back shortly) which implies that Jerome did not consider himself any more fluent in Greek than in Syriac.[16] But once his desert sojourn was ended, he was able to follow the lectures of Apollinarius at Antioch, and not very long after that to start his great series of translations of Greek works.

[12] *Letter* 5, 2. A greatly respected early fourth-century bishop, Reticius attended the council of Arles (314) and wrote against Novatian: see *Famous Men* 82. Jerome was to criticise these commentaries for their blunders in *Letter* 37 (date 384) and to discourage Marcella from reading them: see below p. 95.

[13] So, e.g., Cavallera I, 42. For this usage, with illustrations from inscriptions, see *DACL* I, 1287–1306; also *Thesaurus Linguae Latinae* I, 1794 ad fin.

[14] A. J. Festugière, op. cit., 415 n. 2.

[15] *Letter* 7, 2. The older reading 'barbarus semi-sermo' (= 'the barbarous gibberish'), which has good MS support, seems preferable to 'barbarus seni sermo' ('at my advanced years I must learn a barbarous speech'), which Hilberg adopted.

[16] *Letter* 17, 2.

But the boldest, most surprising of his linguistic enterprises, the one moreover which was to have the most dramatic impact on his career and reputation, was his decision to learn Hebrew. To us it seems a natural enough step for him to take, immersed as he was in scriptural studies; but in fact he was the first Latin Christian to venture into this field, indeed the first Christian of note at all apart from the great theologian and thinker, Origen (c. 185–c. 254). Writing more than thirty years later, he was to give a characteristically ascetic explanation of his initiative: 'When I was a young man walled in by the solitude of the desert, I was unable to resist the allurements of vice and the hot passions of my nature. Although I tried to crush them with repeated fastings, my mind was in a turmoil with sinful thoughts. To bring it into control, I made myself the pupil of a Christian convert from Judaism. After the subtlety of Quintilian, the flowing eloquence of Cicero, the dignified prose of Fronto, the smooth grace of Pliny, I set myself to learn an alphabet and strove to pronounce hissing, breath-demanding words.'[17] Knowing how he was haunted with sex at the time, we need not doubt this frank avowal, but we may suspect that intellectual curiosity, the desire to study the Old Testament in the original, played its part too. As he ruefully recalls, the task he had set himself was no easy one; more than once he gave up in sheer despair, only (fortunately) to redouble his efforts. His struggle was indeed heroic. He was grappling with a language completely different in structure from his own, without any grammar-books or traditions of grammatical or syntactical analysis to help him, and the Hebrew he was struggling with was written exclusively in consonants, without the points which were later invented to indicate the vowels. Yet, with his anonymous Jewish convert to start him off (there were to be later successors), he was to acquire a mastery of the tongue far superior to that of any Christian writer before him (Origen not excluded) or for centuries after him.[18]

Meanwhile letters were flowing to and fro between himself and his friends at Aquileia, Jerusalem, and elsewhere, with Evagrius's mansion at Antioch serving as posting-box. Of the few which have survived we have already mentioned the one to Florentinus requesting parcels of books; a postscript undertaking to have a runaway slave of Florentinus's returned provides a fascinating side-light on the acquiescence of monks in the social order.[19] Of the letters to Aquileia one is to the deacon Julian; Jerome apologises for not having written more often, complains of his

---

[17] *Letter* 125, 12 (date c. 411). The participle 'anhelantia' (lit. 'panting') refers to the drawing of breath required for pronouncing certain aspirate or guttural sounds in Hebrew. Jerome gives a similar account of his difficulties in *Preface to the prophet Daniel* (PL 28, 1291–2). Cf. E. F. Sutcliffe, 'St Jerome's Pronunciation of Hebrew', *Biblica* 29 (1948), 116 f.

[18] On this paragraph see J. Barr, 'St Jerome's Appreciation of Hebrew', *Bulletin of the John Rylands Library* 49 (1966), 280–302.

[19] *Letter* 5, 3.

wretched health, and expresses joy at the news that his sister is sticking fast to her ascetic resolve.[20] It closes with a hint that the rupture between Jerome and his family remains unhealed, and that he is still the victim of maliciously damaging rumours.[20a] There is a much longer letter, over-flowing with affection, addressed jointly to Chromatius, Jovinus, and Eusebius, who have apparently written to him, but much more briefly than he would have liked ('Either you were too bored to write a longer letter or I didn't deserve one'). Jerome dwells with envious admiration on Bonosus, so much purer in spirit than himself ('buried in the tomb of my misdeeds, tied fast with the chains of my sins'), launches a coarse attack on the material vulgarity of Stridon, recommends his sister to his friends' tender care, and ecstatically salutes both the immaculate celibacy of their household and their victorious stand for the orthodox faith. Packed with mannered compliments and pedantic allusions, the letter shows that his privations have not weakened Jerome's command of polished rhetoric.[21]

There are also three letters, respectively to the nuns at Emona, the monk Antony, and his aunt Castorina, all different in tone, but all concerned to break down the wall of hostility which divides him from his relatives and former friends in north Italy.[22] The first, written 'in tears but also anger', with a deep sense of injury, admits that there is no fellowship between the Lord's handmaids and sinners, but humbly begs for pardon, pointing out plaintively that Christ's judgment is quite different from the spite and whispered gossip of human beings. The second is even more bitter: although Jesus was uniformly compassionate in his dealings with sinners, Antony is so stuck up that he has not deigned to answer his injured friend's ten letters with so much as a grunt. The last is a peremptory demand, after repeated rebuffs, for the forgiving attitude Christ requires of his disciples; if Castorina still refuses to reply, Jerome will consider himself absolved.

There are letters to other friends regretting their silence, pathetically begging them to write to him.[23] The whole collection (one or two more remain to be mentioned) represents only a fraction of his correspondence of these years, but lays bare his complex personality in a fascinating way. The warmth of his affections, his passionate desire to be loved, his prickly readiness to take offence, his rapid switches from bitter self-reproach to self-righteous indignation, his intense dislike of being alone—all these traits come to light in them. Often he was disgusted with himself because, in spite of all his fastings and mortifications, he could not rid himself of the

[20] *Letter* 6.
[20a] Cf. his remark about his total ignorance of what is happening at home, his reference to the 'Iberian viper,' and the defiance he flings at men who judge him.
[21] *Letter* 7.
[22] *Letters* 11; 12; 13.
[23] Cf. *Letters* 8 (to the sub-deacon Niceas); 9 (to the Aquileian monk Chrysocomas).

sensual longings which had plagued him since early manhood. 'How often,' he was to lament years later,[24] 'when I was installed in the desert . . . I would imagine myself taking part in the gay life of Rome! . . . Although my only companions were scorpions and wild beasts, time and again I was mingling with the dances of girls. My face was pallid with fasting and my body chill, but my mind was throbbing with desires; my flesh was as good as dead, but the flames of lust raged in it.' Yet in a different mood he could write to Heliodorus at Altinum urging him, in the most ecstatic terms, to change his mind and join him in the desert, brushing aside any excuses he might advance and extolling the spiritual security of the hermit's life.[25] Both in its language and in the deployment of its arguments this is one of the most elaborately contrived of his compositions; in later life he was himself to condemn it[26] (although some pious souls admired it so much that they learned it by heart)[27] as a mere school exercise in rhetoric. But brighter than all its dazzling artifice is the deeply felt love for the austere life he had chosen that gleams through it.

(iii)

Cruel though its effect on his general health, Jerome's desert sojourn seems to have been psychologically beneficial, helping to settle the tensions of his passionate nature. At any rate, while his preoccupation with sex remains, we hear little henceforth of agonies of remorse for having succumbed to its onslaughts. But now (it must have been 376 or the winter of 376/7)[28] an altogether different storm which had been brewing burst over his head. To his surprise and disgust, he found himself dragged by his neighbours in the desert into the acrimonious disputes about the triune Godhead which still convulsed the east and divided it from the west, and which were reflected (as we saw in the last chapter)[29] in the tragic schism fragmenting the Christian community at Antioch. Most embarrassing of all, his own orthodoxy was being impugned, and he was being challenged to declare his adhesion to the description of the Trinity as 'one essence, three hypostases'. At the council of Nicaea (325) 'essence' and 'hypostasis' had been treated as equivalents, and both the west and his

[24] *Letter* 22, 7.

[25] *Letter* 14.

[26] *Letter* 52, 1 (date 394: it was to Nepotianus, nephew of Heliodorus, who was then bishop of Altinum).

[27] So the penitent Fabiola: see *Letter* 77, 9.

[28] For this dating see Cavallera II, 16. It should be noted that *Letter* 15, 3 and 5 implies that the Meletians are denied access to the churches of Antioch (cf. the description of them as 'Campenses'), while *Letter* 16, 2 represents the Arians as installed with government support. Valens revoked his sentence of exile on the orthodox bishops towards the end of 377 in preparation for his campaign against the Goths.

[29] See above p. 38.

friend Evagrius and Bishop Paulinus preferred this older usage. The new, more nuanced formula, however, was becoming widely accepted in the east, and in Syria was strongly backed by Bishop Meletius, at present exiled by the Arianising emperor Valens and cold-shouldered by Pope Damasus, as well as by the great majority of Christians at Antioch and by the hermits around Chalcis.

Jerome's exasperation, and also his blindly stubborn Latin stance, come out in an excited letter he addressed to Damasus asking for guidance.[30] Unknown as he then was, his direct approach to the pope is puzzling; we are bound to wonder whether he had met him in Rome or whether he had been introduced to him by Evagrius, who knew Damasus well and was acting as his agent in the east. The letter is full of scorn for the quarrelsomeness of eastern Christianity, of eulogy for the Roman church (the church of his own baptism, as he proudly recalls) for its inflexible maintenance of the true faith, and of fulsome flattery of Damasus, the occupant of the chair of Peter, the rock on which the Church is built. First, Jerome professes disdain for the three rival bishops of Antioch: 'I do not know Vitalis, Meletius I repudiate, I take no notice of Paulinus.' The only bishops he follows, since he is so far removed from Rome, are certain Egyptian ones whose beliefs, he knows, are identical with the pope's, and whom the emperor has exiled to Syria because of them. Then he comes to the point. All the hubbub is because he, a Roman Christian whose faith should be above suspicion, is being badgered by the followers of Meletius ('the Arian brood') to subscribe their new, unheard-of formula 'three hypostases', or else be branded as a heretic. Jerome is perfectly ready to affirm that there are three subsistent persons in the consubstantial Trinity, but he cannot swallow 'hypostasis' as synonymous with 'person'. Is the creed of Nicaea to be superseded? The whole tradition of the schools is agreed that 'hypostasis' means 'substance' or 'essence'; and to speak of God, who is one and indivisible, as three distinct substances or essences must lead inevitably to the Arian blasphemy. At least, that is how Jerome sees the matter, but he is ready to be guided by the pope both on this matter and also on whom he ought to be in communion with at Antioch. But he warns Damasus that, in pressing for the 'three hypostases' formula, Meletius's followers are craftily seeking the support of his authority for the use of the term 'hypostasis' in its original and proper sense.

This excursion of Jerome's, the first of which we have record, into theological controversy, is instructive. A student of Hilary's *On the Synods*, he was also familiar with the statesmanlike council which Athanasius had convened at Alexandria in 362 to prepare a rapprochement

[30] *Letter* 15.

between the rival parties; he referred to it in the letter. From these and other sources he must have been fully briefed about the development of the doctrinal debate in the east. It was sheer prejudice, or deliberate perversity, to dismiss the adherents of the 'three hypostases' doctrine as Arians. They were just as much opposed to Arianism, with its subordination of the Son to the Father and of the Holy Spirit to the Son and its denial of divinity to both, as he was. The eirenical synod of Alexandria, as he well knew, had acknowledged the legitimacy of both the 'three hypostases' terminology and the 'one hypostasis' terminology, provided each was appropriately safeguarded.[31] Thus, while he had every right to protest against the 'three hypostasis' formula being thrust down his throat, he should have recognised that, in adopting it, the Meletians were only seeking to protect the distinctness of the three equal persons. And he was plainly wrong to insinuate that they were using it as a cunning device for smuggling in Arianism.

The pope did not acknowledge the letter, and a few months later Jerome despatched another, shorter but even more importunate.[32] Once again he recalls his baptism at Rome, obsequiously eulogises Damasus and his apostolic office, and assures him that, if he is now languishing in the Syrian waste, his banishment is self-inflicted and not the result of any sentence passed upon him. An anxious note pervades this letter; Jerome seems to feel himself the object of personal attack. Even in the desert his relentless adversary pursues him. On the one hand there are the Arians, buttressed by government support. On the other hand, each of the three factions into which Christians in Antioch are split strives to seize him for its own. Meanwhile the monks dwelling around menace him with their long established authority. Meletius, Vitalis, Paulinus—all three profess to belong to the pope, but they cannot all be right. For his own part, 'he who is attached to Peter's chair is my man'. So he begs his holiness, by the Lord's cross and passion, to tell him with which of them he should communicate. Like its predecessor, this letter (so far as we know), remained unanswered.

It was not long before Jerome reached breaking-point, and we have one further letter which reveals this.[33] Written to Mark, a priest of the district with whom he was personally on good terms, it is a pathetic mixture of furious indignation, sheer despair, and acceptance of defeat.

---

[31] According to Athanasius, *Tom. ad Antioch.* 5 f. (*PG* 26, 801), the former was accepted on the understanding that the three hypostases were not conceived of as differing in essence but as persons of the one Godhead, the latter on the understanding that 'hypostasis' was synonymous with 'ousia' or 'essence' and that the distinction of the three persons was not obliterated as in Sabellianism.

[32] *Letter* 16.

[33] *Letter* 17. In fact we know almost nothing about this Mark; he may have exercised his ministry among the hermits, and the letter shows that Jerome had good relations with him.

Evidently he has been becoming increasingly the target of abuse and insinuation, and life has been made insupportable. He is being openly denounced as a heretic; despite his tireless protestations that there are three distinct persons in the Godhead, he is being called a Sabellian because he refuses to describe them as 'hypostases'. Every day a statement of belief is being demanded of him, as though the one he had made at his baptism were not sufficient; but whatever statement he furnishes is rejected as unacceptable. Mark too has inquired about his faith, probably trying to help him, and Jerome replies that he has already set it down in writing.[34] Furthermore, every effort is being made to shut him up, as if, with his marvellous fluency in Greek and Syriac (!), there were a danger of his touring the churches and subverting people's faith. And there are whispers of his making improper financial gains. His enemies have even succeeded in ejecting his few sympathetic companions, and Jerome feels that no corner of the desert is being left to him: 'All they want is that I should go away.' This he would be only too glad to do, were he not prevented by physical weakness and the severe winter weather. He begs to be allowed to remain till spring; but if that is considered too long, he will pack his bags forthwith.

We can roughly construct what had happened. The hermits round Chalcis instinctively regarded Jerome as an intruder[35] who was always likely to be a focus of discord in their midst. He was different—a Latin, a highly educated intellectual who attracted an élite group around him, maintained close relations with rich grandees in Antioch, and even in his cavern was surrounded by an extraordinary team of copyists. He was also Jerome—self-willed and sharp-tongued, irascible to the point of morbidity, inordinately proud of his Roman links and contemptuous of his uncultivated, ill-mannered, Syriac-speaking neighbours. The fact that he was a westerner, critical like his friend Evagrius of the new eastern theology, gave them a wonderful pretext for rounding on him. The effect on Jerome was catastrophic. All his starry-eyed illusions about monks dropped from him. These were hypocrites who, for all their filthy robes, mane-like hair, and back-breaking chains, were more arrogant than kings. From their uncouth caves they had the impertinence to pass sentence on bishops and set aside the agreed decisions of councils.[36] A few months

---

[34] Jerome adds that he had given it to 'the holy Cyril', an unknown person. The profession is certainly not to be identified with the obviously much later 'Fides Hieronymi presbyteri' found in MS Vat. lat. 1328, fol. 415 r. and v. and printed in J. A. de Aldama, *El Símbolo Toledano I* (Rome, 1934), 148–50.

[35] The expression is A. J. Festugière's: cf. *Antioche païenne et chrétienne*, 417.

[36] *Letter* 17, 2. What he seems to mean is that, in insisting on the 'three hypostases' formula and theology, they are bypassing, if not rejecting, the creed of the Nicene council, the only creed recognised by himself and those of his way of thinking, which had treated 'hypostasis' and 'essence' as synonymous.

before he had written to Heliodorus, with the enthusiasm of an idealist, 'O desert bedecked with Christ's flowers! O wilderness gladdened by God's intimate presence!'[37] Earlier still he had told the anchorite Theodosius how ardently he longed to settle in 'those spots abandoned by their inhabitants, but transformed into a sort of paradise by the saints thronging them'.[38] Now that he had seen the harsh reality, all that was changed. When his close friends had been edged out by the monks, they had gone gladly, saying that it was better to live among savage beasts than with Christians like that.[39] Shattered and disillusioned, Jerome felt much the same as they did when, having made his decision, he said goodbye to his cell and disconsolately made the journey back to Antioch.

[37] *Letter* 14, 10.
[38] *Letter* 2.
[39] *Letter* 17, 3.

VII

Antioch Again

(i)

For the next phase of Jerome's life, between his humiliating flight from the desert in 376 or 377 and the start of his second, richly creative stay in Rome in 382, we return to the complete lack of contemporary letters and other documentation which baffled our attempts to reconstruct his childhood, youth, and early manhood. From statements or references set down much later we gather that he spent the earlier part of this stretch of years in Antioch, presumably in Evagrius's household, and the concluding part in Constantinople. The detailed chronology, however, is extremely uncertain, and while we can confidently attribute certain events and activities to this period, there are others about which such assurance is impossible, and which might reasonably be assigned to a different date. What is absolutely clear, and what makes the fragmentary character of the information available so tantalising, is that these five or six years were crucial in Jerome's development. Not only did they see a remarkable deepening of his erudition and theological culture, but he now becomes a successful author and (he was approaching fifty) a figure of growing reputation.

One fact which stands out is that, once settled again in Antioch, he abandoned the pose of neutrality towards the schism dividing the Christians of the great Syrian metropolis which he had maintained in the desert. Only a year before he had protested to Pope Damasus that he refused to choose between the three rival bishops, but he now threw in his lot unreservedly with Paulinus, the revered leader of the tiny 'old-Nicene' congregation which affirmed that there were three coequal persons in the Trinity but rejected the description of them as 'three hypostases'. His action was entirely logical; Paulinus's views were identical with those for which Jerome had been hounded by his hermit tormentors, themselves rabid supporters (like the great majority of the orthodox in Antioch) of Meletius and the 'three hypostases' theology. But there was more to it than that. In the meantime Damasus, to the distress of Basil of Caesarea, had come out on the side of Paulinus, corresponding with him as if he were the canonical bishop of Antioch.[1] Evagrius, too, who after his

---

[1] Damasus's letter 'Per filium' (*Ep.* 3: *PL* 13, 356 f. and *PL* 56, 684–6), sent to Paulinus in

diplomatic conversations with Basil at Caesarea in 373 had surprised and disappointed him by cold-shouldering the Meletians on his return to Antioch, had now openly broken with them and joined Paulinus's congregation.[2]

It was natural that Jerome, now that the pope and his patron had so definitely committed themselves, should adopt the same stance. Needless to say, these accessions, especially that of the influential Evagrius (a decade or so later he was to succeed Paulinus as bishop of the little sect, and thus to prolong the unhappy schism) were a tremendous boost to the Paulinians, and Paulinus was quick to follow up his success by persuading Jerome to be ordained priest by him. Evidently Jerome put up a stiff resistance, and when he eventually consented made it clear that his new priestly status was not to interfere with his freedom as a monk, still less shackle him to the church of Antioch.[3] His attitude may seem curious, but in the later fourth century the monastic life, with its (in theory) complete lack of ties and absolute dedication to God, presented itself to many as the most perfect form of Christian vocation.[4] Despite his unnerving experience of what monks could be like in practice, this was the ideal which still captivated Jerome. He was always to profess reverence for the official ministry (although trouncing its unworthy members mercilessly), but he shrank from the pastoral responsibilities, and also the special temptations, it involved.[5] As a result, while reluctantly accepting ordination, he seems to have scarcely ever exercised the sacerdotal functions,[6] and habitually spoke of himself as a monk.

(ii)

So far we have been treading on firm ground, but now we move from certainty to probability. It was during this second stay at Antioch, in all

---

summer 376 and prescribing the terms on which he might admit Vitalis to communion, openly treats him as the sole orthodox and canonical bishop. For Basil's distress and the glee of the Paulinians, see Basil, *Epp.* 214, 2; 216. Cf. E. Schwartz, 'Zur Kirchengeschichte des vierten Jahrhunderts', *ZNTW* 34 (1935), 185.

[2] In 373 he had withdrawn from communion with Meletius: see above p. 39; Basil, *Ep.* 156, 3. The arrival of Damasus's letter to Paulinus must have given him the signal to join his congregation.

[3] Cf. *Against John* 41, where he states that he had accepted ordination on the strict condition that it did not remove his position as a monk 'because of which I abandoned the world'.

[4] Cf. e.g., his remarks to Heliodorus in *Letter* 14, 6, where he implies that the monk is Christ's perfect servant.

[5] He honoured the clergy as those who, 'succeeding to the Apostles, consecrate Christ's body and make us Christians', who feed and judge Christ's sheep (e.g. *Letter* 14, 8). For the temptations to which they are exposed see, e.g., *Letter* 52 (to Nepotian).

[6] Cf. *Letter* 51, 1 (written by Epiphanius in Greek in 394 and translated by Jerome), which reports that, although there was a shortage of priests in his monastery at Bethlehem, Jerome refused, 'for reasons of bashfulness and humility', to exercise the ministry appropriate to a priest.

likelihood, that Jerome, as he was to recall some twenty years later, attended lectures on the Bible given by Apollinarius, bishop of nearby Laodicea (Latakia) on the Syrian coast.[7]

Apollinarius, who was a first-class rhetorician now in his late sixties, had one of the most acute and versatile minds of the century, and was immensely admired both for his championship of Christ's full divinity against the Arians and for his able rebuttal of the Neoplatonist Porphyry's (232/3–c. 305) reasoned attack on Christianity. A voluminous writer, he published a whole library of scripture commentaries as well as more directly theological works;[8] and when Julian the Apostate in 362 forbade Christians to teach literature in schools, he joined with his father in re-writing much of the Bible in classical forms (epic hexameters, tragedies, dialogues, etc.) so that Christian children might not be deprived of a classical education. Latterly, however, his ingenious theory of the union of divine and human in Christ (he held that Jesus had had no human rational soul, its place being taken by the Logos) had fallen under sus-picion and been condemned. For this reason many prefer to back-date Jerome's attendance at his lectures to his earlier residence at Antioch, finding it incredible that such a stickler for orthodoxy should have studied under a heretic. But this is to overlook the fact that, for all the disquiet excited by his Christological views, Apollinarius remained personally a respected figure; and Jerome himself makes the point that, while valuing his teacher's scriptural erudition, he paid no attention to his more debat-able dogmatic opinions.[9] On the more practical level, it is questionable whether in the earlier period Jerome knew enough spoken Greek, or for that matter enjoyed sufficiently good health, to be able to follow difficult, technical lecture-courses with profit.

That he did derive profit from these lectures we need not doubt. He was to spend much of his later life studying and expounding the Bible, and here for the first time he was sitting under a master who could explain it with all the apparatus of scholarship which years before Donatus at Rome had brought to his expositions of Vergil and Terence, but also with less pedantry, greater insight, and disarming eloquence. If we can judge by the substantial fragments of his commentary on St Paul's Epistle to the Romans, Apollinarius was one of the most accomplished and keen-sighted Greek exegetes of his time. He had little use for either the niggling

[7] *Letter* 84, 3 (date 398), where, without fixing the time precisely, he recalls that 'at Antioch I frequently listened to Apollinarius of Laodicea and held him in high regard'.

[8] See Jerome, *Famous Men* 104 (Apollinarius's thirty books against Porphyry 'are reckoned among the best of his works'); Philostorgius, *Hist. eccl.* 8, 14 (they eclipse the earlier refutations of Methodius and Eusebius). Jerome also states (loc. cit.) that he wrote 'volumes without count on the scriptures'.

[9] *Letter* 84, 3: 'While he instructed me in Scripture, I never accepted his disputable dogma on Christ's human mind.'

examination of words popular in some circles or the imaginative allegorism favoured by others. Rather he exerted himself to bring out in all its width and depth what his author was trying to say.[10] Sometimes in his own later commentaries Jerome was to speak slightingly of Apollinarius's work, as if it had consisted of little more than superficial summaries;[11] and he was himself to practise the fanciful allegorical method of Biblical interpretation which was associated with Alexandria rather than Antioch. Even so, it is significant that he was to work on the principle that this allegorical or spiritual interpretation should only be developed after the direct, literal sense of Scripture had been established. We may reasonably surmise that it was at Antioch, from Apollinarius among others, that he learned this respect for the historical approach.

(iii)

Two literary works, marking Jerome's public début as an author, should probably be assigned to this period, although reasonable cases can be argued for dating the one rather earlier and the other much later.

The first, the little *Life of Paul the First Hermit*,[12] introduced an entirely new genre into Latin literature and proved one of the most popular of his writings, as is shown by the production shortly after its publication of six translations into Greek, one into Coptic, one into Syriac, and one into Ethiopic. It is not really a biography, since it deals with only the opening and closing phases of its hero's life, but rather a romantic idealisation of monastic withdrawal, as full of wonders and fabulous creatures as a fairy-tale. Its ostensible object, as the title proclaims, is to prove that the famous Antony of Egypt (d. 356), widely believed to have been the originator of monasticism, had in fact had a precursor in one Paul, of Thebes in Upper Egypt (d. *c.* 341). Indeed, Jerome insists, Antony had acknowledged Paul's priority, visiting him when already 113 years old in his secluded cave, witnessing his death, and (assisted by two grief-stricken but obliging lions) burying his corpse. Once completed, Jerome sent the book to his centenarian friend Paul of Concordia ('I am sending you, Paul so aged, a yet more aged Paul . . . '), and the tone of the accompanying letter,[13] with no mention of the desert and its promise of further compositions if this one proves acceptable, 'along with a parcel of Oriental wares',

---

[10] Cf. K. Staab, *Pauluskommentare aus der Griechischen Kirche* (Münster i.W., 1933), xxiii–xxv, texts in 57–82).

[11] E.g. *Comm. on Hosea* prol.; *Comm. on Malachi* prol.; *Comm. on Isaiah* prol. (CCL 76, 4; 76A: 941–2; 73: 5–6).

[12] See esp. P. de Labriolle, *Vie de Paul de Thèbes et Vie d'Hilaire* (Paris, 1906). For a better text than that in *PL* 23, 17–30 see the edition (unfortunately bowdlerised) by I. S. Kozik, *The First Desert Hero: St Jerome's Vita Pauli* (New York, 1968).

[13] *Letter* 10, 3. For Paul of Concordia see above p. 33.

suggests that Jerome was now at Antioch and not, as has often been proposed, in his retreat near Chalcis.[14]

Outside Jerome's *Life*, no evidence for Paul of Thebes survives,[15] and doubts have been cast on his very existence by modern scholars, as they were (to his intense irritation) by Jerome's own contemporaries.[16] The question scarcely concerns us, but Jerome was obviously convinced that he was dealing with a historical figure.[17] We may readily believe his statement that the identity of the first hermit was a subject of lively discussion, and he may have picked up scraps of information from Nicene-minded Egyptians exiled to Syria because they refused to conform with Valens's compromise religious policy. The idea of writing such a book was probably suggested by his friend Evagrius's free version of Athanasius's much longer, immensely successful *Life of Antony*, which in parts he imitates; and he may have found something specially appealing in Paul because, in contrast to Antony, who had shied away from bookish studies,[18] he was a monk with a first-class education, like Jerome himself! The *Life* is certainly a masterpiece of story-telling; and if he claims to have deliberately adopted a simple style,[19] the simplicity is the product of consummate art, and does not exclude colourful descriptions, carefully chosen words and cadences, and the occasional classical echo. It also tells us something about Jerome himself—his eye for detail, his feeling for the beauties of nature, his credulity and fascination for the marvellous, the ecstatic nature of his piety. Even his obsession with sex comes out in the story, quite unnecessarily introduced but frankly related with relish, of the young martyr whose torture consisted in being intimately fondled by a beautiful harlot and who, when he could no longer control his desires, bit off his tongue and spat it in her face. With its simple message (what Christian would not prefer the poverty and loneliness of Paul to all the glamour of riches?), the book shows that Jerome still cherished a wistful longing for the life of complete self-denial and isolation which he knew in his heart of hearts was not for him.

[14] The earlier date is supported by the reading 'et videre' in ch. 6, which implies that when he wrote Jerome was actually witnessing the mortifications of the desert solitaries. But it is noteworthy that this present infinitive, unlikely in itself, is not reproduced by the earliest Greek translations of the *Life*. For the text of these see W. A. Oldfather (ed.), *Studies in the Text Tradition of St. Jerome's Vitae Patrum* (Urbana, 1943), 143–250.

[15] H. Delehaye argued that there is a clear mention of him in a memorial addressed in 383/4 by the Luciferians Marcellinus and Faustinus to the emperors Valentinian, Theodosius, and Arcadius: *Analecta Bollandiana* 44 (1926), 64–9. But F. Cavallera has shown (*Rev. d'ascétisme et de mystique* 7 (1926), 302–5) that the Paul mentioned there cannot be Paul of Thebes.

[16] Cf. *Life of Hilarion* prol.

[17] *Life of Paul* prol.: cf. *Letters* 22, 36; 58, 5; 108, 6; *Life of Hilarion* prol.; *Chronicle* A.D. 356 (*GCS* 47, 240).

[18] Athanasius, *Vita Ant.* 1: cf. *Life of Paul* 4.

[19] *Letter* 10, 3. For some interesting remarks on the *Life*, including its stylistic features, see E. Coleiro, 'St Jerome's Lives of the Hermits', *VC* 11 (1957), 161–78.

His letter to Paul of Concordia includes a request for a curious assort-ment of books. These are the gospel commentaries of Fortunatianus, a writer whom Jerome flattered now but was later to castigate for actively abetting the emperor Constantius's efforts to force a compromise creed, neither Arian nor Nicene, on a vacillating pope;[20] the recently published sketch of the Roman empire from Augustus to Constantius (*Liber de Caesaribus*) by Aurelius Victor, a pagan 'who disliked Christianity to the point of ignoring it';[21] and some letters of Novatian, the austere Roman theologian who, disgusted by Pope Cornelius's leniency in receiving back Christians who had lapsed under persecution, had set up a splinter church in 251 with himself as anti-pope. After taking in the poison of this schis-matic, he explained, he would all the more enjoy the antidote supplied by Cyprian of Carthage (whose works he was also apparently studying), who had dissociated himself from Novatian and looked on schism with abhor-rence. All this is interesting evidence not only for Jerome's assiduous reading, but for his grappling with issues of church discipline and the nature of the Church itself, in particular the problem whether it is a society of saints (as rigorists like Novatian firmly held) or can make room for sinners who give proof of a change of heart.

It is with this latter problem that the second of the publications to be mentioned here, the *Altercation of a Luciferian with an Orthodox*,[22] is concerned. It is tempting to place this several years later, when Jerome was working in Rome, mainly because the Luciferian sect was active there in the early 380s, and because certain expressions in it (e.g. 'mastruca', signifying the Sardinian skin cloak, and 'montenses', i.e. 'men of the mountain', a Roman nickname for the Donatists)[23] would have been unintelligible at Antioch and seem to presuppose an Italian audience. Against this, however, we should remember that there were pockets of the Luciferians in the east too, and that whatever works Jerome produced in the east, being written in Latin, were really designed for western readers. There are also hints in the pamphlet, notably the remark that the men selected for the episcopate have been brought up on Plato and Aristophanes, which only make sense in the east.[24] A decision is delicately poised, but what swings the balance is, first, the relative gaucherie and

[20] He describes him as 'detestabilis' in *Famous Men* 97 on account of the pressure he had put on Pope Liberius.

[21] So C. G. Starr, *American Historical Review* 61 (1956), 586. The whole article, 'Aurelius Victor: Historian of Empire', is an illuminating study of a neglected author.

[22] Text in *PL* 23, 155–82. There is a good analysis in I. Opelt, *Hieronymus' Streitschriften* (Heidelberg, 1973), 13–27.

[23] For these expressions see *Altercation* 1 and 28. The Donatists were a schismatic group who broke away from the Catholic Church in N. Africa as a protest against the consecration of Caecilian, bishop of Carthage, by a bishop whom they regarded as having betrayed the faith during Diocletian's persecution.

[24] *Altercation* 11. For 'Aristophanes' some read 'Aristotle'.

immaturity of the dialogue's construction, and, secondly, the fact that Jerome himself, in the list of his writings included in *Famous Men*, places it firmly among works which we know he composed in the east before his move to Rome.[25]

Whatever its correct date, the *Altercation* is the earliest of Jerome's controversial pamphlets. Pretending to be the report of an actual debate (a scenario only half-heartedly carried through), it attacks a schismatic sect known after their founder as Luciferians. Lucifer, bishop of Cagliari in Sardinia (d. *c.* 370), had been a fanatical supporter of the Nicene doctrine in its strictest form, and had suffered exile for defying the Arianising Constantius to his face. On the emperor's death in 361 Nicene leaders like Hilary in the west and Athanasius in the east, in the interests of unity, had taken a conciliatory line with the multitudes who, by force or persuasion, had temporarily acquiesced in the watered down creed Constantius had imposed. All they had required of them was to profess the Nicene faith and forswear Arianism. But Lucifer would have none of this. Instead of taking part in the eirenic synod of Alexandria (362),[26] he had rushed off to Antioch, had consecrated Paulinus (to him the sole representative there of pure Nicene orthodoxy) as bishop, and had thereby ensured the continuance of the Antiochene schism. As for those who had made concessions to Constantius, he and his followers were adamant that, while laymen might be received into communion provided they repented of their backsliding, bishops should lose their clerical standing.

One might have expected Jerome, a rigorist who had thrown in his lot with Paulinus, to regard Lucifer as a man after his own heart; and it is true that in the *Altercation* the Orthodox speaks of him respectfully, more in sorrow than in anger. Although the Luciferian is initially aggressive, the dialogue is surprisingly moderate in tone, contrasting strikingly with Jerome's normal polemical ferocity. In the first part (paras. 2–14) the Orthodox has little difficulty in showing up his opponent's inconsistency; if he receives back a penitent layman on the ground that his baptismal status is unimpaired, it is illogical to reject a penitent bishop on the ground that the sacraments he administers are invalid. He is less at his ease when later faced with the case of an extremist Luciferian, the Roman deacon Hilary, who demanded that bishops and laymen who had sold the pass should both alike be rebaptised. This second half of the treatise contains a valuable historical excursus and a discussion of the question (made famous by a clash in 255–7 between Cyprian of Carthage and Pope Stephen I) whether those who have been baptised by heretics need to be rebaptised. In the former the Orthodox recounts how the bishops attending the

[25] *Famous Men* 137. For the later, Roman date see, e.g., Grützmacher 1, 51–9; P. Batiffol, 'Les sources de l'Altercatio . . . ', *Miscellanea Geronimiana* (Rome, 1920), 97–113.
[26] See above pp. 53 f.

council of Ariminum (Rimini) in 359 had been tricked into subscribing an Arian creed but later came to their senses. In the latter he shows how, in spite of Cyprian's efforts to maintain the contrary, the Church had consistently set its face against the rebaptism of heretics. This practice, he claims, is grounded in the scriptural conception of the Church as a mixed society containing, like the Ark, both good and bad; it will be for Christ, on the day of judgment, to separate them and send them their different ways.[27]

The *Altercation* shows little theological originality, but it is an instructive witness to Jerome's understanding of the nature of the Church, his respect for tradition as an independent authority, his conviction of the duty of abiding in the Church founded by the Apostles, his horror of sects and schisms.[28] It also throws light on his literary and controversial methods. Whole sections can be shown to be built up of material, suitably modified, which he has borrowed from authors in whose works he has soaked himself: chiefly Tertullian and Cyprian, but also Hilary, Athanasius and others. This indebtedness is not acknowledged (we shall find this reticence habitual in Jerome), and is discovered only by patient probing.[29] The historical excursus contains a lengthy extract, not available elsewhere, which he has taken (we have his word for it) from the official minutes of the council of Ariminum.[30] On the other hand, he commits serious blunders, does not hesitate to twist or even suppress facts in order to press his argument home, and implies acquaintance with documents (the minutes of the famous council of Nicaea) on which, if they ever existed at all, he is unlikely to have set eyes.[31] His theological prejudice comes out in his caricature of Valens, the court prelate who played a leading part at Ariminum, as an out-and-out Arian, and of the decisions of the synod as equivalent to the adoption of Arianism. In fact Valens repudiated Arianism proper and professed the mediating doctrine favoured by the emperor, and it was that doctrine, not Arianism proper, that the synod endorsed.[32]

[27] *Altercation* 22.

[28] Cf. *Altercation* 22 (the Church); 8; 23; 27 (tradition or 'ancient custom'); 28 (the apostolic Church, the guardian of Scripture; the sects 'synagogues of Satan'). For Jerome's ecclesiology in detail see Y. Bodin, *Saint Jérôme et l'église* (Paris, 1966).

[29] Cf. two exhaustive studies: P. Batiffol, 'Les sources de l'*Altercatio Luciferiani et Orthodoxi* de saint Jérôme', *Miscellanea Geronimiana* (Rome, 1920), 97–113; Y. Duval, 'Saint Jérôme devant le baptême des hérétiques', *Revue des études augustiniennes* 14 (1968), 145–81.

[30] *Altercation* 17 f. He refers readers seeking fuller information to 'the acts of the synod of Ariminum, from which I have extracted this material'.

[31] *Altercation* 20. He appeals also to the list of bishops who had subscribed the Nicene creed, but it seems that the only list to which he had access was the list of the bishops who had been present. See P. Batiffol, art. cit., 111. For other examples cf. Jerome's statements that Arius, whom we know to have been exiled, was received back at the council of Nicaea (*Alterc.* 20), and that the African episcopate repudiated their original decision that heretics must be rebaptised (*Alterc.* 23).

[32] For a good recent account of the synod see M. Meslin, *Les Ariens d'Occident* 335–430 (Paris, 1967).

(iv)

It must have been while at Antioch, or just possibly during his stay in the desert of Chalcis, that Jerome had those dealings with the Nazaraeans settled near Beroea (Aleppo) which, if they ever took place at all, form one of the most obscure episodes of his career. Our knowledge of them derives exclusively from his statement in his *Famous Men* (written 392/3) that St Matthew had composed his Gospel in Hebrew, that it had been translated into Greek by an unknown hand, and that he himself had been allowed to make a copy of the Hebrew original by the Nazaraeans of Beroea, who used it.[33] These Nazaraeans were Jewish Christians, descendants of the primitive community at Jerusalem, who had fled from the city after its destruction in 70; apart from adhering strictly to the Jewish Law, they were orthodox in their Christian beliefs. It is nowadays accepted that there never was a Hebrew original of the First Gospel, but research has shown that there did exist a *Gospel of the Nazaraeans*, written in a Semitic tongue (Aramaic or Syriac), which is attested by the church fathers Eusebius and Epiphanius as well as Jerome, and which showed a certain relationship with the First Gospel.[34] Jerome makes frequent reference to this gospel elsewhere (often alluding to it as 'the Gospel according to the Hebrews'[35] or the like), and in works written between 390 and 398 even claims to have translated it. Unfortunately, while we need not doubt that Jerome had some knowledge of the *Gospel of the Nazaraeans*, the trustworthiness of his more precise statements is open to the gravest suspicion. To take only the case in point, if the Nazaraeans of Beroea really did permit him to transcribe their gospel, it seems incredible that he should have failed to notice the discrepancies between it and St Matthew's Gospel. The conclusion to which most investigators are reluctantly driven is that, as so often, his tendency to exaggerate his learning in his eagerness to impress has led him to transform into actual achievements what were at best plans or wistful hopes.[36] Very likely he knew of the existence of the Nazaraeans, just possibly he visited them during his stay in Syria and observed that they used a gospel written in Semitic characters; but that he actually made a copy of it, much less translated it several years later, we must regretfully rule out.

In contrast to his ordeal in the desert, Jerome's second stay in Antioch was, we may conjecture, a tranquil and happy one. He was immersed in

[33] *Famous Men* 3.
[34] See P. Vielhauer's study 'Jewish-Christian Gospels' in W. Schneemelcher and R. McL. Wilson (ed.), *The New Testament Apocrypha* (ET London, 1963) I, 117 ff.
[35] For a review of Jerome's references in chronological order, see P. Vielhauer, art. cit., 126–32.
[36] See esp. G. Bardy's very important study, 'Saint Jérôme et l'évangile selon les Hébreux', *Mélanges de science religieuse* 3 (1946), 5 ff.

studies and literary projects after his own heart; he must have been conscious of his growing powers. Evagrius too, whose free rendering of the *Life of Antony* had been a best-seller, was trying his hand as an original author. A dozen or so years later Jerome was to record how his 'talented and zealous' friend, while still a priest, had composed and read aloud to him treatises on a variety of subjects, which he had not yet published.[37] But very soon this pleasant interlude came to an end, and Jerome set out once more on his travels. In 379, or possibly 380, we find him in Constantinople.

We can only guess at his reasons for going there. Such information as as we have about his stay in the imperial city consists of much later, disappointingly bare references to people whom he had met there,[38] and throws no light on his motives for the move. Looking to the future, he may have felt that he had been long enough in the east; Rome, and Pope Damasus (to whom he had written so excitedly from the desert), perhaps beckoned him. More immediately, the news that the renowned orator, theologian and ascetic, Gregory of Nazianzus, had arrived in Constantinople early in 379 and, as leader of the small group of hitherto harassed and humiliated adherents of orthodoxy, was expounding the Nicene faith with marvellous eloquence and success, may have attracted him. But it is hard to believe that the dramatically altered situation in the whole of eastern Christendom, and at Antioch in particular, had not some share in determining his plans. The Arianising emperor Valens, who had made Antioch his residence, set up an Arian-minded puppet bishop, and driven Meletius and the orthodox bishops of the east generally into exile, had suffered a catastrophic military defeat by the Goths at the outskirts of Adrianople (Edirne, the Turkish frontier town with Bulgaria) on 9 August 378, and had himself perished in the appalling slaughter which resulted. His western colleague and nephew, Gratian (367–83), was an earnest, Nicene-minded Christian, as was Theodosius I, whom in the terrible crisis under which the empire was reeling Gratian summoned from his Spanish retreat and on 19 January 379 proclaimed Augustus of the east at Sirmium (Sremska Mitrovica, near Belgrade).

These momentous events on the world stage had swift repercussions, and ones not at all to the taste of so committed a supporter of Bishop Paulinus as Jerome, on the balance of power among the tragically disunited Christian groups at Antioch and elsewhere throughout the east. Before setting out from the city to do battle with the Goths ravaging Thrace, Valens had recalled the exiled orthodox clergy and the monks sweating it out in the mines; in the desperate plight of the empire divisions

[37] *Famous Men* 125.
[38] For Gregory of Nazianzus see esp. *Comm. on Isaiah* 6, 1 (*CCL* 73: 89); for Gregory of Nyssa cf. *Famous Men* 128.

over points of theology could only make things worse.[39] One of Gratian's first acts during his brief spell as sole emperor was to proclaim toleration for all except a few extremist minorities.[40] As a result the government policy of favouring a colourless compromise midway between Arianism and the full Nicene doctrine was completely reversed, and the orthodox bishops came streaming back everywhere to the see-cities from which they had been extruded. Meletius was again in Antioch towards the end of 378, being given a tumultuous welcome by the people,[41] and immediately began consolidating his personal position and that of his party in Syria and the neighbouring provinces. In autumn 379, now accepted by virtually the whole east except Alexandria as the rightful bishop of Antioch, he convened an important synod of 153 bishops in the city with the object of reassuring the west, and Pope Damasus in particular, of the perfect agreement of the new orthodoxy of the east with the west in matters of faith.

Jerome can scarcely have viewed these happenings with unalloyed satisfaction. Meletius and his allies were still for him the party of 'the three hypostases', tainted, as he obstinately but wrongly continued to believe, with Arianism. Moreover Paulinus, unyieldingly inflexible, was refusing to come to terms with Meletius, in spite of his generously eirenic overtures. With the detested Meletians triumphant and the outlook apparently hopeless for his friends, it is easy to understand Jerome's decision to depart. It has been further suggested[42] that he may conceivably have judged that he would be in a better position to back Paulinus's claims in Constantinople, where a great council to sort out the theological divisions of the east, including the schism of Antioch, was shortly to be held. This is an intriguing possibility, but can be treated as no more than such, since we do not know either when exactly he left Antioch or when rumours about plans for the forthcoming council began to circulate.[43]

---

[39] *Chronicle* A.D. 378 (*GCS* 47, 249): cf. Rufinus, *Hist. eccl.* 2, 13 (*PL* 21, 522).

[40] Socrates, *Hist. eccl.* 5, 2; Sozomen, *Hist. eccl.* 7, 1: cf. the reference to the decree in *Codex Theod.* xvi, 5, 5.

[41] See John Chrysostom, *Hom. in s. Meletium* 2 (*PG* 50, 517).

[42] E.g. by P. Antin, *Essai sur saint Jérôme* (Paris, 1951), 71; J. Steinmann, *Saint Jérôme* (Paris, 1958)—the latter suggests that Paulinus requested Jerome to accompany him to Constantinople, but I cannot find any evidence that Paulinus went there.

[43] A. M. Ritter (*Das Konzil von Konstantinopel und sein Symbol*, Göttingen, 1965, 33) suggests that, although the imperial letters summoning bishops to the council went out early in 381, talk about it was probably in the air many months before that; indeed it may have been agreed, at least in principle, between the emperors at their meeting at Sirmium in the autumn of 379.

VIII

At Constantinople

(i)

In 379/80 Constantinople occupied a much smaller area than the modern traveller, viewing the battered but spectacular western fortifications linking the Golden Horn and the Sea of Marmara, might suppose. These were to be constructed in 413 by Theodosius II to protect the sprawling overspill of suburbs, but when Jerome arrived the city was still confined within the original landward walls, some 1½ km. to the east, which Constantine had built half a century before.[1] The populace had scarcely recovered from the panic which had seized it when twice in 378, before and then just after the defeat and slaughter of Valens, the Goths with their allies had swept up to the gates and ravaged the suburbs.[2] The air was still full of nerve-racking stories of their savagery and devastation; it may have been about this time, too, that Stridon and Jerome's own family property were engulfed in the irresistible tide.[3] His personal anguish has left a fleeting but poignant impress on the opening pages of his *Chronicle*, which he was to complete at Constantinople in the following year or so. He was content, he remarked, to bring his record to an end with the death of Valens (9 August 378), not because he was afraid to write contemporary history, but 'because total confusion reigns while the barbarians are still roving madly throughout our territories'.[4]

For Christians in the capital the scene was changing dramatically, and during Jerome's stay the city was also the setting of one of the Church's most important, if least orderly conducted, councils. For forty years Constantinople had been dominated by bishops who supported the compromise, deliberately ambiguous theology favoured by Constantius and Valens, and the Nicene loyalists, excluded from the official churches, were reduced to a demoralised handful. Now the tide was flowing powerfully in the opposite direction. The emperors were known to be both keen, Nicene-minded Christians, determined to put down heresies of

[1] For a useful summary of the growth of the city see R. Janin, *Constantinople Byzantine* (2 ed., Paris, 1964), 32; 263–6.
[2] Socrates, *Hist. eccl.* 4, 38; Ammianus Marcellinus, *Res gestae* 31, 16, 4.
[3] See above p. 3.
[4] *Chronicle* pref. (*GCS* 47, 7).

every kind; and on 28 February 380 Theodosius I addressed a rescript to the citizens of the capital insisting that the only form of Christianity to be tolerated was one which acknowledged the full, undivided divinity of Father, Son, and Holy Spirit.[5] Gregory of Nazianzus, the most eloquent of the brilliant trio of intellectuals (Basil of Caesarea, who died on 1 January 379, and his brother, Gregory of Nyssa, were the others) who had worked out the eastern restatement of the Nicene teaching, was now expounding this, at first in a modest house, to enraptured audiences. The triumph of the new Nicene orthodoxy came when Theodosius entered the city in state on 24 November 380, expelled the 'Arian' bishop Demophilus, and handed over the churches of the eastern metropolis to Gregory of Nazianzus.[6]

Then, between May and early July 381, came the stormy assembly which was to be later recognised as the Second Ecumenical Council of the Church. Its first president was Meletius of Antioch, no longer ostracised but recognised by Theodosius himself as leader of the great majority of eastern Christians; but when, to everyone's consternation, he suddenly died, he was replaced by Gregory of Nazianzus, now bishop of the city. Gregory himself, overcome with illness and sheer exasperation, soon resigned. One of his bitterest disappointments had been that the council had rejected his passionate plea (which coincided with the wishes of Pope Damasus and the west) that Paulinus should succeed Meletius as official bishop of Antioch, and instead had given its backing to Meletius's trusted presbyter Flavian. But however interrupted its course and tumultuous its proceedings, the council had noteworthy achievements to its credit. In dogma it reaffirmed the Nicene faith, asserting the full divinity and consubstantiality of the three persons of the Trinity in terms which, while expressing the new 'three hypostases' theology, were carefully devised so as to be acceptable to the west. On the constitutional plane it ratified important canons strictly limiting the jurisdiction of the bishops of the great sees and exalting Constantinople, as New Rome, to the position of second see in Christendom next after Rome.[7]

(ii)

Resident as he was in Constantinople, Jerome must have witnessed these exciting events at close quarters. It is not surprising, however, that he nowhere makes the least mention of the famous council. Presided over by

[5] See *Codex Theod.* xvi, 5, 5 (issued on 3 Aug. 379 by Gratian banning heresies); xvi, 1, 2 (27 Feb. 380).

[6] Socrates, *Hist. eccl.* 5, 6 f.; Sozomen, *Hist. eccl.* 7, 5; Gregory Nazianzus, *Carm. hist.* xi, 1278 ff.; 1303 ff.

[7] Canons 2 and 3. For a recent discussion of them, see A. M. Ritter, *Das Konzil von Konstantinopel und sein Symbol* (Göttingen, 1965), 85–96.

Meletius and packed with bishops of the Meletian party, it must have been a profoundly distasteful gathering to him. His disgust must have been heightened by its contemptuous rejection of Paulinus's claims, perhaps also by the canons mentioned above, which he may have seen as intended to curb the pretensions of Rome and Alexandria. But one of the council's leading figures, Gregory of Nazianzus, won his lasting admiration and affection, and exerted a creative influence on him. Time and again he was to name him, with transparent satisfaction, 'my teacher', recalling the instruction in scripture he had received from him at Constantinople and the discussions they had held together about perplexing passages.[8] One such reminiscence has exposed Gregory to unfair criticism, for Jerome relates that, unable to explain a particularly obscure expression, Gregory had smilingly advised him to come to church and hear him preaching about it; there, amid the wild applause of the congregation, he would understand, or at least imagine he understood, its meaning.[9] The great orator was sufficiently human to be vain about his powers to move an audience, but also realistic enough to appreciate the worthlessness of the persuasion so induced.

The anecdote suggests that the two men enjoyed close relations, but it is noteworthy that Gregory never mentions Jerome either in his letters or in the enormous autobiographical poem he penned in retirement. There is nothing surprising about this; although almost exactly the same age as himself, Jerome was still a person of modest importance. Yet in character, temperament, and interest there were remarkable similarities between them. Both were men of acute sensibility, quick to take offence and to strike back with biting sarcasm; and both suffered from, and were morbidly preoccupied with, ill-health. Both, too, were enthusiasts for asceticism, above all for virginity; and both were fascinated by fine prose, and adepts at writing it; there was no more dazzling stylist in the fourth century than Gregory in Greek or in Latin than Jerome. As was natural, Gregory's influence on the Latin monk was much the greater. It was certainly not as a result of Jerome's persuasions, as some have argued,[10] that he came out so strongly in favour of Paulinus as bishop of Antioch. One might have expected him to back a candidate from the Meletian party, which shared his theology; but Gregory was above all concerned for the restoration of peace at Antioch, and he sincerely (although mistakenly) believed that, now that Meletius was dead, this could best be achieved if Meletius's flock rallied round Paulinus. On the other hand, as

---

[8] *Famous Men* 117; *Against Jovinian* 1, 13; *Apology* 1, 13; 30; *Comm. on Ephesians* 5, 32 (PL 26: 661); *Comm. on Isaiah* 6, 1 (*CCL* 73: 89): also *Letters* 50, 1; 52, 8.

[9] *Letter* 52, 8: the difficult expression was 'sabbaton deuteroproton' given by some MSS at Luke 6, 1. Grützmacher, e.g., speaks of Gregory's 'gelehrte Charlatanerie', which Jerome picked up from him (I, 178 f.).

[10] E.g. Grützmacher I, 180; J. Steinmann, *Saint Jérôme* (Paris, 1957), 100.

an articulate exponent of the 'three hypostases' theology, Gregory may have opened Jerome's prejudiced eyes to its essential orthodoxy. It is likely, too, that he was among those who introduced him to Origen.

It was probably also through Gregory that Jerome made the acquaintance of other distinguished Greek-speaking intellectuals who were in Constantinople for the council. One of these was Gregory of Nyssa, the younger brother of Basil of Caesarea, a theologian of great distinction and originality, and one of the foremost authorities on asceticism and Christian mysticism. He had recently finished at any rate the first two of a series of treatises designed to refute Eunomius, the leader of the new, radical Arianism which taught that the Son was utterly unlike, as well as inferior to, the Father. Not without a touch of complacency Jerome notes in 392/3 that 'a few years ago he [Gregory of Nyssa] read out his books against Eunomius to me and Gregory of Nazianzus'.[11] Another was Amphilochius, bishop of Iconium (now Konya) in Cappadocia, an intimate friend of Basil and the two Gregorys and an advocate of their characteristic theology. He had made his mark by championing the full divinity of the Holy Spirit, which was one of the issues before the council. Jerome records that he too 'recently read to me his essay *On the Holy Spirit*, arguing that he is God, that he is to be worshipped, and that he is omnipotent'.[12]

These are just fleeting glimpses of Jerome's life in Constantinople. The men whom he was meeting (there were doubtless others too) were among the most cultivated Christians of the Greek-speaking world, passionately devoted like him to the ascetic ideal and to theological truth, but far more deeply aware of the intellectual problems of their faith. His intercourse with them must have been stimulating and enriching. But all the time, restlessly curious, he was absorbed by Constantinople itself, the capital which, as he mordantly observed, had been adorned by stripping the cities of the world of their works of art.[13] His *Chronicle*, on which he was working, contains an astonishing number of references to its recent history. Some of the events recorded, e.g. the death and replacement of a notable professor, reflect his scholarly interests, but the majority his concerns as a churchman—the lynching of a military commander who was evicting an orthodox bishop, the reception of the relics of the apostle Timothy, the confrontation of Hilary of Poitiers and Constantius, the dedication of a church or a martyr's shrine, and the like.[14] His fascination for curious phenomena comes out in his exclamation that in 367 a terrible storm had deluged the capital with hail-stones so big that many people

[11] *Famous Men* 128.

[12] *Famous Men* 133. The treatise has not survived. Basil had dedicated his essay on the Holy Spirit to Didymus.

[13] *Chronicle* A.D. 330: 'Dedicatur Constantinopolis omnium paene urbium nuditate' (*GCS* 47, 232).

[14] *Chronicle* A.D. 358; 342; 356; 359; 360; 370 (*GCS* 47, 241; 235; 240; 241 *bis*; 245).

were killed, his eye for the practical in his note that in 373 Clearchus, the new city prefect, had introduced 'a much needed, long and devoutly waited for water-supply'—of which the Aqueduct of Valens, bestriding the traffic-thronged defile between the third and fourth hills of the city, remains to this day a majestic relic.

(iii)

While in Constantinople, Jerome launched out on a fresh branch of literary activity—translation. He now possessed a mastery of Greek, and with the guidance of well-informed friends was familiarising himself with Greek Christian literature. He must have been struck by its vast extent and high quality, as compared with the Latin Christian literature that was available, and he certainly felt the impulse to introduce it to western readers. A remark he made at the time reveals his consciousness of the difficulties of translation: 'If I render word for word, the result sounds absurd; if I make any necessary changes in order or wording, I appear to have abandoned the function of a translator.'[15] He went on to point, as warning examples, to the various Greek translations of the Old Testament—the Septuagint officially used in the Church, the slavishly literal version of the Jew Aquila, Symmachus's free rendering, Theodotion's conservative revision of the Septuagint—all of which failed in different ways to bring out the full flavour of the Hebrew original.[16] His own theory of sound translation, to be consistently observed from now on and elaborated with reasoned arguments in a famous letter years afterwards, was that (except in the case of Scripture, where the actual words and their placing might be pregnant with significance) it should be a paraphrase, reproducing the sense and spirit rather than the letter of the original.[17]

His *Chronicle* was the earliest[18] of these 'translations' carried out at Constantinople, and was in fact an adaptation, with excisions, numerous insertions, and a lengthy supplement, of the admired *Chronicle* (as it is commonly called) of Eusebius of Caesarea (d. *c.* 340), the erudite 'father of church history' who was also the confidant of Constantine the Great. As finally revised, this vast compilation was a chronologically framed com-

---

[15] *Chronicle* pref. (*GCS* 47, 2).

[16] While the Septuagint (LXX) was pre-Christian, the other three Greek versions mentioned were made in the second century A.D. Origen had arranged all four, along with the Hebrew original and the Hebrew transliterated into Greek, in the six columns of his mammoth Hexapla. The four Greek versions were circulated separately as the Tetrapla, and Jerome seems to have had access to this.

[17] *Letter* 57, to Pammachius (date 395/6).

[18] This is suggested by (a) its position in Jerome's list of his writings to date in *Famous Men* 135; (b) its termination with the death of Valens in 378; (c) the mention of it in *Letter* 18A, 1, written prior to the council of Constantinople (cf. *Comm. on Isaiah* 6, 1: *CCL* 73: 89).

pendium of world history from the birth of Abraham, placed in 2016 B.C., down to the twentieth year of Constantine's reign, i.e. 325;[19] it had the propagandist object of showing that the Jewish-Christian tradition stretched back farther than any other. In an introductory section Eusebius had sought to establish a comparative chronology by analysing, with the aid of short surveys of their history, the systems of dating current among the principal ancient peoples (Chaldaeans, Assyrians, Hebrews, Greeks, Romans). The bulk of the work, however, consisted of synchronistic tables of dates (regnal years of kings, emperors, etc., and from 776 B.C. Olympiads, i.e. four-year periods between celebrations of the Olympic Games) set in parallel columns, with miscellaneous noteworthy events, sacred and secular, listed in the intervening space.[20] Eusebius took as his model, and drew largely on, the *Chronicles* of Julius Africanus (d. *c.* 240), a synchronisation of sacred and profane events from the creation to A.D. 221. His work, however, was immeasurably superior to that of Africanus, as of his other Christian and pagan predecessors, not only because he used older and better sources but because of his more critical approach.[21]

Jerome was obviously fascinated by the sweep of Eusebius's achievement; there was nothing to match it in Latin literature, which had lagged noticeably behind Greek in scholarly chronography. Christianity being no longer on the defensive, he had no interest in Eusebius's determination to demonstrate the greater antiquity of the Christian revelation; it was the vast canvas of world history which attracted him, and which he wished to place at the disposal of western students. But to do this successfully he thought it desirable to introduce certain adaptations. First, he cut out Eusebius's prefatory essay explaining the systems of dating used by the leading nations (although the fact that he completely ignores it in his preface may imply that it was already lacking from the edition on which he was working).[22] Secondly, while content to translate Eusebius's historical notices from the birth of Abraham to the sack of Troy, he inserted an increasing number of notices of his own, almost all concerned with Roman history, literature, and scholarship, from the latter date to the end of the book. His sources, he explained,[23] were Suetonius and other celebrated

---

[19] In its first edition it ended at 303. For its revision see D. S. Wallace-Hadrill, 'The Eusebian Chronicle: the Extent and Date of Composition of its early Editions' (*JTS* NS 6, 1955, 248–53).

[20] E. Caspar, *Die älteste Römische Bischofsliste* (Berlin, 1926), 229–98, argued that sacred and secular events were arranged in separate columns right through to the end of the book. But most scholars (cf. esp. R. Helm, *GCS* 47, xxxiii ff.; K. Mras, *Wiener Studien* 46, 1928, 206–8) agree that the two columns were merged after the second year of Darius I and the re-building of the Temple in Jerusalem, i.e. 520 B.C.

[21] For a useful summary account of ancient chronography see the article 'Chronologie' in *RAC* 3, esp. cols. 52–8 (Christian chronography).

[22] So E. Schwartz, PW VI, 1379–80 (art. 'Eusebius').

[23] *Chronicle* pref. (*GCS* 47, 6).

Roman historians,[24] and his understandable motive was to redress Eusebius's pro-Greek bias and make his Latin readers feel more at home. Finally, he added a lengthy appendix ('entirely my own work') covering the span from 325, where Eusebius had stopped, to the battle of Adrianople, obviously drawing heavily on secular and ecclesiastical writers.[25] In the interests of clarity he introduced technical devices like the use of red and black ink for alternate columns of regnal years and for the Olympiads.[26]

It is little wonder that Jerome's book (which he was to retouch in subsequent editions) was an immediate and long-term success. For the first time the west had a conspectus (a very fragmentary and selective one, of course) of universal history annalistically arranged with an apparently scientific chronology. The large number of MSS in which it was circulated, the way later chroniclers either plundered or simply continued it, and the esteem accorded it in the Middle Ages are tokens of its influence. He deserves credit both for his sure instinct in sensing the historian's need for such a manual and for his indomitable industry in producing it. All the greater pity, then, that, on his own confession, he made it 'a rush job', and dictated it (presumably the historical items, for the tables of dates needed only copying out) with excessive speed to his stenographer.[27] It is clear that he devoted thought to its planning and to the technical problems of riveting his readers' attention, and was at pains to maintain his accustomed high stylistic standards (e.g. in the euphonious sentence-endings he cultivated).[28] Even so, his carelessness and haste are evident not only in his numerous errors (even of translation),[29] but also in his apparent indifference to exact dating even where the material for it was provided by

[24] Who these were remains an unsolved problem. Th. Mommsen (*Gesammelte Schriften* VII, 606–32: Berlin, 1909) concluded that he used (i) the survey of Roman history from Romulus to the death of Jovian (364) by Eutropius, one of Valens's secretaries; (ii) the *Breviarium* of Rufius Festus, also a secretary of Valens; (iii) the city chronicle of Rome; (iv) other now lost works of Roman history. Yet it is improbable that he excerpted, in addition to Suetonius (whom he mentions), such an extensive library for a work he admits to have completed in a great hurry. In his massive study 'Hieronymus und Eutrop' (*Rheinisches Museum f. Philologie* 76, 1927, 138–70; 254–306) R. Helm convincingly argued that he cannot have used Eutropius directly; all too often the notices, while at points in verbal agreement with Eutropius, include quite different subject-matter. He concludes that Jerome's source must have been a corpus of Roman history from the beginnings to his own day which Eutropius, Rufius Festus, etc. also used but which has now disappeared. J. W. Ward (*Class. Philology* 35, 1940, 18–21) claimed that Jerome borrowed from Justinus's epitome of the *Philippic History* of Pompeius Trogus; but he does not seem to have proved his case.

[25] Again his sources are obscure. He must also have relied on his own memory.

[26] For these innovations, and also for the technical features he took over from Eusebius, see K. Mras, *Wiener Studien* 46, 1928, 201–8.

[27] *Chronicle* pref. (*GCS* 47, 2), where he speaks of it as 'tumultuarium opus'. It was A. Schöne (*Die Weltchronik des Eusebius*, Berlin, 1900, 77) who first pointed out that Jerome cannot have dictated the synchronistic tables.

[28] For his clausulae see R. Helm, *GCS* 47, xxi; K. Mras, art. cit. 200 f.

[29] For some of these cf. A. Sündermeier, *Quaestiones chronographicae ad Eusebii et Hieronymi chronica spectantes* (Bremen, 1896).

his sources and in his refusal to take the trouble to fill obvious gaps in these.[30] Further, had he not been in such a hurry, or had he been interested, he could have made his chronology of Roman history more precise by incorporating references to the consuls.

No less regrettably, the fresh material he thought it desirable to add, especially the supplement covering 325 to 378, glaringly shows up his weaknesses as an historian. As we should expect, he inserts the names of Latin authors, notes political and military happenings of interest to the west, and pays special attention to the bishops of major sees, persecutions and heresies, and significant developments like monasticism. There is no denying the value of the miscellaneous facts he accumulates, many of them not obtainable elsewhere. But his presentation of them is seriously defective by the standards not only of present-day but even of contemporary historiography. First, he seems unable to distinguish the important from the trivial, so that time and again (to give but one example) he cannot resist the temptation, after mentioning an event or personage of significance, to tack on some irrelevant gossipy detail. Secondly, he continually goes out of his way to highlight his own subjective interests; the prominence he assigns, in what is intended as a world survey, to minor professors or his personal friends (Bonosus, Rufinus, others), or to pseudo-marvellous phenomena, is an illustration. Thirdly and most damaging, his assessment of individuals and movements, especially if they are Christian, is entirely uncritical, being coloured by his violent prejudices. At the end of his preface he remarks that he is projecting a continuous history of his own times; but we need shed no tears at his failure to fulfil his ambition. He was much more in his element writing edifying romances like his *Life of Paul* than serious history.

(iv)

Jerome dedicated his *Chronicle* to two friends, Gennadius and Vincentius, the latter destined from now on to be closely associated with his enterprises and interests. It was this same Vincentius who now urged him to put the writings of Origen into Latin and so 'make available to Roman ears the man who, in the judgment of Didymus, blind but so clearsighted, is second only to the Apostles as teacher of the churches'.[31]

[30] On both these points see R. Helm, 'Hieronymus' Zusätze in Eusebius's Chronik and ihre Wert für die Literaturgeschichte' (*Philologus*, Supplementum 21, 1929), esp. 92 f. He points out that figures such as Propertius, Tibullus, Juvenal, Martial, even Tacitus, are lacking from the list of Latin authors Jerome inserted.

[31] So Jerome in the preface to his translation of Origen's homilies on Ezekiel (*GCS* 33, 318). Didymus was the learned Alexandrian theologian and exegete (c. 313–98), blind from infancy, whose treatise on the Holy Spirit Jerome was later to translate (see below pp. 85; 142f), and under whom he was to study briefly when he visited Alexandria in 386 (see below p. 125). He was condemned as an Origenist by the second council of Constantinople (553).

Origen, who had taught and lectured successively at Alexandria and Caesarea in Palestine until his death about 254, was one of the most profound and wide-ranging thinkers ever produced by the Christian Church, as well as an enormously prolific writer. While the majority of his works were concerned with expounding the Bible, he was a constructive theologian of genius and a brilliant apologist; his contribution to ascetical theology, too, was outstanding. Living in the Greek-speaking world, where Origen's system was keenly debated in the fourth century and formed the intellectual framework of much theological thinking, Jerome must have known about the great man for years. His interest, however, may have been sharpened by Gregory of Nazianzus who, in spite of having reservations about his more daring speculations, admired him as 'the whet-stone of us all'.[32] Before many years there was to be a fierce explosion of anti-Origenism in which Jerome was to be deeply and passionately involved. At present, however, he was under the master's spell, fascinated by his prestigious scholarship and by the skill with which, by lavish use of allegorising and spiritualising methods of exegesis, he had seemingly cleared away many difficulties of the Bible and been able to read a Christian message out of the most anthropomorphic, legalistic, or even morally offensive passages of the Old Testament.

Jerome apparently gave serious thought to translating, not necessarily all, but at any rate a large portion of, Origen's works. In the meantime, as he notes in a prefatory letter to Vincentius,[33] he was prevented from making the progress he could have wished by a painful affliction of the eyes, brought on by incessant reading, and also by the lack of stenographers—'shortage of cash has removed this aid too'. There is a hint here that, because of the swamping of the family estates at Stridon by the Goths, he could no longer count on subsidies from home. As a result he had to content himself with rendering a few of Origen's homilies, short addresses (there were originally as many as 574 of them) on select passages of Scripture delivered at liturgical meetings. In addition to fourteen homilies on the prophet Jeremiah completed some time previously, he now sent Vincentius fourteen more on Ezekiel which he had dictated at intervals as opportunity allowed. A further nine on Isaiah, which have come down without indication of the translator's name, are nowadays attributed to Jerome.[34] This attribution is based partly on his use of them in his later expositions of Isaiah, partly on style and content, but chiefly on Rufinus's testimony that Jerome had translated certain of Origen's homilies on Isaiah and his citation of a passage which is verbally identical

---

[32] So Suidas, *Lexicon* s.v. 'Origenes' (Adler iii, 619).
[33] *Origen's Homilies on Ezekiel* pref. (*GCS* 33, 318).
[34] See the remarks of W. A. Baehrens, *Origenes Werke* viii (*GCS* 33), xlii–xlvi.

with one in the first of these homilies.[35] Because of their clumsiness of form and style, most scholars regard them as the earliest of his renderings of Origen's homilies, but others prefer to place them after 392/3 since he makes no mention of them in a list of his works to date compiled in that year.[36] But perhaps his silence there is best explained by his awareness of their stylistic and other defects.

Jerome put Latin-speaking Christians greatly in his debt by translating these thirty-seven homilies (he was afterwards to translate forty-one more, on Song of Songs and St Luke's Gospel).[37] Without knowing it he performed a service for us too, for owing to the disrepute into which Origen subsequently fell only twenty-one of his 574 homilies, which had great influence on later spiritual and mystical theology, have come down entire in the original Greek. Latin translations of a number of others are extant; but Jerome's share in preserving this precious fragment of the Origenistic heritage is far from negligible. In making his versions he did not follow, as he admits,[38] the author's original order, but selected (so it seems) the ones he found most appealing or most free from the suspect features of Origen's theology. His chief care, he insists,[39] was to preserve the directness and simplicity of the master's sermon style; and, as always, he did not feel bound to produce a word-for-word rendering. We can check his performance in the Jeremiah homilies, for the Greek of these survives.[40] Errors of translation are remarkably few, and although Rufinus was later to charge him with introducing dogmatic rectifications,[41] only one or two examples of these can be detected. On the other hand, side by side with drastic periphrases, abbreviations, and interpolations designed to help the reader's understanding, we come across traces of his incorrigible tendency to heighten or intensify the colour of an expression, to give rein to his personal opinions or prejudices, or to show off his learning. Jerome had to be Jerome; and to this we owe it also that, the Isaiah homilies apart, his translations are more elegant and readable than the originals.

(v)

Although these homilies were translations of another man's work, they provided invaluable experience for one who was to rank among the world's most famous and influential translators. Now, as he was to record

---

[35] Rufinus, *Apol. c. Hier.* 2, 27.

[36] *Famous Men* 135.

[37] See below pp. 86 and 143 f.

[38] *Origen's Homilies on Ezekiel* pref. (*GCS* 33, 318).

[39] See the preface cited in the previous note.

[40] For a discussion see E. Klostermann, *Die Überlieferung der Jeremiahomilien des Origenes* (*TU* xvi, NF 1: 1897), 19–31; also his introduction to *Origenes Werke* iii (*GCS* 6, xvi–xxiii).

[41] *Apol. c. Hieron.* 2, 27.

years later,[42] he decided to put his abilities to the test and produce an essay in exegesis of his own. It was quite a short and, on his own admission, hastily composed one, and the passage of Scripture chosen for examination was one of the most familiar in the Old Testament, the vision which Isaiah had of the Lord God enthroned on high and of the two Seraphim, one of which touched the prophet's lips with a burning coal (Isa. 6, 1–9). As it has come down, this work takes the form of a letter (No. 18) to Pope Damasus, but the structure and contents make it clear that what we have is not in fact a letter but two short pieces, the longer (now called Letter 18A) a straightforward commentary on Isaiah 6, 1–9, and the other (Letter 18B) a rather more technical study of Isaiah 6, 6–9. The heading 'To Damasus' was probably added later when Jerome was in Rome and was submitting specimens of his exegesis to the pope.

These little studies have the special interest of showing the great Biblical commentator serving his apprenticeship. In spite of his working knowledge of Hebrew and his use of it, on occasion, for the discussion of words, he still (as for several years to come) bases his commentary, not on the Hebrew original, but on the Greek Septuagint, in Letter 18B meticulously comparing the other three Greek versions with this. In general he is heavily indebted to earlier expositors, especially Origen (whom he nowhere names), although he once or twice takes a line of his own in the interests of orthodoxy.[43] Characteristically, he makes appeal to the rabbinical exegesis he claims to have picked up from his Jewish teachers; once, indeed, he is caught cheating, when he alleges he has heard a certain interpretation from 'my Hebrew', for he almost certainly got it from Origen.[44] The exegesis itself is extremely figurative and, to modern taste, fanciful, in the manner of Origen. He starts off, admittedly, in a strictly historical vein, giving the facts about King Uzziah (on whose death Isaiah says he had the vision) and fixing his date; but he immediately insists that the literal sense is entirely subordinate to the spiritual one. To give two examples of this, he decides that the two Seraphim 'who called to one another' must denote the Old and New Testaments and the perfect correspondence between them; while their refrain, 'The whole earth is full of his glory', points to the coming of Christ and the world-wide proclamation of his message.[45] In this way, assisted by his exhaustive

[42] *Comm. on Isaiah* 6, 1 (*CCL* 73: 89).

[43] See *Letter* 18A, 4, where he takes the two Seraphim to signify the Old and the New Testaments, not, as Origen had done, Christ and the Holy Spirit. In his view the traditional interpretation implied a subordinate status for the second and third persons of the Trinity. In *Letter* 84, 3 he was to point to this passage as an example of his altering Origen's 'detestable exegesis'.

[44] *Letter* 18A, 15: E. Klostermann has shown (*Die Überlieferung* . . . , 76 ff.) that Jerome must have derived his knowledge of this debate from Origen's 19th *Homily on Jeremiah*.

[45] *Letter* 18A, 4–7.

mastery of the Bible, he is able to discover in the passage a host of profound and edifying Christian suggestions.

Meanwhile poor Jerome, just beginning his fifties but as always an omnivorous student, continued to suffer agonies from his eye trouble. At the end of the first of these two studies he complains that he has not been able to correct the material he has dictated since, as a result of the pain, he can use only his ears and his tongue for his work.[46]

[46] *Letter* 18A, 16.

IX

At the Court of Damasus

(i)

The council of Constantinople broke up shortly after 9 July 381, but Jerome seems to have stayed on in the eastern capital for several months. His mentor, Gregory of Nazianzus, had left even before the close of the council on resigning the see, the other bishops with whom he had associated had now gone home, but his new-found friend Vincentius, the admirer of Origen, was still there, and he was busy with his reading and writing. Then suddenly, in the summer of 382, the golden opportunity was offered him of accompanying Paulinus of Antioch to Rome, the city of his education and baptism, on which he had not set eyes since early manhood. As he was later to put it,[1] 'urgent business of the Church brought me to Rome along with the venerable bishops Paulinus and Epiphanius [of Salamis, now Famagusta, in Cyprus]'.

We have a pretty clear idea of the nature of this business, which was occasioned (as he elsewhere relates)[2] by 'certain dissensions between the churches'. Leading prelates in the west, notably the formidable and ambitious Ambrose of Milan, had in recent months become increasingly exasperated by the course events were taking in the east. The eastern hierarchs were acting much too independently for their liking, and they viewed the whole council of Constantinople with misgiving. In particular, the recognition of Meletius as the spokesman of the east, the brushing aside of Paulinus's claim to the throne of Antioch, and the choice of Flavian instead of him when Meletius died, seemed deliberate slaps in the face. They had other grievances too, such as the appointment of Gregory as bishop of Constantinople and of Nectarius as his successor when he resigned (in fact he was Theodosius's nominee). Ambrose was agitating for a general council to bring matters to a head, and succeeded in persuading the western emperor, Gratian, to convoke one to Rome.[3] A number of western metropolitans assembled there in the summer of 382, but the east declined to cooperate. In fact Theodosius had no wish to see

---

[1] *Letter* 127, 7 (written in 413).
[2] *Letter* 108, 6.
[3] *Letter* 108, 6 ('... imperial letters had brought bishops of east and west to Rome ...').
Cf. also Sozomen, *Hist. eccl.* 7, 11; Theodoret, *Hist. eccl.* 5, 9, 8.

the settlement he was establishing upset by western meddling, and had already re-convened the council of the previous year at Constantinople. When the belated western summons reached them, the eastern bishops gathered there sent a courteous but firm reply, excusing themselves from attending, apart from a token delegation of three, but not yielding an inch on the disputed issues.[4]

Thus Ambrose's scheme for a general council collapsed ignominiously. Nevertheless it had given Paulinus, desperate to have his title to the see of Antioch acknowledged, and Epiphanius, for long his chief supporter in the east, a pretext for coming to Rome. Both must have received a formal summons, and neither had any motive for declining it.[5] In bringing Jerome with them they probably planned to use him as an interpreter, as a personal adviser too in their discussions with Latin prelates. Without intending it, however, they were opening an eventful and decisive chapter in his career. His growing reputation as a writer and scholar apart, Jerome was no stranger to some of the leading personalities at the synod. One of these, for example, was Valerian of Aquileia, around whom, when Jerome had lived there a decade previously, the ardent group of ascetics had gathered. He must have been known as the protégé and intimate friend of Evagrius, who had put Pope Damasus heavily in his debt;[6] and Damasus must have been intrigued to meet the monk who had sent him such passionate, devoted appeals from the desert.

His abilities, scholarship, and personality seem to have made an immediate impression, and from the moment of his arrival in Rome Jerome found himself invited to fill a much larger role than that of interpreter to his Greek-speaking patrons. One of the tasks which the Roman council undertook was the condemnation of Apollinarianism, the heretical theory that in Jesus the divine Logos had taken the place of the normal human mind or spirit. Years later, when the two men were at loggerheads, Rufinus retails a story which underlines Jerome's close involvement in these discussions.[7] According to this, Damasus requested Jerome to frame a formula of belief which Apollinarians would have to sign as a condition of being admitted to communion. In his draft he inserted the expression 'the man who is Lord' ('homo dominicus'). When challenged to justify it, he claimed to have found it in no less an authority than Athanasius, but an unscrupulous Apollinarian tampered with his copy of the work in question, making it look as if Jerome had himself interpolated the controversial words in the text. Commenting on the incident, Jerome

---

[4] For the text see Theodoret, *Hist. eccl.* 5, 9, 1–18.

[5] According to Sozomen, *Hist. eccl.* 7, 11, the western bishops addressed synodal letters to Paulinus, regarding him as legitimate bishop of Antioch, not Flavian. Epiphanius had not been among the bishops attending the council of Constantinople.

[6] See above p. 33.

[7] *De adult. lib. Origenis* 13 (*CCL* 20, 15).

dismisses it as mere dinner-table gossip, but confirms that the pope had entrusted him with 'the dictation [i.e. drafting] of letters on church affairs'.[8]

The Roman synod, as was to be expected, went through the motions (they were, and were bound to be, ineffective) of recognising Paulinus's canonical standing as bishop of Antioch, and for good measure excommunicated the consecrators of his triumphant rival, Flavian;[9] and when the winter was over and the sea-routes open, Paulinus and Epiphanius journeyed back to their respective homes.[10] But it is scarcely surprising, in view of the relations of confidence he now enjoyed with the pope, that Jerome did not accompany him but remained in Rome.

(ii)

His new patron, Damasus, was one of the most remarkable of the early popes. Elected in 366 after bloody hand-to-hand fighting between his own and a rival candidate's supporters, he was the first to give a quasi-royal magnificence to the hitherto modest papal household in the Lateran palace. The truth is that, as a result of Constantine's benefactions and of lavish gifts and legacies that had flowed in since, the bishop of Rome was now an exceedingly rich and prominent social personage, able to give banquets (as a pagan observer dryly commented)[11] surpassing the emperor's in splendour. Despite the ugly rumours that dogged him, Damasus exercised his great office with vigour and success. A forceful character, he pushed through his policies ruthlessly; he stood firmly against the strong opposition to Christianity in senatorial circles; and he was one of the architects of the Roman see's pretensions to supremacy. In tune with the piety of the age he fostered the cult of the martyrs, restored and embellished (as we have seen)[12] the catacombs, and was a builder of churches. Fashionable women adored him, so that gossips nicknamed him 'the matrons' ear-tickler'.[13] But he was also a man of cultivated interests. He organised and re-housed the papal archives,[14] wrote in prose

---

[8] *Apology* 2, 20. Jerome's impatient brushing the story aside was due to the fact that Rufinus had retailed it in support of his theory that the writings of the Fathers had often been interpolated by mischievous hands (see below p. 253).

[9] Sozomen, *Hist. eccl.* 7, 11.

[10] *Letter* 108, 6.

[11] Ammianus Marcellinus, *Res gestae* 27, 3, 11–14. Cf. the jesting remark of the pagan senator, Agorius Praetextatus, to Damasus, 'Make me bishop of Rome, and I'll become a Christian' (Jerome, *Against John* 8).

[12] See above p. 22.

[13] 'Matronarum auriscalpius': *Collectio Avellana, Ep.* 1 (*CSEL* 35, 4).

[14] Cf. his statement that he had built 'a new house' for them at the church of St Lawrence near the Theatre of Pompey (to be known as St Lawrence in Damaso, or in Prasino) in the inscription he set up at the entrance to the church (A. Ferrua, *Epigrammata Damasiana*, Rome, 1942, no. 57: pp. 210–12).

and verse about virginity,[15] and composed and set up on marble tablets sonorous-sounding, if rather vacuous, epigrams inscribed in the elegant lettering devised by his friend Furius Dionysius Filocalus.

Between the ageing pope (he was approaching eighty) and Jerome there quickly sprang up a close, indeed affectionate, relationship. Damasus had already, at the Roman council, found the younger man useful, with his knowledge of languages, his familiarity with eastern church affairs, and his flair for writing. It is clear that the 'drafting of letters on church business' which he entrusted to him continued after the synod's dispersal. According to Rufinus, Damasus regularly employed him for assignments like preparing the anti-Apollinarian formula; and Jerome was afterwards to recall the time when he 'was assisting Damasus, the Roman pontiff, with church documents and dealing with requests submitted by synods of east and west'.[16] The verbs here used are both in the imperfect tense, suggesting that he was in the pope's service in some official capacity. In the fourth century the Roman church had a 'chancery', more correctly a secretarial establishment, and Jerome alludes to its 'chartarium' or record-office.[17] His description of his functions is disappointingly meagre, but seems to hint that he had some responsibility for archives as well as for the preparation of correspondence. It was this activity which inspired one school of late medieval and renaissance artists to depict him, quite anachronistically, in the gorgeous panoply of a Roman cardinal.[18]

The pope was also immensely impressed by Jerome's prestige as an exegete and Biblical scholar, acquainted with the Hebrew of the Old Testament. A fascinating bundle of letters has come down which show him putting, with shrewd practical sense, knotty problems of interpretation to the younger man, and receiving miniature treatises in reply.[19] Once it is a question of the exact meaning in Hebrew of the acclamation 'Hosanna' with which the citizens of Jerusalem welcomed Jesus on Palm Sunday. On another occasion it is the deeper significance of the Parable of the Prodigal Son which troubles him, on yet another a batch of conundrums raised by puzzling texts—conundrums, incidentally, which he must have picked up from a work discussing such texts by a brilliant Roman exegete nowadays known as Ambrosiaster (his true name is lost), whose explanations he had evidently found unsatisfying.[20] In his answers

---

[15] Letter 22, 22.

[16] Letter 123, 9 (date 409).

[17] Apology 3, 20.

[18] For the iconography of Jerome see the convenient summary by Maria L. Casanova, Bibliotheca sanctorum (Rome, 1965), VI, 1132–7.

[19] Letters 19–21; 35–6. The former group seem to belong to 383, the latter to 384: see Cavallera II, 25 f.

[20] On this see the able article by H. Vogels, 'Ambrosiaster und Hieronymus', RB 66 (1956) 14–19. The work in question is Ambrosiaster's Quaestiones veteris et novi testamenti cxxvii (CSEL 50).

Jerome makes great play with his Hebrew learning, shows detailed knowledge of earlier commentators, but freely criticises them where he thinks proper, and also reports rabbinical interpretations supplied him by Jewish informants. In expounding the parable he briefly places it in its gospel context, then elaborately rehearses allegorical exegeses which take it as pointing to the call either of the Gentiles or of sinners in general.

This correspondence throws an intriguing light on aspects of Jerome's personal life. Thus one of the interpretations he offers of the pods which the Prodigal Son, reduced to feeding pigs, was obliged to eat is that these denote 'the songs of poets, the wisdom of the world, the showy displays of rhetoric', which for all their beauty and charm afford no lasting satisfaction.[21] This somewhat arbitrary explanation leads him to complain shrilly that 'nowadays we see even bishops abandoning the Gospels and the prophets to read comedies, hum the erotic words of pastoral poems, and stick fast to Vergil, thus voluntarily making themselves guilty of what schoolboys do under compulsion'.[22] This outburst indicates that, in spite of temptation, he has a clean conscience himself and is strictly observing the oath he swore to the Judge after his frightening nightmare.[23] Later his attitude was to become more liberal, but at this stage he is even doubtful whether Christians may properly study pagan culture at all, and only grudgingly allows them to do so when it has been purged of everything noxious.[24]

In another passage, excusing himself for his delay in answering Damasus's questions, he describes how he had been about to start dictating when a Jewish friend unexpectedly turned up with a parcel of books he had borrowed from his synagogue on the pretext of wishing to read them himself.[25] He was in such a hurry that Jerome felt obliged to throw all his other work aside in order to transcribe the precious volumes. Jerome must have been almost unique in cultivating such close relations with members of the Jewish community in Rome; and the whole incident leaves a powerful impression of his restless energy as a scholar, his determination to deepen his knowledge of Hebrew, and his eagerness to enrich his library with Hebrew texts. We are not surprised to learn from another letter that he was still the victim of painful eye-trouble which, as at Constantinople, prevented him from correcting his amanuensis's drafts.[26]

[21] *Letter* 21, 13.

[22] The remark interestingly reveals that, for boys at any rate, Christians did not dream of abandoning the traditional school curriculum. Cf. H. Hagendahl, 109, who quotes Tertullian, *De idol.* 10: 'How can we give up secular studies, without which divine studies are impossible?'

[23] See above p. 42.

[24] For his later more receptive attitude, see *Letter* 70 (date 397/8), where he produces scriptural authority for reading the pagan classics provided they are suitably purged. See pp. 43 f.; 213.

[25] *Letter* 36, 1.

[26] *Letter* 21, 42. See above p. 79.

(iii)

It is interesting to speculate where Jerome lived and how he supported himself during these few but crowded years in Rome. We may reasonably conjecture that, as he was employing him in various capacities and also recognised him as the intimate of his own friend and benefactor Evagrius, Pope Damasus made himself responsible for him. There is no inconsistency between his accepting such hospitality and his angry denial that he had ever taken money or presents from anyone in Rome.[27] It seems clear, however, that he did not lodge in the Lateran palace, the papal residence since Constantine's time, for we hear of a courier, or a deacon, going to and fro between them with letters.[28] Jerome himself refers in passing to his 'small apartment' ('hospitiolum'), but it was at any rate roomy enough for him to receive groups of friends.[29] A tempting guess, though it can be no more than a guess, is that Damasus placed quarters at his disposal in the 'new buildings' which, in reconstructing the church of St Lawrence near the Theatre of Pompey (on the site of the present Palazzo della Cancelleria), he erected for the papal archives.[30]

As the months went by, the relationship between Damasus and Jerome became increasingly familiar. In one of their exchanges the pope banteringly complained that Jerome had been virtually asleep, spending his time reading rather than writing, and Jerome retorted no less lightheartedly that, so far from dozing, he had been translating Didymus the Blind's celebrated essay *On the Holy Spirit*; when he completed his version, he proposed to dedicate it to the pope, who had pressed him to undertake the task.[31] Alas, by the time it was finished Damasus was dead, and Jerome had forsaken Rome. But he was also extending his study of Origen, especially of his great *Commentary on Song of Songs*, of which he remarked that, while Origen in his other works had surpassed everyone else, in this he had surpassed himself.[32] Again he would have liked to have presented the pope with this profound essay in mystical theology in a Latin dress; but to have done so worthily, he pleads, would have demanded

---

[27] *Letter* 45, 2 (date 385).

[28] *Letters* 35, 1 ('tabellarius'); 36, 1 ('diaconus').

[29] *Letter* 42, 3.

[30] So J. Labourt, *Saint Jérôme: Lettres* 11, 206–8. P. Nautin (*Revue des études augustiniennes* 18, 1972, 218) infers from *Letter* 45, 2 ('Agreed, I lived almost three years with them . . . ') that Jerome must have resided in Paula's mansion ('chez elle'). But 'cum eis vixi' can at least equally well mean, 'I consorted with them' or 'I lived in their company'. His letters to her (esp. *Letter* 30, asking her to salute Blesilla and Eustochium), and *Letter* 31 to Eustochium, also support the view that he did not stay in her home.

[31] *Letters* 35, 1; 36, 1. For the dedication to the pope see his preface to the translation (*PL* 23 : 105).

[32] Cf. the preface to his translation of Origen's two homilies on Song of Songs (*GCS* 33, 26).

'enormous leisure, toil, and expense'. Still, Origen had left two homilies on Song of Songs, much more simple, indeed conversational in style, intended for his candidates for baptism. These Jerome contented himself with translating for Damasus so that from such relatively trifling works he might form some estimate of the immense value of his more important treatises. Although he declares his resolve to aim at a faithful rather than an elegant rendering, his Latin in these homilies is particularly graceful, and he has constructed his sentence rhythms with exceptional care.

Much more far-reaching and memorable than these lesser works was the momentous project on which Jerome now (383/4) embarked, and which was to occupy him off and on for the next twenty-two years. This was nothing less than the revision or replacement of the existing Latin translations of the Bible and the production of a single standard version. The original language of the Old Testament (except such of the deutero-canonical books, or Apocrypha, as were written in Greek) was of course Hebrew, that of the New Testament Greek; but the Old Testament which most Christians at first used in the Gentile world was the Greek version known as the Septuagint (from the tradition that the five books attributed to Moses had been put into Greek by seventy-two translators in the reign of Ptolemy Philadelphus, king of Egypt 285–246 B.C.) carried out at Alexandria in the third and second centuries before Christ. Thus almost as soon as Christianity had caught on in the Latin-speaking west, Latin translations were urgently required. The Old Latin version, as it is called, began being made in the second century, Africa and western Europe being simultaneously its cradle; and by the fourth century it existed in a bewildering variety of forms—almost as many, Jerome declares,[33] as there were codices. This was caused partly by the fact that the task of translation had been undertaken, very probably, by different hands in different areas; but the confusion had been made worse, he explains, by translation slips, the blundering emendations of over-confident critics, careless transcription, and the practice of inserting in one gospel material found in another in the mistaken belief that it must have fallen out. The Latin of these early versions, it should be added, was highly peculiar, and of fascinating interest to modern students. It represented the adaptation of Latin to Christian usage, with the special vocabulary which the new religion required and in its idiom often recalling the Greek on which it was based; and being written for ordinary folk it had a strongly colloquial tang.

We have Jerome's word that it was Damasus who requested him to sort out the multitude of discrepancies and general disorder and provide a uniform text.[34] It was not a completely fresh translation of the original

[33] Cf. the preface to his translation of the Gospels (PL 29, 525).
[34] Cf. the preface cited above.

that the pope wanted, but a revision based on that original. Although Jerome's language does not make it clear, it is likely that his commission envisaged the whole Bible, at all events the whole New Testament, but for the moment he took the four Gospels in hand. As he braced himself for the task, he had no illusions about either its difficulty or the odium he was bound to incur. Among all the competing versions he, and he alone, was to determine the text which agreed most closely with the Greek; and after all his efforts he would be branded as a sacrilegious forger by conservative readers who detected an unfamiliar taste in his revisions. To obviate this, though checking them by 'ancient' Greek manuscripts, he was careful to restrain his pen and introduce corrections only where the sense demanded them.

In the event his revision was a distinctly conservative one; and since he always worked in a hurry and could be extremely careless, it was very far from being consistent, and tended to be more thorough at its earlier than its later stages. He naturally emended what struck him as corrupt or inaccurate, altered finite verbs in the Old Latin to participles where there were participles in the Greek (although more fitfully towards the end of the work than at the beginning), and made intermittent efforts to harmonise the style. But he sometimes deliberately retained expressions for which he knew there were more suitable alternatives in his eagerness to respect tradition. He did, however, substitute the order of the Gospels with which we are familiar, and which he found in the Greek MSS, for the one favoured by the Old Latin (Matthew-John-Luke-Mark), and he was also more radical in his treatment of the actual text. Textual criticism is, of course, a modern science, and he was largely ignorant of its principles; he naturally relied on the 'old codices' which he found to hand. These led him to prefer a text which very often, but not invariably, resembles the type presented by the famous fourth-century codices Vaticanus and Sinaiticus. They also caused him to steer clear, in general, of what modern scholars call the 'western text', with its tendency to paraphrase and assimilate. On occasion, however, one has to admit that his choice of a reading was not governed by any scientific principle at all; it appealed to him, for example, because it was to his taste doctrinally.[35]

To assist readers of the Gospels he appended ten tables, or 'canons', designed to indicate at a glance the passages which were peculiar to each or shared by two or more of them. He borrowed the device, which we should call a harmony of the Gospels, and the lists themselves with their numbered gospel-sections, from Eusebius of Caesarea, who had developed the system (as he informs us) from a simpler but less useful one invented

---

[35] For this paragraph I am indebted, among others, to A. Vööbus, *Early Versions of the New Testament* (Stockholm, 1954), 53–65; H. F. D. Sparks, 'Jerome as Biblical Scholar', *The Cambridge History of the Bible* (Cambridge, 1970) I, 510–26.

by the third-century Alexandrian scholar Ammonius Saccas.[36] Each of the gospel-sections had two numbers placed against it, one in black identifying it and the other in red referring to the canon containing the relevant passage and the parallels in other gospels. This revised edition of all four Gospels was completed and presented, with a characteristic preface setting out Jerome's difficulties and methods, to Pope Damasus in 384. It formed the first instalment of the great Latin Bible which since the council of Trent has been known as the Vulgate.

What about the remaining books of the New Testament—Acts, the Pauline and other Epistles, Revelation? The Vulgate Bible contains all these in a Latin translation which has, in varying degrees, been corrected from the Old Latin. The common opinion formerly was that these revisions too, like the Vulgate revision of the Gospels, represent Jerome's handiwork; they were usually assigned to the latter part of his Roman stay, probably after the death of Damasus on 11 December 384 (this would account for the absence of a dedicatory preface). His own claim, advanced more than once, was in inclusive terms: he had 'restored the New Testament to its Greek original'.[37] Yet in recent years the unlikelihood, not to say impossibility, of this traditional view has progressively forced itself on scholars.[38] The broad fact that stands out is that, where Jerome comments on or quotes from the New Testament outside the Gospels, he seems to ignore the Vulgate text as we know it. Sometimes he uses a text which more or less coincides with the Vulgate, but more often a divergent text; sometimes he passes over or rejects readings admitted by the Vulgate. Equally striking is the fact that in his commentaries on four of the Epistles (Philemon, Galatians, Ephesians, Titus), which he completed in 387 or thereabouts, i.e. shortly after his supposed revision of them, he nowhere attributes the Latin text he is using to himself, but expressly ascribes it to other translators (cf. his repeated reference to the 'Latinus interpres') and on occasion criticises their work. One might add that the stylistic evidence, especially in Acts, is against his authorship. The only tenable conclusion is that Jerome, for whatever reason, abandoned the idea of revising the rest of the New Testament (if indeed he ever entertained it at all) once he had completed the Gospels. In claiming to have corrected the New Testament he may possibly, on a charitable interpretation, have been thinking of the Gospels as the New Testament *par excellence*; but much more probably he was yielding to his habitual

---

[36] *Ep. ad Carpianum* (PG 22, 1276 f.). For useful notes on the 'Eusebian canons' see D. S. Wallace-Hadrill, *Eusebius of Caesarea* (London, 1960), 69 f.; J. Moreau, *RAC* 6, col. 1063.

[37] *Famous Men* 135; *Letters* 71, 5; 112, 20.

[38] See, e.g., F. Cavallera, 'Saint Jérôme et la Vulgate des Actes, des Épîtres, et de l'Apocalypse' (*Bulletin de littérature ecclésiastique*, 1920, 269–92). Some of the points made in what follows are taken from this important article.

tendency to exaggerate. In the passage of *Famous Men*[39] where he makes the claim he also blandly remarks that he had also 'translated the Old Testament from the Hebrew', although at the time of writing he had in fact translated only a portion of it.

There was one further scriptural task which Jerome, again probably at the pope's instigation, undoubtedly carried out at Rome. This was the revision of the existing Latin text of the Psalter on the basis of the Septuagint translation (he had not yet come to appreciate the importance of going back to the Hebrew original). According to his own report, he carried this out hastily, but introduced substantial corrections.[40] Traditionally this work has been identified with what is conventionally known as the 'Roman Psalter', i.e. the special version of the Psalms whose use, once widespread in Rome and Italy generally, has been virtually confined since the sixteenth century to St Peter's basilica. Since 1930, however, this identification has been widely contested; and although not all the objections have been accepted, there is fairly general agreement that the tradition is mistaken.[41] Indeed the truth of the matter seems to be that, while the Roman Psalter is certainly not the version which Jerome produced at Rome in 384 (that is, alas, irretrievably lost), it probably represents the text on which he worked and which he corrected.[42]

(iv)

So far from being immediately popular, Jerome's improved version of the Latin Gospels was greeted with the howl of indignation he had predicted. This is apparent from an angry but revealing letter which he wrote shortly after the work was published.[43] Contemptible characters, he protested, 'asses with two legs' who preferred to lap up muddy rivulets rather than drink the pellucid fountain of the original Greek, were attacking his presumption in flouting tradition and tampering with the inspired words of the Gospels. They were so stupid that they did not realise that he was correcting, not the Lord's sayings, but the manifest faultiness of the Latin codices. To silence them he would blow a trumpet in their ears, since a lyre would make no impression on asses. He proceeded to fling in their teeth three texts from St Paul's Epistles where the renderings he preferred were patently superior to theirs. These examples, as well as the disclosure that his critics emphasised that the Apostles had been simple, uneducated men, indicate that their leader was none other than the distinguished

---

[39] *Famous Men* 135.
[40] Cf. the preface to his later translation of the Psalms from the Hebrew (*PL* 29, 117).
[41] Cf. esp. D. de Bruyne, 'Le problème du psautier romain' (*RB* 42, 1930, 101–26).
[42] See esp. A. Vaccari, *Scritti di erudizione e di filologia I* (Rome, 1952), 211–21.
[43] *Letter* 27, 1.

exegete Ambrosiaster, whom we met a few pages earlier and whom we know to have been a stout defender of the Old Latin version of the New Testament against the Greek original.[44]

As we shall shortly discover, these were not Jerome's only detractors in 384. Nevertheless his star was, temporarily at any rate, splendidly in the ascendant. Respected though he had been on his arrival at Rome, he had risen in the past two years to heights beyond his most ambitious imaginings. Almost without effort he had become the friend and confidant of the pope, who was entrusting him with varied and important responsibilities, and who was constantly making him his mouthpiece.[45] Only a year or so later, when the sky had turned black, he was to recall this as a period when the city resounded with his praises and he was universally applauded for his piety, humble bearing, and eloquence. In the judgment of most people (so he reports) he was being marked down as a worthy successor to the elderly pontiff.

[44] For the identification of the critic with Ambrosiaster see H. Vogels, RB 66, 1956, 16–19.
[45] Letter 45, 3 (from which the other details in the second half of this paragraph are derived). Others take the obscure expression 'Damasi os meus sermo erat' as meaning 'Damasus had me always on his lips'.

X

Marcella, Paula, Eustochium

(i)

Jerome's three years in Rome were, until the closing months, among the happiest of his life. This was in large measure due to the fact that, concurrently with his work for Pope Damasus, a wholly fresh and satisfying field of activity was now opened to him. Hitherto he has appeared in the roles of earnest ascetic, indefatigable student and author, fierce controversialist. At no time (the mysterious, unhappy episode of the virgins of Emona is no exception) have we seen him associating on easy terms of mutual respect and affection with women. Now a great enlargement comes over his experience; he is accepted as spiritual guide and scriptural teacher of a remarkable group of Roman ladies, both mature women and young girls, of exalted rank and considerable wealth.

The comment has been made that, apart from Damasus, we hear nothing of contacts, much less friendships, between Jerome and other men during this period. There must have been many such contacts, and this is confirmed by his dealings in later life with people like the high-born Oceanus, the priest Domnio, and Rogatianus, whose acquaintance he can have made only at Rome.[1] The total silence about them, which at first seems curious, is partly fortuitous, the result of the fragmentary character of the surviving evidence. But it also derives from the fact that, busy as he was with the pope, these exciting and absorbing relationships with women can have left him very little spare time. Strongly sexed but also, because of his convictions, strongly repressed as well, his nature craved for female society, and found deep satisfaction in it when it could be had without doing violence to his principles. He had been fortunate in being introduced, immediately he arrived in Rome, to one or two groups of dedicated Christian women who had embraced, some of them many years back, an extreme type of asceticism modelled, so far as circumstances allowed, on the ideals and practices of the famous desert fathers of Egypt.[2]

---

[1] See below for Oceanus pp. 214; 234 f.; for Domnio pp. 187 f.; for Rogatianus p. 190.
[2] For the spread of Oriental monastic ideals at Rome see G. D. Gordini, 'Origine e sviluppo del monachesimo a Roma' (*Gregorianum* 37, 1956, 220–60); R. Lorenz, 'Die Anfänge des abendländischen Mönchtums im 4. Jahrhundert' (*ZKG* 77, 1966, 3–8).

The leaders of these groups were two aristocratic widows, Marcella and Paula. He almost certainly met Paula first, for he was later to record that, when his party reached Rome in 382, she had entertained Bishop Epiphanius in her house and had treated Paulinus, who was lodging elsewhere, as if he too were her guest.[3] As Jerome was in their entourage, he must have called frequently at her mansion, but several months had to elapse before he became a close family friend.[4] He could certainly never have guessed how intimately, and fatefully, her life was to become intertwined with his. Of illustrious descent and vast fortune, she was now thirty-five (born 5 June 347), and thus some sixteen years younger than himself. A widow with five children, the youngest a boy, she had ceased (Jerome hints),[5] for religious reasons, to have intercourse with her husband, Toxotius, once she had presented him with a male heir. She had been just a girl when she married him, and his death the previous year had been a shattering blow.[6] A Christian already ascetically inclined, she had resolved to devote herself wholly to the Lord's service, withdrawing from the fashionable round and adopting a life which combined ruinously lavish charity with personal seclusion and continuous austerities.[7]

It was Marcella, also a widow but much older than Paula, stronger in character and more practical-minded, who first took Jerome up. Wealthy, high-born, and beautiful, she had lost her husband a quarter of a century earlier, had turned down a tempting offer of marriage in spite of pressure from her mother, and had preferred to consecrate herself to chaste widowhood and a life of simplicity, fasting, and Bible reading.[8] Through the study of Athanasius's *Life of Antony*, then through personal contacts with Bishop Peter of Alexandria when he was living in exile in Rome from 373 to 378, she came to admire the discipline of the monks, virgins, and widows of the Nile valley, and her own way of life increasingly reflected it.[9] Thus she became, Jerome comments, though avoiding in her regimen anything extravagant or unnatural, the first Roman lady of rank to accept 'the monastic profession', and that at a time when it was popularly considered odd and rather degrading. Her home was on the Aventine,[10]

---

[3] *Letter* 108, 6. This letter, the 'consolatio' he addressed to Eustochium on Paula's death in 404, is the source of most of the biographical details given below.

[4] *Letter* 45, 3 : this implies a gap between his arrival and his getting to know Paula's household.

[5] *Letter* 108, 4.

[6] For the view that he died in 381, not (as has been generally held) a year or two earlier, see P. Nautin, *Revue des études augustiniennes* 18 (1972), 218.

[7] *Letter* 108, 5; also *Letter* 45, 3–5.

[8] For most of the following see *Letter* 127, a memoir addressed after her death in 412 to her close friend Principia.

[9] According to Jerome (*Letter* 127, 5), it was Athanasius himself, when a refugee in Rome in 339–42, who had fired her interest in the desert fathers. But this is unlikely as she can have been only a girl of ten or twelve at that time, and in any case subsequently married.

[10] *Letter* 47, 3.

the southernmost of Rome's seven hills and a residential quarter then much favoured by the rich and aristocratic; and living there with her mother Albina, whom she had won over to asceticism, she made it the meeting-place of a whole group of upper-class women and girls inspired by the same ideals.

Both Paula, whose house was now a similar centre, and her third daughter, Eustochium (of whom we shall hear more), had been disciples of Marcella. They looked up to her as their teacher in the higher life, and Jerome reports that 'it was in Marcella's cell that Eustochium, paragon of virgins, was trained'.[11] Paula's eldest daughter, Blesilla, an exuberant girl approaching twenty, was another whom Jerome met, probably in her mother's home. For the moment she was looking forward to a fine marriage, but before long he was to fasten his influence on her. On the other hand, we should include Asella, now almost fifty, in Marcella's circle.[12] As a child of twelve she had dedicated herself to virginity and now lived enclosed in a cell, working with her hands and fasting strenuously; in Jerome's opinion she was the ideal model for young girls. Others, like Marcellina and Felicitas, we know only by name;[13] but there was also Lea, an intimate friend of Marcella's and, like her, a widow who had made a complete break with the world after her husband's death. Always confined to her room, careless of food and dress and amazingly humble, she too had gathered a group of keen disciples around her.[14]

Marcella, Paula, and the rest, as they gaze at us from Jerome's letters, provide an illuminating glimpse of what committed Christianity had come to mean for some enthusiastic believers, mainly women, in Rome between the sixties and eighties of the fourth century. Jerome speaks of 'monastic vocation' and calls Lea 'the leader of her monastery'; and while formal organisation under a rule had yet to come, they were effectively nuns for most practical purposes. For them all, dwelling in their stately houses, meeting for Bible study, and stealing away unobserved to the basilicas or the martyrs' tombs for worship, the Christian ideal found expression, in degrees varying with each individual, in withdrawal from ordinary society, prolonged and rigorous fasting, the wearing of coarse, even squalid clothing, the neglect of personal appearance, and the avoidance of comforts like baths, above all in chastity—the elimination as far as possible of the sexual element. All this, contrasting so strangely with the behaviour of their upper-class contemporaries, Christian or pagan (many of the great senatorial families still held tenaciously and proudly to the old

[11] *Letter* 127, 5: see also *Letter* 46, 1, where Paula and Eustochium speak of her as their mistress and of themselves as her 'discipulae'.
[12] For Asella see *Letter* 24.
[13] *Letter* 45, 7.
[14] For Lea see *Letter* 23.

religion), was eagerly embraced, not for consciously negative or maso-
chistic motives, but because they seriously believed that it brought their
pattern of life closer to that laid down in the gospel. Their devotion was
profoundly Jesus-centred; and they gave it a positive outlet, sometimes
alone in their rooms, sometimes assembled in groups, in sustained prayers,
penitential outpourings, incessant reading of Scripture.

(ii)

Jerome's association with these women, which met a deep-felt need in his
make-up, reveals the warmth of his sympathies, his instinctive skill at
adapting himself to their different personalities and interests, and the hold
he was quickly able to establish over several of them. It also shows him
beginning to make his contribution to the dissemination of asceticism of
the Oriental type at Rome. He was far from being a pioneer in this
respect; as we have seen, the fashion had caught on many years earlier.
But he fanned the enthusiasm of his protégées, sought to bring order and
routine into their observances, and in particular equipped them with a
firm Biblical foundation.

We can imagine their excitement when the news got around that this
ascetic who had fought with demons in the desert, this scholar with a
brilliant reputation, had set foot in the capital. It was Marcella, apparently,
who took the initiative when in his bashfulness (so he says)[15] he was
avoiding the eyes of high-born ladies. She sought him out, plied him
incessantly with scriptural problems, and would go on discussing and
arguing until satisfied. Soon he was a regular visitor to her mansion on the
Aventine, and as the months slipped by session succeeded session of
intensive Biblical study. Usually there must have been others present, for
Marcella had a prudent rule not to see a monk or a cleric alone; and before
long Jerome found himself conducting a whole class of eager students.
With her probing mind Marcella wished to have all the obscurities,
especially the linguistic ones, of the text cleared up; and although their
meetings were frequent, she often insisted on his setting down his solutions on paper. He was content to oblige (his letters thus received wide
publicity), and of the correspondence sixteen letters (none, unfortunately,
by her) survive.

Several of these are highly technical: examinations, for example, of
passages obscurely rendered from the Hebrew, or of Hebrew words or
phrases which the translators of the Latin versions (as of the older
English ones) had retained as they stood. Here Jerome was well placed to
help Marcella, for the correspondence reveals how deeply immersed he

---

[15] *Letter* 127, 7: see this letter for other details of this paragraph.

was in Hebrew studies (so much so that his pronunciation of Latin, he protests, was getting rusty), painstakingly comparing the Hebrew of the Old Testament with the Jew Aquila's literal Greek version.[16] Thus one letter, perhaps the earliest in the collection, seeks to expound the nuances of the ten names given to God by the Jews, and three others the meanings of 'Alleluia', 'amen', and 'Maran atha' (used in 1 Cor. 16, 2), of the musical-liturgical sign 'Selah' which occurs seventy-one times in the Psalter (and still puzzles English readers), and of the terms 'ephod' (generally a priestly garment) and 'teraphim' (cult figures).[17] Marcella had apparently compiled and submitted an extensive dossier on these last alone. Often enough his explanations hit the mark, at other times they break down because the necessary philological equipment was not available to him. In general he relied on comparing the several Greek translations, or on what he had picked up from Origen or Jews he had consulted.

One or two letters contain graphic human touches. His impatience with his 'task-mistress', for example, flashes out in the complaint that, whereas the true function of letters is to bring friends together in mutually delightful intercourse, everything she writes imposes a burden on him.[18] Again, pressed to unravel two baffling phrases in Psalm 127, he confesses that he had been kept up till the small hours dictating his reply, and had broken off only because of violent stomach pains. This same letter[19] shows him correcting the Greek version by the Hebrew original, respectfully criticising even the revered Hilary of Poitiers, and lamenting that Origen's notes on this particular psalm have been lost. In a third letter he flatly refuses to lend Marcella the commentary on Song of Songs by Reticius of Autun.[20] Years before, when in the desert, he had eagerly demanded this very work, extolling it as an eloquent exposition, but now he declares that it abounds in howlers (the ones he quotes are pretty appalling). He reproves the author for not consulting Origen's massive study, much less seeking advice from Hebrew speakers. His high-flown Gallic style was all very well; but the commentator's job is not to make a show of his own eloquence, but to explain the writer's meaning.

In two other letters Jerome seeks to arm Marcella against the propaganda of Montanists and Novatianists.[21] The former were a sect of prophetic enthusiasts and rigorists who believed that the supreme outpouring of the Spirit had not been on the Apostles at Pentecost, but on one Montanus in Phrygia in the late second century; the latter were a splinter-group, also rigorist, which held that Christians who lapsed under stress

---

[16] *Letters* 29, 7; 32, 1.
[17] *Letters* 25; 26; 28; 29.
[18] *Letter* 29, 1: cf. *Letter* 28, 1, where he calls her his 'slave-driver' (ἐργοδιώκτην).
[19] *Letter* 34, 6.
[20] *Letter* 37. See above p. 48 for his earlier demand for Reticius's commentary.
[21] *Letters* 41; 42: generally dated 385.

of persecution could never be re-admitted to the Church, and indeed identified such lapsing with the mysterious 'sin against the Holy Ghost' spoken of in Matthew 12, 32. Marcella had been got at by a Montanist proselytist, and Jerome was clearly afraid that, open-minded and intellectually curious, she might succumb. In his replies he criticises the heretical positions damagingly, defines the differences between them and orthodoxy, and takes a refreshingly humane line on second marriages, fasting, and penitence. He was, of course, combating extreme forms of puritanism, but he was also aware that Marcella, though devoted to asceticism, was a highly practical woman and had personally no use for its more extravagant manifestations. She made a reasonable compromise with her mother, who did not wish her property to go outside the family; she fasted, but in moderation; she even drank a little wine, although Jerome explains that this was for reasons of health.[22]

But their relationship went deeper than the discussion of knotty points of exegesis or orthodox doctrine. When humble, self-effacing Lea died and Marcella was cruelly shaken, Jerome dashed off a moving note of consolation—a note only marred by the savagely jubilant contrast he draws between the fate of Lea, whose life had seemed madness to the world but who was now with Christ, and that of Vettius Agorius Praetextatus, the widely respected consul-designate who had died at almost the same time and who now, according to Jerome, was assuredly in hell because he had been a zealous pagan.[23] It was to Marcella, again, that he poured out his joy that Blesilla's illness had led to her conversion, and his scorn for the critics of his revision of the Old Latin Gospels; to Marcella that he held up to coarsest ridicule a priest who, feeling himself the anonymous target of Jerome's satire, had indignantly complained.[24] Yet there are hints that Marcella disliked, and sought to curb, her friend's petulant and tasteless outbursts which could do him only harm. Intelligent and well poised, she had a firmer character than he; greatly as she liked and admired him, she never had any illusions about him. She was a steadying influence on his impetuosity; without her he might have got into hot water at Rome even sooner than he did.[25]

(iii)

Meanwhile Jerome's friendship with Paula, who also had a Bible-reading

---

[22] *Letter* 127, 4.

[23] *Letter* 24: date sometime between 9 Sept. and 11 Dec. 384 (see Cavallera II, 22 f.). For high opinions of Praetextatus see, e.g., Ammianus Marcellinus, *Res gestae* 27, 9, 8; Zosimus, *Hist. nova* 4, 3, 3. For his distinguished career see *PLRE* I, 722–4.

[24] *Letters* 38; 27; 40.

[25] Cf. his defensive remarks in *Letter* 27, 2. Grützmacher (I, 241 f.) has a discerning sketch of her and her relationship with Jerome.

circle (a sort of 'household church')[26] and who was so modest that she never ate a meal with a man (not even with a bishop),[27] was ripening. In many ways the two were made for each other: she impressionable, soft-hearted, subconsciously seeking someone to lean upon now her husband was dead; and he, for all his touchiness and irascibility, hungry for sympathy and affection. Both had the same simple, Jesus-centred piety; both were enthusiasts for asceticism, she going to even greater lengths than he (she never took a bath except when dangerously ill, preferred to sleep on the bare ground, etc.), so that he sometimes had to restrain her. In the winter of 382/3, when acting as host to Epiphanius and Paulinus, she had had romantic dreams of forsaking home and children to settle as an anchorite in some eastern desert. When they had sailed away in the spring, she had accompanied them in imaginative fantasy. Was it the growing attachment between Jerome and herself, and the influence he was beginning to exert, that held her back?

At any rate, along with her daughter Eustochium, she asked leave to read the Bible under his direction, proving so apt a pupil that eventually she knew much of it by heart. She even set herself to learn Hebrew, becoming proficient enough to chant the psalms in it with an impeccable pronunciation. But her approach to Scripture was not the down-to-earth, literalist one of Marcella; not for her scholarly disquisitions on the meaning of obscure words or phrases. She valued, Jerome records, the historical facts contained in the Bible, but what chiefly excited her were the morally or spiritually edifying messages which, by the deft use of allegory, could be extracted from it. Jerome had no difficulty in supplying these, and we have a breath-taking example of his virtuosity in a letter explaining the significance of the acrostic, or 'alphabetical', psalms (9–10, 25, 34, 37, 111, 112, 119, 145), in which each verse or section is opened by a successive letter of the alphabet.[28] First, he proposes, on the basis of a rather shaky etymology perhaps derived from Jewish advisers, a meaning for each of the twenty-two letters of the Hebrew alphabet. Then he arranges the letters in seven groups, and discovers that each group contains an impressive mystical truth. Thus from the premiss that Aleph denotes 'teaching', Beth 'house', Gimel 'fullness', and Daleth 'of tablets', he deduces triumphantly that the very alphabet proclaims that 'the teaching of the Church, or God's house, is found in the fullness of the sacred books'. If Paula was impressed, we can excuse her credulity; it is less easy to be patient with Jerome in his complacent pride in his self-deception.

[26] *Letter* 30, 14, where he sends greetings to her daughters and the whole 'choir' of virgins who make up her 'domestica ecclesia'.

[27] *Letter* 108, 15. This letter is the source of most of the biographical details in this and the next paragraph.

[28] *Letter* 30.

Only two other letters survive from the many Jerome probably wrote to Paula during these years.[29] One of them contains lists of the writings both of the Roman polymath Varro (116–127 B.C.) and of Origen, the intention being to demonstrate the Christian author's much greater productivity.[30] The compilation of this catalogue, far from complete and unsystematically arranged, raises unsolved problems; it has been suspected that the letter may have been written, or at least revised, some years later in Palestine, where Jerome had access to the library at Caesarea, which possessed Origen's complete works.[31] But wherever it was written (Rome remains the likeliest place), it testifies to Jerome's absorbing preoccupation with Origen, and also to his unqualified admiration (for the moment at any rate) for him. He expresses disgust at the censures the controversial theologian had received in his lifetime, even at Rome, and insists that they were not prompted by any novelty, much less heresy, in his teaching, but by sheer jealousy. It was left to some contemporaries, he sneers, to traduce his orthodoxy, but these are 'mad dogs'. This adulation is all the more surprising as Jerome seems unaware that his friend Epiphanius had recently devoted a substantial section of a massive anti-heretical treatise to exposing Origen's 'errors'.[32]

The second letter, a much more elaborate composition, is intended as a threnody (the first of a great series of such pieces which Jerome was to devote to departed friends) for Blesilla, Paula's eldest daughter, who died in October/November 384.[33] Beautiful and conscious of it, this talented girl of twenty had caused anxious moments to Jerome and her mother. Though a Christian, she enjoyed the gay life of aristocratic Rome, had made a smart marriage, and even when left a widow after seven months had been unable to free herself from worldly ties, lavishing attention on her dress and her appearance. Jerome was deeply worried; he made himself responsible for her, and annoyed her relatives by pestering her with his admonitions. Then suddenly, after a sharp bout of fever from which she recovered, she had become a woman transformed, and had scandalised society as much as she delighted Jerome by undertaking rigorous mortifications and surrendering herself to prayer, penitential outpourings, and the intense study of Scripture. She even mastered Hebrew in next to no time, and made quite exceptional demands on

[29] Cf. *Famous Men* (date 392/3) 54 ('volumes' of letters to Paula); 135 (innumerable, daily letters). The latter may envisage the letters he wrote at Bethlehem, but the former seems to have a wider reference.

[30] *Letter* 33.

[31] For studies of this catalogue and its compilation see E. Klostermann, 'Die Schriften des Origenes in Hieronymus' Brief an Paula' (*Sitzungsberichte der kön. preuss. Akad. der Wissenschaften*, 1897, 855–70), and (esp.) P. Courcelle, *Late Latin Writers and their Greek Sources* (ET, Cambridge, Mass., 1969), 103–13.

[32] Cf. his *Panarion* (*Medicine Chest for Heresies*) 64.

[33] *Letter* 39 (date: the latter months of 384, before the death of Damasus).

Jerome for Bible commentaries.[34] Alas, the strain, emotional and physical, proved too much for her. Before four months were passed she was dead. Paula's anguish was inconsolable, and she collapsed at the funeral.

Jerome, who seems to have regarded Blesilla as now belonging at least as much to himself as to Paula, was shocked by her distress, and took her to task in no uncertain terms. The letter, which he intended as a threnody, and which starts off as a eulogy of Blesilla, soon becomes a rebuke for her mother's excessive grief, and at the same time a terrifying exposure of his own religious attitude. First, he concedes that tears have their place (did not Jesus weep for Lazarus?), but protests that his own agony is no less than Paula's. But the Christian should be able to bear the most shattering blows with meek thankfulness, knowing that God, who controls all things, is good. Secondly, however, the dead man for whom mourning is appropriate is the sinner who has gone down to hell; Blesilla deserves congratulation, for she has passed from darkness to light to meet Christ face to face. Thirdly, Paula should recall that she is not only a mother but a Christian, and a dedicated ascetic at that. The truly Christian reaction to death was that of the heroic Melania:[35] when she lost her husband and two of her sons in quick succession, she shed no tear but, prostrate before Christ, exclaimed with a smile, 'Now I shall serve You, Lord, all the more readily, since You have freed me from this burden.' Finally, Paula's grief is disgraceful to the point of sacrilege. It must be sheer torture to Blesilla, as she consorts with blessed Mary and the saints, to see her own mother behaving in a manner so displeasing to Christ.

This letter to a heart-broken woman (who probably read it with sub-missive penitence because she revered its author and felt sure that his sentiments must be sound), concludes with an empty rhetorical flourish of a piece with much else that is extravagant and artificial in it. As long as Jerome lives, every page he writes will resound with Blesilla's name. Thus she who lives in heaven with Christ will secure an earthly immortality through his writings.

(iv)

Almost as dear to Jerome as Paula, closer to his ideal of Christian perfec-tion, was her third daughter, Julia Eustochium, who (little though either he or she knew it) was to be his devoted companion until her death in

[34] See *Origen's Homilies on Luke* pref. (*GCS* 49, 1), where he recalls that she had asked him to translate Origen's twenty-five volumes on Matthew, his five on Luke, and his thirty-five on John: also *Comm. on Ecclesiastes* pref. (*CCL* 72: 381–2).

[35] Melania the Elder, an aristocratic and wealthy Roman lady. She had left Rome *c.* 372 for Egypt and Palestine (see pp. 40; 121), and in 378, with Rufinus as helper and adviser, had founded a double monastery at Jerusalem. Because of her friendship with Rufinus Jerome's high opinion of her was later to change drastically for the worse: see below pp. 251; 314.

418/19, only a year or so before his own. From the first days of their acquaintance a tender, delicate understanding seems to have grown between the scholarly monk in his early fifties and the shy young girl still in her teens.[36] Along with Paula, and later her sister Blesilla, she attended his Bible classes and joined in singing the psalms in Hebrew. She was gentle and docile, inseparable from her mother, invariably obedient to her.[37] Following her example, in the face of strong counter-pressure from a more worldly aunt and uncle, she refused smart clothes and neglected her hair.[38] But what chiefly thrilled Jerome, with his obsessive esteem for virginity, was the eagerness, humble but quite unswerving, with which she dedicated herself to it from girlhood. Indeed, he congratulated her on being the first young woman of rank in Rome to embrace this stern vocation.[39] How much more blessed she was than her elder sister, who, although she had taken vows of chastity after her husband's death, had by the very act of marrying him lost her irreplaceable crown.

Not that we should picture Eustochium either as repressedly stuffy in her piety or as overawed by her fussily exacting director. On St Peter's Day, probably 29 June 384, she sent him some presents in honour of the feast—bracelets, doves, a basket of cherries, with an accompanying note. We get the impression of an entirely natural girl, happy in her religion and choosing with care, for a day popularly observed at Rome, charming gifts which might please him. Rather it is Jerome who appears in an over-solemn, slightly ridiculous light. In a pedantic letter of thanks he moralises heavily on the mystical significance of the presents, and even more heavily deplores celebrating a martyr's feast with unmixed joyfulness.[40] 'With God nothing pleasurable, nothing merely sweet is pleasing'; a day like this should be kept with exultation of spirit, not abundance of food. Yet he manages to mix with this an almost skittish reference to the colour of the cherries, which recalls a virgin's blushes. The whole tone is patronising, and one is surprised that he was inordinately proud of the artificial piece and once, when he was too busy to write Marcella a full-length letter, sent her this one, along with his letter on the acrostic psalms, in substitute.[41]

In this brief note he counsels Eustochium to bear in mind his 'earlier pamphlet', meaning his famous Letter 22, which he must have completed in the early spring of 384 at latest. While cast in the form of a letter, it is in

---

[36] Her date of birth is unknown, but Jerome speaks (*Letter* 39, 6) of her 'parva adhuc aetas et rudis paene infantia' at the time of Blesilla's death.

[37] *Letter* 108, 27.

[38] *Letter* 107, 5, where Jerome records the divine punishment that speedily overtook the wretched aunt.

[39] *Letter* 22, 15.

[40] *Letter* 31.

[41] See *Letter* 32, 1.

fact a sizeable treatise laying down the motives which should actuate those who devote themselves to a life of virginity, and also the rules by which they ought to regulate their daily conduct. All this for the benefit more particularly of a rich, delicately nurtured girl like Eustochium whose lot is cast in an affluent, pleasure-loving society. Why this young woman, the most responsive of his disciples, should have needed such a massive exhortation is not at first sight apparent. The truth is, this letter should be set in the context of an ascetic campaign which Jerome was carrying on in 383-4, with the pope's approval, not only among his circles of devout ladies but in Rome at large. His letters, like those of other contemporaries, were copied and handed around, and thus attained wide publicity. He was deliberately using this one to Eustochium as a platform for setting out his challenging programme, and also for exposing the rottenness which, as he saw it, was infecting great numbers of would-be Christians in Rome, including many clergy and professed ascetics.

Discursive and lacking regular plan, the letter is brilliant in style and packed with subtle persuasion; one reads with a smile his promise to keep it free from all flattery, all rhetorical display.[42] A whole variety of related themes jostle one another, and several keep recurring. For example, the distinction between a real virgin and a sham one is repeatedly emphasised, and with it the need to repress sensual imaginings immediately they arise in the mind.[43] There is a realistic tirade against wine, insidious because of its liability to stimulate sexual desire; also against rich or abundant food, which can be equally exciting.[44] Again, Jerome urges Eustochium to shun the society of married women and women of the world in general; they can only remind her of things she has renounced.[45] For companions she should choose dedicated women, 'pale and thin with fasting'; and, as far as possible, she should keep to her own room, not even going out to visit the martyrs' shrines. Her days and nights should be filled with prayer (set hours, anticipating the later canonical ones, are prescribed) and Bible reading; prayer should be her armour whenever danger threatens.[46] It goes without saying that she should set no store by money or elegant clothes, should be humble in thought and conduct, and should always take the Blessed Virgin as her example.[47] Mixed up with all these are eloquent reminiscences from Jerome's personal experience (his time in the desert; his terrible dream),[48] searing descriptions of worldly clergy or charlatans who pose as ascetics, and grim catalogues of the inconveniences and

[42] *Letter* 22, 2.
[43] E.g. *Letter* 22, 5; 6; 13; 38.
[44] *Letter* 22, 8-9; 10-11.
[45] *Letter* 22, 16-17.
[46] *Letter* 22, 17-18; 37.
[47] *Letter* 22, 27; 31-2; 38.
[48] *Letter* 22, 7; 30.

positive vexations of marriage. A constant note is the perilous path the virgin treads, the irreparable disaster if she should slip, and the glorious reward if she remains firm till the end.

Jerome inserts an important digression describing for his Roman public the three types of monks to be found in Egypt—solitaries and those living in community, whom he applauds; those moving about in cities in small groups with no fixed rule, whom he dismisses with contempt.[49] But what he is unfolding throughout is a systematic theory of sexuality and its place, or rather lack of place, in the earnest Christian's life. From the second century onwards a widening stream of such essays had been published by Christian writers; in the later fourth century leading thinkers like Gregory of Nyssa and John Chrysostom in the east, and Ambrose and Augustine in the west, were making their contribution. They all draw on a common fund of ideas and expound, though with widely differing nuances, what is essentially the same doctrine. This is that marriage is, on the most favourable interpretation, a poor second best; virginity is the original state willed by God, and sexual intercourse came in only after the Fall. The underlying presuppositions are that the sexual act is intrinsically defiling, and that indulgence in it creates a barrier between the soul and God. If one is married, it is better to abstain from intercourse; a second marriage betokens regrettable carnal weakness. Jerome had, of course, long ago accepted this position; we are not surprised that he presents it here, as elsewhere, in more violent colours and with sharper emphases than most. He protests that his doctrine implies no disparagement of marriage. But almost the only good thing he can see in marriage is that it produces children who themselves may embrace virginity; it is the thorn from which roses may be gathered.[50]

The positive picture of virginity which he presses upon Eustochium is that it is spiritual marriage with Christ. So he declares that she is his 'Lady' since she is the bride of his Lord; and he does not shrink from congratulating Paula on becoming 'God's mother-in-law'.[51] He goes on to develop this congenial theme in frankly erotic imagery borrowed from Song of Songs.[52] Eustochium should remain alone in the privacy of her room, and let her Lover sport with her. 'When sleep overcomes you, he will come behind the wall, will thrust his hand through the aperture, and will caress your belly; and you will start up, all trembling, and will cry, "I

[49] Letter 22, 34-6. The third type he calls 'remnuoth', stating that they formed the majority of ascetics in Italy. It is likely that they represented the survival of an archaic ascetic movement prior to the emergence of monasticism proper. Benedict (Reg. 1, 6) calls them 'sarabaitae', and declares them to be detestable. See R. Lorenz, art. cit. 8.

[50] Letter 22, 19-20.

[51] Letter 22, 2; 20. The latter expression ('socrus dei esse coepisti') was to be castigated by Rufinus as exceeding even heathen profanity (Apol. c. Hier. 2, 10).

[52] See esp. Letter 22, 25-6.

am wounded with love".' Not for her to go gadding about the streets; Jesus is a jealous lover who does not wish her face to be looked upon by others. In the Song she who had been able to say, 'My Beloved is to me a bag of myrrh, and will lie between my breasts', had gone seeking him in the city, only to be wounded and stripped. So let Eustochium wait in her chamber until her Lover knocks and she hears him say, 'Open to me, my sister, my love, my dove, my undefiled.'

Half a dozen years previously Ambrose had exploited the marriage symbolism of Song of Songs in his writings on virginity; Augustine will take up the same ideas in his around 400.[53] But while inevitably present the sexual overtones seem transposed in their exhortations. Jerome makes no attempt to play them down, and it is ironical to reflect that, in urging a young girl like Eustochium to crush the physical yearnings of her nature in the effort to surrender herself the more completely to Christ, he should feed her fantasy with such exciting images.

[53] See, e.g., Ambrose, *De virginibus* 12, 72–4; Augustine, *De sancta virginitate* 55–6.

XI

Triumph and Disgrace

(i)

Several months before addressing his eloquent exhortation to Eustochium, Jerome had publicly entered the lists as a champion of virginity.[1]
Though established in Rome long before his arrival, the Oriental-style
asceticism which he was now eagerly fostering was far from meeting with
unqualified approval. In pagan eyes the monk's withdrawal from the
world, coupled with self-inflicted mortifications, seemed anti-social,
unnatural, sheer madness: all the more so when it was suspected of being
a cloak for self-indulgence.[2] Christian circles were disposed to be more
sympathetic, for from early times there had been a respectable tradition of
asceticism in the Church. Even the ideal of virginity did not strike them,
in general, as outlandish. Ordinary Christians in the fourth century, like
philosophically-minded pagans, were haunted by guilt-feelings about
sexual enjoyment, and cherished an immense respect for self-control,
even complete abstinence, in sex.[3] What alarmed them was the sharp
intensification of ascetic practices, and the growing tendency among
enthusiasts to equate the ascetic way of life with authentic Christianity.
They were particularly disturbed by the campaign of such enthusiasts to
exalt celibacy far above marriage, and to regard those who embraced it as
approaching most nearly to Christian perfection. The arrogance of many
of the monks, and the fact that some of them were palpable charlatans, did
not help their cause.

The opposition in Rome had found an effective spokesman early in 383
in Helvidius, a layman who had been provoked into action (it seems) by a

---

[1] In *Letter* 31, 2, which was written for 29 June 384, *Letter* 22 is referred to as 'my earlier
treatise', and therefore probably belongs to the earlier part of that year. But *Letter* 22, 22
mentions 'the book which I published against Helvidius . . .'. It is plausible, therefore, to
place this controversy in 383. See Cavallera II, 24.

[2] For typical pagan critcisms see Julian, *Ep*. 89b (monks seek solitude whereas man is a
social animal); Libanius, *Or*. 2, 32 ('ascetics only in dress'); 30, 8–11 ('black-robed, more
gluttonous than elephants . . . concealing their vices under an artificially contrived pallor . . .');
Rutilius Namatianus (Prefect of Rome: writing 417), *De red. suo* 1, 439–52; 515–26 (crazed
escapists and masochists who think the divine spark is nourished by squalor). For further
references see P. de Labriolle, *La réaction païenne* (Paris, 1934), Index, s.v. 'Monachisme'.

[3] For detailed references consult the important articles 'Ehe I', by A. Oepke, and 'Enkrateia',
by H. Chadwick, in *RAC* 4 and 5.

pamphlet circulated by a monk named Carterius.[4] Jerome sneers at Helvidius as an ignorant, blasphemous boor, but we have the chronicler Gennadius's testimony (all the more trustworthy because he strongly disagreed with him) that his motives were sincerely religious.[5] He had published a tract seeking to prove that, while Mary had been a virgin in conceiving Jesus, after his birth she had lived a normal married life with Joseph, bearing him several children. His real objective was to reassert the equality of the married and celibate states, for Carterius and other partisans of the latter's superiority were now using the increasingly accepted dogma of Mary's 'perpetual virginity' as a trump card.

Helvidius's literary style may have lacked grace (Jerome ridicules its uncouthness and verbosity), but his case seems to have been logically ordered and impressive.[6] First, he pointed to gospel texts (Matt. 1, 18: 'Before they lived together, she was found to be pregnant by the Holy Spirit'; Matt. 1, 25: 'He did not have intercourse with her until she had borne her son') which seem to imply that Joseph and Mary cohabited as man and wife after the birth of Jesus. Secondly, he appealed to St Luke's description (2, 7) of Jesus as Mary's 'first-born son'; surely this must mean that she later had other children. Thirdly, as confirming this, he listed the numerous passages in which the evangelists mention, and on occasion name, 'brothers' (and 'sisters') of Jesus. Fourthly, he cited the older western tradition, claiming that respected writers like Tertullian and Victorinus of Pettau had drawn similar conclusions to his own.[7] Finally, he pleaded that it did no dishonour to Mary to recognise that she had been a real wife to Joseph. Celibates surely cannot be better than the patriarchs Abraham, Isaac, and Jacob, who had all been married men; and when children are formed in the womb (this was an argument used by Christians against Manichees), it is God who fashions them.

This was straight speaking: courageous speaking, too, for it contradicted the views of powerful figures like Pope Damasus and Ambrose of Milan. It must have gladdened the hearts of the critics of ascetic enthusiasm,

[4] For a skilful attempt to recapture the shadowy form of Helvidius see G. Jouassard, 'La personnalité d'Helvidius' (*Mélanges J. Saunier*, Lyon, 1944, 139–56). He questions whether H. was in fact a layman; Jerome's expression 'solus in universo mundo sibi et laicus et sacerdos' may mean simply that he constituted the entire membership of his sect. For Carterius (v.l. 'Cantherius'; 'Craterius') see *Against Helvidius* 16 (where he is named) and 4 (where H. directly addresses him).

[5] *Against Helvidius* 1. Cf. Gennadius, *De vir. ill.* 33. This work, completed *c.* 480, is a continuation of Jerome's book of the same title.

[6] For his five main points see *Against Helvidius* 3 (i); 9 (ii); 11 (iii); 17 (iv); 18 (v). The work itself is lost except for a few excerpts quoted by Jerome.

[7] He was correct about Tertullian: see his *Adv. Marc.* 4, 19; *De carne Christi* 7; *De monog.* 8; *De virg. vel.* 6. For Victorinus he must have been drawing on his now lost commentary on St Matthew (referred to by Jerome in *Comm. on St Matthew* pref.; *Origen's Homilies on St Luke* pref., but not, oddly enough, in *Famous Men* 74).

just as it scandalised its devotees. Very soon Jerome found himself pressed to produce a rejoinder. At first he held back, fearing (he explains) that publicity would make Helvidius look more important than he was; but too much was at stake for him to stand aside.[8] His *Against Helvidius* (late 383?) is the second of his polemical essays and, probably because his most cherished beliefs were under attack, is far harder-hitting than his *Altercation*. Throughout he insults Helvidius, whom he admits he had never met, and travesties his argument, insisting (to take one point) that it implies that Joseph seized Mary in his lustful embrace the very moment she was delivered of her child.[9] The treatise itself is a dialectical masterpiece. One by one he dissects Helvidius's points, and by cleverly deploying Scripture satisfies himself that the apparent meaning of the gospel texts is neither the only nor in fact the correct one: the 'brothers' of Jesus, for example, were really his cousins. He spurns Helvidius's recourse to tradition: he had misunderstood Victorinus, Tertullian had been a schismatic, and the great body of orthodox fathers had endorsed Mary's perpetual virginity. As for the celibate state, its superiority is proved by the fact that not only Mary, but (so he astonishingly argues) Joseph too, was a life-long virgin. This superiority is confirmed both by St Paul's warning that married people cannot give God their undivided attention, and by the everyday spectacle of the distracting tribulations of marriage.

A point which is often overlooked is that, while fiercely defending the virginity of Mary in her conception and after the birth of Jesus, Jerome was not yet ready to support the view soon to be accepted in the west that she had retained her virginity in the process of parturition, i.e. that the act was a miraculous one involving no opening of her womb.[10]

To all appearances Jerome had scored a major triumph. Helvidius disappeared from the scene, his teaching discredited; the perpetual virginity of Mary became the official orthodoxy; consecrated celibacy was hailed by Catholic Christians as the noblest state; the view of marriage that prevailed was the negative one that it was 'a remedy against sin',[11] to be used exclusively for the propagation of children, certainly not for mutual enjoyment. Jerome's treatment enormously helped to shape both the Mariology of the Latin church and the Christian sexual ethic that was to dominate western civilisation until the Renaissance at least. But on the issues under discussion had he in fact got the better of Helvidius? The New Testament evidence is still debated, but the great majority of critical

---

[8] *Against Helvidius* 1.

[9] *Against Helvidius* 8.

[10] Cf. the realistic description of the gestation and birth in *Against Helvidius* 18: also in *Letter* 22, 39. Many years later, doubtless influenced by Augustine and Ambrose (cf. esp. *Ep.* 42 sent by the latter and his suffragans to Pope Siricius in 390), Jerome came to teach the virginity of Mary *in partu*: cf. *Dialogue against the Pelagians* 2, 4.

[11] So the marriage service of the *Book of Common Prayer*.

scholars are agreed that his interpretation of it, and not Jerome's, is the correct one.[12] Jerome's efforts to get round the obvious meaning of the texts strike most people today as special pleading, the by-product of his prior conviction that sexual intercourse is defiling. His roll-call of ortho-dox fathers who supported him was a dishonest smoke-screen typical of his debating style; it is doubtful whether he had any close acquaintance with the writers he listed, more than doubtful whether they held the views he attributed to them.[13] On the general question his recital of the dis-comforts and humiliations of marriage, for all its brilliance as satire, is an absurdly one-sided caricature which he himself knew to be empty rhetoric;[14] while his distinction between the age of the patriarchs, who obeyed God's command in taking wives, and the Christian era, when it is best to do without them, depends on the acceptance of St Paul's convic-tion that the end of all things is very close. It is significant that he made no attempt to answer Helvidius's argument that the generation of children is an extension of the divine creativity.

(ii)

Jerome's rebuttal of Helvidius, like his letter some months later to Eustochium, exhales supreme self-confidence, disdain too for anyone who presumes to disagree with him. Reading both documents, and recalling the affectionate trust Damasus placed in him, we might suppose that his position in Christian society at Rome was unassailable. Such in fact it was, so long as he had the pope's protection and support. But meanwhile the forces which would undermine it were fast gathering strength. As a newcomer in 382/3 he may well have been, as he suggests, admired and respected by everyone,[15] but every month that slipped by added to the number of his enemies. His correspondence is embarrass-ingly revealing about this. On the one hand, it frankly records, always with an air of injured innocence, the attacks launched upon him. On the other, it is packed with material which, although he seems to have been sublimely oblivious of the fact, was bound to provoke resentment and hostility.

[12] J. B. Mayor's article 'Brethren of the Lord' in J. Hastings, *A Dictionary of the Bible* (Edinburgh, 1898), remains one of the best discussions of the subject. For the conservative Roman Catholic case see, e.g., M. J. Lagrange, *Évangile selon saint Marc* (4 ed., Paris, 1947), 79–93.

[13] P. Courcelle, *Late Latin Writers and their Greek Sources* (ET, Cambridge, Mass., 1969), 91–100, has shown how unlikely it is that Jerome knew the works of Ignatius, Polycarp, Irenaeus, and Justin at first hand. Nothing in their surviving writings suggests that they touched on the precise issues debated here.

[14] *Against Helvidius* 20. In par. 22 he admits that he has been indulging playfully in rhetorical parody.

[15] *Letter* 45, 3: also *Letter* 127, 7 for his reputation then as a student of Scripture.

First and foremost, his campaign for an intensified asceticism was undoubtedly a major cause of the reaction against him. While Roman Christians, in general, were distinctly cool towards the new monasticism, here was Jerome, the apostle of virginity, preaching it in an extreme form and seeking to introduce what was in effect the seclusion of the cloister. A woman like Marcella, though increasingly influenced by Egyptian monastic ideals, still managed to supervise her home, receive visits from friends, and worship at the martyrs' shrines. The programme Jerome put before Eustochium called for something more radical, something revolutionary in western eyes. So far as possible, she should keep to her room, have only virgins like herself for company, submit to far-reaching privations, devote herself exclusively to prayer and Bible study. Jerome confesses, for once ruefully, that his advice to virgins to eschew masculine society had made him a marked man throughout the city, with every finger pointed at him.[16] Again, when Blesilla embraced extravagant mortifications with a convert's fervour, it was he, as her spiritual director, who was widely blamed for her fanaticism.[17] When she died and her mother created a sensation by fainting at her funeral, the indignation of the crowd knew no bounds:[18] 'Isn't this just what we often said? She's weeping for her daughter, done to death by her fastings . . . How long are we to refrain from driving the detestable tribe of monks from the city? Why aren't they stoned, or flung into the Tiber? Unhappy Paula, it's they who have led her astray.' Jerome was the leader of 'the detestable tribe of monks'; the sharpness of his rebuke to Paula for her unrestrained grief sprang from the realisation that he was now the target of widespread hatred.[19]

Equally effective in isolating him was his scornfully denunciatory attitude to the great body of Christians, clerical and lay. By now he had become a consummate master of satire, in the great Roman tradition of Horace and Persius,[20] and his writings of the period, especially the letter to Eustochium, are crammed with blistering portrayals of bogus Christianity. The clergy whose chief motive in getting ordained was to see women more freely and enjoy the pickings of rich, fashionable houses; the psuedo-virgins who had always a crowd of young fops in their train and, using the excuse 'To the pure all things are pure', sought to evade the

[16] *Letter* 27, 2: 'cunctorum digitis notor'.
[17] *Letter* 38, 5.
[18] *Letter* 39, 6.
[19] For his rebuke see above p. 99.
[20] For a thorough, illuminating, readable study of this aspect of his work, see D. S. Wiesen, *St Jerome as a Satirist* (Ithaca, N.Y., 1964). As Wiesen shows in his first chapter, Jerome was well acquainted with these two masters of satire, and, among his Christian predecessors, was steeped in Tertullian, another such master, drawing particularly on his anti-feminism. He argues that he knew Juvenal too, but this is doubtful: see above p. 12.

consequences of their lapses by abortions; the ecclesiastics who made a fuss when the food and wine at their tables fell below standard; the wealthy widows, with their litters, scarlet cloaks, and retinues of eunuchs, on whom clergymen fawned and who, 'after a questionable supper, retired to dream of the Apostles': all these, and many more, became subjects of brilliantly drawn, colourful, devastatingly caustic vignettes.[21] The individuals he was caricaturing (for these sketches were taken from life) must have been cut to the quick. Christians generally were outraged. Not only was Jerome representing the Church, apart from himself and his chosen circle, as a disreputable rag-bag of hypocrites, but he was furnishing delighted pagans with seemingly incontrovertible proof that its members, of every rank and calling, were even more scandalous than they had ever dared to suspect.[22]

What made people the more furious was that Jerome himself did not seem a very convincing censor of morals. Everyone must have noticed how quickly this newcomer from the east had wormed his way into Damasus's confidence. However ready he was to expose worldly Christians, he never breathed a word criticising a pope notorious for his luxury and his toadying to women.[23] Everyone was aware, too, of the niche he had carved for himself in the homes of affluent ladies; hence his passionate, and no doubt justified, denials that he had ever accepted money or presents from anyone.[24] And what of his relations with Paula? That there was a sexual element in them we should be naive to deny; but it would be equally preposterous to infer that either party was aware of, still less gave overt expression to it. It was inevitable, however, especially as he was so censorious of others, that gossip should busy itself with the increasingly frequent meetings of the young widow with her director in his fifties. He himself traces the beginnings of his unpopularity to his intimacy with Paula's household, and in a bitter letter dashed off as he was leaving Rome was at pains to stress the innocence of their friendship:[25] 'The only woman who could give me delight was one whom I never so much as saw at table; yet when I had begun to revere, respect, and look up to her as her conspicuous chastity deserved, at once all my former virtues were held to have deserted me.'

---

[21] *Letter* 22, 28; 13; 40; 16. See also, e.g., *Letters* 21, 13 (bishops reading pagan literature); 27, 2 (Christians living luxuriously); *Against Helvidius* 21 ('virgins' who are adulteresses, monks unchaste, etc.).

[22] Rufinus was later to describe (*Apol. c. Hier.* 2, 5) how pagans vied with one another in copying out *Letter* 22, so full of incriminating matter which they could exploit to the Church's detriment.

[23] Cf., e.g., Ammianus Marcellinus, *Res gestae* 27, 3, 12–15; *Coll. Avell.*, *Ep.* 1 (*CSEL* 35, 1–4).

[24] *Letter* 45, 1.

[25] *Letter* 45, 2; 3.

(iii)

It is extraordinary that Jerome should have been wholly blind to the fact that he had only himself to blame for the progressive worsening of the climate of opinion. Self-knowledge and self-criticism seem to have been almost completely lacking to him. He could misrepresent Helvidius as an uncultivated boor, cover the injured and indignant 'Onasus' of Segeste with foul abuse ('Hide your big nose, and keep your mouth shut: then you'll appear handsome and an excellent speaker');[26] and yet, all innocent, he could ask Marcella, 'What have I said with excessive freedom? . . . Have I ever assailed anyone in bitter terms?'[27] In the present hostile atmosphere, however, there was almost nothing he could do right. Even his revision of the Old Latin Gospels, intended to provide a more reliable text, served only to increase (as we have seen)[28] popular resentment against him. His enthusiasm for Origen, similarly, which Damasus approved and which he communicated to Blesilla before her death,[29] made him still more suspect in influential quarters. While the pope was still alive, these critics probably kept silent, but in a letter written after his death he lampoons as 'mad dogs' people who are now traducing Origen as a heretic.[30]

Several months before that, however, by mid-summer 384, he must have been aware that the tide had turned against him. It was about that time, we recall, that under his influence Blesilla exchanged her life of fastidious elegance for one of prayer and extravagant mortifications. At once, in spite of the pope's patronage, he became the butt of angry murmurings and crude jeering.[31] The open attacks on his gospel revisions began even earlier, probably in the spring of 384.[32] It is likely that Jerome was becoming increasingly conscious of the insecurity of his position, especially as it was obvious that Damasus's days were numbered. It would not be in the least surprising if, in his disillusionment, he was already considering abandoning Rome, which flaunted so much that was repellent to a true ascetic and which, as things were turning out, seemed to hold no future for him. That such thoughts were in his mind at this time is perhaps hinted at in the Preface to his *Commentary on Ecclesiastes* (written 388/9). There he notes that he had begun the work at Rome almost five years previously at Blesilla's request, 'so that in my absence she might

[26] *Letter* 40 (see above p. 96), where he admits, 'It's scarcely surprising if I have offended many by stigmatizing their faults'.

[27] *Letter* 27, 2.

[28] See *Letter* 27 (above pp. 89 f.).

[29] See his Origen's *Homilies on St Luke* pref. (*GCS* 49, 12), where he recalls that she had demanded translations of Origen's vast series of volumes on St Matthew, St Luke, and St John.

[30] *Letter* 33, 5.

[31] *Letter* 38, 5.

[32] For this dating see Cavallera II, 25.

understand what she was reading'.[33] The Latin 'absque me' may signify no more than 'when I was not by her side'. Alternatively it may mean 'when I was gone'; and if this is its sense, it suggests that he was already planning his departure.

Proof that in 384 his mind was preoccupied with the attractions of an anchorite's existence in the desert is contained in a letter to a deacon named Praesidius, which was rejected as apocryphal from the sixteenth to the present century, but which, freed from alien matter which had got attached to it, has impressed a growing number of modern scholars as authentic.[34] By its statement that 'a full year has not yet passed' since the emperor Gratian's slaughter (25 August 383), its date cannot be later than July or early August 384. When he wrote it, Jerome was somewhere in the country north of Rome. Praesidius, who served the church at Piacenza in north Italy, was faced with the task of singing the Exultet, or hymn of blessing on the paschal candle at the Easter Vigil, and had begged the distinguished writer to prepare a suitable text for him. In his reply Jerome excuses himself, mainly on the ground that Scripture offers no material about wax or candles, and then abruptly launches out on an eloquent exhortation to Praesidius to forsake home and family, retire to the desert (has he not visited the angelic settlements of Egypt?), and become a solitary. The fact that he is in orders should not hold him back; he will carry out his functions with less danger to his soul in the earthly paradise, which is what the desert is, than exposed to all the charlatanry and sensuality of a city. There are one or two hints in the letter that in so doing he will be joining up with Jerome.[35]

(iv)

On 11 December 384, a month or so after Blesilla's death, Pope Damasus died. However serious earlier rumours had been that Jerome might succeed him (at the time there was nothing far-fetched in such speculations), there could be no question of that now. The man elected, unanimously and (to obviate trouble with the partisans of Ursinus, long ago

---

[33] *CCL* 72: 381–2.
[34] Printed in *PL* 30, 182–7, with a fragment from the *Physiologus*, an immensely popular collection of edifying fabulous anecdotes from natural history, still attached. It was G. Morin who argued the case for its authenticity: see *RB* 8, 1891, 20–7; 9, 1892, 392–7; *Bulletin d'ancienne littérature et d'archéologie chrétienne* 3, 1913, 52–60 (with critical text). His case has been accepted by H. Leclercq, *DACL* 13, 1569–71 and E. Dekkers, *Clavis Patrum Latinorum* (1957), nos. 620 and 621: also by the editors of *PL Supplementum* 2, 19 (1960). The whole tone, the underlying ideas, and the satiric cuts are all typical of Jerome, as is the style; many expressions found in it recur in acknowledged writings of this time.
[35] Cf. esp. the closing remark: 'Thus against my will I send you back to Piacenza, but on the strict condition, of which you are aware, that as often as you read this you should be reminded that it is your duty to come whither you have promised.'

Damasus's defeated rival) with the express approval of the emperor Valentinian II,[36] was the deacon Siricius. Years later, when he was dead, Jerome was to criticise his 'guilelessness', which caused him to be easily imposed upon.[37] This sneer has often been interpreted as reflecting bitter memories of the new pope's active hostility to the learned, difficult man who had wielded such influence with his predecessor, but this conjecture gains no support from Jerome's correspondence of 385 or elsewhere. On the other hand, since Siricius held the supreme office, the official measures against Jerome of which we shall hear shortly can scarcely have been taken without his cognizance and consent.[38] Whatever his personal attitude, he belonged to and had been elected by the clerical establishment which Jerome despised, with the support of the great body of conventional Christians who were the victims of his satire; he also shared their suspicion of the new asceticism. From the start Jerome must have realised that he could not expect much sympathy from him.

Sympathy was something which he was going to need desperately in the spring and early summer of 385. In the opening months of the year there was an uneasy lull. No hint of the approaching storm appears in his two letters to Marcella about the Montanists and about the sin against the Holy Spirit, which are usually assigned to this period.[39] There is a third letter, however, which reveals him in a despondent, self-critical mood, dissatisfied with his surroundings and eager to escape, and which also contains overtones of disaster.[40] It opens with an envious comparison between the great Origen's ordered routine of work and prayer, and his own tawdry, superficial, self-indulgent, self-seeking existence. Then Jerome comes to his point: 'Since for much of our life so far we have traversed a troubled sea, since our vessel has in turn been struck by furious storms and breached by treacherous reefs, let us as soon as may be find our haven in some rural retreat.' There follows an idyllic description of the charm and healthy frugality of life in the country, and of the opportunities for prayer and for 'cleaving to the Lord' which it provides. There is nothing like this in Rome, with its noisy bustle, licentious theatres and delirious circus, not even in its edifying sessions of pious matrons. The letter is pervaded with a real sense of disappointment and failure, a nostalgia for the unencumbered existence of the anchorite far removed from the corruptions of the great city.

It was in the summer that matters came to a showdown. All the resentment and hatred which his caustic tongue and pen, and his unpopular

---

[36] *Coll. Avell., Ep.* 4 (*CSEL* 35, 47 f.).
[37] Cf. *Letter* 127, 9, where he speaks of the 'simplicity' of the pope, 'who fancied others as guileless as himself', being imposed on by heretics.
[38] Cf. the remarks of E. Caspar, *Geschichte des Papstums* (Tübingen, 1930) I, 260.
[39] *Letters* 41; 42: see above p. 95 f.
[40] *Letter* 43.

propaganda, had aroused, and to which his indiscretions had added fuel, now burst upon him. We have his own extraordinarily frank account in a letter of how people vilified him as 'an infamous rascal, a slippery turncoat, a liar who used Satanic arts to deceive'. They even jeered at his appearance, his manner of walking and smiling, the simple mien he adopted.[41] But worse was to follow. Charges of a disgraceful character, he complains, were falsely brought against him.[42] As the context makes clear, it was his relations with Paula which were causing scandal. His only crime, he declares, was his sex, and this only became a crime when the story got around that she was planning to accompany him to Jerusalem. Finally, there was an investigation into his conduct by the authorities of the Roman church. That this was an official inquiry is implied by a scathing note, jotted down a couple of years later, in which he refers darkly to a meeting of 'the senate of Pharisees' (an expression he uses elsewhere of a formal gathering of Roman clergy) which pronounced unanimously against him.[43] We should probably connect with this inquiry his statement in a contemporary letter that under torture an informant had withdrawn the shameful allegations he had made, for torture was employed in courts to extract the truth from slaves or other witnesses of lowly rank.[44]

Further light is thrown on the outcome of the inquiry by a revealing exchange between Rufinus and Jerome many years later when they were bitterly quarrelling.[45] In a letter which is now lost, but from which Jerome quotes, Rufinus had boasted that, if he wished, he could tell a tale about the circumstances of Jerome's retreat from Rome. More to the point, he could make public the judgment passed on Jerome at the time, the document which was later drafted, and the oath which he had taken. In his blustering but embarrassed reply Jerome challenges Rufinus to produce even a scrap of paper directed against him either by the Roman pontiff or by any other bishop, but he acknowledges both that a judgment had been passed on himself and that a document in writing was subsequently

---

[41] *Letter* 45, 2.

[42] *Letter* 45, 6 ('infamiam falsi criminis inportarunt').

[43] *Translation of Didymus on the Holy Spirit* pref. (*PL* 23: 105). For the expression 'Pharisaeorum senatus' there used of an assembly of the Roman clergy, cf. *Letter* 33, 5 ('Roma . . . cogit senatum'); 127, 9 ('Pharisaeorum turbata est schola') for similar expressions.

[44] *Letter* 45, 2. According to A. Ehrhardt, *PW* XII (1937), 1786, the private torture of slaves by their masters was suppressed in the third century. Ecclesiastical courts dealing, e.g., with the misbehaviour of clerics were recognised by the government in the fourth century (see G. Jolowicz, *Historical Introduction to Roman Law*, 2 ed, 1954, 468–9), and this passage would seem to provide evidence that, like other courts, they employed torture on witnesses of appropriate rank. G. Thür has pointed out (*RAC* 8, col. 111) that the victory of Christianity was not accompanied by any demand for the abolition of torture at trials, which continued to be accepted as a matter of course.

[45] Jerome, *Apology* 3, 21. For the reconstruction of what happened contained in this paragraph, see Cavallera II, 86–8; E. Caspar, loc. cit. Cavallera, however, seems mistaken in concluding that there was no written document.

drafted. When we piece these items together, the conclusion we are bound to draw is that, while Jerome was acquitted of the unsavoury charge, the commission of inquiry reached a formal decision which was communicated to him verbally, and that he was obliged to make an undertaking which was afterwards embodied in a signed document. This undertaking must have been an agreement to depart forthwith.

Clearly the Roman church had had enough of Jerome; he must be got rid of, although (since he was a man of distinction) with as little publicity as was practicable. Disgraced as he was, he had no wish to stay. Rome had now become to him Babylon, the great harlot arrayed in purple and scarlet whose abominations St John had glimpsed in his visions.[46] So once again he set forth on his journeys, never again to set eyes on her. It was August 385, and the rainless trade-winds were blowing from the northwest. His travelling companions were his much younger brother Paulinian (who now comes into the story for the first time), his dear friend Vincentius (who must have come with him from Constantinople), and a handful of monks. As the little party made their leisurely way to the port of Rome, they were escorted (so he tells us) by an impressive crowd of supporters.[47] His last act, before the ship weighed anchor, was to dictate a long letter of protest and self-defence to Asella. Whether she had written to him or sent him some other token of her sympathy, we do not know. Anyway it was to her, the most humble and withdrawn and self-effacing of his women friends, that he poured out his soul in this bitter moment of disillusionment.[48]

Jerome never wrote anything which so starkly laid bare his state of mind. Without any attempt at disguise he described the repulsive portrait of himself and the damaging insinuations about his bearing and conduct which circulated among Roman Christians. With withering scorn he thrust their calumnies aside, scathingly contrasting their present abuse with their hypocritical fawning in happier times. But his indignation and bitterness knew no bounds when he came to the tittle-tattle about Paula and himself. That she of all women in Rome should be singled out as the target of scandal revealed the depths to which squalid envy could sink. Had she chosen the empty life of fashionable ladies, frequenting smart spas, dressing in scented finery, and gorging herself with expensive delicacies, she would have been respected and admired. But because out of devotion to Christ she had given up wealth and family to spend her time fasting in sackcloth and ashes, she had become the victim of malevolent spitefulness. As for himself, Jerome thanked God that he was deemed

[46] Cf. *Letter* 45, 6; *Didymus on the Holy Spirit* pref. ('When I was living in Babylon, a denizen of the scarlet-clad whore . . . '). The image comes from Revelation 17, 1–6.

[47] For these details see *Apology* 3, 22.

[48] *Letter* 45.

worthy of the world's hatred; long before him the Jews had called St Paul a deceiver, Christ a sorcerer. And so he ends: 'Pray that I may return from Babylon to Jerusalem . . . Give my greetings to Paula and Eustochium: whether the world likes it or not, they belong to me in Christ. Greet my spiritual mother Albina, my sisters the two Marcellas, Marcellina too, and good Felicitas. Tell them, "We shall stand before Christ's judgment-seat. There the principles by which each of us has lived shall be revealed." As for yourself, glorious model of purity and virginity, keep me in your thoughts, and calm the waves of the sea with your prayers.'

XII

To and Fro to Bethlehem

(i)

For the next twelve months or so (August 385–summer 386) Jerome was constantly on the move, most of the time in the company of Paula, Eustochium, and their entourage of dedicated women. The rumour that Paula and he were planning to go to the Holy Land together was correct, but in the atmosphere of gossip and suspicion it had excited they had the discretion to make the first part of the journey separately. Jerome rapidly summarises the route he himself took, along with his brother Paulinian, Vincentius, and several others, in a rejoinder made some fifteen years later to insinuations put forward by Rufinus.[1]

From Portus, the harbour of Rome,[2] he sailed to Rhegium (Reggio di Calabria), and the ship anchored briefly in the straits of Messina. Here his imagination (so he claims) was flooded with classical reminiscences of Ulysses lashed to the mast, of the Sirens' melodious but fateful songs, of the insatiable maw of Charybdis. The local inhabitants, he suggests, advised him to avoid the direct route to Alexandria and instead follow the safer one to Jaffa; but he had different ideas. Rounding the perilous promontory of Malea, he passed through the Cyclades and reached Cyprus, there to be received (as he had doubtless arranged) by his venerable friend, Bishop Epiphanius, at Salamis (Famagusta). Thence it was an easy journey to Seleuceia, the great seaport on the Syrian coast, and so to Antioch. Here he renewed communion with his own bishop, Paulinus, in spite of advanced years still head of his tiny, intransigent sect, and probably found hospitality once again with Evagrius.

Neither in this account nor in its sequel after Antioch does Jerome so much as mention Paula and Eustochium. There was no point, in an acrimonious controversy, in making gratuitous reference to long dead scandals. It seems certain, however, that Paula had agreed to meet him either at Cyprus or at Antioch, probably the former. There they would join forces and continue their subsequent journeys together. Jerome was to compose a much lengthier, more elaborately contrived narrative of

---

[1] *Apology* 3, 22.

[2] About 3 km. north of Ostia, the original harbour at the mouth of the Tiber. The new port, made necessary by the silting up of the river, was begun by the emperor Claudius (41–54).

Paula's travels in the obituary on her which he was to address in 404 to Eustochium.[3] Again, for similar motives of delicacy (the letter was intended for a vastly wider audience than Eustochium), he does not bring himself directly into the story. But it is obvious, without much reading between the lines, that at any rate from Antioch onwards he was accompanying the noble widow and her daughter.[4]

Paula must have left Rome several weeks after her spiritual mentor; she also spent rather more time on the journey to Antioch. Jerome paints a highly coloured picture of her departure, with her kinsfolk, her elder daughter, and her little boy Toxotius sobbing on the quay, while 'she herself turned her dry eyes heavenwards, overcoming her love for her children by her love for God'. If the rhetoric seems overdone, it remains a fact that the break she was making with home and family cut far deeper than any sacrifice of his. Hardly at sea, the ship made a short halt at Pontiae, the rocky island in the Gulf of Gaeta to which the emperor Domitian had in 95 banished his niece Flavia Domitilla because (so Christians liked to believe) of her attachment to the faith,[5] and Paula and Eustochium reverently inspected 'the cells in which she had dragged out her long martyrdom'. Like Jerome, they then passed between Scylla and Charybdis, rounded the heel of Italy, and reached the Adriatic, but unlike him they paused at Methone, on the south-west tip of the Peloponnese, to recruit their strength before sailing between Cape Malea and Cythera. Like him, again, they landed at Cyprus, where Paula lodged for ten days with Bishop Epiphanius, once her own guest at Rome, and although she might have relaxed, visited and distributed alms at 'all the monasteries of the region'. Finally, after dropping anchor at Seleuceia, they made their way to Antioch, where Bishop Paulinus received them and, if he had not joined them at Salamis, they found Jerome awaiting them.

(ii)

Once reunited, the two parties did not linger long in the Syrian capital, but under the guidance of Paulinus himself set off for Jerusalem.[6] Though

---

[3] *Letter* 108, 6–14. The details contained in the following paragraphs are derived from this.

[4] Cavallera (I, 123, n. 2), e.g., draws attention (inter alia) to *Apology* 3, 22, where Jerome describes his arrival in Jerusalem 'in the depth of winter', and the identical language used of Paula's arrival there in *Letter* 108, 7. Cf. also *Letter* 108, 10, where he states that he was present when she visited the grotto of the Nativity in Bethlehem.

[5] Cassius Dio (*Hist. Rom.* 67, 14, 1), who names her place of exile Pandateria, states that she and her husband Flavius Clemens were accused of 'atheism', while Suetonius (*Vita Dom.* 15, 1) characterises Fl. Clemens as a man of 'contemptible indolence', which many take as denoting the Christian's deliberate withdrawal. 'Atheism' might equally well stand for an interest in Judaism, but the tradition that they were Christians inevitably grew: so Eusebius, *Hist. eccl.* 3, 18, 4, although he describes Domitilla (probably by sheer error, or as a result of confusion in his source: see *RAC* 4, col. 104 f.) as a niece of Fl. Clemens.

[6] *Apology* 3, 22.

not strictly pilgrims, since they were planning to settle in Palestine, they were in fact making a pilgrimage, though an unprecedentedly elaborate one, in the manner and spirit of the fourth century. Pilgrimages to the Holy Land had begun a long time back. In the middle of the second century we hear[7] of Melito, bishop of Sardis in Asia Minor, and in the third of Alexander, a bishop from Cappadocia, travelling thither, the one to ascertain the correct number and order of the books of the Old and New Testaments, the other 'to pray and gain information about the holy places' of Jerusalem. Again in the third century the famous Origen had made frequent trips to sacred sites in the interests of his biblical studies;[8] and from him we glean the fascinating information[9] that at Bethlehem the cave in which Jesus was born and the actual crib were already on show. By 315 the historian Eusebius could speak[10] of Christian believers streaming to Jerusalem from every corner of the earth. But an enormous boost was given to pilgrimages by the royal tour of Palestine carried out in 324 by Helena, the emperor Constantine's mother, as well as by the lavish restoration and embellishment of the more notable sites by her and her son. In his *Onomasticon*, composed shortly after this, Eusebius provided an admirable biblical gazetteer, with geographical and historical descriptions of each locality as it existed in his day. As early as 333, when an anonymous pilgrim travelled to the Holy Land from Bordeaux and back,[11] the movement was in full swing, with a recognised itinerary covering a rich variety of sacred places and objects.

For our knowledge of Jerome's and Paula's journeyings we are dependent almost exclusively on Letter 108 and the extract from his *Apology* mentioned in the previous section. Although penned many years later, we have no reason to doubt the facts they contain, however much we may suspect that his descriptions of Paula's emotional transports have been written up for effect. Jerome highlights[12] the fact that, although it was the depth of winter and the cold intense, Paula, who had been accustomed to a comfortable litter borne by eunuchs, preferred to ride on a donkey's back. Their travels in the Holy Land fell into three distinct stages. First, they made their way to Jerusalem and Bethlehem, moving in the main down the coast road but taking in every conceivable spot with Old or New Testament associations—Zarephath (Ṣarafand), with the 'little tower' in

---

[7] For these two see Eusebius, *Hist. eccl.* 4, 26, 14; 6, 11, 2. In general for early pilgrimages to the Holy Land (and elsewhere), see B. Kötting, *Peregrinatio Religiosa* (Regensburg-Munich, 1950).

[8] E.g. *Comm. in Ioh.* 6, 40 (204); 6, 41 (211) (*GCS* 10, 149; 150).

[9] *C. Cels.* 1, 51 (*GCS* 2, 102).

[10] *Dem. ev.* 6, 18, 23 (*GCS* 23, 278).

[11] See his *Itinerarium Burdigalense* (*CCL* 175, 1–26). The author fixes the date by giving (571, 6–8) the consuls of the year of his departure.

[12] *Letter* 108, 7. The detailed description of their journeys is contained in pars. 7–14 of this letter.

which Elijah had been miraculously fed[13] (1 Kings 17, 8–24); Tyre (Sur), where St Paul had knelt on the beach in prayer (Acts 21, 5); the Plain of Megiddo, where the good king Josiah had been defeated and slain by Pharaoh Neco (2 Kings 23, 28–30); Caesarea (Quaisāriye), where they were shown the house of the centurion Cornelius[14] and that of Philip the evangelist (Acts 10; 21, 8 f.); Lydda (Lod, now the airport of Tel Aviv), where St Peter had cured the paralysed Aeneas (Acts 9, 33–5); Nicopolis (Amwas), traditionally identified as the Emmaus where the Risen Christ had revealed himself to the two disciples (Luke 24, 28–31); and many more. Jerusalem itself they entered from the north, passing on their left the majestic mausoleum of Queen Helena of Adiabene,[15] famed as a convert to Judaism and for her charity in times of famine.

Secondly, after a stay in Jerusalem and Bethlehem (to which we shall return), they embarked on a fairly thorough survey of the hill-country of south Judah as well as parts of the bleak, waterless Negeb. Among the highlights were the well[16] on the old road to Gaza in which the Ethiopian eunuch had been baptised (Acts 8, 27–39), and the numerous memorials of the patriarchs (their marble sepulchres,[17] Sarah's cell and the cradle of Isaac, the remains of Abraham's terebinth tree)[18] in and around Hebron. Thence they ascended the forbidding heights just west of the southern-most end of the Dead Sea, from which they gazed down on the utter desolation where Sodom and Gomorrah, blasted by God's wrath, had once stood. Paula burst into tears when she recalled how virtuous Lot, while escaping the disaster, had been made drunk and seduced by his own daughters (Gen. 19, 30–8), and warned her virgin companions of the perils of wine. The third and final stage, after a further stop in Jerusalem, brought them to Bethany, with its memories of Martha and Mary and the raising of Lazarus, and so to Jericho, the Jordan, and northwards to Samaria and Galilee. Here they rapidly traversed Nazareth, Cana, and

---

[13] A much later traveller, the archdeacon Theodosius, reports that in 530 a church of St Elias was to be seen there (*De situ terrae sanctae* 23: *CCL* 175, 122). Still later (570), Antonius of Piacenza was shown Elijah's room and bed, and the trough in which the widow prepared his bread (*Itin.* 2: *CCL* 175, 129).

[14] The Bordeaux Pilgrim mentions the bath in which Cornelius had been baptised (*Itin. Burdig.* 585: *CCL* 175, 13).

[15] She had been sister and wife of Monobazos, king of Adiabene (in north Mesopotamia). For her magnificent tomb, a landmark till the end of the fourth century at least, see Josephus, *Ant. Iud.* 20, 95; *Bell. Iud.* 5, 55; 119; 147; Pausanias, *Graec. descr.* 8, 16, 5; Eusebius, *Hist. eccl.* 2, 12, 3 ('its splendid columns are still shown in the suburbs of Aelia'). It has often been placed at the so-called Tombs of the Kings, just off the Nablus Road about 1½ km. north of the Damascus Gate.

[16] The Bordeaux Pilgrim was shown this well (*Itin. Burdig.* 599, 1–2: *CCL* 175, 20).

[17] For the marble and fine workmanship, see Josephus, *Bell. Iud.* 4, 533. See also *Itin. Burdig.* 599, 8–9; Antoninus Plac., *Itin.* 30 (*CCL* 175, 20; 144).

[18] For the terebinth, see Josephus, *Bell. Iud.* 4, 533. The Bordeaux Pilgrim, who was also shown it, adds that Constantine built a fine basilica there (*Itin. Burdig.* 599, 3–6: *CCL* 175, 20).

Capernaum, crossed Lake Tiberias recalling its associations with Jesus, penetrated the wilderness where he had miraculously fed the hungry thousands, and even clambered up Mount Tabor (Jebel eṭ-Ṭôr), the scene of his Transfiguration.

Jerome disclaims[19] the intention of writing a mere travelogue, but there is no escaping the fact that, urged on by what he calls Paula's incredible faith, the enthusiastic band were making, perhaps a little hurriedly at times, one of the most exhaustive explorations of the Holy Land carried out to date. His narrative confirms, fascinatingly and much more graphically than the Bordeaux Pilgrim's bare notes, the enormous number of sites which had been identified, with whatever degree of accuracy, by the mid-eighties of the fourth century, and leaves a powerful impression of the wonder and awe felt by Christians as they came face to face with the actual spots, as they believed them to be, at which the signal events of sacred history had been enacted. If Paula was the more excited emotionally, Jerome clearly felt their spell as well. He was also, richly informed and eager student of the Bible as he was, laying the foundation of the more wide-ranging scriptural studies that lay ahead of him. As he was later to remark,[20] 'Just as Greek history becomes more intelligible to those who have seen Athens, and the third book of Vergil to those who have sailed from Troas by Leucata and Acroceraunia to Sicily and so on to the mouth of the Tiber, so that man will get a clearer grasp of Holy Scripture who has gazed at Judaea with his own eyes and has got to know the memorials of its cities and the names, whether they remain the same or have been changed, of the various localities.'

(iii)

It was Jerusalem, however, Jerusalem with Bethlehem 9 km. south of it, which had been their original goal, and which remained their base between these various excursions. As at Cyprus and Antioch, both had friends there to welcome them on their first arrival in winter 385.[21] The proconsul of Palestine, probably to be identified with the Flavius Florentius whose name is fleetingly mentioned in contemporary documents, had been closely acquainted with Paula's family in Italy.[22] The provincial seat of government was at Caesarea, the superbly equipped city on the coast which Herod the Great had re-built and named in honour of Augustus,

---

[19] *Letter* 108, 8.

[20] *Preface to Chronicles* (LXX) (PL 29, 401A).

[21] For this date, late 385 rather than early 386, see P. Nautin, *Revue des études augustiniennes* 18 (1972), 216.

[22] *Codex Theod.* x, 16, 4: also an inscription (*Supplementum epigraphicum Graecum* xviii, no. 626) recording the thorough restoration of aqueducts at Caesarea in 385 or shortly thereafter. For his friendship with Paula's family see *Letter* 108, 9: from which the other details.

but when the proconsul heard of her approach he despatched members of his staff to meet her with orders for his official residence in Jerusalem (on the site of the present Citadel, near the Jaffa Gate) to be placed at her disposal. With the self-effacement appropriate to the role she had chosen, she declined his invitation and preferred to lodge, like other pilgrims, 'in a humble cell'.

As for Jerome, Melania the Elder, whom he had recently held up as an example to Paula and (although he had not met her until now) had hailed as 'the noblest of Roman matrons',[23] and Rufinus of Aquileia, the dear companion of his youth, had been settled in Jerusalem for several years. Aristocratic, wealthy, and strong-willed, Melania had lost her husband and two of her three sons when only twenty-two, and had gone off to Egypt in 372. There she had visited the desert fathers, and had courageously assisted the victims of the persecution which savaged the supporters of Nicene orthodoxy in Egypt on the death of Athanasius[24] (May 373). It was there too, it seems, that she had met Rufinus, who himself shared in the persecution and was able to describe its horrors as an eyewitness.[25] Their next few years are extremely obscure, but Melania moved up to Palestine giving financial aid to orthodox confessors exiled to Diocaesarea in Galilee,[26] while Rufinus stayed in Egypt studying under Didymus the Blind and having frequent contacts with desert ascetics.[27] The darkness lifts about 378, for it is around this time that we find Melania in charge of a convent for fifty women on the Mount of Olives.[28] About 381 Rufinus also was in Jerusalem, collaborating with her and supervising an associated monastery for men. They were thus the first Latins to start ascetic foundations in the Holy Land, and for some twenty-seven years their twin house was to be renowned as a centre of edification and generous hospitality.[29] Jerome mentions neither of them in his report of his and Paula's arrival in Jerusalem, but as he composed it when his relations with both had been tragically disrupted his silence is easily explicable. It is impossible to believe that, devoted friend of Rufinus as he still was, he did not call on them, inspect their pioneer establishment at first hand, and pick up information and advice about the future expeditions (especially that to the Egyptian desert) he was planning.

For the moment, however, and during their stays in Jerusalem between

---

[23] *Chronicle* A.D. 374 (*GCS* 47, 247): cf. *Letter* 39, 4. Later, according to Rufinus (*Apol. c. Hier.* 2, 26), Jerome was to erase her name from his personal copies of his *Chronicle*.

[24] For this account cf. Palladius, *Hist. Laus.* 46.

[25] *Apol. ad Anast.* 2; *Hist. eccl.* 2, 2–4.

[26] Palladius, *Hist. Laus.* 46.

[27] Rufinus, *Apol. c. Hier.* 2, 12; *Hist. eccl.* 2, 4.

[28] Palladius, *Hist. Laus.* 46: for the date see F. X. Murphy, 'Melania the Elder: a Biographical Note' (*Tradition* 5, 1947, 59–72).

[29] Palladius, *Hist. Laus.* 46.

their excursions, Jerome's and Paula's overriding concern was to do the full round of places and objects connected with Jesus's birth, passion, and resurrection. Ancient Jerusalem had been razed to the ground in 70 and an exclusively Roman city, Aelia Capitolina, built over it in 135 by Hadrian, but a host of these had been re-discovered, or with credulous ingenuity conjured into existence, after Constantine's adoption of Christianity as the favoured religion. Chief among them, of course, were Calvary and the rock-hewn tomb in which the dead Jesus had been placed and from which he had risen. Originally just outside the north wall, they had been brought within the city when Herod Agrippa (40–4) extended it northwards, and, lying to the west of the main north-south artery of Aelia, had been exposed by Constantine's architects and enclosed in a magnificent complex of buildings[30]—fragments of them are still visible in the present, Crusader-built Church of the Holy Sepulchre. Like countless others, Jerome and his companions passed from the column-lined boulevard through a great triple gateway into a porticoed atrium open to the sky, and thence into an ornate five-aisled basilica known as the Martyrium, or Place of Witness. Beyond this, on the south side of a second open court, they gazed with awe at the 'little hill' of Calvary surmounted with a cross, while still further east they entered a circular, columned building called the Anastasis because it contained, surrounded with grills, the cave of rock which had been the scene of the burial and the resurrection.[31] Jerome describes[32] the ecstasy with which Paula prostrated herself before the cross,[33] entered 'the tomb of the resurrection', and covered both the stone[34] which the angel had removed from its mouth and (like millions today) the slab on which the Lord's body was presumed to have lain with kisses.

There were numerous other marvels to be venerated in Jerusalem, such as the blood-stained column tied to which Jesus had been scourged[35] and

---

[30] Primary authorities for the lay-out of Constantine's buildings are Eusebius, *Vita Const.* 3, 33–40; *Itin. Burdig.* 593 f.; *Itin. Eger.* 24–30 (*GCS* 7, 93–5; *CCL* 175, 16 f.; 67–77). For accessible modern accounts, with plans, see, e.g., *DACL* VII, 2312–18; *New Catholic Encyclopaedia* 13, 97 f.; J. D. Wilkinson, *Egeria's Travels* (London, 1971). See also E. Wistrand, *Konstantins Kirche am heiligen Grab in Jerusalem* (Göteborg, 1952).

[31] For the rock-hewn cave rising from the levelled ground, cf. Eusebius, *Theophaneia*, frag. 3 (*GCS* 11 (2), 14). Cyril of Jerusalem, preaching *c.* 350, describes the rock, recalling that before the decorations applied by Constantine there was a cave in front of it (*Cat.* 14, 9).

[32] *Letter* 108, 9.

[33] This was not the 'true cross' allegedly discovered by Helena and exposed for veneration on certain days, but the commemorative cross placed on the summit of the little hill identified as Calvary or Golgotha, which in consequence was popularly known as 'Crux'. Cf. H. Vincent and F. M. Abel, *Jérusalem* (Paris, 1912–26) II, 185–9.

[34] For this stone see Cyril of Jerusalem, *Cat.* 10, 19. In *Cat.* 13, 39 he speaks of 'the stone which was laid on the door, which lies to this day (350) by the tomb'.

[35] The Bordeaux Pilgrim reports (*Itin. Burdig.* 592, 4–5: *CCL* 175, 16) that the column was in Sion, i.e. the sacred hill where tradition placed the upper room in which the Last Supper took place. Egeria also mentions the column (*Itin. Eger.* 37, 1: *CCL* 175, 80), also locating it in Sion.

the spot where at Pentecost the Holy Spirit had descended on the assembled believers. During a later stay they were to visit also the complex church called Eleona, on the Mount of Olives, built by the Empress Helena above a grotto in which Jesus was believed to have instructed his disciples before his passion,[36] and nearby the octagonal sanctuary which had been erected about 375 to mark the place from which he had ascended to heaven.[37] Their first stay concluded, however, Paula distributed alms, and the party made straight for Bethlehem some 9 km. south and slightly to the west. Here again there was much to be seen: the age-old tomb of Rachel at the fork of the road before one ascends to the village,[38] the field in which the angel had announced the Saviour's birth to the shepherds,[39] the site of the slaughter of the Holy Innocents. But the chief attraction, a little apart from Bethlehem itself, was the basilica[40] built at Constantine's behest shortly before 330 over the cave in which, according to ancient tradition, Jesus had been born.[41] By Jerome's account Paula, deeply conscious of her sinfulness, was abashed by the privilege of being accounted worthy to kiss the manger, and in his hearing protested that she could see the infant in his swathing-clothes, his foster-father Joseph, and the shepherds coming by night to adore him.

Modern students are sometimes tempted to smile at these ecstasies, and they brush aside Jerome's emotionally embroidered recital of their visits

[36] With the churches at Bethlehem and over the tomb of the resurrection this was the third of Constantine's great constructions: cf. Eusebius, *Vita Const.* 3, 43 (*GCS* 7, 95 f.). The 'mystic cave' where Christ was thought to have 'initiated the disciples, as authentic history tells, into the hidden mysteries', was held in highest honour among early Christians: cf. *Itin. Burdig.* 595, 5–6 ('where the Lord taught his disciples before his passion'); *Itin. Eger.* 30, 3 (*CCL* 175, 18; 77).

[37] Built by a pious matron, Poemenia or Pomnia, and itself named Imbomon. See *Itin. Eger.* 31 (*CCL* 175, 77): also Vincent-Abel, op. cit. II, 460–73; 374–92. The cupola was open at the centre, being supported on a colonnade. Its plan inspired the architect of the Dome of the Rock (Qubbet es Sakhra) built on the Temple site between 687 and 691. For the glittering cross which surmounted it, see Jerome, *Comm. on Ezekiel* 11, 23 (*CCL* 75: 112).

[38] This age-old shrine is still an object of pilgrimage for Jews, Muslims, and Christians. Rachel was buried here according to post-exilic Jewish belief as expressed in the glosses on Gen. 35, 19; 48, 7. The older tradition was the Ephrath, where she died and was buried, lay about 10 miles north of Bethlehem. For a mention see *Itin. Burdig.* 598, 5 (*CCL* 175, 20).

[39] Not mentioned in *Itin. Burdig.* but in *Appendix ad Itin. Eger.* L, 1, which adds that there was a church called Ad Pastores with an altar on the spot where the angel appeared to the shepherds (*CCL* 175, 96). Jerome states (*Book of Places: GCS* 11 (1), 43) that the tower of Ader which Paula climbed in the shepherds' field was 1000 paces from Bethlehem. The field is shown today in the broad valley east of Bethlehem beyond the village of Beit Sahur. For descriptions see C. Kopp, *The Holy Places of the Gospels* (ET, Freiburg, 1963), 35–47; R. W. Hamilton, *The Church of the Nativity, Bethlehem* (Jerusalem, 1947), 100 f.

[40] For the Church of the Nativity see below p. 131, with note.

[41] As we saw above, Origen reports that the cave and the manger were shown in his time. The cave is mentioned in the middle of the second century by Justin (*Dial.* 78) and the *Protoevangelium of James* 18 ff. (E. Hennecke, *New Testament Apocrypha*, ET, London, 1963, I, 383 ff.).

to these and other hallowed places. But such impatience is in danger of missing an essential, profoundly characteristic feature of the piety of fourth-century Christians, not least of Jerome and Paula. When they came face to face with the actual localities which, as they accepted without question, had been the scene of God's saving intervention, they were filled with awe and rapture, uncritical and credulous perhaps, but absolutely overwhelming in their effect. As Jerome was to put it in a terse sentence,[42] 'I entered Jerusalem, I saw a host of marvels, and with the judgment of my eyes I verified things of which I had previously learned by report.' To understand and participate in the emotion he experienced, we need to read sympathetically the letter[43] which, in the name of Paula and Eustochium, he wrote a few years later to Marcella urging her to join them in Jerusalem. Here he portrays with extraordinary vividness the impact which all the sites of the Holy Land, especially those associated with Jesus himself, had on the believing tourist. The whole sacred story suddenly came alive for him, he felt he was actually witnessing the amazing events as they were enacted, above all as he gazed at the cave in which Jesus had been born he felt sure he could say with the author of Song of Songs, 'I have found him for whom my soul searched; I shall hold him fast and not let him go.'

(iv)

One final act in this year-long drama of exhausting travel and sight-seeing remained. After seeing all there was to see in Palestine, Jerome, Paula, Eustochium, and their numerous escort set forth on the southerly route, much of it through desert, to Egypt. Again they were following the religious fashion of the times. For devout travellers to the Holy Land it was the most natural thing in the world either to complete their tour by a trip to the desert cradle of monasticism in the Nile valley or, if they were westerners who had made the direct sea-voyage to Alexandria, to make a preliminary diversion to it. Jerome and Paula, too, were eager to see the heroes of asceticism at close quarters, but he matched her pious enthusiasm with a more strictly scholarly objective. As he was to note[44] two or three years later, 'My chief concern in journeying recently to Alexandria was to see Didymus and interrogate him on points I found obscure throughout the Bible.' We have already noticed[45] his admiration for this Alexandrian scholar, blind from about five years old and so unable to read, but renowned for his theological learning, enormous literary production, and

---

[42] *Apology* 3, 22.
[43] *Letter* 46.
[44] *Comm. on Ephesians* prol. (PL 26: 539–40).
[45] See above p. 85.

asceticism.[46] Now Paula's decision to visit Egypt gave him a golden opportunity of making his personal acquaintance and studying under him. Henceforth he was to salute[47] him proudly as (like Gregory of Nazianzus) his 'master', and, recalling how frequently he had attended his lectures, to acclaim[48] him as 'the most erudite man of his epoch'.

In the course of their later quarrel Rufinus, who off and on had spent about eight years under Didymus's tutelage, was to taunt[49] Jerome with not having stayed more than thirty days in Alexandria in his whole life. If this is correct (even Jerome did not contest the fact), he must have haunted the blind exegete's lecture-hall and kept him inordinately busy. Perhaps the two men's passion for scripture enabled them to establish firm relations immediately. At any rate Jerome several times recalls[50] that, at his request, Didymus had dictated for him three volumes expounding the prophet Hosea (thus filling, he says, a gap left by Origen), and in addition five expounding the prophet Zechariah. Didymus was an ardent disciple of Origen, sharing those daring speculations about the pre-existence of souls and the ultimate salvation of even the most wicked for which the great teacher was to be condemned; and, like Origen's, his exegesis of scripture was highly allegorical, paying little attention (as Jerome was to remark[51] regretfully) to its literal, historical sense. At this stage, however, his influence on Jerome was profound; grey-haired as he was (he was in fact fifty-five), he was not ashamed to become a student again under such a professor.[52] Years later, when he had himself broken with Origenism and embraced a narrower orthodoxy, it was inevitable that he should censure Didymus for adopting some of Origen's 'errors'. Even so, he was to applaud his correct views on major doctrines like the Trinity, and was to continue to call him his master[53] and go out of his way to stress their one-time friendship.[54]

We have no evidence whether Paula and her party remained in Alexandria while Jerome attended Didymus's school. Her own keen interest in scriptural exegesis, especially of the mystico-allegorical kind, combined with her affectionate dependence on Jerome, makes it likely that she did;

[46] Cf. Palladius, *Hist. Laus.* 4. Owing to his condemnation as an Origenist by the second council of Constantinople (553), very little of his vast literary output has survived, although some of his commentaries were retrieved in 1941 at Toura, south of Cairo, when the British army was clearing some caves of rubbish in order to make an ammunition dump.

[47] *Letter* 50, 1.

[48] *Comm. on Hosea* prol. (*CCL* 76: xxii).

[49] *Apol. c. Hier.* 2, 12.

[50] *Comm. on Hosea* prol.; *Comm. on Zechariah* prol. (*CCL* 76: xxii; 76A: 777–8); *Famous Men* 109.

[51] *Comm. on Zechariah* prol. (cited above).

[52] *Letter* 84, 3.

[53] *Apology* 3, 27; *Letter* 84, 3.

[54] *Comm. on Isaiah* prol. (*CCL* 73: 5–6).

while her keenness to press on to the monastic settlements may explain why Jerome had to limit his studies under Didymus to a single month. At any rate, whether together or with Paula preceding him, they were at Nitria in the spring or early summer of 386. Their journey there had not been lengthy or trying, for Nitria[55] (now the village of Pernoudj) lay only 65 km. south of Alexandria, in the Nile Delta on the edge of the Western Desert, and like other pilgrims they probably reached it by water.[56] Here the pioneer Amoun, who had spent his wedding night persuading his young wife that they should not consummate their marriage and then lived with her for eighteen years in chastity, had built himself two domed cells in the lonely desert around 330. By 386, however, some thousands[57] of ascetics were settled there, some living alone, others in pairs, others still in larger groups.[58] With its unusual organisation[59] (it had its own priests, and blended the eremitical and communal modes of life), the community attracted curious visitors from all over the world.

The arrival of Paula, of aristocratic descent and vast fortune, had evidently been heralded beforehand. A huge procession of monks, Jerome reports,[60] led by the confessor bishop Isidoros and including many priests and deacons, streamed out to receive her with appropriate honours. If their excitement was intense, so must have been their wonderment at the noble lady's bashfulness and humility in face of their magnificent welcome. Clearly her raptures knew no bounds as she explored the cells in which these ascetics, to her the living embodiments of Christ, dwelt; and as she poured out gifts upon them, she rejoiced to think she was bestowing them upon her Lord. Jerome's enthusiasm does not seem to have been quite equal to hers. He dryly observes that, in her eagerness to make her home, along with her attendant girls, among so many thousands of celibate men, she was in danger of forgetting her sex and the weaknesses which belong to the flesh. As for himself, he compressed his personal account of the tour into a terse, biting sentence:[61] 'I went on to Egypt, surveyed the monasteries of Nitria, and noticed vipers lurking among the throngs of dedicated men.' Unfortunately the remark tells us nothing about his real reaction at the time. Dictated in 402, it reflects the aversion he had by then conceived for the teaching of Origen—an aversion of which he was innocent in 386—and also the knowledge which he was

---

[55] Its correct geographical location was established by H. G. Evelyn White in his *The History of the Monasteries of Nitria and of Scetis* (New York, 1932), chap. 2.

[56] Cf. *Hist. monach. in Aeg.* 20, 5 (Festugière, 120), where the verb used is 'we put in at' (κατήχθημεν).

[57] Rufinus (*Hist. eccl.* 2, 3) describes their number as 'three thousand or more' in 373; Palladius (*Hist. Laus.* 7) saw five thousand when he was there twenty years later.

[58] Cf. *Hist. monach.* 21 (Latin version: *PL* 21, 443).

[59] For this see H. G. Evelyn White, op. cit. above, 170 ff.

[60] *Letter* 108, 14.

[61] *Apology* 3, 22.

later to acquire that Origenism was rampant among the monks of Nitria.[62]

(v)

Their visit to the desert was, apparently, of short duration; there is no hint, for example, that they went on to Scetis (Wadi-el-Natrûn), 64 km. south, or any of the other popular monastic colonies. We need not doubt Jerome's statement (he was writing to her daughter, who had been with her at the time and could recall the facts) that Paula was initially so captivated by the ascetic settlements at Nitria that she had serious thoughts of permanently joining them. The project, however, bristled with impracticabilities, and we may be sure that Jerome, who wielded such influence over her, did not find it at all to his taste. Ascetic withdrawal could take many forms, and it is unlikely that he had any wish to resume the form he had experienced to his cost in the Syrian desert. Much more congenial, much more serene and emotionally satisfying, was the relationship he had been building up for several years now with Paula, Eustochium, and their like-minded female companions. At Nitria that relationship would have to be shared with other ascetics, some more venerable and looked up to than himself, more liable perhaps to impress the susceptible Paula. And Jerusalem and Bethlehem, he implies, had set a special spell upon her as well as upon him. At Jerusalem, too, they must have observed at close quarters the ascetic foundations which Melania had established, with Rufinus as her counsellor, and which corresponded much more closely than Nitria to the form of life which, he must have realised, would best meet his spiritual and scholarly needs.

So back to Palestine they went; we may suspect that Paula, who had found the holy places so inspiring, was not difficult to persuade. As it was mid-summer and the heat well-nigh insupportable, it seemed impracticable to return by the sun-scorched land-route across the desert to Gaza. Instead they went by ship from Pelusium, at the eastern mouth of the Nile, to Maiuma, the sea-port 4 km. west of Gaza, accomplishing the journey, as Jerome picturesquely puts it,[63] with the speed of a bird. Their far-ranging pilgrimages were now over; it was time to embrace the life of prayer, study, and mortification to which they were vowing themselves.

Contrary to what had seemed their original intention, it was not at Jerusalem but at Bethlehem that they decided to settle, at first, pending the

---

[62] Cf. *Letter* 92 (translation of a synodal letter of Bishop Theophilus in Greek: date 400), which deplores the propaganda in favour of Origen's 'errors' rampant among the monks of Nitria.

[63] *Letter* 108, 4 ('. . . with such speed that one would suppose her a bird'). Of himself he simply remarks (*Apology* 3, 22), 'I returned to Bethlehem with great rapidity'.

construction of the monastic buildings they were planning, in modest temporary lodgings.[64] Their choice has sometimes intrigued scholars: had Jerome's once passionate affection for Rufinus already turned sour? There is no evidence of this; as we shall see,[65] such hints as survive suggest that relations between the two establishments on the Mount of Olives and at Bethlehem continued cordial for some years. There may be some truth in the guesses that, whether they admitted it to themselves or not, Jerome had no wish to be a disciple, overshadowed by a much more experienced pioneer like Rufinus, while Paula instinctively felt the wisdom of placing a certain distance between herself and the devout but imperious Melania.[66] The decisive factor, however, was probably Bethlehem itself. Far removed from bustle and corruption, it was more suitable for monks than Jerusalem. Above all, Bethlehem had the grotto of the Nativity, and this had a special fascination for them both. Here they were to dwell, not in tranquillity (Jerome was not born for that), but in relative contentment, for the long remaining years of both their lives.

[64] Letter 108, 14.
[65] See below p. 136.
[66] E.g. J. Steinmann, Saint Jérôme (Paris, 1958), 171; F. M. Abel, Miscellanea Geronimiana (Rome, 1920), 137 (citing R. Génier).

XIII

The Monasteries at Bethlehem

(i)

Today Bethlehem, set on a limestone ridge just east of the Jerusalem–Hebron highway, is a busy town of about 20,000 inhabitants, looking out with its close-packed, white buildings on fertile, hilly country of idyllic beauty. When Jerome and Paula settled there, it was a tiny village, more properly a hamlet (a 'villula', as he called it),[1] with its sparse population given over to agriculture (corn, vines, sheep-farming), although year by year it was becoming increasingly a tourist draw. At the southern end of the spur, originally a short distance from the village, stood the splendid church which Constantine had had built over the cave in which Jesus was believed to have been born. Until its construction the spot had been thickly wooded,[2] and Jerome laments[3] that 'Bethlehem, which is now ours . . . used to be overshadowed by a grove of Tammuz, that is Adonis, and in the grotto where the Christ-child once cried people mourned for Venus's lover-boy.' Whether this was an act of deliberate desecration, as Jerome and others suggest,[4] the cult had inevitably been suppressed when Constantine, who took drastic measures against it elsewhere,[5] restored and embellished the sacred site.

For three years (386–9), Jerome records,[6] Paula stayed in a minute hostelry 'until she could build the cells and monasteries, and found a hospice for travellers because Mary and Joseph had not been able to find shelter'. Whether he shared her lodgings or put up somewhere else, we have no means of knowing; but the latter is much more likely, both intrinsically and because there was at least one religious house for men

---

[1] *Letter* 46, 12. Augustine, writing *c.* 400 (*De cat. rud.* 40), says that 'it was so small that even today it is called a "villa" '.

[2] Cyril of Jerusalem (*c.* 350) remarks (*Cat.* 12, 20), 'A few years ago the place was densely wooded (δρυμώδης).'

[3] *Letter* 58, 3.

[4] Jerome, *Letter* 58, 3; Paulinus of Nola, *Ep.* 31, 3. The latter, if not the former, attributes the profanation to Hadrian. A. M. Schneider (*RAC* II, col. 226) points out that Origen does not hint at any such desecration, and concludes that it may therefore have taken place in the persecution of Decius (250–1).

[5] Cf. his eradication of it at Aphaka (Afka) and Heliopolis (Baalbek) in Lebanon: Eusebius, *Vita Const.* 3, 55; *Laus. Const.* 8, 5 f. (*GCS* 7, 102 f.; 216 f.); Socrates, *Hist. eccl.* 1, 18.

[6] *Letter* 108, 14.

already established in the village. We know[7] that Jerome's younger contemporary, John Cassian, who years later was to found communities for both men and women at Marseilles and whose influence on western spirituality was to be profound, had spent several years (380–6?), with a fellow-countryman named Germanus, in a monastery near the cave of the Nativity before going down to Egypt for a longer sojourn. Indeed, his departure seems to have almost coincided, or even overlapped, with Jerome's arrival; but although he mentions Jerome once or twice in his writings,[8] he betrays no hint (despite obvious admiration) of having been personally acquainted with him.

It was Paula, clearly, who, with her ample fortune, paid for the cost of the new constructions. The first to be completed was a monastery for men,[9] of which Jerome himself took charge, and then came a more complex convent for women. Tradition placed the monastery to the north-west of the village,[10] and this is about as near as we can get to its location. Scholars have tried to fix it more precisely from hints in his writings, but all in vain. In one passage,[11] for example, dating from 396, when Bishop John of Jerusalem had forbidden him entrance to the Church of the Nativity, he protests that he can 'only see the Lord's cave and, standing at a distance, groan as heretics walk in'. The reference here, however, is not to the position of his monastery, but simply to the fact that, owing to his bishop's ban, he has to be content with merely gazing at the hallowed spot without actually entering it. Again, in one of his commentaries he remarks[12] that he daily sets eyes on Tekoa (8 km. south of Bethlehem); but nothing can be built on this since the hill-town of Tekoa is clearly visible from most parts of Bethlehem. Elsewhere[13] he describes the tomb of Herod Archelaus, who became king of Judaea on Herod the Great's death (4 B.C.), as being the point on the main road where a track led up to his 'cells'; but since all trace of the tomb (or cenotaph, since Archelaus died in Gaul) has vanished, the only hard fact we can glean from this is that the monastery stood some distance from the highway. On the other hand, we have his explicit statements[14] that Paula's

---

[7] Cf. his *Inst.* 3, 4, 1; 4, 31; *Coll.* 11, 1; 11, 5; 19, 1, 3 (*CSEL* 17, 38; 70; 13, 314; 317; 535).

[8] *Inst.* pref. 5; *C. Nest.* 7, 26 (*CSEL* 17, 5; 384).

[9] *Letter* 108, 20 ('post virorum monasterium . . . plures virgines . . . in tres turmas monasteriaque divisit').

[10] So the *Life* of Jerome once attributed to Gennadius but nowadays regarded as an anonymous work of the eighth or ninth century (*PL* 22, 180). In what follows I am much indebted to B. Bagatti, *Gli antichi edifici sacri di Betlemme* (Jerusalem, 1952), 158 f.

[11] *Against John* 42.

[12] *Comm. on Jeremiah* 6, 1 (*CCL* 74: 882).

[13] *Book of Places* (*GCS* 11 (1), 45): a note added to Eusebius's original text.

[14] *Letter* 108, 20 ('ad ecclesiam . . . ex cuius habitabant latere'); 14 ('diversorium peregrinorum iuxta viam').

convent stood alongside the Church of the Nativity, and that the pilgrim's hospice, as indeed its purpose dictated, was 'next to the main road'.

The basilica[15] was to be the focal point of their existence. Built in the late 320s by the empress Helena, it reproduced on a smaller scale the main features of the Church of the Resurrection at Jerusalem, being far simpler in design, as well as much more beautiful, than the ungainly, fortress-like complex the visitor sees today. One approached it through a colonnaded atrium, open to the sky, which has long disappeared but which occupied part of the present paved square west of the church. From this, after ascending some steps, a majestic façade with triple doors admitted one to a broad, almost square nave divided into five aisles by four rows of columns. Immediately east of this, connected with it by a flight of steps, an octagonal sanctuary (its detailed arrangements remain obscure) rose above the subterranean grotto in which the Saviour had been born. Access to this was either by stairways on the north and south (as today) or by a single stairway leading down from the steps to the sanctuary, and in the dim, irregular vault the believer, by the light of lamps, could pick out the very spot where Mary was delivered of her child and, a few paces south, the manger in which she had laid him. Jerome reports,[16] with unconcealed regret, that by his time the original earthenware trough had been replaced by a sumptuous silver replica. Under Justinian, in the 530s, the church, which had been devastated, was drastically remodelled, and subsequent additions and alterations have confused the earlier plan still further. But in the nave, with its columns of local red limestone,[17] the general impression one gets must be much the same as Jerome and Paula received, the rich mosaic pavement they trod so frequently can still be glimpsed 75 cm. beneath the floor that was later superimposed, and the underground cavern with its vulgar trappings and ornate illumination remains the shrine they entered with awe and rapture.

(ii)

Despite the alarms and upsets of barbarian invasions, these two monasteries were to be the homes of Paula, Eustochium, and Jerome until their deaths in 404, 419, and 420 respectively. Initially quite unpretentious, the fame of their occupants caused the number of their inmates to grow, and Palladius, the historian of monasticism, reports[18] that when Paula died and Eustochium took over the convent contained some fifty nuns.

[15] See esp. B. Bagatti, op. cit., esp. chaps. 1 and 3. For a more popular but scholarly account, based on the excavations in the 1930s, see R. W. Hamilton, *The Church of the Nativity, Bethlehem* (Jerusalem, 1947).

[16] *Christmas homily* (*CCL* 78, 524 f.).

[17] Because they show no sign of damage many believe these cannot be the original columns (so R. W. Hamilton, op. cit., 51); but cf. B. Bagatti, op. cit., 51 f.

[18] *Hist. Laus.* 41.

We have a vivid, if slightly idealised, picture of Paula's community from Jerome's own pen.[19] Her girls came from a whole variety of provinces, and as they differed widely in social background she divided them into three groups according to rank, each with its own hostel. Thus they worked and took their meals separately, but worshipped together. Their practice was to recite the psalter in turn at dawn, at the third, sixth and ninth hours, at evening, and at midnight. The intervening hours they filled with Bible reading, the menial tasks of the convent, and manual tasks—mainly sewing. On Sundays and festivals they all trooped to the basilica for mass, each social group shepherded by its mother-superior. They all dressed alike, and apart from food and clothing none possessed anything she could call her own. Paula was quick to pounce on faults like quarrelsomeness, talkativeness, pilfering, and over-attention to dress ('a clean body and clean clothes betoken an unclean mind'), was wonderfully tactful when sisters got on each others' nerves, personally attended to the sick, but was quite ruthless when she detected any stirrings of sexual desire—her infallible nostrum for this was redoubled fasting. Writing in 398, Jerome describes[20] how she and Eustochium, 'shabbily and sombrely clad, positive heroines in comparison with their former selves, trim lamps, light fires, sweep floors, clean vegetables, put cabbage heads into the boiling pot, lay tables, hand round cups, serve food, and run to and fro to wait on others'.

Unfortunately no such graphic description of Jerome's daily round has come down to us, and we have to piece together scattered hints. Certainly he was no solitary, as tradition has sometimes represented him, but busily engaged in supervising his monastery as well as maintaining multifarious contacts with the wider world. Much as he objected[21] to the new-fangled Syriac title 'abbot' (i.e. 'father': had not Jesus ruled that none was to be called 'father' except God?), that was what in fact he was; and in addition he was constantly advising and assisting Paula, not the strongest of women, and acting as spiritual guide both to her and to her community. He also had, perhaps officially, but more probably through sheer force of personality, some kind of leadership among the Christians of the village generally. At any rate Postumianus, a native of Aquitania who spent six months with him in the early 400s, told[22] his friends at home that 'Jerome directs the church there as presbyter, the place itself being under the jurisdiction of the bishop of Jerusalem'.

At the start his monastery must have been relatively small; the monks who had accompanied him from Rome seem to have preferred to stay in

[19] *Letter* 108, 20.
[20] *Letter* 66, 13.
[21] *Comm. on Galatians* 4, 6 (*PL* 26: 451).
[22] Cf. Sulpicius Severus, *Dial.* 1, 8 and 9 (*CSEL* 1, 159; 161).

Jerusalem.[23] But it grew steadily; in 394 Epiphanius could speak[24] (perhaps exaggerating a little) of 'a multitude of dedicated brothers', while a year later it had no fewer than five priests.[25] To judge by his sermons,[26] it included a sprinkling of Greek-speaking Orientals as well as Latins. We have hardly any clues to its routine, except that (like Paula's nuns) the monks met together six times daily to recite what we should call the offices, and went to mass in the basilica on Sundays and holy days.[27] For the rest, Jerome seems to have followed the pattern of community living which had recently excited his enthusiasm in Egypt, upon which he had expatiated approvingly in his famous letter to Eustochium, and which St Pachomius was held to have inaugurated *c*. 320 at Tabennisi in the Nile valley. His monks lived in cells (sometimes, perhaps, shared); they assembled in common rooms for meals, prayers, instructions; obedience to superiors was inculcated[28] (Jerome himself, ironically, never obeyed anyone except when it suited him); agricultural and other work played a prominent part.

Not that Jerome felt obliged to copy the Pachomian model slavishly and in detail; it was probably never intended to supply more than guidelines. The fact that he did not translate[29] the Rule attributed to St Pachomius into Latin until 404, and then, in the first instance at any rate, for the benefit of Latin monks ignorant of Greek and Coptic who were joining religious settlements in Egypt, is significant. In fact, he and Paula seem to have interpreted it pretty freely, with adaptations suited to their circumstances as well as to the Latin temperament. Liturgically, for example, we find him observing the Saviour's birth at Christmas, 25 December, the date favoured at Rome and increasingly in the west since the beginning of the century, rather than at Epiphany, 6 January, still the preferred date in Jerusalem and much of the east, and robustly defending the usage with characteristically Latin arguments.[30] Again, at Bethlehem, as in Palestine generally, the brethren met for their offices at regular intervals throughout the day and night, in contrast to the Egyptian practice of not meeting till the ninth hour (i.e. the third before sunset) on the theory that prayer should be continuous.[31] Institutionally, there is no evidence that Jerome's

---

[23] *Apology* 3, 22 ('along with . . . other monks who now reside in Jerusalem').

[24] Jerome, *Letter* 51, 1 (a translation of Epiphanius's original Greek).

[25] *Against John* 42.

[26] *Tract. on Ps.* 143 prol.; *Homily on Matthew* (*CCL* 78, 313; 503; 504).

[27] *Tract. on Ps.* 119, 7 (*CCL* 78, 257). For the Sunday mass Jerome's sermons (see below) provide ample evidence.

[28] See esp. *Hom. on Obedience* (*CCL* 78, 552–5). The comment on Jerome's personal practice is suggested by P. Antin, *Recueil sur St Jérôme* (Brussels, 1966), 108.

[29] For his translation of Pachomius's *Rule* see below p. 280.

[30] Cf. *Christmas Homily* (*CCL* 78, 527).

[31] Jerome, *Letter* 22, 35 and 37 (defence of fixed hours); Cassian, *Inst.* 3, 1–3 (contrast between eastern and western practice: *CSEL* 17, 33–8).

monks were regimented in houses of between twenty and forty inmates, as were the Egyptians[32] (there was probably no need with his much smaller numbers); and while at a village like Bethlehem they must have worked in the fields, there was greater emphasis on intellectual labour (study, copying of books, etc.) than in strictly Pachomian circles. Jerome himself, with typical individualism, though warmly encouraging manual toil in other monastic aspirants,[33] did not soil his own hands with it. He would have escaped much criticism, he ruefully confesses,[34] if he had earned his living by weaving baskets or plaiting palm-leaves; but because he had spent his time producing a corrected version of Scripture, he had brought down nothing but abuse on his head.

(iii)

Postponing for the moment his literary and polemical activities, we catch a few glimpses, isolated but informative, of how Jerome occupied himself at Bethlehem. In the earlier years, for example, we find him taking energetic steps to improve his knowledge of Hebrew. He spared neither trouble nor expense over this, retaining as his teacher a Jew named Baraninas who, fearing the wrath of his co-religionists, used to visit him under cover of night.[35] This practice, for which Rufinus was to upbraid him unreasonably,[36] was invaluable preparation for his later work as a Biblical translator and exegete; and he from time to time supplemented it by persuading Jewish scholars (at no small cost, he claims) to help him to unravel obscure texts like the Book of Job.[37] He also reports that, with the object of acquiring an exact knowledge of Biblical sites, he had made a point of traversing Palestine with 'very erudite Hebrews' accompanying him, and recalls being conducted by guides around Elkosh, in Galilee, the supposed birthplace of the prophet Nahum.[38] This has led scholars to picture him undertaking extensive topographical expeditions from Bethlehem in the late 380s. It is much more likely, however, in view of the mistakes he makes about places and the curious gaps in his knowledge of them, that these references are to his pilgrimage with Paula in 386, and that after that he spent most of his time at home in his monastery.[39]

---

[32] For the Egyptian house system see *Vita Prima* (in F. Halkin, *S. Pachomii Vitae Graecae*: *Subsidia hagiographica* 19, Brussels, 1932) 28; 58 f.; 94 f.; 110; 121: also Jerome, *Rule of St Pachomius* pref. (in A. Boon, *Pachomiana Latina*, Louvain, 1932).

[33] E.g. *Letter* 125, 11 (advice to the young monk, Rusticus of Toulouse).

[34] *Preface to Job* (LXX) (*PL* 29, 61): written *c.* 390.

[35] *Letter* 84, 3 (date 398).

[36] *Apol. c. Hier.* 2, 12.

[37] *Preface to Job* (Vulgate) (*PL* 28, 1081).

[38] *Preface to Chronicles* (LXX) (early 390s); *Comm. on Nahum* prol. (391–2) (*PL* 29, 401; *CCL* 76A: 535–6).

[39] In *Revue biblique* 81, 1974, 245–57 (an article he kindly showed me in draft), J. Wilkinson.

One city he did occasionally visit was Caesarea (Quaisāriye), the ecclesiastical and civil metropolis of Palestine. What drew him there was its magnificent library, the richest then extant in its collection of Christian writings, which, reorganised by Pamphilus (d. 310), went back to the days of Origen, and which Bishop Euzoius (deposed 379) had recently attempted to restore by replacing the badly worn papyrus rolls with parchment codices.[40] Among its chief treasures was the original copy of Origen's famous Hexapla, i.e. his edition of the Old Testament presenting most of the books in six parallel columns: the Hebrew consonantal text in Hebrew letters, a transliteration of this into Greek characters, the Greek version of Aquila the Jew (*c*. 132), the Greek version of Symmachus (late second century), the pre-Christian Greek version known as the Septuagint, and the Jewish Christian Theodotion's revision of this. For certain books up to three further Greek versions were added. Jerome was to claim (*c*. 387) to have gone through the Hexapla thoroughly so as to obtain a corrected text of the Old Testament, and later still he speaks of his 'reading it through again'.[41] Other references attest his familiarity with the great library;[42] and once he recalls having come across and studied there the *Defence of Origen* which the martyr Pamphilus had composed while in prison for the faith (307–10), and which after his death Eusebius of Caesarea had completed.[43]

His contacts with nearby Jerusalem must have been vastly more frequent, in the early years indeed regular. The liturgical ties between Jerusalem and Bethlehem, each the setting of signal events in Christ's career, were inevitably close, and for certain festivals the bishop of Jerusalem, escorted by his clergy and crowds of the faithful, went out to Bethlehem to take part in the ceremonies.[44] Some of Jerome's sermons, too, leave the impression of having been preached in Jerusalem.[45] One

demonstrates how slight is Jerome's personal knowledge of places in Palestine outside his pilgrimage route with Paula; such knowledge as he does show is much more easily explained in other ways than by the assumption that he travelled around the country.

[40] *Famous Men* 113.

[41] *Comm. on Titus* 3, 9 (PL 26: 734 f.); *Comm. on Ps.* 1 (G. Morin, *Anecdota Maredsolana* iii, 1, 5).

[42] E.g. *Famous Men* 3 (it contains 'the Gospel according to the Hebrews'); 75 (it contains the great majority of Origen's works transcribed by Pamphilus himself).

[43] *Apology* 3, 12. Having now become an anti-Origenist, Jerome describes it as the work of Eusebius in order to discredit him and save the reputation of the martyr Pamphilus: see below p. 252. In *Famous Men* 75, when he still admired Origen, he attributes the book to Pamphilus. Photius (*Bibl. cod.* 118) reports that five of the six books were by Pamphilus.

[44] Cf., e.g., *Itin. Eger.* 25, 6–12 (CCL 175, 71 f.) which, although the vital leaf of the MS is missing, indicates when supplemented by the Armenian Lectionary that the bishop and faithful assembled at Bethlehem for the solemn vigil of Epiphany, returning to Jerusalem just before dawn to celebrate the feast there. See J. Wilkinson, *Egeria's Travels* (London, 1971), 80–2.

[45] Cf. esp. *Tract. on Ps.* 119 (where he speaks of seeing the ruins of the Temple); *Tract. on Mark* 11, 15–17 (where he describes the multitudes gathering at Jerusalem for Easter) (CCL 78, 247; 492).

way or another, he must have had abundant opportunities of meeting his diocesan, the young (he was in his early thirties), brilliant, and masterful John, an admirer like himself of Origen, who had recently been appointed to the see.[46] Everything suggests that their relations were, to start with at any rate, cordial; a decade later, when they were at their lowest ebb, Jerome was to exclaim,[47] 'Let him show himself what he used to be, when using his own judgment [i.e. uninfluenced by others] he loved me.' Much closer and warmer, because of much longer standing, were his relations, for a few years at least, with Rufinus, installed in his monastery next to Melania's on the Mount of Olives. We have Rufinus's statement that numbers of his monks were employed copying out works of Cicero for Jerome (apparently weaned now of his aversion for the pagan classics), and receiving a much better price for them than the current rate.[48] In the same passage he explicitly mentions a visit Jerome paid him bringing a dialogue of Cicero's along with one of Plato's. There can be no doubt that this was only one of many visits. The general view at this time was that they were fast friends, and Jerome was later to complain that he had been considered a heretic (i.e. an Origenist) precisely because of his friendship with Rufinus.[49]

(iv)

Trips to Caesarea apart, Jerome was kept extremely busy at Bethlehem itself. For one thing, he frequently preached in the basilica—in Jerusalem, too, as we have noticed. By singular good fortune we have almost a hundred of his addresses, restored to their true author after being denied to him for hundreds of years.[50] Most of them explain passages of psalms which have been sung in the liturgy, others deal with gospel excerpts or with notable festivals. Their frequent reference to the 'errors' of Origenism, as well as other features,[51] impose a date after 400; but there can be no doubt that Jerome was delivering homilies like these throughout the whole of his residence at Bethlehem. What immediately strikes any reader accustomed to his normal literary elegance is their unadorned colloquialism, their crudities of style, the errors in assigning Biblical texts in which they abound. Evidently they were pulpit improvisations, taken down in

[46] The general view is that Cyril of Jerusalem, John's immediate predecessor, died on 18 March 386, i.e. before Jerome's arrival. P. Nautin has argued (RHE 56, 1961, 35) that in fact he died on 18 March 387. If he is correct, Jerome must have known Cyril.

[47] Letter 82, 8 (2).

[48] Apol. c. Hier. 2, 11.

[49] Apology 3, 33.

[50] This identification was the brilliant achievement of G. Morin: see his Anecdota Maredsolana iii, 2 and 3 (1897 and 1903); also Études, Textes, Découvertes (Maredsous, 1913). They have been reprinted in CCL 78 (1958).

[51] For a discussion see G. Morin, Études, Textes, Découvertes, 233 f.

shorthand by admirers and never corrected.[52] As if to silence sceptics of their origin, they are also packed with turns of phrase and mannerisms which belong unmistakably to Jerome—including sharp attacks on heretics and pagan learning, and numberless references to the Hebrew original, the several Greek versions, and other philological matters which must have been far above the heads of his (for the most part) modestly educated, as well as racially mixed, congregation. This was composed of monks, and the homilies are as remarkable for their ecstatic exaltation of the monastic vocation as for their down-to-earth appreciation of its practical difficulties. Every page, too, radiates Jerome's passion for Scripture (he compares[53] it to the consecrated bread of the eucharist); and their very simplicity and directness issue from time to time in bursts of moving eloquence.

Two other activities which occupied Jerome as head of his monastery during these long years were teaching and the supervision of the hospice. As regards the first, he took a personal interest, presumably with others assisting him, in the instruction of candidates for baptism. In 396 (the fact slips out in a bitter protest he was making against Bishop John)[54] there were some forty of these of both sexes. One or two of his homilies are specifically addressed to catechumens, others[55] presuppose the presence either of catechumens or of recently baptised persons in the congregation. More surprisingly, we find him running a sort of secondary school for children. We owe our knowledge of this to Rufinus, who jeers[56] (the date is 400) that, for all his solemn oath that he would be guilty of disowning Christ if he so much as glanced at the pagan classics, 'once he had installed himself in his monastery, he set up as a schoolmaster, lecturing on his beloved Vergil, the comic and lyrical poets, and the historians, to young boys who had been entrusted to him to learn the fear of the Lord'. Rufinus professes to be shocked by this, but to us it is not only evidence of Jerome's return to a more balanced attitude to pagan literature, but reveals a trait in his character which we have not noticed before, his genuine interest in and concern for children.

The hospice for strangers was clearly both a chore and a worry, becoming all the more so as the fame of the monastery spread. In 398 we find him lamenting[57] that so overwhelmed is he with monks flocking in from all over the world that he can neither abandon the enterprise nor summon

---

[52] Cf. *Letter* 48, 2 (date 394), where he complains that, for very different reasons, his admirers and his ill-wishers alike are in the habit of taking down and publishing his 'trifles' without giving him a chance to make corrections.

[53] *Tract. on Pss.* 145; 147 (*CCL* 78, 326; 337 f.).

[54] *Against John* 42.

[55] E.g. *Tract. on Mark* 13; *on Ps.* 41 (*CCL* 78, 496 ff.; 542 ff.).

[56] *Apol. c. Hier.* 2, 8 (2).

[57] *Letter* 66, 14.

the strength to carry it out properly. More cheerfully, but carried away by his own rhetoric, he boasts[58] in 400 of every day welcoming monks from India, Persia, and Ethiopia. Letter after letter[59] names individuals coming from remote countries and staying, sometimes for prolonged periods, in the guest-house—Augustine's friend Alypius from North Africa (394); Vigilantius, later to assail his most cherished teachings, from Aquitania (395); Eusebius of Cremona in North Italy (395-8); the Egyptian monk Theodore; others too. Indeed, scarcely a decade after its inception, the original building was proving much too small for the ever-growing demands made upon it. He had been obliged, Jerome confesses[60] in 398 to his friend Pammachius, to send his younger brother to Stridon to sell what remained of the family properties after the barbarian devastations, so as to obtain the funds needed (Paula's fortune had by now been frittered away) for further constructions. He had no wish, having once set his hand to it, to give up this charitable service to Christian people and so (he winds up with a characteristic snarl) become a laughing-stock to the evil-tongued and envious.

(v)

Although he was never to be free from turmoil, his monastery at Bethlehem opened up for Jerome a new, profoundly satisfying phase in his personal history. The ascetic ideal, the challenge of complete severance from the world, of surrender to Christ in poverty and chastity, had haunted him ever since he had glimpsed it at Trier. To be a monk was for him to possess the Lord and absolutely nothing else, and in return to be himself possessed by the Lord.[61] He saw the monk, like the martyr, undergoing a second baptism, a total immolation of self which cleansed him from all the sins committed since the first.[62] His attempt to capture the ideal as a hermit, or near-hermit, in the desert of Chalcis had ended in humiliating failure. At Rome he had experimented with being a monk in the world, directing his devout women friends and busy in the pope's employ and with his own studies. But Rome, as he was uneasily aware, with its noise and glamour, its dubious but demanding social round, 'was entirely alien to the dedication and seclusion of a monk'.[63] At Bethlehem, close to the

[58] *Letter* 107, 2.

[59] *Letters* 56, 1 (Alypius: the letter is from Augustine); 58, 11 (Vigilantius); 53, 11 (Eusebius: for his departure see *Apology* 3, 24); 89, 1 (Theodore).

[60] *Letter* 66, 14.

[61] *Letter* 52, 5: cf. *Letter* 14, 6 ('The perfect servant of Christ has nothing but Christ; if he has anything but Christ, he is not perfect').

[62] *Letter* 39, 3 (of Blesilla after her conversion); *Tract. on Ps.* 115, 17 (*CCL* 78, 245). Cf. E. Dekkers, 'Profession-Second Baptême: Qu'a voulu dire saint Jérôme?', *Hist. Jahrbuch* 77, 1958, 91-7.

[63] So *Letter* 46, 12. For his attitude to city life see P. Antin, *Recueil sur St Jérôme* (Brussels, 1968), 375-89. The same volume contains useful studies of his views on monasticism.

humble cave in which the infant Christ had uttered his first cry, he had at last discovered a practical form of 'the perfect life' which corresponded both to his own needs and the gospel pattern. As a young man he had written[64] with romantic ardour of the isolation of the anchorite, alone in the desert with Christ. He was never to relinquish his admiration for the solitary existence. But with experience he came to understand its dangers and temptations, and to appreciate that for most people, himself included, the monastic vocation found its most satisfactory fulfilment in an organised community.

His personal development apart, we should not overlook the contribution of Jerome's monasteries to the emergence of monastic institutions in the west. We should link with them, of course, the houses of Rufinus and Melania the Elder on the Mount of Olives, for these had preceded his by several years. In western Europe monasteries proper, organised communities under the discipline of a rule such as dotted the Christian east (especially Egypt and Syria) in their hundreds, were only now, hesitantly and sporadically, beginning to appear. As we saw in Chapter Four, the clergy of Aquileia formed an ascetic fellowship about 370, and a community of virgins existed then at Emona. In the early 380s there was a group of male monks under Ambrose's surveillance outside the walls of Milan;[65] there were also sisterhoods at Bologna and Verona.[66] A decade or so earlier groups of semi-hermits were settling around Martin of Tours in Gaul.[67] But these seem to have been relatively primitive, amateurish initiatives, many of them probably ephemeral. When Jerome lived at Rome from 382 to 386, there were apparently no communities for men, and the only communal life for women with ascetic leanings was provided by certain noble ladies turning their mansions into retreat-houses. Only in 387 Augustine reports[68] having seen several 'communal lodging-houses' ('diversoria') in the capital, both of men and of women, with their inmates practising the ascetic life under direction. So at least a start was then being made. The time was to come, early in the fifth century, when properly organised monasteries would be planted and take root in the west; but as yet the ground was ill prepared for what was still, in origin and general character, an essentially Oriental phenomenon. A stimulus was required, and also living illustrations of how the forms of community

[64] *Letter* 14: in *Letter* 52, 1 (date 394) he was to be less happy about these youthful raptures.
[65] So Augustine, *Conf.* 8, 6, 14 f.
[66] Cf. Ambrose, *De virginibus* 1, 60; *Ep.* 5, 19.
[67] Sulpicius Severus, *Vita Martini* 10. For the development of monasticism in the west, see esp. R. Lorenz, 'Die Anfänge des abendländischen Mönchtums im 4. Jahrhundert', *ZKG* 77 (1966), 1–61.
[68] *De mor. eccl. cath.* 1, 70. For monasticism in Rome in the fourth century, see R. Lorenz, art. cit.; G. D. Gordini, 'Origini e sviluppi del monachesimo a Roma', *Gregorianum* 37 (1956), 220–60.

living developed in the east could be moulded to western habits and temperaments. Many factors played their part, but these foundations of Rufinus and Jerome, Latin outposts on eastern soil which had absorbed and adapted eastern experience, were prominent in showing the way.[69] Thousands of travellers from western lands visited them and returned home with reports. At the same time the two leaders, Rufinus returning to Italy in 397 and Jerome with his voluminous correspondence, were to carry on an active and successful campaign of information and advice.

[69] See the discussion in G. D. Gordini, 'Il monachesimo romano in Palestina nel iv secolo', *Studia Anselmiana* 46 (1961), 85–107.

XIV

Translator and Commentator

For the first phase of Jerome's residence at Bethlehem, from autumn 386 until early 393, there is an almost complete gap in his correspondence. Of the numerous notes (daily, he alleges)[1] which passed between him and Paula and Eustochium not one survives. It is certain that he kept in regular touch with friends in Rome, but the only letter which remains is an eloquent, emotional appeal,[2] written in the name of Paula and her daughter but manifestly by Jerome himself, to Marcella, their spiritual mother, to forsake the corrupt metropolis and settle with them in this most sacred spot in the whole world. We cannot fix a precise date for it, but a natural one would be shortly after the death[3] of her mother, Albina, some time in 388/9. It is an idyllic piece, radiating spiritual serenity and contentment, and an almost ecstatic joy in their nearness to the Saviour's birthplace, and stands in striking contrast with the querulous, often vituperative note which sounds through many of the prefaces to his formal publications during these years.

Actually this was a period of prodigious, sometimes feverish literary activity. Over and above his other preoccupations, Jerome was pouring out a spate of books—translations, commentaries, scholarly studies and compilations, even an outline history of Christian literature. With one or two exceptions it is impossible to establish absolute dates for these. Their relative dating, too, is in most cases uncertain, for although he lists them in *Famous Men* (in the section[4] devoted to himself), he does so in an order which sometimes clashes with the evidence of their prefaces. No doubt it was a relief, after his humiliations at Rome, to immerse himself in pursuits so congenial and so suited to his talents; but we shall discover that occasionally spite and personal animosity played their part. As usual, he worked rapidly, dictating to secretaries because (he explains)[5] the weakness of his eyes, indeed of his 'whole wretched body', precluded writing with

---

[1] *Famous Men* 135.
[2] *Letter* 46.
[3] See below p. 145.
[4] *Famous Men* 135.
[5] *Comm. on Galatians* III pref. (PL 26: 485–6).

his own hand. This was expensive; but he was lucky enough, in the early days at any rate, to have some money of his own, and to be able to draw on Paula's fortune. In 398 we find him thanking[6] Bishop Chromatius, of Aquileia, for help in financing his stenographers and copyists.

(ii)

One of his earliest tasks, we may conjecture, was to complete the translation of Didymus's *On the Holy Spirit* which he had begun at Rome for Pope Damasus[7] but laid aside on his death. The preface, dedicating the finished work to his younger brother Paulinian, exudes such virulent hatred for Rome ('the scarlet-clad whore', etc.), such contempt for its clergy ('the senate of Pharisees'), and such heartfelt relief at having at last found his true home in Bethlehem, that we get the impression of wounds still fresh and bleeding.

Didymus's treatise, which argues for the full divinity of the Spirit against the view that he is a creature, was a pioneer work of originality and acuteness. A close analysis of its argument indicates that it dates from the beginnings of the great debate in the Church about the status of the Spirit in the Godhead, perhaps from as early as 355-8.[8] As with most of his writings, the Greek original has perished because of his condemnation for Origenism by the Fifth General Council (553), and we know it exclusively through Jerome's translation—which, incidentally, secured its diffusion and influence in the west.[9] We have every reason to suppose that, with his boundless admiration for Didymus at this time, his version was an extremely faithful one. To be sure, he must have corrected a verse from the prophet Amos[10] which readers of the Greek Septuagint could twist in an unorthodox sense (Didymus knew no Hebrew); but elsewhere he reproduces even his master's mistakes in quoting Scripture. It used to be argued[11] that, with his horror of the 'three hypostases' theology, he must at least have carefully eliminated any trace of this from his version. But if, as now seems probable, the treatise ante-dates the Synod of

---

[6] *Preface to Solomon's Books* (Vulgate) (PL 28, 1241).

[7] *Letter* 36, 1: see above p. 85.

[8] For this date, much earlier than G. Bardy's 'before 381' and 'perhaps contemporary with Basil's *De spir. s.* (373)' (*Didyme l'Aveugle*, Paris, 1910, 20 f.), see E. Staimer, *Die Schrift 'De spiritu sancto' von Didymus dem Blinden von Alexandrien* (Munich, 1960), esp. 117-71.

[9] Augustine, e.g., refers to it in 419 (*Quaest. in Hept.* 2, 25: PL 34, 604), and B. Altaner (*VC* 5, 1951, 116-20) shows that he probably knew it as early as 393-4. A little later the author of *De eccl. dogmatibus* 20 (PL 42, 1216) criticises a point in it. At the council of Florence (1439) the Latin fathers appealed to it by name (*Acta Latina conc. Flor.* [Rome, 1955] VI, 210 [*Sess. Flor.*, coll. viii, univ. xxi]).

[10] In par. 15 (PL 23: 123) he points out that the Hebrew of Am. 4, 13 differs from the LXX and implies that the verse means that God creates the wind, not the Holy Spirit.

[11] E.g. by J. Leipoldt, *Didymus der Blinde* (TU 29: 1905), 10 f., and G. Bardy, op. cit., 21 f.; 73 f.

Alexandria (362) and the acceptance of the new technical vocabulary, the most natural explanation of its absence is that he did not find it in Didymus's original.

For reasons which will shortly become clear, this is the place to mention another translation which Jerome carried out three or four years later, probably in 389/90. This was a rendering of thirty-nine homilies by Origen on select parts of St Luke's Gospel. It was at the urgent petition of Paula and Eustochium, he announces,[12] that he undertook this task, interrupting other work on which he was engaged. Once again he was placing posterity in his debt, for the Greek original of these addresses, short and superficially simple (they show Origen, as Jerome puts it, 'playing children's games'), but rich in mystical spirituality, has disappeared apart from a mass of fragments. Where these are reliable, they confirm that Jerome has followed his avowed policy of reproducing the sense rather than the exact words of his original.[13] Rufinus (he was defending his own practice) was to charge[14] him with introducing 'countless' doctrinal corrections; but while he quotes two examples, the only one that can be checked is entirely trivial. What in fact astonishes us is the large number of passages in which he has incorporated unaltered either theologically dubious speculations of Origen (e.g. about the ultimate transformation of the blessed into angels, or the pre-existence of souls and their incarceration in bodies as the result of a pre-temporal fall), or opinions (e.g. about the need of Mary, indeed of Jesus, for purification) which he must have known to be offensive to contemporary orthodoxy.[15]

What links these two works, apart from their being translations, is the fact that both were deliberately planned as damaging onslaughts on Ambrose of Milan. 'I have preferred,' he remarks[16] of the former, 'to come forward openly as the translator of another man's book than to deck myself out, as certain people do, like an ugly crow with someone else's plumes.' Recently he had read an essay on the Holy Spirit which was sheer plagiary from Greek authors, and incompetent plagiary at that; slick and smooth on the surface, but devoid of dialectical rigour and the power to convince. He similarly confesses[17] that Paula and Eustochium had

---

[12] *Origen's Homilies on Luke* prol. (*GCS* 49, 1). The date must have been somewhere between 387/8, when Ambrose finished his exposition of St Luke, and early 393, when the Origenistic quarrel began.

[13] For his translation policy see *Letter* 57, esp. par. 5. For his translation of these homilies see the remarks of M. Rauer (*GCS* 49, xiii–xv) and H. Crouzel (*SC* 87, 85–7).

[14] *Apol. c. Hier.* 2, 27.

[15] For the former cf. *Hom.* 4; 23; 31; 35; 39 (*GCS* 49, 23; 147; 178; 205; 217). The inclusion of these 'errors' is all the more curious as he was careful to exclude some of them in his earlier commentaries on Pauline epistles (see below). For the latter cf. *Hom.* 14; 17 (*GCS* 49, 85 f.; 106).

[16] *Didymus on the H. Spirit* pref. (*PL* 23: 105).

[17] *Origen's Homilies on Luke* pref. (*GCS* 49, 1 f.).

begged him to translate Origen's homilies because they were so disgusted by a commentary on St Luke which they had been reading. Stylistically frivolous, this had been obtuse in its ideas; its author was an ill-omened, croaking crow which, all darkness itself, was resplendent with bright hues filched from other birds. As Rufinus was to point out with indignation,[18] the unnamed target of these sallies was none other than the revered bishop of Milan, the foremost leader of the Christian west. In 381 Ambrose had written three books on the Holy Spirit, borrowing extensively but without acknowledgment from Greek authorities, especially Didymus and Basil the Great. Some time between 388 and 390 he had published an *Exposition of St Luke's Gospel*, a vast, untidy compilation consisting mainly of addresses delivered from 377 onwards,[19] and again he had made lavish use of Greek sources, including Origen, sometimes incorporating great slabs of borrowed material in a near-literal translation.[20]

This aversion of Jerome for Ambrose has a certain piquancy in his biography. In 376, in the desert of Chalcis, he had coupled[21] Ambrose with Pope Damasus as a pillar of orthodoxy. When he compiled his *Chronicle* in 380/81, he had noted[22] his election as bishop as marking the defeat of Arianism in Italy. In 383/4 he had enthused[23] to Eustochium over 'our own Ambrose's' writings on virginity. From this time onwards, with a very few exceptions which can be explained in terms of self-interest, his references to Ambrose become at best cool, at worst savagely hostile. How are we to account for this sudden reversal of attitude? There was something personal in the vendetta, and it is noticeable that the volte-face first becomes visible, and that the animosity is at its fiercest, during the early years at Bethlehem. The most plausible explanation so far suggested,[24] and one that is in itself very plausible, is that instead of siding with Jerome (as he perhaps expected) during his ordeal at Rome, Ambrose had given his approval to the sentence of expulsion passed by the 'senate of Pharisees'.

(iii)

Not content with mere translation, Jerome now presented himself before the public as a Biblical commentator. The role was not completely new to

[18] *Apol. c. Hier.* 2, 23 f.

[19] For its date and character see F. Homes Dudden, *The Life and Times of St Ambrose* (Oxford, 1935) II, 692–4; G. Tissot, *Ambroise de Milan: Traité sur l'Évangile de Luc* (Paris, 1956), 10–14.

[20] H. C. Puech and P. Hadot have demonstrated (*VC* 13, 1959, 204 ff.) that among the works of Origen he used in this way was the *Dialogue with Heracleides*, which only came to light in 1941.

[21] *Letter* 15, 4.

[22] *Chronicle* A.D. 374 (*GCS* 47, 247).

[23] *Letter* 22, 22.

[24] So A. Paredi in his able article 'S. Gerolamo e S. Ambrogio', *Studi e Testi* 235 (*Mélanges Eugène Tisserant* 5, 1964), 183–98. He has assembled there all the relevant texts.

him. Years before, at Antioch, he had produced a commentary on the prophet Obadiah, which was later to cause him embarrassed blushes,[25] while at Rome in 384, just before Blesilla's death, he had begun preparing one for her on Ecclesiastes.[26] As usual, the pressure now came from Paula and Eustochium, who, ever persistent, clamoured for expositions of St Paul's epistles. At first he resisted; then consented to try out his hand on the last and shortest of them, Philemon.[27] A few days after completing this, he thrust other tasks aside in order to tackle a much more important epistle, Galatians. Just at this moment the sad news reached him from Rome that Albina, Marcella's aged mother, had died, and that her disconsolate daughter yearned for some scriptural medicine for her grief.[28] This gave him a special incentive for pressing on with his new commentary, a sprawling work in three books. Once it was finished, again to meet the demands of Marcella as well as of Paula and Eustochium, he got down to a third commentary, also in three books, on Ephesians.[29] He was now working at breakneck speed, sometimes dictating as many as a thousand lines a day.[30] Finally came a fourth, on the medium-sized Epistle to Titus. The whole enterprise, which occupied only a few months,[31] should probably be assigned to 387/8, for in 401 Rufinus speaks[32] of the commentary on Ephesians as having been written about fifteen years previously.

Although they abound in characteristic personal touches, these four commentaries are in their content largely compilations from earlier exegetes, chiefly Origen. In *On Galatians* and *On Ephesians* Jerome makes some acknowledgment of this. Conscious of his own feeble powers, he states,[33] he had followed Origen, and had also had the expositions of Didymus, Apollinarius and others stored in his mind as he dictated; the alert reader would detect that the resulting product was partly his own work, partly other men's. In *On Ephesians*, where numerous, often lengthy fragments of Origen's original Greek survive[34] and where Rufinus was to pounce on almost a score of passages which slavishly incorporated questionable items of Origenistic theology, the enormous extent of his indebtedness, going far beyond anything his admissions might suggest,

[25] See above pp. 44 f.

[26] *Comm. on Ecclesiastes* pref. (*CCL* 72: 381–2).

[27] *Comm. on Philemon* 1 (*PL* 26: 746).

[28] *Comm. on Galatians* prol. (*PL* 26: 367–8).

[29] *Comm. on Ephesians* II prol. (*PL* 26: 586).

[30] Loc. cit.

[31] Cf. his reference in *Comm. on Titus* 1, 11 (*PL* 26: 704) to his having dictated his Galatians commentary 'a few months back'.

[32] *Apol. c. Hier.* 1, 36.

[33] *Comm. on Galatians* prol.; *Comm. on Ephesians* prol. (*PL* 26: 369–70; 543–4). In the latter passage he confesses to have followed Origen 'in part'.

[34] Cf. *JTS* 3 (1902), 233–44; 398–420; 554–76, where J. A. F. Gregg published a reconstructed text of the Origen fragments with references to the parallel passages in Jerome. C. H. Turner summarised the results in J. Hastings, *Dictionary of the Bible*, extra vol. (1904), 493–5.

is demonstrable. That it was hardly less far-reaching in *On Galatians*, as also in the two smaller commentaries (where he names no authorities), is intrinsically probable, and is confirmed wherever checks are possible.[35] His borrowings from other Greek predecessors, though much less in quantity, were also considerable, and can occasionally be identified.[36] Admittedly, when taxed by Rufinus, Jerome retorted[37] that it was the accepted practice of commentators, whether of Scripture or of secular works, to set down other men's interpretations alongside their own; but we could wish that, after pillorying Ambrose so unmercifully, he had himself been more candid.

His method in all four commentaries is similar. Each has its own prologue; in the case of the two lengthier works each of the three books into which they are divided has its separate one. These contain personal messages to Paula and Eustochium, references to himself, his manner of writing, or his sources, critical discussions (e.g. of the authenticity of Philemon), a summary of the argument, or notes on the circumstances of the letter. The body of the commentary consists of continuous exposition, a verse or group of verses being set down and then discussed. Digressions are frequent, and Jerome repeatedly criticises the Old Latin text before him in the light of the Greek original. He apologises for his colloquial, unliterary style—the result, he pleads,[38] partly of his long unfamiliarity with the classics and preoccupation with Hebrew, partly of his eye-trouble and the impatience of the stenographers to whom he is consequently obliged to dictate, partly of the speed of his composition. But this is conventional self-depreciation. In fact, while unadorned and matter-of-fact as befits a commentary, his prose is generally of high quality, and it is only occasionally that his precipitate hurry leaves an imprint of carelessness.

The exegesis itself, usually derivative, varies in character with the source used as well as with the material commented on. On Philemon and Titus, where the subject-matter scarcely lends itself to allegory, it is mostly practical and to the point. Even so Jerome cannot resist the temptation, at the end of the former, of throwing in quite gratuitously a pseudo-explanation (almost certainly cribbed from Origen) of all the proper names used in the epistle, and then drawing an edifying lesson from their supposed symbolism.[39] In *On Galatians* and, still more, *On Ephesians* we find him, in agreement with his theory, serving up two or more interpre-

---

[35] Cf., e.g., A. Harnack, 'Origenistisches Gut . . . in den Kommentaren des Hieronymus zum Philemon-, Galater-, Epheser-, und Titusbrief' (*TU* 42, 1919, 141–68).

[36] E.g. E. M. Buytaert, *L'héritage littéraire d'Eusèbe d'Émèse* (Louvain, 1949), 175–7, has shown his close dependence on the few fragments that survive of Eusebius of Emesa's commentary on Galatians.

[37] *Apology* 3, 11.

[38] *Comm. on Galatians* III prol.; *on Ephesians* III prol. (PL 26: 485–6; 586).

[39] *Comm. on Philemon* 25 (PL 26: 764).

tations of a passage and leaving the reader to take his pick. Apart from some fanciful etymologies of proper names and an excursion into the symbolism of numbers,[40] there are only sporadic instances of allegorising in *On Galatians*; most of it is an honest, painstaking attempt to discover the Apostle's meaning, and Harnack was justified in describing[41] it as 'the most interesting Latin commentary we possess'. By contrast *On Ephesians* has a more chaotic air, the result partly of its rushed composition, partly of the sheer difficulty of this baffling epistle. Allegorical or 'spiritual' exegesis is slightly more in evidence, but in the main (following perhaps Apollinarius)[42] Jerome struggles valiantly to establish the literal sense.

What is chiefly disappointing, especially in expounding Galatians and Ephesians, is Jerome's failure to understand, much less present adequately, the profound theological issues with which these letters are concerned. As regards his own standpoint, while he is still under the spell of Origen, copying out ideas and interpretations from which he would later recoil, we observe him beginning to reject certain of his master's more controversial speculations.[43] Very characteristic is the way he seizes every opportunity to air his personal opinions or prejudices. Thus he rebukes with relish contemporary bishops who drink to excess, or are so stuck up that they scarcely deign to look at ordinary mortals, or educate their children in secular literature and encourage them to read lewd comedies.[44] Again, he declaims against the increasingly elaborate music of church services; and, faced with St Paul's ban on observing fixed days and seasons, he produces a sophisticated defence of Christian holy days and festivals.[45] Particularly interesting is his view that in the apostolic age the terms 'bishop' and 'presbyter' were synonymous, each church being governed by a committee of coequal presbyters. The emergence of the episcopate proper, he argues (much to the embarrassment of Catholics down the centuries), was due, not to any ordinance of the Lord, but to ecclesiastical custom, with the object of excluding divisions.[46] But we

---

[40] For etymologies cf. *Comm. on Galatians* 1, 7; 1, 21; for number symbolism cf. *Comm. on Galatians* 1, 18 (*PL* 26: 382; 397; 395).

[41] For allegorising cf. *Comm. on Galatians* 1, 17; 5, 17 (*PL* 26: 394; 502 f.). For Harnack's opinion see *TU* 42, 147.

[42] Cf. Grützmacher II, 40. For Apollinarius's exegesis see above pp. 54 f.

[43] For a good discussion see Grützmacher II, 38–40. As illustrating Jerome's changed attitude he cites his rejection of Origen's theories that all souls pre-existed and that God's punishment for sin consists in the sin itself and the anguished conscience (*Comm. on Ephesians* i, 4; 5, 6: *PL* 26: 550; 644).

[44] *Comm. on Titus* 1, 7; *on Galatians* 4, 13; *on Ephesians* 6, 4 (*PL* 26: 699 f.; 458 f.; 666).

[45] *Comm. on Ephesians* 5, 19; *on Galatians* 4, 10 (*PL* 26: 652; 456 f.). Many of these 'personal' comments are likely to have been borrowed from Origen or others.

[46] *Comm. on Titus* 1, 5 (*PL* 26: 694 f.). For another strong expression of the same view, see *Letter* 146 (to Evangelus). For Roman Catholic discussions attempting to save Jerome's orthodoxy, see J. Forget, art. 'Jérôme', *DTC* VIII, 965–76; Y. Bodin, *Saint Jérôme et l'église* (Paris, 1966), 196–204.

should look more closely at his treatment of Gal. 2, 11–14, for, years later (as we shall discover),[47] it was to land him in a protracted debate with Augustine.

In this famous passage St Paul states that he had rebuked St Peter at Antioch 'because he was in the wrong'. After eating food with Gentile converts (conduct reckoned defiling under the Jewish Law), he had drawn back through fear of Judaising Christians and reverted to separate meals. At great length Jerome contends that there was no real difference, either of principle or of practice, between the two Apostles. Both were fully aware that, as Christians, the Law was no longer binding on them. St Peter's apparent backsliding, he explained, was a tactical measure temporarily adopted by the Apostle of the circumcision to win Jews over to Christianity. St Paul's rebuke, similarly, was not seriously intended or taken as such; he could scarcely censure St Peter since he himself, on several occasions recorded in Acts, deliberately feigned compliance with the Law for precisely the same purpose. Thus St Peter was not 'in the wrong' in his eyes, but in the eyes of the Gentile Christians with whom he had formerly eaten. St Paul deemed it politic, however, in order to reassert the primacy of grace over the Mosaic Law, to go through the motions of anger—'to correct St Peter's pretence of observing the Law . . . by himself pretending to reprimand him'. This exegesis strikes modern students as a tortuous and fantastic evasion of the plain sense of the passage, but it was one which Jerome had taken over from Origen and a long succession of Greek commentators.[48] Their reason for resorting to it, as Jerome points out, was to provide an answer to pagan critics, especially the formidable Porphyry (*c.* 232–*c.* 305), who had exploited the clash of the two Apostles, and the inconsistent behaviour of the Prince of the Apostles, in their efforts to discredit the Church.[49]

An intriguing question, the answer to which can only show Jerome in an unflattering light, is raised by his remark[50] that no one had written a Latin commentary on Galatians before him. He qualifies this by immediately adding that he was of course aware that Marius Victorinus, the Neoplatonist professor and convert who had lectured at Rome when he was a boy, had published commentaries on some of St Paul's letters, but dismisses these on the ground that, for all his secular culture, their author

[47] See below pp. 218 f.; 269–72.

[48] Thus in *Letter* 112, 4 and 6 Jerome informs Augustine that he had followed Origen, and mentions others who had taken the same line (Didymus the Blind, Apollinarius, Eusebius of Emesa, Theodore of Heraclea, John Chrysostom).

[49] The most accurate and satisfactory discussion of Jerome's exegesis is P. Auvray, 'Saint Jérôme et saint Augustin: La controverse au sujet de l'incident d'Antioche' (*Recherches de science religieuse* 29, 1939, 594–610). He skilfully refutes the widely held view that Jerome presupposes collusion or concerted action between the two Apostles.

[50] *Comm. on Galatians* prol. (*PL* 26: 368 f.).

was an ignoramus in Scripture studies. What is puzzling here is Jerome's complete silence about the anonymous scholar who, because his writings were for centuries attributed to Ambrose, was designated Ambrosiaster by Erasmus, and who about 380 had produced at Rome the first exposition in Latin of all thirteen of the epistles, including Galatians. This remarkable work, much more original than Jerome's and utterly unlike it in its terseness, astringency, and undivided concern for the literal sense, must have been known to him; indeed his familiarity with it, as with other products of Ambrosiaster's pen, is demonstrable.[51] Yet not only does he here in effect deny its existence, but when he came to write *Famous Men*, supposedly a complete catalogue of Christian writers, he excluded, we must infer deliberately, this unquestionably outstanding exegete.

It is not easy to find reasons for his attitude, and the obscurity in which Ambrosiaster's personality and life are shrouded does not help. The problem seemed to be solved when the mysterious exegete was identified with Isaac, the converted Jew who had brought a charge of adultery against Pope Damasus; Jerome might fairly be expected to ignore his patron's traducer. But this identification cannot be sustained.[52] It has sometimes been proposed that Jerome may have been jealous of his brilliant predecessor; but if it had been merely a matter of rivalry, it is much more likely that he would have castigated an author who had neglected the whole rich tradition of Greek exegesis. Something deeper and more personal, we may be sure, was involved, and the clue is provided by Ambrosiaster's outspoken preference for the Old Latin version of the New Testament to the Greek original. We recall[53] how infuriated Jerome had been by the 'two-legged asses' who had criticised his attempts to improve the Old Latin of the Gospels. There is convincing evidence that Ambrosiaster was one of them, and that the two scholars clashed on precisely this issue. We may consider the issue scarcely worth getting worked up about; but in the eyes of one so sensitive, and so petty-minded, as Jerome, his opponent amply merited relegation to oblivion.[54]

(iv)

Jerome sometimes spoke[55] as if he planned commentaries on all St Paul's letters, but after finishing his study of Titus he suddenly threw up the project, and never again came back to it. Instead, spurred on (we may

---

[51] Cf. H. Vogels, 'Ambrosiaster und Hieronymus', *RB* 66 (1965), 14–19.

[52] For the affair see *Coll. Avellina, ep.* 13: 'disgraceful calumnies' (*CSEL* 35, 56 f.); *Liber pontificalis* 39: 'adultery' (ed. L. Duchesne, 212). For a discussion see C. Martini, *Ambrosiaster* (Rome, 1944), 154–9.

[53] See above pp. 89 f.

[54] For a good discussion see H. Vogels, art. cit. above.

[55] So *Comm. on Philemon* 1 (PL 26: 746).

suspect) by his growing mastery of Hebrew, he took in hand an Old Testament book, the fascinating but profoundly worldly Ecclesiastes, with its refrain 'All is vanity' and its advice to enjoy life's pleasures while one can. In the preface[56] he reminds Paula and Eustochium that at Blesilla's request he had made a start on this commentary about five years earlier at Rome, but had abandoned it in the anguish of her sudden death. This enables us to date the work to approximately 389. In the same preface Jerome explains his method. This was not to follow any previous authority, but to make his own translation from the Hebrew, adapting it however to the familiar language of the Latinised Septuagint where this did not differ substantially from the original, and also to take account of the rival Greek versions (Aquila, Symmachus, Theodotion). This somewhat arbitrary compromise reveals that Jerome had now reached an important turning-point. He had become aware of the paramount authority of the Hebrew, but was not yet prepared to base himself exclusively on it. His motive, he confesses, was to avoid discouraging his readers by too much novelty (he had bitter memories of the hostile reaction to his revision of the Gospels) without betraying what his scholarly conscience knew to be the truth.

The remark that he had followed no previous authority thus refers to the independence of his translation, not (as many have inferred)[57] of his exegesis. The commentary itself refutes the latter interpretation, for it abounds in references to, occasionally direct quotations from, earlier exegetes. Sometimes Jerome names them (Origen, Apollinarius, Gregory Thaumaturgus, Victorinus of Pettau, Lactantius), sometimes he is content with a vague 'as others say', 'as many think', etc. Apart from direct references, his large-scale borrowings from Origen in particular are easily recognisable throughout. For example, he reproduces[58] as if it were his own Origen's suggestion that of the three books attributed to him Solomon had intended Proverbs for children, Ecclesiastes for adults, Song of Songs for the elderly, and that they are related to each other as ethics, physics, and logic in philosophy. Again, he cites,[59] without a hint of criticism (although he was later to deny this), Origen's speculations about the sun being a living spirit and about human souls being imprisoned in bodies as the penalty for pre-temporal sin. An original feature is the extensive use he makes of contemporary rabbinical exegesis, which he had picked up from the Jew with whom he read the book in Hebrew. From this he had learned of the doubts the Jewish authorities had had

---

[56] *Comm. on Ecclesiastes* prol. (*CCL* 72: 381–2).

[57] E.g. O. Zöckler, *Hieronymus* (Gotha, 1865), 166; A. Penna, *S. Gerolamo* (Turin-Rome, 1949), 149.

[58] *Comm. on Ecclesiastes* 1, 1 (*CCL* 72: 383 f.).

[59] *Comm. on Ecclesiastes* 1, 6; 4, 3 (*CCL* 72: 388; 419). For his denial see *Against John* 17.

about the propriety of including Ecclesiastes in the canon: only the magnificent finale, 'Fear God and keep his commandments; for this is the whole duty of man', had earned it a passport.

In trying to expound Ecclesiastes Jerome faced much more formidable difficulties than he knew; no one in the fourth century, Jew or Christian, possessed the equipment for the task. In view of its apparent claim he was bound to assume that King Solomon was its author, and not (as now seems likely) a pessimistic rationalist of 250–180 B.C. whose belief in a personal God had grown dim. The only way he could wrest a Christian message from its melancholy fatalism was by the wholesale use of allegory, and from this, devout Origenist as he still was, he did not shrink. He even sometimes suggests,[60] though without following the line consistently through, that it is Christ himself who speaks to us in the guise of the Preacher. His general procedure is to propose a broadly literal interpretation of a passage, and then move on to one or more alternative 'spiritual' ones, thus 'not neglecting the poor matter-of-fact sense in our pursuit of its spiritual riches'.[61] An example chosen at random is the Preacher's statement that 'one generation goes, another comes . . . The sun arises and the sun goes down'. Its straightforward meaning is as obvious to Jerome as to us, but he prefers[62] to read the first half as a reference to the supersession of the Synagogue by the Church, the second as pointing to Christ, the sun of righteousness which rises for God-fearing men and goes down for false prophets. His treatment[63] of 'Go, eat your bread joyfully, and drink your wine with a merry heart', is typical. If the words are to be taken as they stand, he argues, the Preacher is graphically rehearsing the teaching of Epicurus, only to expose its hollowness in the sequel. But a far more satisfying interpretation is that men whose deeds are pleasing to God can never lack spiritual enjoyment. Even the food and drink the Preacher bids us treat as a gift from God should properly be understood as Christ's body and blood, on which we feed both in the eucharist and in our reading of Scripture.[64]

On every page we come across similarly breath-taking transformations of the plain meaning of the Preacher's musings, all set out in colourful and rhythmic prose. Stylistically as in imaginative virtuosity, this commentary surpasses those on the Pauline letters. For the modern student, intent on discovering what Ecclesiastes is really about, Jerome's brilliant exegetical essay is worse than useless. But judged by the standards of his age, when Christian men took it for granted that the true sense of the Old Testament

---

[60] E.g. *Comm. on Ecclesiastes* 1, 1; 2, 7 (*CCL* 72: 385; 399).
[61] *Comm. on Ecclesiastes* 2, 24–26 (*CCL* 72: 406).
[62] *Comm. on Ecclesiastes* 1, 4 f. (*CCL* 72: 387).
[63] *Comm. on Ecclesiastes* 9, 7 (*CCL* 72: 461 f.).
[64] *Comm. on Ecclesiastes* 3, 13 (*CCL* 72: 413).

was the spiritual one lurking beneath the surface which pointed forward to Christ and his Church, it was a *tour de force* of edification and illumination. The author of Ecclesiastes would have been surprised had he known it, but Jerome had never doubted that, by using the magic key of allegory to unlock its secrets, he could fortify Blesilla in her ascetic resolve.[65] In the same assurance he dedicated it now to her memory and offered it to Paula and Eustochium as a handbook to the life of Christian withdrawal.

---

[65] *Comm. on Ecclesiastes* prol. (*CCL* 72: 381–2). He says that he read the book with her 'in order to challenge her to despise this world (ut eam ad contemptum istius mundi provocarem)'.

XV

From Septuagint to Hebrew
Verity

(i)

Even by themselves these earlier commentaries eloquently attest the consuming interest Jerome was now devoting to the Bible. They were accompanied or quickly followed, still within these first half-dozen years at Bethlehem, by further works which show how he was widening his range, deepening his grasp of Scripture, and gaining a firm sense of direction.

First came a trilogy which modern readers find dryly technical, but which greatly enhanced his scholarly reputation. Ostensibly intended to supply the west with aids it had hitherto lacked, we may suspect that Jerome also found it invaluable in his own studies. It comprised an etymological dictionary of Biblical proper names, a gazetteer of places mentioned in Scripture, and a critical examination of difficult passages of Genesis. The prefaces indicate that this was their order of publication, but the references they severally make to each other suggest that he was working on all three simultaneously. This must have been somewhere around 389/91, for the third, *Hebrew Questions*, was the work he temporarily interrupted when, to comply with the entreaties of Paula and Eustochium (more accurately, to give vent to his spite against Ambrose), he made his translation of Origen's homilies on St Luke.[1]

His *Hebrew Names*, or *Onomasticon*, belonged to a genre much favoured in antiquity not only by Christians but, long before them, by pagans and Jews.[2] Homer, Hesiod, the Old Testament (to mention but a few) demonstrate how fascinated ancient man was by etymologies, especially of personal names and place-names. For Christians the fascination was intensified by their belief that the names used in the Bible contained hidden meaning which, as Augustine claimed,[3] were wonderfully helpful in solving its mysteries. This (reinforced by pressure from friends), and not

---

[1] See above p. 143. For their date and mutual relation see Cavallera II, 28.

[2] For a useful summary consult I. Opelt, 'Etymologie', *RAC* 6, cols. 797–844.

[3] *De doct. christ.* 2, 58; 141 (*CSEL* 80, 50; 74). Cf. also Origen, *Comm. in Ioh.* II, 33 (*GCS* 10, 90 f.).

philological interest as such, was Jerome's motive in compiling his book: he knew just how useful exegetically it would be.[4] Thus he lists the names alphabetically, treating each of the selected books separately, and setting down against each name its presumed meaning, or alternative meanings, on the assumption that it is derived from Hebrew. Jerome firmly believed that he was restoring, and vastly improving, a similar work by Origen, who had himself revised and, by adding New Testament names, christianised a much earlier compilation by Philo, the famous Jewish exegete and thinker (d. 45). It is today accepted that, while his assumption of a Philonic-Origenistic original was mistaken, the word-lists on which he worked (he speaks of several confused, mutually discordant 'exemplars') went back at any rate to the third century.[5] This is confirmed for the New Testament section by the inclusion of the Epistle of Barnabas, which both Eusebius and Jerome (when writing on his own) rejected from the canon.[6]

This accumulation of 'etymologies' makes an extraordinary impression on anyone even moderately acquainted with Hebrew. It is obvious that, while a minority of the derivations are correct or nearly so, the great majority are erroneous, often to the point of fantasy. Particularly bewildering is the way in which Greek or Latin names are assigned meanings on the basis of similar Hebrew sounds. To be fair, Jerome frequently corrects his sources, proposing alternative, sometimes superior derivations; and he labours to restore the original Hebrew name-forms. On occasion he confesses that such-and-such a meaning can only be extracted from a Greek or Latin name 'by violence', and that a straight Greek or Latin derivation is more natural. Even so, the suspicion is unavoidable that, with his extensive knowledge of languages, he should have steered clear of the more blatant of these absurdities. Yet if we are not to be anachronistic, we should temper criticism by recalling three simple facts. First, Jerome took it for granted,[7] like most Christians of the early centuries, that all languages descended from Hebrew, the original speech of mankind until the presumptuous building of the tower of Babel. Secondly, neither he nor his authorities could have the slightest understanding of scientific etymology, much less of the special problems raised by the formation of Hebrew names. They had therefore to rely on arbitrary guesswork. Thirdly, their primary aim was to discover meanings which were instruc-

---

[4] So the preface: 'rei ipsius utilitate commotus' (CCL 72: 1–2). The preface is the source of other details in this paragraph.

[5] Cf. F. Wutz, Onomastica Sacra (TU 41: 1914). Every student is indebted to this thorough and masterly examination.

[6] Cf. Eusebius, Hist. eccl. 3, 25, 4; 6, 13, 6; Jerome, Famous Men 6; Comm. on Ezekiel 43, 19 (CCL 75: 531).

[7] E.g. Letter 18A, 6; Comm. on Zephaniah 3, 18 ('... linguam Hebraicam omnium linguarum esse matricem') (CCL 76A: 730). Cf. also, e.g., Origen, Hom. in Num. 11, 4; Augustine, De civ. dei 16, 11, 1 (GCS 30, 84; CSEL 40, 146).

tive or edifying. This Jerome did with no small success, and it is not surprising that his manual was avidly studied all down the middle ages, indeed until the birth of scientifically based Hebrew scholarship.

The gazetteer, or *Book of Places*,[8] was a reasonably close rendering of Eusebius's widely used *Onomasticon*, published *c.* 330. There was already a Latin version in existence, but it was a slovenly one, Jerome alleges,[9] by a scarcely literate translator (his name, perhaps mercifully, is lost). Eusebius had listed the place-names alphabetically, with brief topographical and historical notes; and his catalogue included not only towns and villages mentioned in Scripture, but mountains, plains, rivers, even a few heathen gods (e.g. the Ammonite Milcom mentioned at Jeremiah 49, 1). Even so it was sadly incomplete, for the New Testament (for example) drawing only on the Gospels and neglecting Acts, with its multitude of place-names. As a result it was neither a straightforward name-list of the Holy Land nor an exhaustive catalogue of Bible places.

Jerome's preface suggests that he had made radical changes, both of omission and of correction, in Eusebius's text. The omissions are in fact surprisingly few; even the heathen gods, which seem clearly out of place, are retained. He has, of course, rearranged the work to comply with the Latin alphabet. On the other hand, he does not supply the many names left out by Eusebius; and while he corrects a large number of his mistakes, he leaves far more either without comment or with a reference (not always verifiable) to a fuller treatment in his *Hebrew Questions*. Many of his alterations are trivial: abbreviations, explanatory glosses, a reminiscence or two of Roman history or a Latin author. There is some interesting fresh material consisting of local information derived either from Jews he has conversed with or from personal information; but these latter items are curiously meagre, except for the sites he had visited with Paula on their pilgrimage, and bear out the view that he did not make the extensive trips throughout Palestine which are often attributed to him. Still, he provides useful notes on churches which have been built (e.g. at Sychar, where Jesus talked with the Samaritan woman), or holy places which have been identified (e.g. Sebaste, with the remains of John the Baptist), since Eusebius's time. For all its defects the work speedily became an indispensable guidebook for pilgrims and an authoritative manual on Palestine for western scholars.

The third, perhaps most interesting, member of the trilogy, the *Hebrew Questions*, has a special significance in Jerome's evolution as a Biblical

---

[8] This is the name ('Liber locorum') he gives it in the preface to *Hebrew Names* (CCL 72: 3–4).

[9] Cf. his preface, printed with the rest of the book in E. Klostermann's critical edition of Eusebius's *Onomasticon* (GCS 11). Much of this and the following paragraph is based on Klostermann's Introduction, esp. xxiv–xxix.

scholar. Like the glossary of names, it belongs to a genre much in vogue in the early centuries (we have an example from Augustine's pen which can be usefully compared with it), taking the form not so much of a continuous commentary as of a pointed discussion of problem texts— selected in this case from Genesis.[10] Since Jerome speaks of planning to extend this to the whole Bible,[11] many have inferred that what has survived is only a fragment of a much vaster whole; but while there are pointers to his having made a start on such an enterprise, it is unlikely that he ever got very far with it.

What gives the book its distinctive character is, first, the large-scale and, on the whole, sympathetic use it makes of contemporary rabbinical exegesis. This must have been an eye-opener to the Christian public of the day, to which 'the Hebrew traditions' (as he calls them) were largely a sealed book. Equally striking is its deliberate avoidance of mystical or allegorical exegesis. In his commentaries on the Old Testament Jerome was to give free rein to this in his effort to discover the underlying sense of Scripture, but here for once we observe him sticking firmly to questions of fact—linguistic, geographical, historical—or establishing what he believes to be the true text and its literal signification. It is intriguing to notice that a high proportion of the explanations he supplies are taken textually from the *Antiquities* (Book I) of Josephus (*c.* 37–*c.* 100), the only non-Christian historian he knew thoroughly and whom he had hailed as the Greek Livy, but whom he here avoids mentioning except to criticise him.[12] Most important of all, however, is the fact that, in discussing his difficult passages from Genesis, Jerome invariably scrutinises them in the light of the Hebrew original. When commenting on Ecclesiastes, he had been at a transitional stage, still preferring the familiar Septuagint when it did not deviate too drastically from the Hebrew. In the *Questions*, having lost faith in the inspiration of the Seventy, he was opening a deliberate campaign in favour of 'the Hebrew verity' ('Hebraica veritas'), as he was henceforth to call it, by seeking to remove the widespread suspicion and distrust people felt for it.

He was fully alive, of course, to the outcry he was bound to provoke by seeming to cast doubts on the Septuagint-based version universally used by Christians and commonly believed to be divinely inspired. His preface reveals that he was already being called upon to answer for his

[10] Cf. F. Cavallera's essay in *Miscellanea Agostiniana* 2 (Rome, 1931), 359–72: also C. G. F. Heinrici, 'Zur patristischen Aporienliteratur' (*Abhandl. der philol.-hist. kl. der kgl. sächs. Gesellsch. der Wissenschaft* 27: Leipzig, 1909).

[11] *Hebrew Questions* pref. (*CCL* 72: 301–2). Cf. the references in *Book of Places* and *Hebrew Questions* itself to discussions not found in the text as it stands.

[12] On this see P. Courcelle, *Late Latin Writers and their Greek Sources* (ET, Cambridge, Mass., 1969), 83. Many, but by no means all, of the borrowings are indicated in the footnotes in *PL* 23. In *Letter* 22, 35 Josephus is called the Greek Livy.

presumption.[13] Exceptionally long, it opens with a fiercely abusive attack on the 'filthy swine who grunt as they trample on pearls'. Then he protests that his work should not be deemed to imply any disparagement of the Septuagint. Its authors, the famous Seventy, he ingeniously argues, had felt obliged to suppress the true drift of the Old Testament, especially its prophecies of Christ, to avoid giving Ptolemy Philadelphus (285–246 B.C.), for whom they made their translation, the impression that the Jews worshipped a second God instead of being, as he admiringly believed, monotheists. He makes the further point that, when the evangelists, St Paul, and Christ himself cited the Old Testament, they used texts which often differed from the ones found in the ordinary Christian's Bible. Finally, he pointed to the great Origen, who in his popular addresses had followed the Septuagint, but in his more scientific studies had resorted to 'the Hebrew verity'.

(ii)

Two very different works, both on the Psalter, belong to much the same date: seven tractates on Psalms 10–16, and a series of notes (*Commentarioli*) covering the majority of the Psalms. The former he lists with his writings to date in *Famous Men*;[14] they were probably serious expositions, Origenistic in character, but have all disappeared save possibly that on Psalm 15.[15] He had compiled the latter, he explains,[16] because, when reading through Origen's *Enchiridion* on the Psalter with a close friend (it is a tempting guess, but only a guess, that this was Rufinus), he had come across a host of passages either touched on superficially or not treated at all; he had therefore collected the master's comments on them from his larger works and set them down summarily. Origen was thus his exclusive source, and he did not hesitate to incorporate his 'dubious' opinions without hint of criticism.[17] He also included frequent, usually hostile, references to rabbinical exegesis; and his Latin text of the Psalms, it is worth noting, was not identical with any existing version, either by himself or anyone else, but was a fresh rendering from the Greek with careful attention to the Hebrew.[18] For whatever reason (did he consider it too slight a work?) he refrained from mentioning it in *Famous Men*, although in controversy

---

[13] *CCL* 72: 301–4.

[14] *Famous Men* 135.

[15] Text in G. Morin, *Anecdota Maredsolana* III, iii (Maredsous, 1903), 10–31.

[16] *Short Comments* prol. (*CCL* 72, 177 f.). They were rediscovered by G. Morin and published in *Anecdota Maredsolana* III, i. xix–114 (Maredsous, 1895): reprinted in *CCL* 72.

[17] For examples see *Short Comments on* Ps. 78, 34; 136, 1 (*CCL* 72, 216; 241: the incarceration of souls in bodies).

[18] See A. Vaccari, *Scritti di erudizione e di filologia* I (Rome, 1952), 213 f.

with Rufinus in 401 he specifically speaks[19] of his *Commentarioli* in a context which implies that they antedated his translation of the Psalter from the Hebrew.

Both these are relatively unimportant productions. Indeed not only they, but all the other works discussed in this and the preceding chapter fade into insignificance when compared with the formidable project to which he now set his hand, but which had probably been occupying his thoughts at least since he first settled in Bethlehem. This was nothing less than a thorough-going revision of the current Latin version of the entire Old Testament. At first he seems to have been undecided as to the principles on which he should carry this out. The conviction was steadily forcing itself upon him that the original Hebrew must be its basis, but for a time he was either not ready or reluctant to accept the challenge. Instead he set about revising the accepted version based on the Greek Septuagint, applying, however, critical methods and making comparisons both with the other Greek versions and with the Hebrew. He was greatly helped by the ready access he now had, in the library of nearby Caesarea, to Origen's Hexapla,[20] which contained all these, and in its fifth column presented a critical text of the Septuagint with signs (obeli and asterisks) indicating where the Greek was redundant or defective as compared with the Hebrew. A feature of his amended edition was the transference of these bodily into it.

This cautious half-measure, which nevertheless exasperated conservative susceptibilities,[21] must have been undertaken in the earlier half of our period (386–92); Jerome must have judged it pointless once he had been seized of the overriding claims of 'the Hebrew verity'. The Psalter was the first book he tackled. He had already prepared a revision of the Old Latin Psalter at Rome,[22] but the discovery of Origen's more scientific text and his own advance in critical skill had opened his eyes to its defects. Little though he could have guessed it, this second revision had a dazzling future in store for it. Introduced into Gaul and thus designated the Gallican Psalter, it gradually triumphed over his later translation of the Psalms from Hebrew, and became the Psalter both of the Vulgate and of the Roman Breviary (only to be superseded by the New Latin Psalter in 1945). In addition he produced similarly amended Latin versions of Job, 1 and 2 Chronicles, and the books attributed to Solomon (Proverbs, Ecclesiastes, Song of Songs). For Chronicles, which abounded in proper names defectively reproduced in the Greek and Latin codices, he received

---

[19] *Apology* 1, 19. Some regard the omission from *Famous Men* 135 as proof that the work was posterior to 392–3. But apart from the clear pointer of *Apology* 1, 19, it is unlikely that it would have contained such adulation of Origen if it had been later than *Famous Men*.

[20] For this see above p. 135.

[21] Cf. his laments in the prefaces to Psalms, Job, Chronicles (*PL* 29, 120; 61; 403 f.).

[22] See above p. 89.

special assistance from a learned, highly respected Jew from Tiberias, who read the book through with him from start to finish.[23]

Although the question remains open, it is very unlikely that he carried his revision of the Latinised Septuagint beyond these books. He himself often speaks[24] as though he had corrected the whole Old Testament, but his generalised language is probably attributable in part to his habitual exaggeration, in part to an apologetic eagerness to impress critics with the devoted work he had done on the Septuagint. What is significant is that, when he later recommended his revision of this to readers reluctant to use his translation from the Hebrew, the only books he named were the ones mentioned above.[25] The likelihood is that, by the time he had finished them, he was already convinced of the supreme authority of the Hebrew, and realised the futility of tinkering with what was, after all, only a translation of a translation. This fading of interest may also explain his failure both to mention this abortive revision in *Famous Men* and to go to the trouble of preserving the portion of it he had completed. While the Psalter, Job (in two MSS), and Song of Songs (in a single MS)[26] have survived, 1 and 2 Chronicles and the Salomonic books have entirely disappeared; and in 416, when Augustine asked to see his revised Septuagint, Jerome was reduced to confessing[27] that he had lost practically all of it (had he kept only one copy?) through someone's sharp practice.

(iii)

It was around 390 that Jerome at last took the plunge ('with my eyes open I thrust my hand into the flame'),[28] and embarked on an entirely fresh translation of the Old Testament based directly on the Hebrew. His intensive Biblical studies over the past decade had finally convinced him that, however revolutionary it might seem and whatever hostility it might provoke, the only ultimately satisfying Bible for Christians was one which reproduced the Hebrew original. In principle, of course, he was entirely right, even allowing for the fact (which he could not possibly know) that, being older, the Septuagint in many passages preserves a more ancient reading than the currently accepted Hebrew text (substantially the same as

---

[23] *Preface to Chronicles* (LXX) (*PL* 29, 401 f.). This preface, it should be noted, contains the only passage in which Jerome seems to admit that the LXX is inspired by the Holy Spirit: an admission he probably makes in deference to the views of the two Roman friends to whom he dedicated the revision.

[24] E.g. *Apology* 2, 24; 3, 25; *Letters* 71, 5; 106, 2.

[25] Cf. *Prefaces to Psalms, Job, Chronicles, Solomon's Books* (Vulgate) (*PL* 28, 1126; 1084; 1326; 1245 f.).

[26] *Vat. Lat.* 5704 (sixth century). Its identification was made only in the early 1950s by A. Vaccari: see op. cit. II, 121–46.

[27] *Letter* 134, 2.

[28] *Preface to Isaiah* (Vulgate) (*PL* 28, 772).

our 'Massoretic' text). But he had an apologetic inducement which carried even more weight. It had become translucently clear, to himself and certain close friends, that their only hope of demolishing the arguments of Jewish critics was to take their stand on a text of the Old Testament which both parties agreed was authentic. 'It is one thing,' he declared,[29] 'to sing the psalms in churches of Christian believers, quite another to make answer to Jews who cavil at the words.' His whole object, he claimed,[30] in sweating over this translation from a strange tongue was to stop the Jews once for all from taunting the Church with the falseness of its Scriptures. He wished to deprive them of their present vantage-point for deriding Christians, and to refute them on their own ground by appealing, when controversy arose, to a version which they had to acknowledge as indisputably accurate and which nevertheless spoke unmistakably of the coming of Christ.[31]

Jerome's conversion to 'the Hebrew verity' carried with it an important corollary—his acceptance also of the Hebrew canon, or list of books properly belonging to the Old Testament. Since the early Church had read its Old Testament in Greek, it had taken over without question the so-called Alexandrian canon used in the Greek-speaking Jewish communities outside Palestine. This had included those books (Wisdom, Ecclesiasticus, Judith, etc.) which are variously described as deutero-canonical or as the Apocrypha. Around the end of the first century, however, official Judaism had formally excluded these, limiting the canon to the books which figure in English Bibles as the Old Testament proper. Since Origen's time it had been recognised that there was a distinction between the Jewish canon and the list acknowledged by Christians, but most writers preferred to place the popular and widely used deutero-canonical books in a special category (e.g. calling them 'ecclesiastical') rather than to discard them. Jerome now takes a much firmer line. After enumerating the 'twenty-two' (or perhaps twenty-four) books recognised by the Jews, he decrees[32] that any books outside this list must be reckoned 'apocryphal': 'They are not in the canon.' Elsewhere, while admitting that the Church reads books like Wisdom and Ecclesiasticus which are

[29] *Preface to Psalms* (Vulgate) (PL 28, 1123–8): addressed to his friend Sophronius, who had had difficulties with a Jew who claimed that the texts to which he appealed read differently in the Hebrew.

[30] *Preface to Isaiah* (Vulgate) (PL 28, 774).

[31] *Preface to Joshua*; *to Isaiah* (Vulgate) (PL 28, 464; 773 f.); *Apology* 3, 25. Augustine, who himself disapproved of Jerome's project (see below pp. 218; 264; 266), had to admit that, while the Jews found the LXX full of errors, they acknowledged the accuracy of Jerome's version (*De civ. dei* 18, 43: CSEL 40, 336).

[32] *Preface to Samuel and Kings* (Vulgate) (PL 28, 555–7). The number twenty-two was obtained by grouping two or more books (e.g. the twelve Minor Prophets) together as one; it had the attraction of being the number of letters of the Hebrew alphabet. He reached the number twenty-four by including Ruth and Lamentations separately.

strictly uncanonical, he insists[33] on their being used solely 'for edifying the people, not for the corroboration of ecclesiastical doctrines'. This was the attitude which, with temporary concessions for tactical or other reasons,[34] he was to maintain for the rest of his life—in theory at any rate, for in practice he continued to cite them as if they were Scripture.[35] Again what chiefly moved him was the embarrassment he felt at having to argue with Jews on the basis of books which they rejected or even (e.g. the stories of Susanna, or of Bel and the Dragon) found frankly ridiculous.

To judge by his statement in *Famous Men*,[36] 'I translated the Old Testament from the Hebrew,' one might infer that he had completed the gigantic task by the end of 392. Such a sweeping claim, however, is entirely in character and should be treated with reserve. We know that it was not until 405/6 that he reached his goal. Nevertheless the amount he achieved in these two or three years was impressive by any standard. To us moderns his logical course would have been to start with Genesis and then treat the other books in the order in which they stood in the Hebrew Bible; but Jerome's order was dictated by the needs of the moment, even more by the demands (often agitated) of friends. Thus the books of Samuel and Kings seem to have been the first to appear in his new version. Although this has been questioned,[37] it is made practically certain by their preface,[38] which envisages the Old Testament as a whole, defining its contents and limits and setting out Jerome's programme. Thus he pointedly describes it as 'this prologue to the Scriptures, this helmeted (so to speak) exordium to all the books I am translating from Hebrew into Latin'; and goes on to add, 'Read therefore first my Samuel and Kings.' It was perhaps the relative ease of these historical books that persuaded him to try his prentice hand on them. Very soon, however, he was at work on the Psalter, the Prophets, and Job. In *Famous Men*[39] he reports that his friend Sophronius had already made an 'elegant Greek translation' of his renderings of the former two from Hebrew; while from a letter[40]

---

[33] *Preface to Solomon's Books* (Vulgate) (*PL* 28, 1242 f.).

[34] E.g. in defending himself against Rufinus he suggests that his objection to the passages in Daniel which do not appear in the Hebrew does not represent his personal opinion but the criticism of Jews (*Apology* 2, 33). Again, he translated the non-canonical Judith only to satisfy the insistent requests of Chromatius and Heliodorus (*Preface to Judith*: *PL* 29, 37–9). For his consistency in theory, cf. the advice he gave Laeta in 400–1 on the education of the younger Paula: 'Let her steer clear of the apocrypha' (*Letter* 107, 12).

[35] See the impressive, albeit selective, list given by Penna, 387–9 (often introduced by 'it is written', 'Scripture says', etc.).

[36] *Famous Men* 135.

[37] E.g. by Cavallera: II, 28 f.

[38] *PL* 28, 547–58. He describes it as 'helmeted' ('galeatus') because in it he is arming himself in advance against possible critics. For the meaning of the term see I. Cecchetti, 'S. Girolamo e il suo "Prologus galeatus"', *Miscellanea Antonio Piolanti* II, 81–90 (*Lateranum* 30: Rome, 1964).

[39] *Famous Men* 134.

[40] *Letter* 48, 4.

despatched to Rome in 394 we learn that copies of the two latter were already available for the borrowing.

When eventually completed, this new version of the Old Testament, along with his earlier revision of the Gospels, was to be Jerome's crowning literary achievement. By a gradual process extending from the sixth to the ninth century it was to become accepted (with the rest of the New Testament revised by an unknown hand or hands) as the standard, or 'Vulgate', Latin text of the Bible, and as such to exert an incalculable influence not only on the piety but on the languages and literature of western Europe. In the Old Testament, with which we are here concerned, we see him at his most characteristic, since he was not revising but translating afresh. He preened himself on the fidelity of this version, and indeed challenged readers to compare it with the original.[41] To ensure accuracy he went to immense pains—using, for example, Aquila's slavishly literal rendering as a constant check, and drawing on the help of Jewish experts. Modern students are agreed that his translation is in general faithful, certainly much more so than the Old Latin it was to displace, but they would add certain qualifications.[42] First, in numberless passages he either interpolated a few explanatory words to assist the reader or abridged the original so as to avoid tedium. Secondly, where the Hebrew presented difficulties or inconsistencies (often due to the composite character of the text), he frequently papered them over by deft re-writing. Thirdly, he tended to take greater liberties with the books he translated latest, so that while he justly scorned[43] any suggestion that his Samuel and Kings could be described as a paraphrase, his version of Judges (404/5) comes pretty near to being one. Fourthly, he translated a large number of passages in such a way as to give them a much more pointedly Messianic or otherwise Christian implication than the Hebrew permitted.

Although in 395 he was to inform Pammachius[44] that Scripture ought to be translated word for word, his guiding principle in practice was that a good translation should express the meaning, not the actual words, of the original. Since the idioms of one language could not be reproduced in another, he felt justified in preserving the characteristic elegance of Latin so long as he did not alter the sense.[45] Hence in the interests of 'grace' and

[41] *Preface to Samuel and Kings* (Vulgate) (PL 28, 557f.).
[42] For examples see especially A. Condamin's important article 'Les caractères de la traduction de la Bible par saint Jérôme', *Recherches de science religieuse* 2 (1911), 425–40; 3 (1912), 105–38. A much fuller, more comprehensive catalogue can be found in K. J. R. Corneley, *Historica et critica introductio in utriusque Testamenti libros* 1 (Paris, 1885), 423–44. A valuable summary is provided by H. F. D. Sparks in 'Jerome as a Biblical Scholar', *The Cambridge History of the Bible* 1 (Cambridge, 1970), 510–41, esp. 524–6.
[43] *Preface to Samuel and Kings* (Vulgate) (PL 28, 557f.).
[44] *Letter* 57, 5.
[45] For this theory of translation see *Letters* 57, 5; 106, 3; 26; 29 f.; 54 f.; *Preface to Job* (Vulgate); *to Judith* (PL 28, 1081; 29, 39). For 'grace' and 'euphony' see *Letter* 106, 3; 29; 55.

'euphony' he consistently rearranges in more complex groupings the paratactic sentences favoured in Hebrew, and goes to every length to eliminate, by the substitution of synonyms, the monotonous but distinctively Hebrew repetition of words and phrases.

What surprises us, however, is that, with these principles and with his reverence for the classical models, he never dreamed, apparently, of translating the Bible into the cultivated literary prose of which he was a master without rival among his contemporaries. For all the corrections and embellishments he introduced, the Latin of his new version was essentially that special 'Christian Latin', with its strong Hebrew colouring, which as a young man in the desert had repelled him (as it repelled many an educated Christian) as barbarous and uncouth. The explanation of this paradox was in large measure practical: he had no wish that his Old Testament should deviate more than absolutely necessary from the style and general tone, indeed from the actual wording, of the familiar version hallowed by centuries of usage. At a more theoretical level he, like other Christian intellectuals, was persuaded, first, that what mattered in Scripture was the content, not the literary form;[46] and, secondly, that, being intended for ordinary folk, it was appropriate that it should be expressed in the simple, even crude language which most of them appreciated.[47] Later generations have good reason to be grateful for Jerome's decision, for in spite of inequalities (stylistically, for example, his Pentateuch stands out as supreme, while Job is about the least satisfactory of the books), his Old Testament raised the vulgar Latinity of Christians to the heights of great literature.

(iv)

While still immersed in this giant task, Jerome was busily preparing commentaries on the books he was translating. Just as he had started off on St Paul's letters with the briefest, he now took in hand five of the shorter of the twelve Minor Prophets—first Nahum, then in rapid succession Micah, Zephaniah, Haggai, Habbakuk. Once again the seemingly haphazard order reflects the demands made by friends or his own sense of his capacity.[48]

---

[46] Cf., e.g., his remarks in *Comm. on Galatians* I, 11 f. (PL 26: 386 f.).

[47] See *Letter* 53, 10; *Comm. on Ezekiel* 47, 1–5 (CCL 75: 590), where he apologises for using the incorrect 'cubiti' instead of 'cubita' on the ground that it is the form customarily used among 'simple, uneducated folk who form the majority in church congregations'; *Origen's Homilies on Jerem. and Ezek.* (PL 25: 741 f.), where he speaks of 'the simple, pure style which alone can be of use to churches'. On the whole matter see the interesting discussion of G. Q. A. Meershoek, 'Le Latin biblique d'après saint Jérôme', *Latinitas Christianorum Primaeva* 20, esp. 4–14 (Nijmegen-Utrecht, 1966).

[48] For this order see *Comm. on Amos* III prol. (CCL 76: 309), where he explains that he has not followed the canonical sequence but has written 'as I was able and as I was asked'. He lists them differently in *Famous Men* 135 and *Comm. on Jonah* prol. (CCL 76: 387–8), giving the canonical order in the latter.

The method he adopted, dictated by his anxiety to leave no loophole to malicious critics,[49] but also by its usefulness to his exegesis, was the highly peculiar one of setting down (except where discrepancies were minimal) his new rendering from the Hebrew and the traditional Latin version of the Septuagint side by side, and then commenting on each separately. As always, he was an unashamed plunderer, drawing chiefly (though not exclusively) on Origen and contemporary rabbinical interpretations. He made no concealment of the latter, valuing them particularly for textual points and historical details, but reacting violently against some of their assumptions, e.g. that the Messiah had still to come and that, when he did, Jerusalem would be rebuilt and would dominate all nations.[50] Origen he nowhere names, although an evasive 'I read in someone's book'[51] occasionally gives us a clue. But we have his frank admission[52] that, when he came across Origen's twenty-five books on the Minor Prophets in the library at Caesarea, he gleefully reckoned himself the possessor of Croesus's treasures. Readers of these commentaries also accused him of plagiarising Origen, only to receive the retort[53] that, so far from being a calumny, this was a compliment, since everyone admired Origen. Here and there[54] his borrowings are demonstrable, but in countless other passages the practised eye can detect the Origenistic background.[55] It is noticeable, however, that he has become distinctly cooler to the master's heterodox opinions; and once or twice a suggestion of Origen's is only stated to be dropped.[56]

The five prophets selected were a motley group—Nahum exulting over Nineveh's downfall (612 B.C.); Micah (late eighth century B.C.) denouncing social unrighteousness and finding the essence of religion in justice and humble communion with God; Zephaniah (end of seventh century B.C.) proclaiming the terrible Day of the Lord; Haggai (520 B.C.) urging the people to rebuild the ruined Temple; Habbakuk (probably *c*. 600 B.C.) concerned with the mystery of evil, but finally concluding that acceptance of God's will is the answer to it. Jerome could not know that they often combine oracles of widely separated dates; for him they are all unities. More disappointing, however, is his failure to explore each pro-

---

[49] Cf. *Comm. on Nahum* 3, 8–12 (*CCL* 76A: 572).

[50] E.g. *Comm. on Micah* 4, 11–13; 5, 7–14; 7, 8–13; *on Zephaniah* 2, 12–15 (*CCL* 76: 485; 498; 522 f.; 76A: 709).

[51] E.g. *Comm. on Micah* 1, 16; *on Habbakuk* 2, 9–11 (*CCL* 76: 448; 76A: 619).

[52] *Famous Men* 75.

[53] *Comm. on Micah* II prol. (*CCL* 76: 480).

[54] E.g. *Comm. on Habbakuk* 3, 14 (LXX) (*CCL* 76A: 659): cf. Origen, *In Ies. Nave hom.* 15, 5 (*GCS* 30, 389 f.).

[55] For examples see Grützmacher II, 115–18.

[56] Cf. esp. *Comm. on Haggai* 1, 13 (*CCL* 76A: 751), which mentions Origen's theory (see *Comm. in Iob.* II, 31: *GCS* 10, 88 f.) that John the Baptist and other prophets were angels in human form.

phet's profounder message; his exposition tends to be a mosaic in which each section is treated on its own. His procedure is to take a verse or two and explain the literal sense, or what he calls 'the history' (a technical expression he had picked up in the schools of Antioch), basing himself for this on his new translation and on information supplied by Jewish mentors. Then he passes to the allegorical or 'spiritual' interpretation, using now the Septuagint-based Old Latin and (often with Origen as his unacknowledged guide) relating the prophet's words to Christ, the Church, or the destiny in store for believers or sinners, or drawing from them moral or ascetical lessons.

He is clearly aware of the tension involved in this twofold exegesis. 'I am compelled,' he writes,[57] 'to steer my course between the literal and the allegorical senses like a sailor threatened with shipwreck by the reefs on either side.' The scrupulous attention he pays to the former is the fruit mainly of his early training at Antioch, but partly too of the factual material supplied by Jewish advisers. In these commentaries this is invariably his starting-point, and we note his theory[58] that the literal sense often includes a further 'metaphorical' one which does not coincide with the allegorical one, as when a particular individual symbolises a whole people. Except in the Habbakuk commentary, however, where he makes a special effort to satisfy Chromatius's appetite for a 'historical exposition', he in general assigns more space to the spiritual interpretation, and at this stage finds it more satisfying. To describe it he uses various terms—allegory, 'anagogê', tropology—which were later to be used technically to denote subdivisions of the spiritual sense, but he himself seems to use them indifferently for the most part. The trouble was, of course, that the allegorical method of interpretation lent itself to abuse, and Jerome was fully conscious of this. The literal sense, he confessed,[59] left no room for arbitrary options, but the spiritual sense was open-ended unless controlled by such rules as tendency to edify, conformity with the context, and strict avoidance of contradiction. In his own practice, however, whatever Christian meanings or salutary messages could be extracted from the text were in order.[60]

To conclude with one or two illustrations. He explains Nahum's triumphant outpourings over Nineveh as intended, 'according to the

---

[57] *Comm. on Nahum* 2, 1 (*CCL* 76A: 549).

[58] *Comm. on Habbakuk* 3, 14–16: 'frequenter historia ipsa metaphorice texitur': also his later remark in *Comm. on Hosea* 10, 11 that 'the divine word is in the habit of expressing the historical truth by means of tropology and metaphor' (*CCL* 76A: 658; 76: 115).

[59] *Comm. on Habbakuk* 1, 6–11 (*CCL* 76A: 599).

[60] For Jerome's exegesis see esp. A. Vaccari, 'I fattori dell' esegesi Geronimiana', *Biblica* 7 (1920), 458–80: reprinted in *Scritti di erudizione e di filologia* II (Rome, 1958); A. Penna, *Principi e carattere dell' esegesi di s. Gerolamo* (Rome, 1950). But in fact no satisfactory study as yet exists.

letter', to raise the spirits of his fellow-Jews groaning under the Assyrian yoke. Christians, however, may read them as dire warnings of the doom awaiting those who defy God and spurn the refuge of his Church.[61] Haggai's call to erect an even more magnificent Temple accurately paints the historical situation, as well as containing (verse 7) a distinct prophecy of the Messiah. But 'the discerning reader can rise from this to a more sublime understanding': in Joshua the high-priest he can see Jesus, God made man, and realise that what is really being spoken of is the replacement of the synagogue by his glorious Church.[62] When Habbakuk declares (2, 11) that the very stone of the wall and the tie-beam will cry out, Jerome takes this literally as a rebuke to the Assyrian pillager's rapacity. But since the Septuagint substitutes 'beetle' for tie-beam, he is able, with tortuous ingenuity and a sly dig at an inept interpretation of Ambrose's,[63] to read the passage as referring to the rantings of heretics (beetles being creatures which crawl out of dung).[64]

Most fascinating, however, both as an example of his exegesis and as an eye-witness glimpse of fourth-century Jerusalem, is his discussion of Zephaniah's warning (1, 15 f.) that the Day of the Lord will be a day of wrath, distress and anguish, ruin and devastation to fortified cities. Spiritually understood, this is a description either of the consummation of the world or of the end of each individual, when God's avenging anger will be terribly manifested and even the righteous will be saved only after being tested in fire. But for once Jerome spreads himself, with eloquence throbbing with almost personal indignation, on the 'historical' exposition which precedes this. The prophet, he explains, is foreseeing the sack of Jerusalem whether by Nebuchadnezzar in the sixth century B.C. or by the Romans in the first century A.D., a disaster which it amply deserved for slaying God's servants and finally God's own Son. Indeed, Zephaniah's horrifying imagery finds its fulfilment in the wretched plight of the Jews of Jerome's own day, virtually excluded from the city that was once their pride and admitted once a year, on the anniversary of its capture and destruction, and then only for a fee, to gaze, weeping and wailing, under the watchful eyes of Roman guards, at the ruined Temple site with its

[61] *Comm. on Nahum* prol. (*CCL* 76A: 533–6) and *passim*.

[62] *Comm. on Haggai* 2, 2–10 (*CCL* 76A: 754–8).

[63] *CCL* 76A: 617–19. Jerome rejects as 'impious' the exegesis of some who believe that the beetle which cries from the wood (= the cross) is Christ. He mentions no names, but this is an interpretation which Ambrose, whom he so much disliked, had given in *Expos. ev. Luc.* 10, 113 (*CSEL* 32, 4, 498). He does not seem to have been influenced by Jerome's criticism, for he was to produce the same exegesis in his funeral oration on Theodosius I on 25 Feb. 395 (*De obitu Theod.* or. 46: *PL* 16, 1401B): For a full discussion see F. J. Dölger, *Antike und Christentum* 2 (1930), 230–40.

[64] *Comm. on Habbakuk* 2, 11 (*CCL* 76A: 618 f.). Pliny describes how a species of beetles nests their grubs in balls of manure (*Hist. nat.* xi, 34, 98).

shattered altar. For them this is the prophesied day of calamity and misery, of darkness and gloom. But in the midst of their shame the Church of the Resurrection shines resplendent, and the cross rises triumphant on the Mount of Olives.[65]

---

[65] *Comm. on Zephaniah* 1, 15–16 (*CCL* 76A: 691–3). The glittering cross was the one which surmounted Imbomon, or the church covering the spot from which Jesus was believed to have ascended to heaven. Jerome reports (*Comm. on Ezekiel* 11, 23) that in his day it was in full view of the ruined Temple site.

XVI

Propagandist History

(i)

Strangely contrasting with the renown Jerome's great translation of the Old Testament was later to bring him were the distress and indignation it excited in his lifetime. A limited circle of friends—Paula and Eustochium, of course, Sophronius, Chromatius of Aquileia, a few others—understood his motives, applauded his principles, encouraged his efforts. The great majority, including (as we shall learn) responsible and deeply respected figures like Augustine, were appalled by his irreverent tampering, as it seemed to them, with the traditional version hallowed by its use in the Church's life and worship and accepted as inspired by the Holy Spirit.

The vivid and poignant evidence of this embittered reaction stands before us in all the prefaces to his new translations. On the one hand, we find him inveighing[1] with his accustomed violence against 'the howling dogs who rage savagely against me', 'the biting multitude who, egged on by envy, disparage what they cannot themselves attain', 'the perverse creatures to whose shrieks of disapproval I have delivered myself'. On the other hand, we observe him tacking skilfully to adopt a defensive position. It was never his intention, he protested,[2] to belittle the older version, but simply to clear up its obscurities and restore what had either dropped out or been altered by the mistakes of copyists. A few years later he was to argue[3] that there would have been no need for a fresh translation from the Hebrew if the Septuagint had retained its pristine purity; but the variety of editions current throughout the world, all in different degrees corrupted and all omitting key-texts quoted by the Apostles and Jesus himself, had made drastic reform necessary. In any case no one was compelled to read his new translation from the Hebrew. The older version was freely available; for some books there was also his revision of the Septuagint. Each reader could take his choice.[4]

Some of the attacks on him were more personal. Gossipy tongues were

---

[1] *Preface to Samuel; to Isaiah; to Psalms* (Vulgate) (PL 28, 558; 772; 1125 f.).
[2] *Preface to Job* (Vulgate) (PL 28, 1082).
[3] *Preface to Chronicles* (Vulgate) (PL 28, 1323–6). Date 396.
[4] *Preface to Job* (Vulgate) (PL 28, 1083 f.). Cf. his later defence of his practice to Augustine: *Letter* 112, 20 (date 404).

poking fun at his habit of dedicating his writings almost exclusively to women (four of his five commentaries on the Minor Prophets were addressed to Paula and Eustochium). In a pedantically laboured apologia[5] he pointed to the remarkable women both of classical antiquity and of the Bible, and further recalled that it was to women that the Lord had first appeared after his resurrection. These flattering comparisons must have consoled his outraged protégées; but the fact remains that the commentaries he dedicated to them were less thorough than the one on Habbakuk he offered to the more exacting Chromatius, which included many more notes on the readings of the several Greek versions as well as learned quotations from classical literature.[6] Then there were the 'bloated bulls' who jeered at his wholesale plundering of Origen. They should hold their tongues, he retorted,[7] and remember that famous Latin authors like Vergil and Cicero had borrowed freely from the Greeks, as had Hilary of Poitiers from Origen in his commentary on the Psalms.

There was one individual whose criticisms Jerome found particularly exasperating; it was the desire to deflect them, he explains,[8] that had prompted his decision to comment on the Septuagint alongside the Hebrew. He flits through the early commentaries under various insulting soubriquets—Sardanapalus (the Assyrian king whose name was a byword for effeminacy), a hissing snake, the fury Alecto, the Lernaean hydra whose ever-sprouting heads Jerome threatens to smite with the prophet's battle-mace. Once he mentions that he was recently, as a punishment from God, afflicted with dropsy.[9] Although certainty is impossible, the suspicion is hard to avoid that his unnamed tormentor was none other than Rufinus, once his student friend and fellow-seeker after the higher life, now his neighbour in Jerusalem. We know that Rufinus thoroughly disapproved of his revolutionary translation of the Old Testament from the Hebrew, and it would not be like him to keep his disapproval to himself. We know, too, that a few years later Jerome was to besmirch him with the same or similar spiteful descriptions. The objection that, in dedicating his Habbakuk commentary to Chromatius, Jerome could not have spoken so abusively of one he knew to be so dear to him can be dismissed. Chromatius may not have guessed the identity of the man pilloried; alternatively, assuming he did guess it, he also knew Jerome, and may have shaken his head sadly. If this conjecture is correct, however,

---

[5] *Comm. on Zephaniah* prol. (*CCL* 76A: 671–2).

[6] As Grützmacher (II, 112) noted. Some of the classical citations are so lengthy as to suggest that he must have looked them up: see H. Hagendahl, *Latin Fathers and the Classics*, 134.

[7] *Comm. on Micah* II prol. (*CCL* 76: 480). The 'bloated bulls' are an echo of Ps. 22, 12.

[8] *Comm. on Nahum* 3, 8–12 (*CCL* 76A: 572).

[9] *Comm. on Habbakuk* II prol.; *on Zephaniah* 3, 20; *on Haggai* 3, 24; *on Micah* 1, 1; II prol. (*CCL* 76A: 631; 734; 773; 76: 434; 480). Cf. *Comm. on Nahum* 3, 1–4 (*CCL* 76A: 564) for the reference to dropsy.

we must infer that the two friends began drifting apart rather earlier than is usually supposed, and we must trace the initial cause of their estrangement (which need not for the moment have interrupted their day-to-day relations) to Jerome's attachment to 'the Hebrew verity'.[10]

(ii)

As if to compensate Jerome for the unpopularity which he incurred through his Biblical revisions and translations, three other works which he published in this first period at Bethlehem were an instant success and brought him increasing fame. All three were, to a greater or less degree, historical essays (he had long fancied himself as a historian),[11] and it is remarkable that, at a time when his energies were so stretched on Scripture studies, he was also apparently seriously planning to write a history of the Church with a characteristically polemical bias. This was to start, he explains,[12] with the coming of Christ and the age of the Apostles, and then describe how the Church had acquired strength and a glorious crown through persecutions and martyrdoms, but in 'the dregs of this present time' had grown rich and powerful but declined in virtue. In other words, it was to be a history which would give full scope to his caustic pen for belabouring the organised Christianity of his day for its failure to live up to his own severely ascetic standards. The project never came to fruition, but he regarded the first two of the three books we have mentioned as preparatory exercises for it.

Both these were lives of monastic heroes closely similar, in genre and in treatment, to the *Life of Paul the First Hermit* he had written many years before at Antioch. Like it, they are not strictly biographies at all, but propagandist pamphlets presenting the monastic ideal in persuasively attractive colours. The earlier of the two is almost certainly the *Life of Malchus the Captive Monk*. Some, indeed, consider[13] it the very first of his literary productions at Bethlehem, on the basis of his statement that he is wiping the rust off his tongue after a long period of enforced silence. But in the next paragraph he refers to his old friend Evagrius as a bishop ('papa'), an office he did not assume until the death of Paulinus in 388/9, when he became leader of the small, old-Nicene group at Antioch.[14] We must therefore date the *Life of Malchus* somewhere around 390/91, and

---

[10] For Rufinus's objection to Jerome's translation of the Old Testament from the Hebrew see *Apol. c. Hier.* 2, 32–5.

[11] See above p. 75.

[12] *Life of Malchus* 1.

[13] So, e.g., Cavallera II, 27, who speaks of 'une longue inaction littéraire'. But what Jerome actually says is 'diu tacui', i.e. 'I have been silent long', which in the context suggests that he has abstained from controversy, not that he has written nothing.

[14] *Life of Malchus* 1 and 2. According to Theodoret (*Hist. eccl.* 5, 23, 2–4), Evagrius's consecration was uncanonical, for the dying Paulinus consecrated him on his sole authority.

find some other explanation of his remark about at last breaking his silence. The most natural one is that he regarded these works (and the church history to which they were to lead up) as marking the resumption, not of literary activity (he had been busy writing books for years), but of the public campaign for asceticism which his Roman critics had obliged him to suspend. It fits in with this that he compares his work on them to the battle-training marines undergo when preparing for a sea-fight, and also expresses the hope that his vilifiers will leave him alone now he is living in exile shut up in a monastery.

The *Life of Malchus* is, just as much as the famous Letter 22 to Eustochium, a paean in praise of life-long chastity. Malchus was an old man whom Jerome had come across many years before at Maronia, a village some forty-eight km. from Antioch belonging to Evagrius, and who had described to him how he had been able to preserve his virginity intact in spite of temptations and terrifying dangers. The son of well-off parents at Nisibis, he had resisted their attempts to marry him off and thereby 'betray his chastity', had fled from home, and had settled in a monastery in the desert of Chalcis. Many years later, his father being now dead, he decided to return home and enjoy at any rate part of his inheritance. His abbot had warned him that no good could come of this defection and, sure enough, as he was travelling along the dangerous highroad he was seized by marauding Saracens and, along with a woman in the same party, reduced to slavery and set by his master to tend sheep.

For a time he was idyllically content, praying and singing psalms and thanking God that in the barren country he could live the monk's life he had been tempted to abandon. Then, to his horror, his master, as a reward for his exemplary service, insisted on his marrying the female slave who was his fellow-captive. This he could not bring himself to do: he would not only be sacrificing his virginity but, since she already had a husband (he had been sold to a different master), would be committing adultery. In his despair Malchus was on the point of killing himself, but at last yielded to the woman's suggestion that they should live together as celibates pretending to be man and wife. They successfully maintained this charade for a time ('I never saw her naked body, never touched her flesh'); but eventually a yearning to return to his monastery seized him, and after making careful plans the pair made their escape by night. Their master, however, was soon hot on their tracks with a servant, and although they took refuge in a cave he would certainly have captured and slain them but for the timely intervention of a lioness, which savaged first the servant and then the master to death. Finally the two landed up safely at Maronia, and lived there under the same roof like Zechariah and Elizabeth in the gospel, except that there was of course no John the Baptist since they resolutely abstained from intercourse.

The *Life* is only a few pages long, but is one of the most exciting examples of Jerome's flair for story-telling.[15] The narrative flows rapidly, abounding in telling phrases and accurately observed details of locality, custom, and climate (Jerome had vivid memories of his own time in the desert). Although the style is of studied simplicity, it glows with brilliant descriptions. People sometimes label it a romantic legend, but this is to miss the point. There is a minimum of miracle, and there is no reason to question the substantial truth of the tale. Touches like the mention of Sabinianus as 'commander of Mesopotamia',[16] and of the need for travellers on the main road from Beroea (Haleb) to Edessa to form convoys, bear this out. The story gives precious eye-witness information about monastic conditions in mid-fourth-century Syria—the freedom of movement of monks, the lack of tight discipline in monasteries, the control a monk might still have over his worldly goods, the practice of a monk and a woman living chastely together (to be sternly frowned upon by the later formal Rules) without exciting scandal, etc. But its true importance, for the student of Jerome, is the renewed plea he presents in it, after all the rebuffs he had received, for complete sexual abstinence. So he concludes by saying that, old man as he is, he has told this tale of chastity courageously preserved to give his readers a model to imitate and in their turn to pass on to others.

The *Life of Hilarion* is not only a lengthier work, but is much more carefully constructed on the lines of ancient encomiastic biography as remodelled to suit Christian hagiography.[17] Born in 291/2 at Thabatha, some 7½ km. south of Gaza, Hilarion had been sent to school at Alexandria, had become a Christian and spent two months with the renowned Antony in the desert studying his method and mode of life, and while still a lad of fifteen had returned to Palestine, stripped himself of all possessions, and settled as a hermit in the brigand-infested wilderness by the sea-shore south of Maiuma, the port of Gaza. For twenty-two years he lived in solitude, quelling fleshly desires, fighting off demons, and submitting to extraordinary privations. By now his fame had spread abroad, people flocked to him from Syria and Egypt, monasteries began springing up around him, and like Antony in Egypt he became the

---

[15] Some have suspected that the *Life* is not Jerome's original work, but a translation made by him from the Greek. But P. van den Ven (*Le Muséon* NS 1, 1901, 413–55; NS 2, 1902, 208–326) showed conclusively that the Greek text is a free translation of Jerome's Latin. This is confirmed by the way it tightens up details of monastic practice and behaviour so as to bring them into conformity with later stricter standards.

[16] *Life of Malchus* 10. For the office see A. H. M. Jones, *The Later Roman Empire* (Oxford, 1964) II, 609. For the possible identification of Sabinianus with the man of that name who was *Magister equitum per Orientem* 359–60, see *PLRE* I, 788 and 789.

[17] Cf. P. Winter, *Der Literarische Charakter der Vita beati Hilarionis des Hieronymus* (Zittau, 1904): summarised, with a useful general discussion of the *Life*, by S. Schiwietz, *Das Morgenländische Mönchtum* (Mainz, 1913) 2, 95–119, esp. 102 f.

inaugurator of the monastic life in Palestine.[18] By the time he was sixty-three, however, his popularity, the crowds pestering him with their needs, and the monks clustering around him made him feel that, though outwardly a monk, he was really living in the world; he had lost the solitude for which he craved. So, resisting the entreaties of thousands, he made his escape, journeying first to the desert spot where Antony had died, then to the vicinity of Alexandria, to Sicily, to Dalmatia, never able to shake off people and be alone with God. At last he found a rugged, inaccessible but beautiful mountain hideout in Cyprus,[19] and there, at the age of eighty, he died in 371. A devoted disciple, Hesychius, secretly conveyed his body to Maiuma, and both there and at his garden retreat in Cyprus miracles continued to be wrought daily.

The bulk of the *Life* consists of the recital of the holy man's exorcisms, cures, acts of clairvoyance, wondrous exploits and sayings, all graphically related and interspersed with colourful descriptive passages. The existence of Hilarion has been unnecessarily questioned. Jerome had among his sources a widely circulated letter by Bishop Epiphanius, who had known Hilarion personally;[20] and the historian Sozomen, who was also a native of the region near Gaza, while using Jerome's *Life*, supplies a good deal of supplementary information about the saint and his disciples.[21] Jerome of course idealises his hero, directing the flood-light exclusively on him, leaving his collaborators mere shadows, even setting him up as the equal of the prestigious Antony. All this, as well as the persuasive rhetoric of the presentation, was in the hagiographical tradition. For the historian his narrative is a fascinating revelation not only of local conditions in contemporary Palestine,[22] but even more of the credulity, the belief in demons, miracles and magic, and the veneration of the holy man as a spiritual giant, which Christians of all classes (Aristaenete, wife of Helpidius, praetorian prefect of Oriens in 360–1, is an intriguing example)[23] unquestioningly shared. So far as Jerome himself is concerned, the *Life* (like that of Malchus) eloquently confirms how deeply his mind continued to be obsessed with the challenge of absolute abandonment of worldly goods and surrender to Christ, as well as with contempt for the popularity and vulgar éclat which the conventional Christians he despised clutched at so

[18] *Life of Hilarion* 14. One of Jerome's aims was to make propaganda for Palestinian monasticism.

[19] According to Sozomen (*Hist. eccl.* 5, 10), it was called Charbyris, and the date was 367, i.e. soon after Epiphanius was elected bishop of Salamis in Cyprus.

[20] *Life of Hilarion* 1.

[21] *Hist. eccl.* 3, 14; 5, 10.

[22] E.g. F. Millar has drawn attention (*Journal of Roman Studies* 61, 1971, 7) to the evidence it provides for the mixture of languages in fourth-century Roman Syria.

[23] For Hilarion's cure of her children see *Life of H.* 14. Ammianus Marcellinus (*Res gestae* 21, 6, 9) gives an account of Helpidius, commenting on his repugnance to cruelty and bloodshed. For his career see *PLRE* 1, 414.

eagerly. 'Nothing,' he confessed,[24] 'more amazes me than the way Hilarion spurned popular esteem and honour . . . All he wanted was to withdraw and be alone.'

(iii)

The last book Jerome published in this astonishingly productive period was also a work of propagandist history, his object this time being not to win men to the asceticism he cherished so dearly but to persuade them of the riches of the Church's literary inheritance.

Entitled *Famous Men* (*De vivis illustribus*),[25] it was a catalogue, in one hundred and thirty-five paragraphs of very varying lengths, of as many Christian authors and their writings, beginning with St Peter and ending with himself. The period covered, he explained,[26] was 'from the passion of Christ down to the fourteenth year of the emperor Theodosius'; and in the closing section he echoed these last words, saying that he is listing the books he has written 'as far as the present year, i.e. the fourteenth of the emperor Theodosius'. There is general agreement, therefore, that, since Theodosius I was proclaimed Augustus on 19 January 379, the work should be dated somewhere between 19 January 392 and 18 January 393, probably towards the close of the span. Because of apparent chronological difficulties raised by his later *Commentary on Jonah*, which seems to suggest[27] that certain of his works listed in *Famous Men* belong in fact to the middle of 393, it has been argued that Jerome must be computing the years of Theodosius's reign, not from his actual accession, but from his first assumption of the consulship, i.e. 1 January of the following year. This would allow us to assign *Famous Men* to the second half of 393. The chronological problems, however, can be solved otherwise, and we have no need to attribute to Jerome a mode of calculating an emperor's regnal years which is in itself unnatural and does not square with his practice, for example, in his *Chronicle*.[28]

As we learn from its preface, Jerome had been pressed to undertake this work by a distinguished friend, Nummius Aemilianus Dexter,[29] a

[24] *Life of Hilarion* 29.
[25] The best critical edition is E. C. Richardson's in *TU* xiv (1896). S. von Sychowski, *Hieronymus als Litterarhistoriker* (Münster, 1894), is indispensable for its analytical introduction and very full notes.
[26] *Famous Men* prol. and 135.
[27] *Comm. on Jonah* prol. (*CCL* 76: 387–8). Cf. *Letters* 60 and 77, 1.
[28] For the revised date 393, see P. Nautin's ingenious article in *RHE* 66 (1961), 33 f. For criticism of it and the solution of the chronological problems cf. T. D. Barnes, *Tertullian* (Oxford, 1971), 235 f. This appendix, along with pp. 4–12, contains a valuable discussion of aspects of *Famous Men* which I have used with profit. A date late in 393 is harder than one late in 392 to reconcile with Jerome's statement in 401 (*Apology* 2, 23) that he had written *Famous Men* 'almost ten years ago'.
[29] For his career see *PLRE* I, 251.

keen Christian and son of a bishop of Barcelona, who had been proconsul of Asia some time between 379 and 387 and was to become praetorian prefect of Italy in 395. It is a sobering reminder of the gaps in our knowledge that, beyond the fact of his having inspired the writing of *Famous Men*, we know absolutely nothing of Jerome's relations with this highly placed and powerful official. He had suggested, probably during some visit to Bethlehem, that Jerome should perform the same service for Christian literature as Suetonius had for classical Latin literature when he published *c*. 100 a collection (also called *Famous Men*) of short biographies of noteworthy writers. The moment was well chosen for such a propagandist boost, for recent imperial legislation banning the public celebration of pagan cults had set the seal on the Church's dominant position in society.[30] As if to dazzle the reader, Jerome reeled off in his preface the names of several others, Greeks and Romans (it is pretty certain that the Greeks at any rate were mere names to him),[31] who had composed similar biographical handbooks, and ruefully contrasted the rich sources available to them with his own lack of any predecessor. All he had had at his disposal was Eusebius's *Ecclesiastical History*, which he admitted had been a great help to him, and the writings of the authors themselves. Nevertheless he felt sure the book would be of signal apologetic value by demonstrating to contemptuous pagans, who dismissed the Church as a boorish society with no worthwhile thinkers or fine writers to its credit, how abysmally wrong they were.

This aim at any rate Jerome came some way to achieving. Despite certain significant omissions, the array of authors, Greek as well as Latin, he was able to muster was impressively numerous; and, as with his *Chronicle*, he seems to have inserted a few more entries in later editions.[32] True, he included a few non-Christians (Jews like Josephus and Philo, the pagan Seneca), and, stickler though he was for orthodoxy, a number of heretics, some of them (e.g. the extreme Arian Eunomius) notorious. For the former he could plead special reasons: e.g. there existed an exchange of letters, since recognised as apocryphal, between Seneca and St Paul, while Josephus seemed to have acknowledged the messiahship of Jesus in his *Jewish Antiquities*.[33] But his chief motive was to swell the army of famous writers who, by hook or crook, could be claimed for the Church. It was this consideration, doubtless, and not a sudden access of

---

[30] *Codex Theod.* xvi, 10, 10 (date 24 Feb. 391).

[31] Cf. P. Courcelle, *Late Latin Writers and their Greek Sources* (ET, Cambridge, Mass., 1969), 78 f.

[32] Cf. A. Feder, *Studien zum Schriftstellerkatalog des hl. Hieronymus* (Freiburg im B., 1927), 158–60. Some MSS contain additions which, Feder argues, are in Jerome's style.

[33] *Ant.* 18, 63 f. The passage (the 'testimonium Flavianum') is very early, being cited by Eusebius (*Hist. eccl.* 1, 11, 7 f.; *Dem. ev.* 3, 5, 105), but is agreed either to be an interpolation or to have been doctored in a pro-Christian sense.

liberal tolerance, which caused him to swallow his repugnance for heretics —and later earn a rebuke from Augustine, who complained that, if he had to include them, he should at least have underlined the pernicious aspects of the irteaching.[34] To reinforce the high quality of the Church's contribution to letters, he was profuse in sprinkling laudatory epithets like 'elegant', 'distinguished', or 'extremely beautiful', even in cases where we have reason to suspect that he had never read the works concerned.

Not surprisingly, this pioneer patrology, with its wide sweep and apparently unassailable apparatus of learning, was not only an immediate success, but from the fifth to the fifteenth century inspired no fewer than nine continuators, beginning with Gennadius of Marseilles (*fl.* 470). It also added greatly to Jerome's reputation for erudition. Despite the lack of a consistent chronology and the meagreness of many of the notices, it was clearly an immense advantage to have so much information about the Church's literary figures assembled for the first time in a compendious, readable form. Much of it was inevitably derivative. For example, the first three centuries were shrouded in darkness, and so for most of the first seventy-eight authors, from St Peter to Bishop Phileas of Thmuis (d. *c.* 307) Jerome was heavily dependent on Eusebius. Indeed, this dependence went much further than his frank acknowledgment in the preface would suggest, for in the majority of entries he was content to copy out, often word for word, the literary notices scattered throughout Eusebius's *History* and *Chronicle*. For the earlier Latins, of whom Eusebius's knowledge was minimal or non-existent, he had their works, facts generally remembered or passed down in hagiography, and, in the important case of Cyprian, an early life as well. In the second half of the book (chaps. 80–135), which dealt with fourth-century authors, he had no Eusebius but could rely on what he had read (sometimes less than one would expect) or heard of their writings, on the mass of data about them which must have been current knowledge, and in several cases on personal acquaintance with the men themselves.

Famous Men could have been, and for centuries was accepted as being, a superb scholarly achievement. Unfortunately, as the analyses of modern investigators have made plain,[35] its pretentious façade is largely a sham. This is not to deny that it has real merits and usefulness. Much of the independent information it contains is unobtainable elsewhere. Jerome reports on books which he had read but which are now lost, and on writers of whom we should have otherwise been ignorant. Here and there he inserts an acute critical comment. But the defects are so glaring that the

---

[34] *Ep.* 40, 9: written in 397. See below p. 219.
[35] See esp. S. von Sychowski, op. cit., 18–35; 49–73; C. A. Bernouilli, *Der Schriftstellerkatalog des Hieronymus* (Freiburg and Leipzig, 1895). See also T. D. Barnes, op. cit., 6–12; 236 f. (useful for Jerome's knowledge of early Latin authors and for his use of Eusebius).

book needs to be read (as many have remarked) with a cautionary commentary by one's side. For example, while Jerome rightly leaned heavily on Eusebius in the earlier part, he used him quite uncritically, never questioning his reliability or bothering to correct his mistakes even when he might have done so. Several times, through sheer carelessness, he misunderstood him or mistranslated him. Even worse, he attempted to conceal his dependence, taking up his master's statements or opinions and shamelessly reproducing them as if they were his own.[36] And when he ventured (as he frequently did) to supplement or improve on the information he found in his source, more often than not his additions and alterations either were untrustworthy or show him representing as firm facts what Eusebius had more prudently reported to be rumours or possibilities.

The faults which stand out in the second half are of a different order. First, Jerome seems to have become more and more hurried and careless as the work progressed, and the reader is disappointed by the culpable inadequacy of many of the entries. Basil of Caesarea, for example, and Gregory of Nyssa, two of the outstanding writers of the age, receive only perfunctory notices with lamentably incomplete bibliographies, although with a little trouble Jerome could easily have provided complete ones. Secondly, his personal prejudices are more in evidence in this section. On the one hand, he assigned a place, and complimentary remarks, to friends who were relatively insignificant as writers—Pope Damasus, Evagrius, Dexter (to whom he dedicated the work), Sophronius. On the other hand, he either completely omitted people he disliked (e.g. Ambrosiaster),[37] or dismissed them with a cursory mention (e.g. John Chrysostom—again one of his greatest contemporaries) or even a contemptuous epigram (so Ambrose of Milan: 'I shall refrain from giving my opinion on him, lest I should be accused either of toadying to or speaking the truth about him'). His personal bias is all the more regrettable because, side by side with these inequalities, he filled this section with a mass of biographical and literary information, and obviously could have supplied much more if only he had taken pains and not been blinded by partiality. But self-centred subjectivism reaches its height as the book draws to its close. Increasingly in these last paragraphs Jerome stresses the contacts of the worthies mentioned with himself; and the finale is a lengthy, circumstantial notice (for which posterity is grateful, but which contrasts strangely with the rushed summaries which were all that most others received) describing himself and his own publications to date.

[36] A notorious example is the notice (no. 11) on Philo, in which, by saying 'there exist other monuments of his genius which have not come into my hands', he seems to imply personal acquaintance with all the works of Philo he has just enumerated. But the list is copied direct from Eusebius, and while he knew some of the books mentioned it is certain that he did not know them all. See Sychowski, op. cit., 69, qualified by Courcelle, op. cit., 81 f.

[37] See above p. 149.

Yet however disappointing and exasperating to the historian, *Famous Men* remains an especially precious source to the biographer. It confirms (to give but one important example) the undiminished admiration Jerome still had for the 'immortal genius' of Origen.[38] And it lays bare, almost more than any other of his writings, the character and psychology of the man himself. Here we observe his scholarship, genuine and wide-ranging (there was no more learned man alive at the time), but defective in both originality and self-criticism, and all too often marred by partiality, carelessness, unwillingness to take trouble. We see his pride in the Church and its achievements, which made him swallow even his horror for heretics, and his generosity to his friends; but side by side with these his unfairness, the pettiness with which he allowed his critical judgment to be blinded by personal antipathies. Fascinating, too, is the light the book throws on his pious concern[39] (a concern which reflects the rapidly growing cult of relics) for the burial-places of saints and famous Christians (St Peter, St Luke, St Andrew, Ignatius, Origen, the martyr Lucian, even a relatively recent figure like Eustathius of Antioch). But perhaps the most vivid impression it leaves is of his conceit and vanity. It was these which led him not only to conceal his sources in ways which deserve to be called dishonest, but to give such exaggerated prominence to himself in the closing section. Shortly after he was to explain,[40] with an affectation of modesty, that after listing the long line of Christian writers he had felt obliged to mention himself on the very last page, the appropriate place for one who was 'as it were an untimely birth, the very least of all Christians'. But the ordinary reader, he must have realised, was bound to conclude that the subject of this fulsome notice, with its long catalogue of varied works, could scarcely be the most insignificant of the literary figures who had 'founded, built up, and adorned' the Church.[41]

---

[38] *Famous Men* 54.
[39] This point is made by Grützmacher (II, 141).
[40] *Letter* 47, 3: written 393. The expression 'quasi abortivum' is, of course, borrowed from St Paul's self-deprecating language in 1 Cor. 15, 8 f.
[41] Cf. the remarks of S. von Sychowski, op. cit., 25 ff.

XVII

Champion of Chastity

(i)

While Jerome, now in his early sixties, was preparing his commentaries and *Famous Men*, important events were taking place in the empire which were to have their effect both on Christian society and on his own career. On the frontiers the barbarian menace was steadily worsening, and the policy of settling whole tribes in the outer provinces was already bearing bitter fruit. In the west the seemingly secure position of Christianity was momentarily imperilled when Eugenius was proclaimed Augustus in August 392 by the commander-in-chief, the Frankish Arbogast, after the death, probably by assassination, of Valentinian II on 15 May. Nominally a Christian, the usurper was eager to rally pagans to his side. His leading supporters, Arbogast and the praetorian prefect Nichomachus Flavianus, were both out-and-out pagans, the latter indeed openly restoring pagan cults and predicting the speedy collapse of Christianity; and something like a pagan revival, with numerous career-interested Christians lapsing, got under way.[1] The alarm felt by serious Christians was intense until the situation was restored by Theodosius's victory over Eugenius at the river Frigidus on 6 September 394. Theodosius, however, died on 17 January 395, being succeeded by Honorius, aged ten, in the west, and Arcadius, aged seventeen or eighteen, in the east. Supreme power thus passed effectively to two great officials who will later appear briefly in these pages: the Vandal general Stilicho (whom Theodosius had in fact appointed guardian of both his sons) in the west, and Flavius Rufinus, a zealous Christian from Gaul, whom the late emperor had made praetorian prefect of the east in 392.

Jerome himself had now lived in Bethlehem for about eight years. He had, of course, maintained contact with Rome, but by the exchange of letters with personal friends rather than by official correspondence. Between him and Marcella, for example, the flow of letters, all now lost, was regular and frequent.[2] The sole survivor of this private exchange is a

[1] For Nichomachus Flavianus see the very full notice in *PLRE* I, 347–9. For the pagan revival see, e.g., H. Bloch, 'The Pagan Revival in the West at the end of the Fourth Century', *The Conflict Between Paganism and Christianity in the Fourth Century* (ed. A. Momigliano, Oxford, 1963), esp. 198 ff., and the references there given.

[2] So he records in *Letter* 127, 8 (his obituary on her). I am excluding *Letter* 46, written for Paula and Eustochium.

letter[3] despatched early in 393, just after the completion of *Famous Men*, inviting two old friends, Desiderius and Serenilla, married but now living together as brother and sister, to come to the Holy Land—still revered by him as the soil which 'the Lord's feet trod'. So far as the official clergy of the capital were concerned, he remained an outcast, and his resentment comes out in *On Ephesians* (387/8) in the sneer[4] that he cannot expect 'the senate of doctors' there to read it. Nevertheless, for all his contempt for the social distractions, artificialities, and moral degradation of 'Babylon', a nostalgia for the city of his baptism was stirring in him. St Paul, he emphasised, had complimented (Rom. 1, 1) the ordinary folk of Rome (the 'Romana plebs', as he significantly puts it) on their faith; and nowhere else, he boasted,[5] did the crowds rush so eagerly to churches and martyrs' shrines, nowhere else did the worshipping congregation shout such thunderous 'Amens', nowhere else could such simplicity of devotion and belief be found. He must therefore have been deeply gratified when, perhaps early in 393, an urgent approach was made to him by a group of ascetic-minded Roman Christians. It was almost certainly Pammachius,[6] the patrician friend of his schooldays and now Paula's son-in-law, a leading member of the Senate, who took the initiative, and in so doing revived a relationship which, it seems, had lain dormant for many years.

(ii)

This démarche took the form of an appeal to him to refute, 'with evangelical and apostolic vigour', the teachings of one Jovinian; copies of his writings were enclosed. As we know Jovinian only through the caricatures of his detractors ('the Epicurus of Christians', Jerome labels him), it is not easy to piece together a reliable portrait of him. What is certain is that he was the instigator of a campaign at Rome against the extremist, Oriental-style monasticism of which Jerome had been the over-ardent propagandist several years earlier and which was still, apparently, making headway in certain circles. He himself was a monk, and had begun as an enthusiast of this rigorous school. For a time he had gone about barefoot and dirty, clad in a filthy black tunic and pale from his sparse diet of bread and water. Then he had undergone a complete change, deciding that mortifications like these had nothing to do with true Christianity. Without ceasing to be a monk or abandoning celibacy, he adopted a more normal, comfortable mode of life, taking care about his dress and appearance, developing a taste for good food, frequenting the public baths,

[3] *Letter* 47.
[4] *Comm. on Ephesians* II prol. (*PL* 26: 586).
[5] *Comm. on Galatians* II prol. (*PL* 26: 427–8).
[6] See above p. 19. For the date 393 see Cavallera II, 43f.

mixing freely with women.[7] What was more disturbing, to win converts to his views he prepared a reasoned presentation of them backed with plentiful citations from Scripture and secular authorities. It was this pamphlet (or pamphlets)[8] that Jerome's worried friends sent to him, no doubt judging him uniquely well qualified to demolish its baneful doctrines.

As reported by Jerome, Jovinian advanced four principal theses.[9] First, it makes no difference, so far as spiritual perfection is concerned, whether Christians who have been baptised and give proof of the reality of their baptism are married, widowed, or single. Secondly, Christians who have received baptism with full adhesion of faith cannot henceforth fall under the dominion of the devil. If they sin, they can be spared the effects of sin by repentance. Thirdly, Christians who mortify themselves by fasting are in no way superior to those who eat and drink freely while offering thanks to God. Fourthly, on the day of judgment there will be no differentiation of rewards among Christians who have preserved their baptism, but they will all enjoy equal blessedness. Although Jerome fails to bring it out, what gave a theological basis and inner cohesion to these propositions was Jovinian's stress on the element of faith in baptism, and his conviction that the transformation effected by it not only rescued a man from the power of sin but created a unified, holy people in which considerations of merit were irrelevant.[10] From Ambrose and Augustine[11] we learn that he also taught that, while Mary conceived Jesus virginally, she must have lost her virginity in the physical process of bearing him.

It is unlikely that Jovinian was the voluptuary that Jerome represents him. He was evidently a serious thinker whose critique of celibacy and fasting, indeed of the whole conception of a more perfect life attainable by ascetic practices, stemmed from a high estimate of baptismal regeneration and an interpretation of Christianity completely at variance with current orthodoxy. His propaganda met with considerable success, perhaps not unconnected with the disarray into which the pagan revival was throwing Christians at Rome. He gained many disciples there, and we hear of

[7] For these details see *Against Jovinian* 1, 40; 2, 21; 36. The original descriptions are full of satirical distortions.

[8] Jerome speaks of 'Commentarii' or 'Commentarioli' (*Against Jovinian* 1, 41; 1, 1). We should probably identify the pamphlet with the 'scriptura horrifica' mentioned by Pope Siricius in *Ep.* 7, 3 (*PL* 13, 1171).

[9] *Against Jovinian* 1, 3. For discussions of Jovinian's teaching see W. Haller, *Iovinianus* (*TU* XVII, 1897), 132–59, and (much better) F. Valli, *Gioviniano* (Urbino, 1953), 75–121. For a thorough analysis of the argument of *Against Jovinian*, see I. Opelt, *Hieronymus' Streitschriften* (Heidelberg, 1973), 37–63.

[10] Cf., e.g., his insistence (*Against Jovinian* 2, 19) that there is no difference of grades among Christians since Christ is equally present in all and all form the temple (not temples) of the Holy Spirit (1 Cor. 3, 16; 6, 19). So the Church, like the Trinity (John 17, 20–3), is a single, tightly-knit body.

[11] Ambrose, *Ep.* 42, 4–7 (*PL* 16, 1125 f.); Augustine, *De nupt. et concup.* 2, 15; *C. duas epp. Pelag.* 1, 4; *C. Iul.* 1, 4; *De haer.* 82 (*CSEL* 42, 267; 60, 425; *PL* 44, 643; 42, 46).

dedicated virgins abandoning their vows to get married.[12] The ascetic party took fright, and, led by Pammachius, denounced him to the pope. Although himself no admirer of extreme asceticism, Siricius felt obliged to take action. Jovinian's doctrines were condemned by a Roman synod as 'contrary to Christian law', and he and eight close associates were excommunicated.[13] At once he betook himself to Milan, only to have his excommunication endorsed there by Ambrose,[14] a passionate supporter of virginity. The chronology of these events is obscure, but the Roman synod cannot have been held earlier than late 392, more probably in 393, for Jerome would certainly have made the most of Jovinian's disgrace in his diatribe against him (written after *Famous Men*) had he had the least inkling of it. What seems most probable is that Pammachius despatched Jovinian's incriminating treatise to him about the same time (spring or early summer 393 ?) as he was denouncing him to the pope.[15]

(iii)

Jerome responded to the appeal of his Roman friends with alacrity. He genuinely considered Jovinian's conception of Christianity, especially his disparagement of celibacy and other ascetic practices, a degrading refusal to face the challenge of the gospel. Nothing could be more congenial to him than to expose the worldliness and immorality to which, he was sure, it was bound to lead, and to refute the arguments advanced in its favour. But the invitation must have been doubly welcome as demonstrating that his special abilities were again recognised at Rome, and as offering him a wonderful opportunity of rehabilitating himself in responsible Christian circles there. So he poured all his dialectical skill and rhetorical art, all his learning and formidable powers of invective and satire, into the composition of *Against Jovinian*. The lengthiest of all his polemical pamphlets, in two unequal books, this is also the most accomplished of them, and marks the full revival of his unrestrained use of the pagan classics and of 'rhetoric'. Granted the limitations of his premises and approach, it is one of his most effective productions. It is commonly stated,[16] though without evidence, that he polished it off in a matter of weeks. But the essay itself,

[12] *Against Jovinian* 2, 36 f.: also Siricius, *Ep.* 7, 3; Augustine, *De haer.* 82; *Retract.* 2, 48 (22) (*PL* 13, 1170; 42, 45 f.; *CSEL* 36, 156 f.).

[13] Siricius, *Ep.* 7, 4 (*PL* 13, 1171).

[14] Ambrose, *Ep.* 42, 14 (*PL* 16, 1128).

[15] For a discussion of the chronology see F. Valli, op. cit., 30–5. Jerome first mentions Jovinian's condemnation in *Letter* 49, 2 (date 394). A date for the Roman synod in early summer 393 might explain why Jovinian went to Milan. He must have expected short shrift from Ambrose, but he might reasonably have looked for sympathy from the usurper Eugenius, whose plans for moving from Gaul to Milan must have already been known (he reached the city in late summer 393).

[16] So L. Duchesne, *The Early History o the Church* (ET, London, 1922) II, 445, followed by others. But cf. F. Valli, op. cit., 36 n. 2.

with its careful structure, skilfully deployed argument, and stylistic brilliance, betrays none of those signs of haste so obvious in other writings which we know he rushed.

Clearly what shocked Jerome most was the claim that the sexually abstinent are in no way superior to married people who enjoy normal sexual relations. So he devoted the whole of his first book (some typical, quite unfounded jibes against Jovinian's prose-style apart)[17] to its rebuttal. Jovinian had appealed to divine blessings on marriage (e.g. Gen. 1, 28: 'Be fruitful and multiply'; Matt. 19, 5: 'What God has joined, let not man put asunder'); to revered figures in the Bible (e.g. Solomon and St Peter) who had married; to statements attributed to St Paul (e.g. Heb. 13, 4: 'Marriage is honourable . . . '); to the respect accorded to wedlock in classical antiquity; to the implicit Manichaeism of those who denigrated sex. Step by step Jerome follows him, pointing out that Adam and Eve embarked on marriage only after their sin, and that while marriage was intended to 'replenish the earth' (Gen. 1, 28), 'virginity replenishes paradise'.[18] With great ingenuity he explains away the marriage, even the polygamy, of the patriarchs, but claims that the figures closest to God in the Bible were all virgins (Joshua, Elijah, John the Baptist, etc.). Solomon's was an awkward case, but the sharp things he said about marriage in Proverbs and Ecclesiastes, above all his hymn in praise of chastity (so he interprets Song of Songs), prove that he had learned his bitter lesson.[19] St Peter's marriage took place before he heard the gospel; his statement (Matt. 19, 27), 'We have left all and followed You,' proves that, once a disciple, he abandoned it. Even so, Jerome asserts,[20] his marriage made him less dear to Jesus than the unmarried John, and even the blood of martyrdom could not wash its 'defilement' away. But it was St Paul whom he made his chief oracle, twisting the famous texts of 1 Corinthians 7 and 1 Timothy to wrest from them an even greater aversion to marriage and second marriages than they contain: 'I suspect the goodness of something which can only be reckoned a lesser evil because of the extreme evil of something else.'[21]

[17] Jerome habitually accused his opponents of literary uncouthness. So Helvidius (*Against Helvidius* 1); Vigilantius (*Against Vigilantius* 3: he was praised as a stylist by Gennadius, *De vir. ill.* 36); Rufinus (*Apology* 1, 30; 3, 6; 10: in fact he was an excellent writer); the unnamed earlier translator of Eusebius's *Onomasticon* (above p. 155). I agree with Valli that the surviving fragments of Jovinian's work reveal him as an expert prose-writer, remarkable for the vigour and trenchancy of his diction (op. cit., 65).

[18] *Against Jovinian* 1, 16.

[19] *Against Jovinian* 1, 28–31.

[20] *Against Jovinian* 1, 26.

[21] *Against Jovinian* 1, 9 (at the end). For his discussion of St Paul (1, 6–15) he drew lavishly, without admitting it, on Tertullian's (Montanist) treatise *De monogamia*: cf. F. Schultzen, 'Die Benützing der Schriften *De monogamia* und *De ieiunio* bei Hieronymus, *Adv. Iovinianum*' (*Neue Jahrbücher für deutsche Theologie* 3, 1894, 485–502).

He brought the book to a close by recalling notable pagan women celebrated for their chastity,[22] and then retailing a depressing catalogue both of the disagreeable aspects of marriage and of notorious wives who had plagued or deceived their husbands. These sections, we should note, were largely borrowed,[23] without acknowledgment and as if he had read the original texts himself, from Seneca, Plutarch, and a lost treatise of Porphyry. The charge of Manichaeism he brushed aside[24] by protesting that he had not absolutely condemned marriage, but only placed it on a lower level than virginity.

Jerome despatched Jovinian's other three theses in his second book. He did not waste much time on the second. Interpreting it as implying that the baptised Christian cannot be *tempted* by the devil (earlier he had used the probably more exact expression 'overthrown'), he had little difficulty in showing[25] that the New Testament is full of warnings against sin, and that the saints of both Testaments had been tempted and sinned; some, indeed, though baptised, fell away irreparably (Heb. 6, 4 f.). He devoted much more space[26] to the third, which denied the spiritual worth of fasting on the grounds that everything had been created for man's enjoyment, and that St Paul had encouraged (1 Tim. 4, 3–5) the eating of every kind of food since God had intended it to be received with thanksgiving. Jesus, too, had attended dinners and feasts, drunk wine, and even made it the sacramental type of his blood. With an imposing parade of learning (second-hand, alas, for although he pretended to have read his authorities, he in fact cribbed most of his information from the pagan Porphyry),[27] Jerome cited natural scientists to prove that, while living creatures had all been made for man's benefit, they were not necessarily meant for his stomach, and philosophers and medical writers (he had read at least Galen) who had applauded abstemiousness. Then, basing himself on Tertullian[28] (again without naming him), he argued that it was through eating that Adam fell and Esau lost his birthright, that Moses, Joshua, Saul, Elijah, Daniel, John the Baptist, etc. had set the example of fasting, and that Jesus had consecrated Christian fasting by fasting forty days himself. He crystallised the dangers of indulgence in the characteristic sentence, 'Eating meat, drinking wine, having a well-filled belly—there you have the seed-bed of lust.'[29]

[22] *Against Jovinian* 1, 41–6.
[23] See E. Bickel, *Diatribe in Senecae philosophi fragmenta* 1 (Leipzig, 1915), esp. 325 and 357.
[24] *Against Jovinian* 1, 3.
[25] *Against Jovinian* 2, 1–4.
[26] *Against Jovinian* 2, 5–17.
[27] Cf. P. Courcelle, *Late Latin Writers and their Greek Sources* (ET, Cambridge, Mass., 1969), 73 f.: he gives the references to Porphyry's *De abstinentia*.
[28] This time his *De ieiunio*: cf. F. Schultzen, art. cit.
[29] *Against Jovinian* 2, 7.

To support his fourth thesis Jovinian had appealed to the many passages of Scripture which divide mankind into two undifferentiated classes, the good and the bad. This was the implication, he contended, of the stories of Noah and the Flood, of Sodom and Gomorrah, of the Israelites and the Egyptians at the Red Sea, of the foolish and the wise virgins, above all of our Lord's description of the final judgment, when the sheep will be separated from the goats, the righteous from the wicked. Jerome's reply consisted, in part, in arguing[30] that, while these broad distinctions are valid, they do not exclude gradations within each category. There are sheep and goats, but the individual members of each flock differ vastly from each other in all sorts of respects. But, further, St Paul, by calling himself 'the least of the apostles', had conceded that even apostles can be of higher or lower rank; while in other passages[31] he had clearly taught that each man will receive a recompense proportionate to his merits. Jovinian's elimination of differentials in rewards, which he justified[32] by the equal treatment meted out to the Prodigal Son and his elder brother and to all the Labourers in the Vineyard, seemed to Jerome the height of perverse ingenuity. In his reply he complained that Jovinian was adopting a Stoic stance,[33] protested against the unfairness of not recognising degrees of sin and goodness, recalled that St John himself had singled out a 'sin unto death',[34] and produced far-fetched explanations of the two awkward parables.[35] His parting taunt was that, if Jovinian's immoral doctrine were true, we might as well all sin, confident that after repenting we shall be on the level of the apostles.[36]

A surprising omission in the treatise is any discussion, indeed any mention, of Jovinian's claim that Mary's virginity had been impaired by the physical process of bearing the child Jesus. Surely Jerome would have torn such an impious assertion to shreds had he come across it, especially as he had held Mary up as a model of virginity in *Against Jovinian* 1, 32. One possible explanation of his silence is that the offensive proposition did not feature in Jovinian's pamphlet, either because he developed this teaching after his condemnation at Rome when he fled to Milan, or because he propagated it verbally rather than in writing.[37] What many have

[30] *Against Jovinian* 2, 22.

[31] E.g. 1 Cor. 15, 22 f; 39; 2 Cor. 5, 10; 9, 6. Cf. *Against Jovinian* 2, 23.

[32] *Against Jovinian* 2, 20: cf. Matt. 20, 1–16; Lk. 15, 11–32. For Jerome's critique see *Against Jovinian* 2, 21–32.

[33] *Against Jovinian* 2, 21; 35. So too Augustine, *De haer.* 82 (' . . . sicut Stoici philosphi'). For the Stoics the only good was to be virtuous, i.e. to live in harmony with reason, and the only evil was not to be virtuous. The actual deeds men do are purely accessory products of the spirit which is good, or evil, in this sense; there is no gradation between them, any more than in truth and falsehood.

[34] 1 Jn. 5, 16 (*Against Jovinian* 2, 30).

[35] *Against Jovinian* 2, 31 f.

[36] *Against Jovinian* 2, 34 (at the end).

[37] For the former explanation see W. Haller, *Iovinianus*, 127; for the latter A. Penna, 184.

overlooked, however, is that Jerome might have had difficulty in attacking Jovinian on this particular issue, since he himself shared the view that in bringing Jesus into the world Mary had undergone all the normal birth-pangs.[38] What he was passionately concerned to maintain were the theses (a) that she had conceived Jesus virginally, and (b) that after, as before, his birth she had had no carnal intercourse with Joseph. We know that Jovinian upheld the former point, and there is not a particle of evidence that he denied the latter one. Jerome may well have found Jovinian's inference that, since the parturition was physically normal, Mary's virginity was undermined highly objectionable; but since he himself accepted the major premiss, he may reasonably have decided not to do battle with him on this matter, but deliberately to pass it over as one of the points raised by him which, as he states,[39] 'it would be unprofitable to discuss'.

(iv)

Jerome was a hard-hitting fighter, and did not mince his words. His treatise abounds in coarse abuse, describing, for example, Jovinian's book as 'vomit which he has thrown up', and the man himself as 'the debauchee preacher'.[40] It also contains robustly libellous caricatures,[41] depicting him as wantoning in pleasure gardens, or in baths where men and women bathe together, surrounded by pampered favourites of both sexes, while the true followers of Christ, pale through fasting and squalidly clad, languish like strangers in this world (which is what in fact they are). For all its polemical bravado, however, for all its technical expertise, *Against Jovinian* seems to modern readers singularly superficial and unconvincing. Where he has a useful card (e.g. St Paul's misogynism in 1 Cor. 7), he overplays it. Where he is at a disadvantage, as with the marriages of St Peter and other Apostles, he resorts to an unnatural exegesis to distort the scriptural record. On the level of discussion adopted he inevitably makes plenty of effective points, but at least as often he either cheats in argument or reaches his desired conclusion by a non-sequitur or by special pleading. But what is most disappointing is that he nowhere comes to grips with, nowhere seems to understand Jovinian's fundamental thesis, viz. that baptism received with genuine faith really does abolish original sin and effects a total regeneration, creating a unified, holy community in which distinctions based on merit are without meaning.

---

[38] See above p. 106.
[39] *Against Jovinian* 1, 5. In this paragraph I have been greatly helped by F. Valli, op. cit., 125–42.
[40] *Against Jovinian* 1, 4 ('voluptuosissimus concionator').
[41] *Against Jovinian* 2, 36.

Here was a challenge to the conventional Catholicism of the day which deserved to be debated at a deeper level.

Naturally Jerome's contemporaries would not apply the same critical standards in assessing his work as we do. The great majority, not just the extreme ascetic group, were outraged by Jovinian's questioning of such almost universally accepted tenets as the superiority of virginity to marriage and the spiritual value of ascetic practices like fasting. So when Jerome despatched his brilliant treatise to Rome, he could be confident that it would be greeted with applause. Certainly it was widely read, in Palestine as well as the west,[42] but its reception was the reverse of what he had expected. Jovinian, it is true, disappeared from the scene,[43] but more as the result of his double condemnation by the pope and Ambrose than of Jerome's tirade. Even so, his ideas continued to be canvassed sympathetically, though not openly, at Rome, and to be disseminated more brazenly at Vercelli, in north Italy.[44] But even Jerome's friends, the devoted Christians who had begged him to pulverise 'the Christian Epicurus', were filled with consternation when they read what he had written. They were shocked by the violence and crudity of his language, and by his eagerness to crush Jovinian rather than persuade him,[45] but even more by the derogatory view of marriage which his hysterical exaltation of virginity entailed. While some of his dicta were moderate (e.g. marriage differs from virginity as what is good from what is better),[46] others condemned intercourse between spouses as an obstacle to prayer and reception of the eucharist, an evil which was only to be tolerated because fornication was worse.[47]

The people who found these passages offensive were not necessarily frivolous worldlings. In a letter[48] to his friend Domnio we hear of a young monk at Rome, a former barrister who had now turned to the religious life and was lecturing to fashionable ladies (Jerome's jealousy comes out very

[42] So Jerome, *Letter* 48, 2. He adds that once he has written anything, his admirers and ill-wishers, for opposite motives, immediately ensure its circulation.

[43] There is a mystery about his end. *Codex Theod.* xvi, 5, 53 suggests that he was banished by imperial decree, after a thorough flogging, to an island off Dalmatia; but this can be accepted only if the date given (412) is altered to 6 March 398. The only firm fact we know is that he was dead by 406 when Jerome wrote *Against Vigilantius* 1, where he states that he had, 'amid feasts of pheasants and pork, I shall not say breathed out, but rather belched out, his spirit.

[44] Cf. Augustine, *Retract.* 2, 48 (22); Ambrose, *Ep.* 43, 7 f.: to the church at Vercelli (*CSEL* 36, 156 f.; *PL* 16, 1191 f.).

[45] Jerome, *Letter* 49, 2 and 14.

[46] *Against Jovinian* 1, 13.

[47] *Against Jovinian* 1, 7: also the whole section 7–13. Cf. his reference (1, 26) to the 'defilement' ('sordes') of St Peter's marriage.

[48] *Letter* 50. For the identification of the monk with Pelagius see G. de Plinval, *Pélage* (Lausanne, 1943), 51–5. His case, accepted without question by J. N. L. Myres, 'Pelagius and the End of Roman Rule in Britain', *Journal of Roman Studies* 50 (1960), 22 and 24, has been greatly strengthened by the detailed argument of R. F. Evans in his *Pelagius: Inquiries and Reappraisals* (London, 1968), 31–7.

clearly) on morals and Scripture, who, while denouncing Jovinian, was
also publicly attacking Jerome's negative teaching about marriage. He
was a fine figure of a man, of massive and athletic build, and Jerome and
he had known each other previously (presumably at Rome in 382–5) and
had crossed swords in argument. Although he is not named, it is as
certain as can be that this was none other than the great Pelagius, the
arch-heretic who twenty or so years later was to clash with both Jerome
and Augustine on the issues of grace and free will. The letter suggests that
he was a formidable disputant, relying on ordered reasoning rather than
on a parade of learning; and while jeering at him as self-taught, in contrast
to his own highly professional training in logic, even Jerome had to admit
his eloquence. His criticisms had evidently struck home, for Jerome was
reduced to shrilly denying that he had ever condemned wedlock and to
challenging Pelagius, instead of ranting against him in general terms, to
put pen to paper and publish a treatise to which he could reply. He professed to believe that he secretly held the same views as himself, but was
inspired by envy to denigrate him.

There was panic among Jerome's friends. His exaggerated claims and
unbridled language, they were quick to see, were doing incalculable
damage to the very cause both he and they wished to uphold. Pammachius
made valiant efforts to withdraw as many copies of the embarrassing
pamphlet from circulation as he could,[49] and at the same time wrote
asking him to produce a reasoned defence of his views.[50] Domnio, the
Roman friend who had alerted him to the campaign Pelagius was mounting against him, was equally perplexed, and excerpted a collection of
passages which were causing scandal, and sent them to Jerome requesting
him either to amend or to explain them.[51]

For Pammachius he prepared an enormously long, carefully argued
pièce justificatif.[52] Without retreating one inch from his previous position,
but tactfully moderating his language and highlighting whatever concessions he had made to the admissibility of marriage, he protested that
none of his remarks should be construed as condemning marriage for
those who could not aspire to something better. (Thus he had ended his
letter to Domnio about Pelagius by remarking, with stinging irony and
an allusion to Song of Songs 3, 8: 'Finally, to make my meaning plain to
him, I want everyone to take a wife who cannot sleep alone because, I
suppose, of "the terrors of night".') True, he had extolled virginity to the
skies (not, alas, as one who possessed it, but as one who admired what he
had lost); but the Parable of the Sower indicated that it is virginity which

[49] *Letter* 48, 2.
[50] *Letter* 49, 1.
[51] So Jerome reports in *Letter* 50, 3.
[52] *Letter* 49 (in Vallarsi, reproduced in *PL* 22, numbered 48).

yields a hundred-fold, while chaste widowhood yields sixty-fold and marriage only thirty-fold. So far from his doctrine being novel, it had the support of older writers in the Church, including Ambrose (in his dire straits he did not hesitate to cite his *bête-noire* as a witness). In defence of his pugnacious style he reminded Pammachius that the conventions of rhetoric permitted greater licence in a polemical than an instructional work. In conclusion, 'Christ and Mary, both virgins, consecrated the pattern of virginity for both sexes'. His reply[53] to Domnio, his informant about the activities of the unnamed Roman monk, consisted largely of a virulent attack on the latter, in which abuse and innuendo, coarse sneers and indignant threats, combine in a disagreeable but, alas, characteristic mixture.

(v)

Notwithstanding the brave front he put up to Pammachius and Domnio, Jerome must have been bitterly disappointed by the hostile reaction to *Against Jovinian* in Rome. Nevertheless its publication marked the re-opening at last of relations between himself and the west, particularly the western capital. On the one hand, we observe him seizing the opportunity to impress his achievements as a Bible scholar on leading western churchmen. On the other, evidence begins to accumulate from now onwards that, austere though his programme might be, his standing as an ascetic counsellor and as an authority on the life to be followed by dedicated Christians was becoming increasingly recognised.

Under the former heading, we note that in a covering letter[54] which he sent with his apologia to Pammachius he included an exhortation to his old friend to study his commentaries on the Prophets, and also his translations of the Old Testament from the Hebrew, comparing these latter with versions based on the Greek Septuagint. The difference, he would find, was that between truth and falsehood. He also suggested that he should borrow a copy of his recent translation of Job from Marcella. She was still, apparently, his Scripture taskmaster, and we have a letter[55] from this period in which he attempts to clear up five Biblical conundrums which were worrying her. The most interesting were what St Paul had meant (1 Cor. 2, 9) by the things which no eye has seen or ear heard, whether we are to suppose that those who are alive at the Second Coming will escape death and be taken up in their actual bodies to meet Christ

---

[53] *Letter* 50 (an invaluable source, in spite of its distortions, of information about Pelagius at this time in Rome).

[54] *Letter* 48, 4.

[55] *Letter* 59 (date uncertain, but probably shortly after *Against Jovinian*, which it mentions in par. 2).

(1 Thess. 4, 15–17), and whether before his ascension the risen Christ was present only with his disciples or was omnipresent. The solutions Jerome provides are instructive examples of his exegesis, careful to smooth out apparent discrepancies in Scripture, strictly orthodox (e.g. in affirming the omnipresence of the risen Christ), still Origenist in accepting the transformation of the resurrection body.

Jerome, however, had been writing to Marcella along these lines for years. More significant is his dedication of his new translations of Ezra and Nehemiah (394/5) to his Roman friends, Domnio and Rogatianus (otherwise unknown), and of Chronicles (395) to Chromatius of Aquileia.[56] Both prefaces bear painful witness, in Jerome's bitter complaints and expostulations, to the venomous fury which his return to 'the Hebrew verity' continued to excite among prejudiced people who ought to have known better—so much so that he bids Domnio and Rogatianus keep his versions strictly to themselves and such enlightened people as could appreciate them. But they equally confirm that he now had in the west at least some intelligent, well-informed admirers who were positively insistent that he should carry on with the great enterprise.[57] It was their encouragement which made him conclude the former preface with a spirited expression of his determination to do so: 'Though the serpent hiss and "victorious Sinon hurl his fire-brand", with Christ's help my mouth will never be shut. Cut off my tongue, and it will still manage to stammer something.'[58]

His letters to Nepotian, Furia, and Amandus[59] fall under the second heading, and illustrate the uncompromising rigour of his advice. Nepotian was the nephew of Heliodorus, whom twenty years earlier Jerome had vainly begged to share his experience as a desert hermit.[60] Now he was bishop of his home town, Altinum, his nephew had served in the palace guard (though with sackcloth under his brilliant uniform), but had resigned and given all his pay to the poor,[61] and Heliodorus had ordained him priest. In response to his entreaties Jerome sent the young man an

[56] The date of the former can be deduced from its preface (PL 28, 1404), which suggests that he was then working on *Letter* 57 (date 395); of the latter from its preface (PL 28, 1325), which states that he had 'recently' composed *Letter* 57.

[57] This is made clear by the prefaces just mentioned. Chromatius took a great interest in the work, and provided funds to help Jerome to carry it out: see below p. 284.

[58] The 'serpent' is probably Rufinus: see above p. 169. The quotation is from Vergil, *Aeneid* 2, 329. Sinon was a Greek who, pretending to be a deserter, told the Trojans a lying story about the Trojan Horse, and once it was within the city released the soldiers it contained and himself joined in the sack of Troy.

[59] *Letters* 52, 54, 55. The first states (52, 17) that it was composed ten years after *Letter* 22, i.e. in 394. The second (54, 18) dates from 'amost two years' after *Against Jovinian*, i.e. 395–6. The third gives no clue, but must be prior to *Comm. on Matthew* (398), for Jerome would surely have referred to this when dealing with the first of Amandus's problems.

[60] See above p. 44.

[61] Cf. *Letter* 60, 9 (the threnody on Nepotian).

affectionate, polished essay, decked with classical quotations and allusions, setting out (he rightly knew it would not be popular) the austere pattern of the priest-monk. No friend of the establishment, he interspersed it with caustic digs at priestly cupidity and worldliness, and at stuck-up bishops (there is but one ministry of priests and bishops). Humility, poverty, sombre attire, constant Bible study, regular pastoral activity, avoidance of gossip, sparse diet, above all strict continence in sexual matters (rarely if ever should a woman cross his threshold, nor should he encourage girls to marry, still less widows to re-marry)—these are the ideals he inculcates. The letter, incidentally, opens with one of Jerome's most audacious feats of exegesis. It would be crudely literalistic, he assures Nepotian, to regard Abishaig the Shunamite, whom (so I Kings 1, 1–4) David's courtiers procured to sleep with the ageing king and warm his chilled body, as having been a real girl. What she stands for in the story is the wisdom which glows in an old man, such as Jerome himself (he was sixty-three), and in a young man of dedicated life.

Furia, too, had sought his guidance. A Roman aristocrat recently widowed, she had decided against re-marriage, and Jerome congratulates her on her resolve to have only Christ as her spouse. Having experienced the vexations of marriage, why should she be like the dog which returns to its vomit? But if she is to remain steadfast, she must turn a deaf ear to self-interested servants who press her to marry; she must dress soberly, throw away cosmetics and jewelry, eat and drink frugally (excess in either respect stimulates lust); she must steer clear of young men and have only dedicated widows and virgins as her companions. As a horrifying example he cites the scandal caused by a wealthy, pampered widow who had recently travelled over the whole east (evidently a pilgrim) keeping such indiscriminate company and such a luxurious table, wearing such sumptuous clothes, that one might take her for the bride of Nero or Sardanapalus.[62] To Amandus, a priest otherwise unknown who had put some questions to him, Jerome repeats his familiar doctrine that excess in food and drink enflames the passions, finds authority in Christ's commendation of those who make themselves eunuchs for the kingdom of heaven (Matt. 19, 10–12) for the superior blessedness of celibacy, and insists that even a woman who has abandoned her husband because of his revolting debauchery and has been taken by force to be another man's wife must be excluded from communion as an adulteress while her original husband is still alive.

---

[62] Often taken to be a reference to Egeria, the rich and noble lady from Aquitaine whose travel-diary (*Peregrinatio Egeriae*) of the Holy Land is one of the most vivid and informative documents of the period. But P. Devos, 'La date du voyage d'Égérie', *Anal. Boll.* 85 (1967), 165–94, seems to have established that she left Jerusalem on Easter Monday 384, i.e. before Jerome's arrival in the city.

Specially interesting, as evidence of his prestige in the west but also for their own sake, are two letters which Jerome sent in 394 and 395 respectively to Meropius Pontius Paulinus.[63] A Christian by family, noble, rich and cultivated, a polished writer himself, Paulinus had been born at Bordeaux c. 355, had been governor of Campania (where he owned estates) in 381, but in 389 had been baptised and with his wife had adopted strict asceticism, abandoning his career in the world and resolving to dispose of his wealth for Christian purposes. Ordained priest against his will at Barcelona at Christmas 393, he was soon to settle at Nola (23 km. east of Naples), but meanwhile had written to Jerome (to Augustine too), being eager to open up friendships with committed Christians from whom he could learn and who shared his interests. The immediate purpose of his letter, which he accompanied with small gifts, seems to have been to commend to Jerome its bearer, Ambrose, who was on pilgrimage to the Holy Land. But in it he recalled his reading of Jerome's Biblical writings, dwelt on his own zeal for sacred studies, and touched on his determination to renounce the world and rid himself of his vast property, although he stressed that this would take time unless he was to sell it at a loss and thus deprive Christ's poor of their full due.[64]

In his elaborate reply Jerome welcomes this new friendship, cemented by common devotion to Scripture, and presses his friend to join him at Bethlehem. Eusebius of Cremona, who is already there with him, has expatiated on Paulinus's nobility of character and love for Christ; the letter he has received is ample proof of his literary skill. Paulinus's zeal for Scripture is wholly admirable, but the Bible is full of mysteries, and it is a mistake to assume that one can do without a guide. He must also eschew false guides, such as professors who learn from women what they are to teach to men, and even then explain to others what they do not themselves understand (a palpable hit at Rufinus, who relied on the theological expertise of Melania).[65] He should be wary, too, of imagining that a good classical education, such as he and Jerome possess, automatically provides a key to the Bible. Then, after an extended survey of the books of the Old and New Testaments designed to illustrate their difficulties, Jerome urges Paulinus to live with them and meditate on them. He himself would not offer himself as a master, but would be delighted to be a fellow-

---

[63] Letters 53 and 58. Cavallera's widely accepted view (II, 89–91) that Letter 58 is the earlier of the two has been shown to be incorrect by P. Nautin: see his 'Études de chronologie hiéronymienne (393–7)', Revue des études augustiniennes 19 (1973), 214 ff. I am much indebted to this article both for the dating of the letters and for their contents and Jerome's replies. For Paulinus's career see PLRE I, 681–3. For his personality, ideas, etc. see P. Fabre, Saint Paulin de Nole et l'amitié chrétienne (Paris, 1949).

[64] Paulinus's letter is lost, but its outline can be deduced from Jerome's reply in Letter 53: see P. Nautin, art. cit. 224 ff.

[65] Letter 53, 7. So Nautin understands the passage.

student with him. He concludes with a summons to sell his property at once, even if it entails a loss, and set out on the journey; Jerome will welcome him with open arms.

Jerome's second letter maintained the same complimentary tone, but a vein of hardly concealed criticism and irritation ran through it. Paulinus had written in the meantime explaining that he had now finally quitted the world and settled as a monk at Nola, and asking advice on the way to organise his life. Dearly though he wished he could come to Jerusalem, he was held back by his ties with his wife, with whom he now lived as a brother. He enclosed a copy of a panegyric he had composed in honour of the emperor Theodosius (d. 17 January 395), and warmly commended to Jerome the priest Vigilantius, who was carrying the letter and who was charged to distribute alms on his behalf. This Vigilantius will come again into the story, and it was he (we may suspect) who was the cause of Jerome's irritation. Not only had his behaviour during an earthquake made him a laughing-stock, but he had made his stay with Jerome indecently short; it is likely, too, that he had lodged and associated with Melania and Rufinus on the Mount of Olives.[66]

In his response Jerome congratulated Paulinus on translating his vow of renunciation into action, but warned him of the incompatibility of the monkish garb with the retention of a vast income, warned him also of the danger of leaving the distribution of his wealth to others and of doling it out to people who already had ample means. The former point expressed his dissatisfaction with Paulinus's policy of keeping possession of his property while devoting it to alms-giving, the latter was a thrust at Vigilantius, who seems to have given less of the money he brought from his master to Jerome than he had hoped, and more than he thought proper to Melania and Rufinus.[67] As for Jerusalem, there was no special advantage in living there. God is not confined to any one spot, none of the heroes of monasticism had ever set eyes on the Holy City, the places which witnessed the crucifixion and resurrection profit only those who take up their own crosses daily. A monk would in fact do better to live in seclusion in the country than in Jerusalem, which was a crowded metropolis swarming with the scum of the earth. Jerome then gave Paulinus useful practical advice on how he and Therasia should live as ascetics, eulogised

[66] Paulinus's letter does not survive, but its contents can be reconstructed from Jerome's reply in *Letter* 58. For Vigilantius's panic during the earthquake see *Against Vigilantius* 11; also below p. 289. As P. Nautin points out, it was only natural that, after his curtailed visit to Jerome, he should stay with Melania and Rufinus, for she was a relative of Paulinus and he must have recommended him to her as well as to Jerome. The latter was to claim (*Apology* 3, 19) that it was they who had stirred up Vigilantius against him.

[67] For these two points see *Letter* 58, 2 and 6 f. The advice in par. 7, 'Do not, by an error of judgment, give what belongs to the poor to those who are not poor', hints at the well-off Melania and Rufinus (P. Nautin). For Jerome's disappointment with the alms his communities received from Vigilantius, cf. his sneering language in *Against Vigilantius* 13.

his panegyric in extravagant terms, and urged him to crown his remarkable talents and literary flair by acquiring a thorough, discerning knowledge of Scripture, thereby becoming as eminent in the Church as he had been in the Senate. He ended with some biting comments on the unexpected brevity of Vigilantius's stay; he had been a mere 'passer-by', fretting to be on the road again.[68]

These letters to friends have little, if any, of the crudity and violence of *Against Jovinian*. But if Jerome moderated his language, he did not water down his doctrine in the slightest, although he was fully aware that by re-opening his campaign for extreme asceticism he was exposing himself to 'the stabs of every tongue'.[69] As always, he was the inflexible champion of chastity, the brightest jewel, as he saw it, in the committed Christian's crown. As always, he was the preacher of total renunciation of wealth, position, personal comfort, of the joyful acceptance of privations in order 'naked to follow the naked cross'.[70] Where he had changed in this second letter to Paulinus was in his attitude to Jerusalem. When he had written to Marcella in the name of Paula and Eustochium, his enthusiasm for the Holy Places was lyrical; it was still the same when he wrote a year or two before this to Desiderius and Serenilla.[71] In his first letter to Paulinus in 394 he had eagerly invited him to come to Bethlehem. In the following chapter we shall discover the painful factors, cruelly affecting his own position, which caused him to swing, temporarily at any rate, to the opposite extreme.

---

[68] *Letter* 58, 11. Almost certainly the reason for his cutting short his stay was his discovery that Jerome and his monastery were (as we shall later learn) at this time under the ban of the bishop of Jerusalem. As a loyal Catholic this must have alarmed him.

[69] So he confesses to Nepotian: *Letter* 52, 17.

[70] *Letter* 58, 2.

[71] *Letters* 46 and 47: see above pp. 141 and 180.

XVIII

Jerome, Rufinus, John

(i)

Early in 393, even before he set to work on *Against Jovinian*, Jerome found himself caught up in a controversy of extraordinary bitterness which, despite attempts at reconciliation, was to rumble on for more than a decade, bring out the worst in his nature, poison friendships of long standing, and fill the Christian world with abashed consternation. What sparked the controversy off was an essentially theological dispute, but in each of its phases the flames were fanned by a tragic clash of personalities.

Along with Jerome the leading characters in the first act of the drama were Rufinus, Bishop John of Jerusalem, and the elderly Epiphanius, bishop of Salamis in Cyprus. Until 393 Jerome's relations with Rufinus had been, officially and so far as the general public could perceive, cordial,[1] and with John at least correct. Yet there is reason to suppose that ominous cracks were rapidly developing behind the façade. However polite their exchanges, Jerome could not forget that John's theological background was that of his predecessor Cyril and of Meletius of Antioch, both associated in his mind with Trinitarian views not far removed from Arianism.[2] John too, monk though he was, lived in the grand manner and exercised his office with masterful disdain: traits which Jerome, who had no love for prelates anyhow, found highly objectionable.[3] With Rufinus, of course, his friendship went back to boyhood and had once been of the tenderest kind. The two men were vastly different in temperament, however; and while this did not matter when they were young, it became a critical factor now that they were ageing, hardened in their attitudes after living apart for decades. Learned and greatly respected, Rufinus was less brilliant and versatile than Jerome, but also more cautious, more deliberate, more steadfast. Jerome's was a much more passionate, impulsive, egotistical disposition, sensitive to the point of morbidity. He was also, to

---

[1] See above p. 136.

[2] Cf. his harsh comments on Cyril and Meletius in *Chronicle* A.D. 348; 329; 360 (*GCS* 47, 237; 232; 241 f.). For his belief that John had a pro-Arian past see his insinuations in *Against John* (e.g. 3 and 4).

[3] These points come out in, e.g., *Against John* 4; 14; *Letter* 57, 12. See also below p. 308.

judge by a comment of Palladius[4] (admittedly no friend, but he had lived in Jerusalem from 386 to 388 and the remark chimes in with our other impressions), intensely possessive, suspicious of and hostile to people who did not yield to his spell.

It was natural that the two Latin monastic settlements, at Bethlehem and on the Mount of Olives, should start off on good terms with each other. With hindsight, and reading Jerome's early commentaries, we may suspect that, before many years, relations had become distinctly cool, not to say strained. The high reputation Rufinus and Melania enjoyed must have grated on the jealous Jerome. So too must the friendship and mutual esteem which existed between Rufinus and Bishop John (who had probably ordained him priest). More practically, Jerome seems to have considered the ascetic standards observed on the Mount of Olives much laxer and less demanding than he deemed suitable.[5] Melania, for example, had not stripped herself of her wealth, but husbanded it for charitable purposes. Rufinus for his part, with his primly ecclesiastical outlook, was scandalised by Jerome's return to the reading of pagan literature, as also by his giving lessons in it to local children.[6] He was outraged, too, by Jerome's tampering with the sacrosanct Septuagint and by his preference for the original Hebrew in translating the Old Testament. It is fairly certain, as we have seen,[7] that he had already felt the lash of his friend's tongue on this score.

The intellectual issue which brought these smouldering animosities to a blazing quarrel was the theology of Origen. Until 393 all three had been devoted admirers of the great third-century thinker, the most outstanding theologian so far produced by the Church; in *Famous Men* Jerome had recently applauded his 'immortal genius'. Origen had been primarily an exegete, the perfecter of a method which, studying Scripture at different levels, discovered in the personages, events, and prescriptions of the Old Testament Spirit-directed pointers to the saving mysteries of the Christian revelation. He was also, however, a constructive theologian, and his vision of the triune Godhead as a hierarchy of divine persons had (despite its intrinsic subordinationism, ultimately Middle Platonist in inspiration) a pervasive impact on the currently accepted orthodoxy, especially of the east. In addition, in trying to solve the baffling problems of existence and providence, he had propounded (as we have noted from time to time)

---

[4] *Hist. Laus.* 36, 6: cf. 41, 2 (of the unhealthy hold he had over Paula). The term he uses is βασκανία, i.e. 'jealousy', 'malignity', 'envy'. Contrast his remarks in *Hist. Laus.* 46, 5 on Rufinus's 'consistency', 'solidarity of character': 'a man more spiritually discerning or more balanced could not be found.'

[5] This can be deduced from his sneers at Rufinus's wealth, luxurious life-style, etc. (e.g. *Comm. on Nahum* 3, 8; *Apology* 3, 4; *Letter* 125, 18—'Grunnius . . . bene nummatus').

[6] *Apol. c. Hier.* 2, 4–8.

[7] See above pp. 169 f.: also *Apol. c. Hier.* 2, 32–5.

speculative opinions which were as far-reaching as they were original. From the first he had had hostile critics, some offended by particular features of his teaching, others convinced that he had adulterated the gospel with Platonic philosophy. Emotions were particularly excited among the monks of Egypt, some of whom (e.g. at Nitria) were enthusiasts for Origen, while others rejected his allegorism and spiritualising tendencies, inclining themselves to take the corporeal language used about God in the Bible literally, and thus incurring the charge of 'anthropomorphism'. In general, however, the leading Greek theologians of the second half of the fourth century valued Origen's contribution and assimilated what they found useful in it. His more questionable views, it is important to note, found no reputable supporters, and his admirers tended to turn a blind eye to them.

The great exception was Epiphanius,[8] the fanatical bishop of Salamis whom Jerome had accompanied to Rome in 382 and whose hospitality he and Paula had enjoyed in Cyprus when journeying to the east in 385. Born near Eleutheropolis (37 km. south-west of Jerusalem) between 310 and 320, he had served his monastic apprenticeship among (apparently) anti-Origenist monks in Egypt, had founded his own monastery at Besanduc, close to his birthplace, and in 366 had become bishop of Salamis, the principal see of Cyprus. Able but anti-intellectualist, of wide but ill-digested learning and intransigent zeal for 'correct' doctrine, he was inordinately lacking in judgment, tact, and charity, but also inordinately venerated for his force of personality, impressive bearing, and rigorous asceticism. He had decided that Origen was an arch-heretic, the man who, blinded by Greek culture, had been the intellectual father of Arius; and he had denounced him as such in works published almost twenty years previously. He had there assembled a dossier of opinions attributed, in a garbled form, to the master, the more alarming being that, just as the Son could not see the Father, so the Holy Spirit could not see the Son, that human souls had pre-existed as angelic spirits and then been incarcerated in bodies as a result of the Fall, that in support of this the Bible language about the coats of skin with which Adam and Eve were clothed after their expulsion from Eden was to be interpreted allegorically as meaning bodies, that at the resurrection the bodies with which men will rise will not be real flesh but ethereal, and that the Devil will in the end repent and be restored to his former dignity.[9] Epiphanius was determined to extirpate the pernicious heresy wherever he found it, and especially in

---

[8] There are admirable summary studies of Epiphanius in *DHGE* 15, by P. Nautin, and in *RAC* 5, by W. Schneemelcher.

[9] Epiphanius had dealt with Origen in his *Ancoratus* (374), and much more fully in his *Panarion* 64 (374–6). He was to summarise the more objectionable features of his theology in his famous letter to John (translated by Jerome as *Letter* 51: see below p. 201 f.).

his native Palestine, where he had discovered to his dismay that Origen's admirers were numerous and included the bishop of Jerusalem himself.

(ii)

Not ready as yet for a confrontation with Bishop John, Epiphanius first attempted to purge the Latin settlements at Jerusalem and Bethlehem. Rufinus made no secret of his sympathy for Origen; he had learned to admire him during his six years' study under Didymus at Alexandria and during his sojourn at Nitria. Jerome, too, was an obvious suspect, not only (as he alleged)[10] because he was Rufinus's friend, but because of the praise he had lavished on Origen (even after the publication of Epiphanius's attack on him)[11] and the wholesale use he had made of his writings. At Epiphanius's instigation, therefore, early in 393 a band of monks led by one Atarbius presented themselves at both Jerome's and Rufinus's monasteries demanding a formal abjuration of Origenism.[12] Jerome complied without hesitation. Biographers have been puzzled by his alacrity, attributing it to his eagerness to brush off the slightest suspicion of unorthodoxy. But he was at least equally swayed by keenness to re-establish himself in the good books of Atarbius's patron, his octogenarian friend Epiphanius. Perhaps, too, he felt he could disavow the 'dogmas of Origen' with a clean conscience since his veneration for him had been largely based on his marvellous exegesis, not on his dogmatic writings, which up to the present he does not seem to have studied closely.[13] Rufinus, however, was not going to be bullied or cajoled. Having learned so much from Origen, he was not the man 'to accuse or change his teachers'.[14] He kept his gate barred and refused to see Atarbius, letting him know, however, that unless he took himself off he would have him driven from the premises with cudgels.

Rufinus's contemptuous reaction to Atarbius, so different from his own, infuriated Jerome against his old friend (his later taunts make this clear).[15] For Rufinus the position cannot have been helped by the fact that

---

[10] *Apology* 3, 33.

[11] It is unlikely that he had read until now Epiphanius's *Ancoratus* or his *Panarion*. The brief notice in *Famous Men* 114 cursorily mentions the latter work in a way which suggests that he did not know it directly. His comment on Epiphanius ('He survives to the present day . . . in extreme old age') makes one think that he cannot have had much contact with him since stopping with him briefly in 385 on the way to the east.

[12] Our entire knowledge of the incident derives from Jerome's later (401) *Apology* 3, 33. Most biographers assume that Atarbius was acting on his own initiative, but Jerome clearly alludes to someone whose agent he was, and it can hardly be doubted that this was Epiphanius.

[13] So in *Apology* 3, 9 he implies that he had admired Origen's Biblical learning when he was young and knew nothing of his heretical teaching.

[14] For the remark see Jerome, *Apology* 3, 18.

[15] *Apology* 3, 33.

(in Jerome's words) Atarbius continued 'howling against him' at Jerusalem. But this incident was only the first move in Epiphanius's campaign against Origen's admirers in Palestine, the chief of whom was, of course, Bishop John. A few weeks, more probably months, later he appeared in person in Jerusalem to take part in important liturgical celebrations. The accepted view is that this was Easter 393, but at that season he must have been in Cyprus presiding over the administration of baptism in his cathedral. It is much more likely that it was the Dedication festival in mid-September, which we know was observed with exceptional solemnity over several days at Jerusalem, with crowds of monks from far and near and numerous bishops attending.[16] Epiphanius was staying in John's house adjacent to the Church of the Resurrection, and, when invited by his brother-bishop to preach (John no doubt felt obliged to ask him in view of the popular expectation), made his sermon a violent onslaught on Origen's errors. But, as Jerome boasts, if his oratorical javelins were ostensibly aimed at Origen, their intended target was really John.

The scene was one of high drama, and we can recapture it through Jerome's graphic, if heavily biased, description.[17] As the aged Epiphanius fulminated, John and his clergy (so he alleges) were grinning like dogs, tapping their foreheads, nodding to each other, and muttering, 'Silly old man'. Eventually exasperated, John took the unprecedented step of sending his archdeacon to Epiphanius with the request to shut up. When his turn came, at an afternoon service, John himself declaimed against the simple-minded Anthropomorphites who took literally the Bible references to God's eyes, hands, and body (sophisticated Origenists liked to caricature their opponents as such). His looks and gestures made it plain that it was Epiphanius he had in view. But, for once, Epiphanius exercised superb self-control. Indicating that he wished to say a few words, he expressed entire agreement with everything 'my brother in office, my son in years' had said against Anthropomorphites, but insisted that if that heresy was to be condemned, it was only fair that its direct opposite, Origenism, should be anathematised as well. When he sat down, the church rang with mingled laughter (at John) and applause (for Epiphanius).

Despite what had happened, there was as yet no open rupture between the two. Epiphanius stayed on in Jerusalem, perhaps hoping to induce the bishops present to censure John for heresy. At any rate John seems to have felt his position imperilled, for a day or two later, taking his cue from the Scripture lection, he thought fit to deliver in public a complete exposition of the Christian faith in all its aspects. The statement seems to have impressed people as wholly satisfactory—as well it might: there is no

---

[16] For this date see the convincing argument of P. Nautin in *Revue des études augustiniennes* 19, 1973, 69–73. He refers to the description of the festival in *Itin. Eger.* 49, 1–2 (*CCL* 175, 89).

[17] *Against John* 11.

shred of evidence that John, or indeed Rufinus, believed Origen's 'perverse dogmas'. Epiphanius himself, invited to speak, was obliged to concede that it was the authentic Catholic faith.[18] This was a check to his campaign, and he realised it. Abruptly quitting John's palace, he made his way to Jerome's monastery at Bethlehem. Jerome, however, quickly sensing that matters were getting out of hand, persuaded him (against his will,[19] it seems) to return in the evening. At midnight, however, Epiphanius was again on the road, this time making for his own monastery at Besanduc.

(iii)

This clash between the two bishops inevitably involved their devoted supporters, Rufinus and Melania being drawn in on the side of John, Jerome and his monks on that of Epiphanius. The latter, according to Jerome, withdrew into himself, brooding silently over his supposed wrongs and only pleading with John to forswear his erroneous beliefs (beliefs which, as has been emphasised, he had never held). Not that this withdrawal prevented him from despatching letters critical of John to the Bethlehemite monastery or from praying during divine service (secretly, he insisted, but gossip said openly), 'Lord, grant John correct belief'.[20] It was not long, however, before he took an extraordinary step (not that it seemed so to him) which brought him into head-on collision with John, as well as making relations between John and Jerome impossible.

For many months the community at Bethlehem had lacked priests to celebrate mass and perform other sacerdotal functions. Previously they had used the local clergy, but now they were reluctant to do so because their attachment to Epiphanius (as he frankly admitted) and his flood of letters to them had made them loath to have any communion with John.[21] They had, of course, Jerome and Vincentius, both priests; but these declined to exercise their priestly office because they regarded the pastoral ministry as incompatible with their isolation as monks:[22] probably also because it would have brought them into clerical obedience to the bishop of Jerusalem. Epiphanius had been apprised of the situation for some time, and had noted that John was doing nothing to remedy it. Then in early summer 394, when he was again at Besanduc, a delegation of monks and

[18] For the scene see *Against John* 14.

[19] Jerome reports (*Against John* 14) that he went back only because 'entreated by the whole monastery' to do so. He seems to have been incensed at the monks' reluctance to keep him, and this was probably the grievance he had against them to which he refers in *Letter* 51, 1 (see below).

[20] For his withdrawal see *Against John* 14; for his letters and prayer for John see *Letter* 51, 1 and 3.

[21] *Letter* 51, 1 (this is Jerome's translation of Epiphanius's letter to John).

[22] *In Letter* 51, 1 Epiphanius says that they were unwilling to offer mass 'because of bashfulness and humility'. Paulinian's ordination is narrated in the same paragraph.

deacons from Bethlehem, including Jerome's brother Paulinian (he was twenty-eight) arrived with the object of putting right some grievance he had against them. Whether what happened was pre-arranged or not, Epiphanius had the young man seized during divine service, and in spite of his energetic resistance proceeded to ordain him, first deacon and then priest.

John's indignation can be easily imagined. Besanduc was outside his jurisdiction, being under the bishop of Eleutheropolis,[23] but since Paulinian had been ordained to serve in Bethlehem he had good reason to consider his rights infringed. This was not the first time that Epiphanius had taken the law into his own hands on his territory. Not long before these events, when accompanying John to Bethel, he had noticed a curtain embroidered with a portrait of Christ or a saint hanging before a church door, and in his iconoclastic zeal had pulled it down and torn it in pieces.[24] John therefore expostulated sharply to Epiphanius through the latter's clergy, pointing out that he had broken his solemn promise not to ordain anyone in his diocese. He threatened to denounce his uncanonical behaviour to the ends of the earth, meaning to Rome, and made the further point that Paulinian was below the prescribed age for ordination, 'a mere youth'.[25] At the same time or soon after, angered by the collusion of Jerome and his monks with Epiphanius and their hostile attitude to himself, he took the drastic step of excommunicating them, forbidding the local clergy to administer the sacraments to them (or to any who recognised Paulinian's ordination), and banning entry to the Church of the Nativity to them. 'From that day to this,' Jerome was to write in 397, 'we can only see the Lord's cave, and from a distance groan as heretics walk in.' Meanwhile Paulinian's position had become impossible, for if he were to exercise his ministry he would be flagrantly defying the bishop of Jerusalem. Jerome therefore arranged for his brother to leave Bethlehem and settle for the time being, apart from occasional visits, in Cyprus, 'subject to his bishop', i.e. Epiphanius.[26]

Epiphanius's reaction to John's protests and threats was typical. In a lengthy letter[27] he first rejected the charge of inflicting injury on his brother-bishop by ordaining Paulinian. What he had done he had done to supply the dire needs of the Church, and he had in no way contravened

[23] Jerome makes this point in *Letter* 82, 8.

[24] Epiphanius tells the story, without a blush, in *Letter* 51, 9. He was one of the leading denouncers of the cult of images in the fourth century: see W. Schneemelcher, *RAC* 5, cols. 925 f.

[25] An age of at least thirty was prescribed by the council of Neocaesarea, canon 11 (314–25), and reaffirmed by the Sixth General Council, canon 14 (Constantinople, 680). The rule does not seem to have been rigidly observed, but John was infuriated by its violation in this case, complaining to Epiphanius (*Against John* 44) and to Rome (*Letter* 82, 8).

[26] *Against John* 42 (for John's ban on Jerome and his monks); 41 (for Paulinian's withdrawal to Cyprus).

[27] *Letter* 51 in Jerome's collection (it is Jerome's Latin translation of the Greek original: see below p. 203).

the canons since the monastery at Bethlehem was a foreign one outside John's jurisdiction. Indeed, he deserved John's gratitude for succeeding in ordaining someone he had been unable to get hold of himself. In Cyprus he and his fellow-diocesans acted together in a spirit of Christian cooperation, and in circumstances like these were only too glad to welcome men ordained in their dioceses by neighbouring bishops. After this he turned to the offensive and professed to find the root of John's indignation in his devotion to Origen, 'the spiritual father of Arius'. The body of the letter then consisted of a detailed exposure of Origen's heresies, and an earnest summons to John to repudiate them. The letter was widely circulated ('All Palestine fought for copies of it'),[28] but failed to elicit a response from John, who probably disdained to furnish any statement which could be interpreted as a confession of guilt. In his fury Epiphanius wrote round to the monasteries branding the bishop as a heretic and warning them against holding communion with him.[29]

The rival Christian groups in Palestine were thus, at the end of 394 and throughout the whole of 395 and 396, in a state of declared war. Relying on the backing of Epiphanius and his demagogic appeal, Jerome and his monks were denouncing Bishop John and demanding recantations from him. At the same time, while on good terms personally with the village clergy, they were prevented by John's ban even from burying their dead, and were obliged to send their catechumens to Diospolis (Lydda, now Lod) for baptism.[30] As for Rufinus, relations between him and Jerome were at breaking-point. Not only were he and Melania hand in glove with John, but in his letter Epiphanius had singled out Rufinus as especially needing to be purged of Origenism.[31] The arrival of Vigilantius in 395, carrying Paulinus of Nola's second letter, served only to exacerbate feelings. As we have seen, he incensed Jerome by cutting down his stay with him to a minimum; his reason, as we can now appreciate, was that he could not properly associate longer than necessary with excommunicated people. Worse still, it seems clear that, before coming to Bethlehem, he had lodged with Melania, a relative of Paulinus, and Rufinus at Jerusalem, and had learned from them that, in spite of his present posture, Jerome had always been an admirer of Origen. At any rate, Jerome deemed it prudent, during his brief stay, to preach a sermon in his hearing on the reality of the resurrection body in order to convince him that he was not an Origenist.[32]

[28] *Letter* 57, 2.

[29] *Against John* 39 and 44.

[30] *Letter* 82, 11 (on good terms with the local clergy); *Against John* 42 f. (the effects of their excommunication).

[31] *Letter* 51, 6.

[32] For Vigilantius's visit see above p. 193. For the sermon see *Letter* 61, 3 (to Vigilantius, recalling the incident). I am relying on P. Nautin's discussion in *Revue des études augustiniennes* 19, 1973, 213–39.

On top of all this came the incident of Jerome's Latin translation of Epiphanius's famous letter to Bishop John. By his own account he had made it at the entreaty of his Greek-less guest, Eusebius of Cremona, adding (it seems) caustic comments in the margin, and had insisted that Eusebius should keep it for his private use. In the latter months of 395 the letter was mysteriously extracted from Eusebius's desk, and soon found its way into the hands of John and Rufinus. Going through it with a fine comb, they discovered that, so far from making a literal translation, Jerome had (in addition to inserting marginal comments) both toned down Epiphanius's expressions of courtesy to John and accentuated his accusations.[33] Jerome was to protest that Rufinus and Melania had engineered the theft by bribery;[34] but if Eusebius had really been bound to secrecy, it is difficult to deny his complicity. In any case the accusation that he had produced a falsified, damaging version was quickly carried to Rome and excited criticism (instigated, he hinted, by Rufinus).[35] Jerome judged it advisable to justify what he had done to Pammachius, ever anxious for the reputation of his turbulent friend. The result was his important letter on *The Principles of Good Translation*.[36] The real object of this was to set out his own version of events and to emphasise the trifling character of the deviations of his Latin from the Greek original. At the same time he developed the view that, except when dealing with Scripture, the intelligent translator should always seek to render the sense rather than the words. This was the principle, he argued, which he himself had always followed, and upon which the great classical and ecclesiastical writers, and even the inspired authors of the New Testament, had consistently acted.

(iv)

Jerome's preparation of a Latin version of Epiphanius's letter, and his dispatch of a copy to Rome along with his apologia, seem to have struck John as the ultimate defiance. However specious the explanations he put out for his actions, the bishop must have interpreted his real motive as being to expose him to the west as an obdurate heretic. He therefore decided to get rid of him once for all and, making an approach to Flavius Rufinus, the all-powerful minister and effective guardian of the young emperor Arcadius, procured an order, probably in autumn 395, expelling

[33] For Jerome's account of the circumstances of the translation, and of the attacks made on it, see *Letter* 57, 2.

[34] *Apology* 3, 23.

[35] *Letter* 57, 12, where he remarks that the blame for the criticism should not lie with those who merely passed it round, but with their 'instructors', presumably Rufinus and Melania, whose names appear in some MSS.

[36] *Letter* 57.

Jerome and his monks from Palestine.[37] But the order was never put into effect. In July and the months following all Palestine was in turmoil as hordes of trans-Caucasian Huns poured through the Caspian Gates and, rushing southwards through the Armenian highlands and the plains of Mesopotamia, carried desolation into Syria. Antioch prepared for siege, and from Jerusalem, rumoured to be the invaders' goal, there was a flood of refugees to the coast.[38] The attention of the government was directed to this much more important menace. Then, on 27 November 395, came the downfall and death of Flavius Rufinus. Outside Constantinople, before the eyes of Arcadius, the hated minister was cut to pieces by the eastern army returning from the civil war in the west under Stilicho's general, the Goth Gaïnas.[39]

In spring next year, shortly before Easter (13 April), an attempt at mediation was made by a prominent layman, 'the count Archelaus, a most accomplished and Christian man'.[40] Our sole knowledge of this comes from Jerome, who in an obviously partisan account describes how John excused himself, for derisory reasons, from attending meetings which had been arranged. We may surmise that, however well-intentioned Archelaus was, John did not consider him a suitable arbitrator in an ecclesiastical dispute between himself and an excommunicate monk of his diocese. In any case, his manoeuvre to get Jerome expelled having collapsed, he had already taken the step of approaching Theophilus, the bishop of Alexandria, for help in finding a solution. Jerome was to complain that, if he wanted an adjudicator, he should have appealed either to the bishop of Caesarea, the metropolis of Palestine, or to the bishop of Antioch, the patriarchal see of the whole region (Oriens).[41] Neither of these, however, was in the least acceptable. Apart from the fact that Jerome was still in communion with the bishop of Caesarea, Jerusalem, 'the mother of the churches', was already beginning to assert itself as an independent patriarchate, and John was not likely to commit any act which implied a subordinate status for it.[42] His choice of Theophilus was probably sugges-

---

[37] *Against John* 43 (he 'set specially at our throats that powerful monster who menaced the throats of the entire world'); *Letter* 82, 10 (' . . . recently he demanded exile for us, and obtained it').

[38] Jerome supplies a vivid, factual account in *Letter* 77, 8 (date 399). For a popular narrative see E. A. Thompson, *A History of Attila and the Huns* (Oxford, 1948), 26–8.

[39] For the killing of Fl. Rufinus, probably at Stilicho's orders, see Zosimus, *Hist. nova* 5, 7, 5–6; Jerome, *Letter* 60, 16; Socrates, *Hist. eccl.* 6, 1, 5–7 (he supplies the exact date); Sozomen, *Hist. eccl.* 8, 1, 3; Claudian, *In Ruf.* 2, 343–427 (a blood-thirsty poetic description).

[40] *Against John* 39. Many books describe Archelaus as 'governor of Palestine'. He is possibly to be identified with the Archelaus who was Augustal Prefect of Egypt in 397 (*Codex Theod.* 2, 1, 9; 9, 45, 2).

[41] *Against John* 37: cf. canons 6 and 7 of Nicaea (Hefele-Leclercq, *Histoire des conciles*, Paris, 1907 ff., 1, 553; 569).

[42] At Nicaea (325: canon 7) Bishop Macarius obtained for Jerusalem, still called Aelia, an honorary precedence immediately after the patriarchates of Rome, Alexandria, and Antioch,

ted to him by Rufinus, who had been his pupil at Alexandria many years back, and who was now keeping him informed of the controversy.[43] The fact that Theophilus was, at this stage, sympathetically disposed to Origen must have seemed an additional advantage.

Theophilus's first attempt at mediation was a complete failure. The priest whom he appointed to represent him, Isidore, and who arrived in Jerusalem in June 396, had committed the astonishing gaffe of writing in March to John, Rufinus, and their allies encouraging them to stand fast in the true faith and not to be terrified into altering their opinions: the adversary would soon be dissipated like smoke in the air or wax in fire.[44] By accident, or perhaps by some ruse, this compromising missive was delivered, not to its addressees, but to Jerome's friend and fellow-monk Vincentius, who naturally kept hold of it. Not surprisingly, Jerome and his supporters were outraged by such partisanship in one who was supposed to be a conciliator. When Isidore arrived, three meetings were held, with Jerome demanding to see his letters of credence and John forbidding him to show them. The debate resolved itself into repeated requests from Jerome for proofs of John's orthodoxy, and offers by John to forget the past if, recognising the irregularity of Paulinian's ordination, the monks would resume canonical obedience to their bishop.[45] Clearly nothing could be achieved, and Isidore returned to Alexandria.

He did not, however, return empty-handed, but carrying a lengthy letter, in the preparation of which he had himself taken a hand, from John to Theophilus. Known as John's Apology, it is lost, but we can get some idea of its contents from extensive citations from it or references to it made by Jerome.[46] Much of it consisted of a circumstantial account, from John's point of view, of the whole lamentable affair. Fulsomely deferential to Theophilus, it did not spare Jerome and his monks, but its confessed intention throughout was pacific. John played the doctrinal issue down, claiming that it had not arisen until he had protested about Paulinian's ordination; and he made the shrewd point that Jerome had himself been

---

though still subject to the jurisdiction of the bishop of Caesarea. John was pushing the claims of Jerusalem to be an apostolic see, and Jerome charges him with this aspiration *Letter* 82, 10 ('apostolicam cathedram tenere se iactans'). Bishop Juvenal, after failing at the council of Ephesus (431), succeeded at Chalcedon (451) in getting the see of Jerusalem elevated to a genuine patriarchate, independent of Antioch.

[43] *Apology* 3, 18. Jerome denies that Rufinus had been Theophilus's pupil, but his denial is not convincing.

[44] For this letter, and what happened to it, see *Against John* 37. Jerome makes clear in *Apology* 3, 16 that Rufinus was among the addressees.

[45] Cf. Jerome's account of events in *Against John* 38–40.

[46] The letter, which Jerome calls 'Apologia' (*Against John* 1; 38; *Letter* 82, 8), can be in part recovered from *Against John*, which quotes substantial fragments of it. *Letter* 82 also gives a general idea of its contents. These fragments and allusions were collected by F. Caspari, *Ungedrückte, unbeachtete und wenig beachtete Quellen zur Geschichte des Taufsymbols und des Glaubensregels* (Christiana, 1866), I, 166–72.

an admirer and translator of Origen. It was Jerome, he contended, who was splitting the Church by his contumacious attitude. Yet he conceded that, although Jerome might seem to be separated from him, the two were really in communion with each other through Rome and Theophilus. Agreeably with the fashion of the times, he included a comprehensive statement of his personal beliefs, and this repudiated, explicitly or by implication, the chief Origenistic errors. This was in itself an olive-branch, but one which he preferred to extend to the patriarch rather than directly to Epiphanius or Jerome.

The Apology speedily found its way to Rome. Either Melania and Rufinus or John himself must have arranged for its transmission and diffusion there. The latter is the more likely explanation, for Jerome suggests that John sent envoys to Rome to denounce Paulinian's ordination and put pressure on the pope.[47] We hear also of a letter addressed about this time by Epiphanius to Siricius; and as it seems to have been a letter of self-defence, we may conjecture that the pope had intervened to reproach his fiery colleague from Cyprus.[48] Whoever its bearer, the Apology made a deep impression in the capital; with opinion there generally hostile to Jerome, it must have shocked people as further evidence of his intransigence. Pammachius was sufficiently disturbed to write to his friend requesting an explanation.[49] Jerome was all the more embarrassed because news had reached him that his transitory guest Vigilantius, who had now returned to Italy, had apparently forgotten his assurances and was branding him and his close associates as full-blooded Origenists. Nothing could be more awkward for Jerome, whose attacks on John and Rufinus on precisely this score were now notorious.

His reaction was immediate and characteristic. First came a withering letter to Vigilantius, argued with moderation in its opening paragraphs but progressively degenerating into coarse sneers at his detractor's stupidity, ignorance, social origins, blasphemous doctrines—even his name.[50] The solid case it presented was one to which Jerome was to have frequent recourse in years to come: like other orthodox writers before him, he had freely exploited the admirable things in Origen, especially his remarkable exegesis, but he had consistently 'either excised or corrected or passed over in silence' his many blatant errors. In short, he had studied

---

[47] *Letter* 82, 8 ('he stirred the ears of western bishops'); *Against John* 14 ('You send your dignified envoys hither and thither and bestir the sleeping old man to reply'). See P. Nautin, *Revue des études augustiniennes* 19, 1973, 81 f.

[48] *Against John* 44 ('one recently to the bishop of Rome'). In par. 14 he refers to what seems to be an earlier letter.

[49] *Against John* 1.

[50] *Letter* 61. 'Vigilantius' suggests watchfulness; Jerome sneers that it must have been given to him out of contrariety, since he is intellectually a sluggerhead. He hints that Vigilantius's father was a mere inn-keeper.

Origen as he had studied Apollinarius and other heretics, sifting with careful discrimination the acceptable from the unacceptable.

Then, early in 397, he prepared for Pammachius the ferocious philippic known as *Against John of Jerusalem*.[51] He had remained honourably silent, he claimed, for three years; the report that people at Rome were disturbed by John's Apology forced him to speak out and demolish it. Section by section he went through the Apology, tearing it to pieces and heaping insults on its author. Much of the pamphlet is therefore a scornful critique of John's version of events from Epiphanius's intervention to Isidore's mission, highly tendentious in tone, abounding in brilliantly abusive or satirical sallies, but invaluable for the factual information (however distorted) it contains. Mixed up with this is a sustained exposure of the bishop's statement of his beliefs, which Jerome professed to find dangerously ambiguous, avoiding the real issues and riddled with heresy. He contemptuously dismissed John's claim that Theophilus had approved it. He had been challenged by Epiphanius to clear himself on eight cardinal points of Origenism, but he had touched superficially on only three and had ignored the rest.[52] On the crucial matter of the state of the body, of Christ and of Christians, after the resurrection Jerome tried to show, in an extended analytical passage, that John's teaching was hopelessly inadequate; he had spoken always of the resurrection of the body, never of the resurrection of the flesh.[53] Throughout he ridiculed his grovelling adulation of Theophilus, castigated his arrogance both to Epiphanius and to himself, and nailed the blame for schism firmly on his insufferable pride.

(v)

The final section of *Against John* breaks off with an unfinished air, and although Rufinus had clearly read it before leaving Palestine in 397, even so close a friend as Oceanus had to wait until 416 before obtaining a copy from a visitor from Bethlehem.[54] The fact is that, despite the appearance of deadlock, Jerome must have known as he wrote that peace was only round the corner, and may have judged it wiser not to circulate so explosive a pamphlet. Although his agent Isidore's mission had collapsed miserably, Theophilus was taking his role as mediator seriously, and he

[51] For the date see P. Nautin, *Revue des études augustiniennes* 18, 1972, 210–15. I. Opelt, *Hieronymus' Streitschriften* (Heidelberg, 1973), 64–82 provides a detailed analysis of the argument.

[52] Jerome lists the eight points in *Against John* 7. S. Jannacone, 'La genesi del cliché antiorigenista ed il platonismo origeniano nel contra Iohannem Hier. di S. Girolamo' (*Giornale italiano di filologia* 17, 1964, 14–28) has demonstrated that Jerome's immediate source for these eight points was Epiphanius's *Panarion* 64.

[53] *Against John* 23–36. Y. M. Duval, *Revue des études augustiniennes* 17, 1971, 227–78 has shown how extensively Jerome drew on Tertullian for this section.

[54] Cavallera showed (II, 95 f.) that Rufinus, writing in 401 in *Apol. c. Hier.* 1, 16, revealed a close acquaintance with the text. For Oceanus see Augustine, *Ep.* 180, 5 (date 416).

had been favourably impressed by John's Apology and had sensed the irenic note in it. Now he addressed a diplomatically balanced letter, which carefully avoided blaming either side, to Jerome and his dissident monks. Recalling the humility of Christ and the Scripture teaching about peace and brotherly charity, he urged them to be reconciled with their bishop.

The letter has not survived, but the immense impact it made on Jerome is discernible in every line of his deeply emotional reply.[55] Originally resentful of the intervention of Alexandria, he now threw himself at Theophilus's feet: 'You caress as a father, instruct as a teacher, enjoin as a bishop ... You do not demand subjection from your monks; they are therefore all the more subject to you. You offer them a kiss, and so they bow their necks.' Jerome repeats his charges against John, complains of his churlish treatment of himself, questions his version of events; but the bluster is muted, the attacks less vehement. Throughout the letter runs Jerome's weariness with the controversy, his longing for a settlement: 'Peace is what I wish for—not only wish for but demand ... Let them show themselves peacemakers, and peace will follow at once ... I repeat what I said at the outset, that it is Christ's peace that I desire, true concord that I long for, and that I beg you to urge him not to extort peace from me but to will it ... Let him be as he used to be when he loved me of his own choice ... If he shows himself like that, gladly I hold out my hands and stretch my arms to him. He will have in me a friend and a kinsman, and will find that in Christ I am as submissive to him as to all my Christian brothers.' In sum, there was nothing he yearned for more than to serve his bishop so long as he behaved like a bishop, not a domineering master.

Thus, with sporadic warning growls, the quarrel between John and Jerome moved to its uneasy close. The bishop's dignified refusal to be drawn into doctrinal wrangling had played its part as well as Theophilus's astute diplomacy. The actual steps by which the reconciliation was effected remain obscure to us; but John seems to have recognised Paulinian's ordination, no doubt requiring canonical obedience, and he restored the monasteries at Bethlehem to communion, while Jerome and Epiphanius desisted from their attacks on his orthodoxy. There remained, of course, the tragic rift between Jerome and Rufinus. Obscure but ominous hints in Jerome's letter to Theophilus, as well as in his earlier letter to Pammachius defending his translation of Epiphanius's attack on John, reveal that he regarded Rufinus as the bishop's evil genius, the man who had sowed hostility in his mind.[56] It rankled with him, too, that Rufinus and

---

[55] *Letter* 82.

[56] *Letter* 82, 9 ('he is acting at the instigation of another'); 11 (hints that he has allowed himself to be used by someone else); *Letter* 57, 12 (John is acting a part for which those who prompt him, Rufinus and Melania, must bear the blame).

Melania had incited the stolid Vigilantius against him, suggesting that he was an Origenist.[57] Now, however, that there was peace between John and Jerome, now that Christian charity and brotherly love were on everyone's lips, it was neither logical nor sensible that these personal animosities between old friends should fester on.

Just conceivably Rufinus's patroness, Melania, played a mediating role. In his note about her Palladius records that she was instrumental in healing a schism that had to do with one 'Paulinus' and over four hundred monks.[58] Many have thought that this must be a mistaken reference to the split between the two Latin settlements caused by Paulinian's ordination. But if this must remain a guess, there can be no doubt that a reconciliation was somehow patched up. In their later writings, after they had become once again, even more disastrously, embroiled, there are several references to their 'friendship restored' at this time—restored, according to Rufinus, 'with great difficulty and much sweat'.[59] From two of these passages, shot through though they are with bitter reproaches, we catch a vivid glimpse of what happened. In one Jerome recalls that they had shaken hands together in the Church of the Resurrection at the Easter mass in 397.[60] In the other he relates how, when a few months later Rufinus was taking his departure for the west, he had accompanied him part of the way in the courteous manner of the age, and the two had wished peace to each other on the understanding that neither was anything but a sound Catholic Christian.[61]

---

[57] See *Apology* 3, 19 for his conviction that Rufinus was responsible for the view Vigilantius took of him. Also see above p. 202.

[58] *Hist. Laus.* 46. This explanation of the puzzling passage goes back to Tillemont.

[59] *Letter* 81, 1; *Apology* 1, 1; 3, 24; 3, 33; Rufinus, *Apol. c. Hier.* 2, 37.

[60] *Apology* 3, 33 ('. . . in Anastasi, immolato agno, dextras iunximus', where the mention of the slaying of the Lamb gives the clue to the Easter festival).

[61] *Apology* 3,24.

XIX

Letters, Threnodies, Commentaries

(i)

The reconciliation painfully effected at Easter 397 was to prove short-lived, and the controversy over Origen was to be re-opened and continued, in an intensified form and with Jerome and Rufinus as the protagonists, beyond the end of the century. Before tracing these unhappy developments, we may fittingly pause and collect together such scraps of information as are available about Jerome's literary and other activities (apart from the quarrel with Bishop John) from 394 till 400. A few have already been reported;[1] the rest, apart from the books he wrote, are sporadic snapshots, usually unrelated and out of context, provided by his letters and the prefaces to his biblical studies.

Most interesting, both as an episode in his life and for the light it sheds on his character, is the tantalising story of his relations with Fabiola.[2] This rich, aristocratic Roman matron had been married as a young girl to a notorious debauchee, had divorced him, and in his lifetime, Christian though she was, had taken a second husband—an adulterous union in Christian eyes. His early death brought about an extreme revulsion of feeling, and in the days preceding Easter (we do not know the year) she presented herself in the Lateran basilica in the ranks of the penitents, deploring her sin in sackcloth and ashes before pope and people. Eventually restored to communion, she devoted herself and her wealth to the needy, founding a hospital for paupers picked up in the streets and personally nursing the most repulsive patients. All of a sudden she decided to visit the Holy Land, and turned up there in autumn 394 with her own and Jerome's close friend Oceanus. First she stayed at Jerusalem, probably under Melania's wing, then at Bethlehem with Jerome and Paula. Here she fell under his spell, studied the Bible assiduously with him, and finally began planning to settle there. Then in summer 395 came news of the Huns devastating Syria. Panic gripped the monastic settlements, and Jerome, Fabiola, and many others fled to the coast and chartered ships, all ready for an evacuation. When calm returned, their attachment to the

---

[1] See above pp. 189 ff.

[2] Her family was the 'gens Fabia' (*Letter* 77, 2). All our information about her comes from *Letters* 64 and 77, the details of this paragraph being derived from the latter.

holy places kept Jerome and Paula there, but Fabiola had no such firm ties and returned to Rome. Joining forces with Pammachius, now a widower, she set up a hospice for travellers at Portus,[3] the harbour of Rome.

It was not just restlessness, nor even dread of the Huns, that had determined Fabiola's departure. A delicate hint which Jerome drops[4] makes it certain that she was disillusioned by the squabbles by which she found the Christian communities rent. He felt her loss keenly, for some-how (not just because she was a high-born lady who might have eased his financial difficulties) she had made a special impression on him. Writing about her after her death, he was to display, for one normally so inflexible, an astonishingly sensitive understanding of her second marriage. She had sinned terribly, he agreed; but she was young, her physical passions were at their height, she was wise to accept 'the shadow of a wretched marriage' rather than indulge in sex without marriage.[5] When she had gone, they kept up a correspondence, one piece of which survives—an enormous, minutely detailed examination[6] of the priestly sacrifices, vestments, and ornaments prescribed in the Pentateuch, including a brief exposition of their mystical significance. Incorrigible as ever, Jerome professed to have dictated this in a single short night, but this was bragging to impress. The composition of the laborious little treatise, with the collection of learned material for it, must have taken time. But it has the interest of revealing that Jerome still cherished hopes of luring Fabiola back. Perhaps, he hinted, she felt a nostalgia for Bethlehem; and he added that peace had been restored, and that he could again hear the infant Christ crying in his manger.[7]

In 400 he was composing an even longer letter-treatise[8] for her, this time elucidating the spiritual meaning of the forty-two stages, or camp-sites, of the Israelites on their journey from Egypt to the Promised Land, as set out in Numbers 33. Years before, at Bethlehem, in her new-found passion for Scripture, she had demanded such an explanation. Now at last he furnished it, ingeniously proposing edifying, if largely far-fetched, etymologies for all the bizarre-sounding place-names, and interpreting the

---

[3] For Portus see above p. 116.

[4] *Letter* 77, 8 ('At that time there was a division among us, a domestic struggle which put the war with the barbarians into the shade'). Cf. *Letter* 64, 8 ('You found our company displeasing . . . at last peace has been restored').

[5] *Letter* 77, 3. Contrast the advice he had given Amandus with regard to another woman in a similar situation (*Letter* 55, 4: see above p. 191).

[6] *Letter* 64. He probably drew on Origen for the exegesis, as in *Letter* 78 (see below).

[7] *Letter* 64, 8. Many take the reference to the restoration of peace, etc. as meaning the departure of the Huns and Jerome's return to Bethlehem. But the letter seems to have been written in 397, and Jerome was back in Bethlehem long before that. Clearly what he had in mind was the settlement with John and the lifting of the ban on his entering the Church of the Nativity.

[8] *Letter* 78. See *Letter* 77, 7 for its sending to Oceanus. For the date see Cavallera II, 46.

camp-sites as symbolising the pilgrimage of the Christian, the true Israelite, from earth to heaven. For the broad lines of his mystical exegesis, though not for the detail, he drew largely on a homily of Origen's (he was careful, of course, not to breathe his name) which is preserved, ironically, in a translation by Rufinus.[9] Fabiola was dead by the time he completed the elaborate essay; but he sent it to Oceanus as a funeral offering to one (as St Paul expressed it: Rom. 5, 20) 'in whom sin had abounded, but grace had much more abounded'.

(ii)

Exegesis occupied quite a large part of Jerome's correspondence in these years. His reputation as a biblical scholar was now so great that requests to clear up difficulties came pouring in not only from Rome, but from north Italy, Pannonia (roughly, modern Hungary), and other regions. Thus in 397 we find him sending Principia, Marcella's youthful friend and devoted companion till death, a mystical exposition of Psalm 45.[10] With a great display of learning Jerome interpreted this lovely greeting to a prince on his wedding-day, which Jewish exegetes understood as pointing to the Messiah, as referring to Christ and his bride, the Church; he was even able to transform it into a panegyric of virginity.

Four letters to three priests, three written the following year and one of unknown date, grapple with problems raised or illuminated by Scripture.[11] Evangelus was disturbed by the opinion he had heard voiced that deacons were superior in rank to priests. In refuting this Jerome developed, with the support of texts from Acts and the Epistles, his famous theory that in the primitive Church 'bishop' and 'priest' were different names for the same office; the emergence of a presiding priest, or bishop, had been occasioned by the need to exclude schism.[12] Evangelus was also concerned at a suggestion, almost certainly Ambrosiaster's,[13] that the Melchizedek mentioned in Genesis 14, 18–20 was the Holy Spirit. After reviewing the authorities Jerome, who heartily disliked 'Ambrosiaster', rejected this as an ignorant howler, and argued that the mysterious king was a real man and prefigured Christ. Vitalis, almost certainly a Pannonian, found it puzzling that, as he read the chronological data, both Solomon and Ahaz had become fathers at the age of eleven. Jerome replied

---

[9] *Hom. in Num.* 27 (*GCS* 30, 255–80).

[10] *Letter* 65. For the date see Cavallera II, 44.

[11] *Letters* 146 (to Evangelus: of unknown date); 73 (to Evangelus, on Melchizedek); 72 (to Vitalis); 74 (to Rufinus of Rome). The difficulty raised by Vitalis had previously occurred to Jerome (*Letter* 36, 10).

[12] For the theory see above p. 147.

[13] Cf. Ambrosiaster, *Quaest. vet. et nov. test.* 109 (*CSEL* 50, 257–68). See C. Martini, *Ambrosiaster* (Rome, 1944), 46. For Ambrosiaster and Jerome's dislike of him, see above p. 149.

that he was perfectly prepared to accept their alleged precocity because many things in Scripture which sounded incredible were none the less true, and 'nature cannot resist the Lord of nature'; but he personally deprecated wasting time on such trivial questions. To one Rufinus (a Roman, not Rufinus of Aquileia) he wrote explaining the judgment of Solomon (1 Kings 3, 16–28) as a spiritual parable, the two harlots being figures of the Synagogue and the Church respectively and Solomon of Christ.

But Jerome's letters were not concerned exclusively with the Bible. In 397/8 one of his Roman admirers, Tranquillinus, wrote to inform him of the stand Oceanus was making against Origenists in the capital (we shall hear more of this later), and to ask whether any parts of Origen's works could be safely studied. Jerome's reply was a judicious one.[14] Origen was not to be condemned *en bloc*; as with other heretics, 'we should pick out what is good and reject what is bad'. From about the same year we have a letter to Flavius Magnus, official professor of rhetoric at Rome, defending his practice of using quotations from secular writers—and ending with a bitter sneer at an unnamed critic (Rufinus for sure) who he suspects has made Magnus his mouthpiece.[15] To 397 belongs also a charming note to Castricianus, a keen Pannonian Christian who, in spite of blindness, had set out on a pilgrimage to Bethlehem to visit Jerome, but at the Dalmatian coast had been held back by the entreaties of anxious friends.[16] Jerome thanks him for his brave intention, and to console him for his affliction relates a *bon mot* of the desert hero, St Antony, to the effect that no one need lament the loss of eyesight, which men share with ants, flies, and gnats, provided he possesses spiritual vision.

Jerome's fame as a learned writer had spread to the remote west, and in 397 Lucinus, a Spaniard of rank and fortune, had sent copyists all the way to Bethlehem to transcribe the great man's principal writings for him. Being dedicated Christians, he and his wife Theodora had vowed to live together without sexual relations, and they now proposed to travel to Bethlehem themselves. From 398 we have an excited letter[17] from Jerome to Lucinus, apologising for any mistakes in the copies the scribes had made (he had been too ill, and too busy with pilgrims, to supervise their work), giving rulings on points of church practice Lucinus had submitted to him, but above all welcoming him to Bethlehem and inviting him to settle there. There is a clear hint, in his exhortation to Lucinus to strip

[14] *Letter* 62. For the date see Cavallera II, 45.

[15] *Letter* 70. Its date must be after Rufinus's arrival in Rome in spring or summer 397; Jerome explicitly blames him in *Apology* 1, 30. For Magnus see *PLRE* 1, 535. A sarcophagus said to be his can be seen in the Capitoline Museum, Rome.

[16] *Letter* 68. For its date, and the dates of the other letters mentioned in this section, see Cavallera II, 45 f.

[17] *Letter* 71.

himself of his wealth, that Jerome saw him as a munificent potential benefactor for his and Paula's convents. Finally, there is a letter[18] (about 400) to Oceanus, who had sought his backing in a protest against an elderly Spanish bishop, Carterius, who had violated (so he alleged) St Paul's ruling (1 Tim. 3, 2) that a bishop should be 'the husband of one wife', i.e. only once married. Jerome indignantly refused his support, pointing out that Carterius's first marriage had been contracted and his wife had died before his baptism, and that by baptism a Christian becomes a completely 'new man', his previous life being abolished. If the most disgraceful excesses are washed away by baptism, it would be paradoxical that a marriage he has entered into before baptism precisely in order to avoid those excesses should continue to count against a man; such a principle would indeed encourage catechumens to indulge in every form of depravity so long as they abstained from marriage. Jerome proceeded to lash out against bishops who, in the luxury and show of their lives, offended flagrantly against the more relevant standards laid down by the Apostle; for good measure, he added a snide cut at Ambrose of Milan, who had been elected a bishop while still a catechumen. The intriguing background of this discussion, which recalled controversies in which Jerome had been involved at Rome a dozen years earlier, was that both Ambrose, whom he hated, and Pope Siricius, between whom and him there was no love lost, had publicly pronounced in favour of the view which he rejected.[19]

(iii)

Several consolatory letters which Jerome wrote during these years merit special consideration, both because of their intrinsic interest and because they were literary efforts over which he took great care and on which he prided himself. Such compositions, usually concerned with death but also with exile and other misfortunes, were much in vogue in Greek and Roman antiquity. They were an accepted genre, with its distinctive plan, rules, and stock arguments and reflections. Jerome was very conscious of standing in the great tradition, and when he and other cultivated Christians (e.g. Augustine and Paulinus of Nola) took it over from their school training, they modified it very freely in the light of the Christian attitude to death and the teaching and illustrations provided by the Bible.[20]

[18] *Letter* 69: written after Oceanus's departure from Bethlehem (after 395) but before 401, when Jerome notes in *Apology* 1, 32 that it was being subjected to criticism.

[19] Cf. Ambrose, *De offic. min.* 1, 50 (PL 16, 97: after 386—he died in 397); Siricius, *Ep. ad Himerium Tarrac. episc.* 10 f. (dated 11 Feb. 385: PL 13, 1143 f.). In para. 2 Jerome refers to the earlier discussions in which he had taken part at Rome. For his cuts at Ambrose see paras. 2 and 9 ('heri catechumenus, hodie pontifex').

[20] On the whole subject see Ch. Favez, *La consolation latine chrétienne* (Paris, 1937).

The earliest in our period (an earlier one still, of course, was the lament on Blesilla he had sent Paula),[21] and also the most famous, is the elaborate letter which he addressed in 396 to Heliodorus, bishop of Altinum, on the premature death of his nephew Nepotian, the young officer turned priest to whom only two years before he had sent a short treatise on the priestly life.[22] Here Jerome deploys all his stylistic brilliance, all the sleights of rhetoric at his command. The solace he offers is the Christian assurance that by his resurrection Christ has conquered death, that Nepotian is alive with God and, unseen, still grasps his friends' hands, and that though they may grieve his loss they should rejoice that he has escaped from a world crumbling in ruins. The conventional eulogy of the departed has become a glowing panegyric of the gifted young man who gave up all for Christ, who was as eager in embracing ascetic privations himself as in relieving Christ's poor, and who now enjoys his reward with the saints. The whole is a set-piece of almost baroque splendour, pervaded with deeply religious feeling and unaffected sorrow. Its sombre backcloth is the steady collapse of the empire, weakened by indulgence and effeteness, before the barbarian invasions.

Another such threnody, nominally at any rate, is Letter 66, sent to Pammachius shortly after Easter 398 on the death of his wife Paulina (Paula's third daughter) in the winter of 395/6.[23] It is an odd example of the genre, for Jerome assigns only a third of his space to the deceased woman. The remainder he turned into a eulogy of Pammachius himself, who after her death had felt free to embrace monasticism in the most rigorous form, wearing his monk's black habit unashamedly in the Senate and expending his life and fortune on charitable works. Even the few paragraphs on Paulina read cold and perfunctory, and contain more praise of her mother, sister (Eustochium), and husband than of herself. The explanation of these curious facts, as of Jerome's long delay in preparing his *consolatio*, is plain. Christian though she was, Paulina had not been a Christian after his heart. 'Not daring to aspire to either her sister's virginal felicity or her mother's continence', she had been content to be a normal wife, attempting to bear her husband children. After a series of mis-carriages she had died childless, but Jerome flattered himself that in Pammachius, chaste at last and a recruit to total monastic commitment, he could discern the virgin offspring she had secretly yearned to bring forth.[24]

[21] *Letter* 39 (see above pp. 98 f.).

[22] *Letter* 60 (the treatise is *Letter* 52: see above pp. 190 f.). T. Barnes (*Tertullian*, Oxford, 1971, 235 f.) suggests that it might well have been written in spring 396 rather than, as commonly accepted, summer of that year.

[23] For the date, instead of the closing months of 396 proposed by Cavallera (II, 159), see Ch. Favez, op. cit., 26 n. 1.

[24] *Letter* 66, 3 f.

An 'epitaphium' which stands out, both for its graphic descriptions and for its depth of feeling, is that on Fabiola,[25] which Jerome sent in 400 to Oceanus. Here the consolatory element is at a minimum; almost the entire letter is a hymn of praise for his heroine, 'the soul who had fallen among thieves, but was carried home on Christ's own shoulders'. But the genre, with its commonplaces and stock reflections, lent itself to mannered artificiality. The letter (No. 75: date 399) to Theodora, the wife of Lucinus, the rich Spaniard who had planned to come to Bethlehem, on her husband's sudden death is an example. Reading Jerome's extravagant phrases about the grief the news has caused him, and the fulsome praise of the man himself, one would scarcely credit it that he had never set eyes on Lucinus. He is more himself when he slips in a veiled exhortation[26] to Theodora to persevere in the vow of chastity she took with Lucinus when he was alive: 'Victorious now and free from care, he is looking down from on high and supporting you in your struggle.' (Just to be quite sure, he took the opportunity, when writing[27] to a blind Spanish priest named Abigaus, to ask him to keep an eye on Theodora and see that she did not grow weary of the course on which she had embarked.)

The most intriguing of these threnodies (Letter 79: date 400) is addressed to Salvina, daughter of Count Gildo, governor of Africa, who had revolted in 397 and been killed the following year. Her recently deceased husband, Nebridius, was nephew to Flacilla, first wife of Theodosius I and mother of the reigning emperors, Arcadius and Honorius, with whom he had been brought up. Theodosius had arranged the marriage in the hope of ensuring Gildo's loyalty. The letter follows the pattern we should expect from Jerome—a eulogy of young Nebridius for his amazing chastity, his contempt of riches and bounty to the poor, his lack of all pride, prince though he was, etc.; an assurance that he is 'asleep with the Lord', but (a graceful touch) that his features can be recalled in those of his delightful children; an extended admonition to Salvina to honour his memory by bringing up the children well, practising strict asceticism, and, above all, remaining a chaste widow without thought of a second marriage. This advice is interspersed with gauche protestations that it should not be taken to imply any reproof of Salvina personally. But how did Jerome come to make this uninvited approach to a royal lady who was, as he acknowledges, a total stranger? After producing a couple of unconvincing excuses, he reveals[28] that he has been put up to it by 'my son Avitus'. Whoever this man was, it is likely that he was a leading figure in the strictly monastic circles which Nebridius had cultivated in the

[25] *Letter* 77: composed (para. 1) four summers after the threnody on Nepotian.
[26] *Letter* 75, 2.
[27] *Letter* 76, 3.
[28] *Letter* 79, 1.

court at Constantinople. It was he, probably, who had informed Jerome of the young man's readiness to sponsor their interests with the emperor,[29] and had emphasised the importance of influencing his widow in the right direction. And Jerome, conscious of and revelling in the power he wielded over aristocratic ladies, could scarcely refuse to respond to Avitus's request.

(iv)

To this period, too, belong the beginnings, admittedly somewhat abortive, of a correspondence which, carried on at intervals over a quarter of a century, was to prove, from the psychological, intellectual, and religious points of view, one of the most fascinating in antiquity. This was the interchange of letters between Jerome and his younger contemporary Augustine.[30] As it happened, both men, to be acclaimed by later generations as the most gifted Latin Christians of their day, had been in Rome in 383/4. But Augustine had been a disillusioned Manichee flirting with philosophical scepticism, while Jerome was immersed in the pope's business and in directing his circle of pious ladies. Not surprisingly, their paths had not crossed. Now Augustine was a Christian, having been baptised by Ambrose in April 387, and was settled at Hippo in north Africa, a priest clearly marked out for advancement. He was an avid reader of Jerome's works, and although he had never set eyes on him he felt sure that he knew him since through them (a characteristically Augustinian thought) he had made contact with his mind.[31] Further, his closest friend, indeed his alter-ego, Alypius, had in 393 visited Bethlehem, and had brought back a glowing description of the famous scholar-monk, a description so vivid that it seemed to bring Jerome's physical presence before him.[32]

So in 394 or 395 Augustine wrote (Letter 28A)[33] to Jerome. His immediate purpose was to commend to him an African priest, Profuturus; but he soon got down to his real business. This was, first, as spokesman of the intellectually alive element in Christian Africa, to encourage Jerome to

---

[29] Cf. para. 5, where Jerome dwells on his readiness to press the interests of bishops, widows, poor people, etc. with the emperors, and their readiness to accede to his requests.

[30] The nineteen letters are conveniently printed, with introduction and notes, in J. Schmid, *SS. Eusebii Hieronymi et Aurelii Augustini epistulae mutuae* (Florilegium Patristicum xxii), Bonn, 1930. There are full discussions of them and the questions they raise in Grützmacher, Cavallera, Penna, etc. For dating, critical problems, etc. see Cavallera ii, 47–50, and especially D. de Bruyne, *ZNTW* 31 (1932), 233–48.

[31] Augustine, *Ep.* 40, 1: cf. also *Ep.* 28, 1, which reveals his acquaintance with Jerome's writings.

[32] Augustine, *Ep.* 28, 1.

[33] In Jerome's correspondence it figures as *Letter* 56. To lessen confusion Augustine's letters in this correspondence will in the text be marked A, Jerome's J.

continue making the great Greek Bible commentators—'especially that one [Origen] you mention in your writings with particular pleasure'— available in translation to western readers. Secondly, to request him, with surprising bluntness, when translating the Old Testament, not to go back to the Hebrew but, as he had done so successfully with Job, to stick to the Septuagint as corrected by Origen for his Hexapla, inserting Origen's diacritical signs to mark its differences from the Hebrew. The authority of the inspired Septuagint was without question paramount; and this was borne out as much by the amazing unanimity of such a numerous band of translators as by the discrepancies and obscurities found in later versions based on the Hebrew. These latter suggested that Jerome himself might not be immune from mistakes. Finally, and at great length, Augustine gave vent to his shocked dismay that Jerome, in his *Commentary on Galatians*, should have represented St Paul's rebuke to St Peter at Antioch as deliberately simulated. It was not just a question of whether lying was in any circumstances permissible. Once one admitted that a single passage of Scripture contained a falsehood, however exalted the motive, the veracity of the Bible as a whole was fatally imperilled. Although he does not say so, what had probably instigated Augustine to raise this particular issue was that he himself had recently completed (perhaps was still working on) a short exposition of Galatians, and had doubtless been studying Jerome's larger work.[34]

Augustine was profuse in expressions of affection, of yearning for intellectual communion with Jerome. He softened his reproof by welcoming criticisms of his own writings, of which he enclosed copies. Nevertheless, had he received it, Jerome would have been cut to the quick by this letter, with its double attack on his exegesis and his attachment to 'the Hebrew verity'. It failed to reach him, however, for its bearer, Profuturus, before setting out for the Holy Land found himself elected bishop of Cirta (Constantia, in Algeria), and shortly afterwards died.[35] Some time between 395 and 397, however, a letter did reach him from Hippo from a close friend of Augustine's, probably Alypius, with a postscript by Augustine in his own hand. The subject of this postscript was an inquiry about the nature of Origen's errors; news of the turmoil in Jerusalem must have reached north Africa. Jerome for his part despatched a brief reply to Augustine. Without being specific he expounded his familiar thesis that Origen's writings contained orthodox ideas which merited acceptance, but also mischievous ones which should be rejected. Both

[34] For Jerome's account of the clash of the two Apostles see above p. 148. Augustine combated it, without mentioning names, not only in his exposition of Galatians (394: *PL* 35, 2105–48), but also in *De mendacio* (written shortly after) and in *C. Faustum Manichaeum* (*c.* 400).

[35] Cf. Augustine, *Epp.* 40, 8; 71, 2. He was to send Jerome copies of both *Ep.* 28 and *Ep.* 40 along with *Ep.* 71 in 403.

these letters have disappeared. We learn of their existence, and can deduce their subject-matter, from Augustine's next letter (40 in his correspondence), which he wrote *c.* 398 in response to Jerome's lost letter, and in which he referred to 'the full-size letter (though much shorter than I could wish from such a man)' which he had sent in answer to a mere postscript.[36]

In Letter 40A, as well as inquiring about the correct title of *Famous Men* (he had been told it was *Epitaphium*, but suspected this must be a mistake), Augustine repeated, with more detail and enhanced cogency, his objections to Jerome's interpretation of the clash between St Peter and St Paul at Antioch—he knew, of course, that Letter 28A had not reached Bethlehem. Without more ado he asserted his principle that, if false statements, even false statements made for honourable ends, have really crept into the Bible, its veracity everywhere must be open to question. St Paul, he pointed out, had introduced his narrative with a solemn oath (Gal. 1, 20) that what he was writing was no lie. Admittedly, he had claimed (1 Cor. 9, 20) to have behaved 'as a Jew to the Jews'; but there had been no intentional deceit in this, only a compassionate desire to save them. In any case St Paul was a Jew, and as such was entitled to observe the practices prescribed by the Law, so long as he did not regard them as mediating salvation. St Peter, however, was compelling Gentiles to observe the Law, as if it were still necessary for salvation; and for this St Paul properly corrected him. Augustine therefore begged Jerome drastically to revise his views and, like Stesichorus of old, 'sing a palinode'.[37] Not content with this, he sharply pointed out that Jerome had not answered his query about Origen. He had no need to be told that one should applaud a writer's innocuous opinions and condemn his erroneous ones. What he had wanted, and still wanted, was to be told by Jerome, out of his wisdom and learning, the specific matters 'in which that remarkable man is convicted of having deviated from the truth'. As a parting shot he suggested that, since Jerome had thought fit to include a number of heretics in *Famous Men*, he could make the book much more useful by inserting notes warning readers of the teaching for which they should be shunned.

Though courteously expressed, with flattering compliments and requests for regular correspondence, this was a firm and forcefully argued letter, not the sort of letter Jerome was likely to read with relish. By an unhappy coincidence, however, like its predecessor, it failed to find its way to him for several years, and when it did it was in the form of a copy which he declined to accept as authentic. The explanation was that the

[36] For the reconstruction of these letters see D. de Bruyne, art. cit.

[37] *Ep.* 40, 7. The reference is to the poet Stesichorus, who, having been blinded as a judgment for writing an attack on Helen of Troy, had his sight restored when he wrote a recantation. 'Christian truth,' Augustine remarked, 'is incomparably more lovely than the Grecian Helen.'

courier, one Paul, fearing the hazards of a sea-voyage, altered his travel-plans without Augustine's knowledge, and stopped in Italy without going on to Palestine.[38] What happened to it after that belongs to a subsequent chapter. The fact that he received neither of these respectfully critical effusions of Augustine's accounts for the friendly, even warm tone of the sole surviving letter of Jerome's to Augustine from this initial phase of their correspondence (if indeed it should be assigned to this phase).[39] This is a brief note commending the deacon Praesidius to Augustine, making a passing reference to the vexatious troubles by which he was being assailed (the dispute, perhaps with Bishop John), and sending respectful greetings to 'our godly and right reverend brother, Pope Alypius'.

(v)

For several years, occupied as he was with *Against Jovinian*, his controversy with Bishop John, and the apologetic writings they called forth, distracted too by swarms of visiting monks, Jerome had produced no major work on Scripture apart from his translation of Ezra-Nehemiah and Chronicles.[40] Now, early in 396, although his imbroglio with Bishop John was at its height, he prepared commentaries on two more of the Minor Prophets, Jonah and Obadiah, and in 397, at the request of a Pannonian bishop, Amabilis, a closely literal exposition of Isaiah's ten visions (Is. 13–23). He sent this to Amabilis by the bishop's deacon Heraclius, the bearer of his letter (see § ii above) to the blind Castricianus, but it will be more conveniently discussed when we come to his great Isaiah commentary. Then in 398, in the lull before the renewed storm over Origen, he tackled the last of his New Testament commentaries, on St Matthew's Gospel.[41]

Jonah was a figure who fascinated Christians of the early centuries. Taking their cue from Jesus's comparison (Matt. 12, 40) of Jonah's three nights in the whale's belly to his own forthcoming three days' entombment, they regarded him as prefiguring Christ and his resurrection, as also the resurrection of believers, and delighted to portray him in popular

[38] For these mishaps see Jerome, *Letter* 102, 1; Augustine, *Ep.* 73, 5.

[39] *Letter* 103. The date of this letter is uncertain and much controverted. If Jerome's mention of his being 'tossed to this side and that by stormy waves' refers to his dispute with John, it will belong to 396–7. But D. de Bruyne made out a good case for 402. See the discussions in Cavallera (II, 49 f.), Schmid (op. cit., 2 f.; 37 n.), de Bruyne, art. cit., 235 f.

[40] Cf. the significant remarks in *Comm. on Jonah* prol., esp. 'detained by other work I could not complete what I had begun . . . Thus, resuming my true status after such a lapse of time, I make a start by commenting on Jonah'. For the crowds using the hospice see *Letter* 66, 13 f.

[41] In its preface he states that he wrote the *Comm. on Jonah* 'about three years—circiter triennium' after the commentaries on the five Minor Prophets tackled earlier. He wrote the *Comm. on Matthew* just before the departure of Eusebius of Cremona for the west at Easter 398.

art. Jerome applied particular care to his exposition of the story; he was dedicating it, after all, to his exacting friend Chromatius. As usual, he adopted the plan of a double translation (from the Hebrew, and the Old Latin of the Septuagint), and a double exegesis (first literal or historical, then spiritual or 'tropological'). Most moderns believe the book to be a picturesque parable, written long after the 'Jonah, son of Amittai' (eighth century B.C.), mentioned in the opening verse, with the object of warning contemporary Jews against exclusivist nationalism and of proclaiming the universality of God's mercy. Jerome, as we should expect, treated it as genuine history (not all Christians of his day did),[42] and produced a spirited defence of the possibility of Jonah's having actually spent three days in the whale's belly. On the spiritual plane he saw Jonah as a type of Christ, but in his preface frankly avowed that the parallelism could not be followed through systematically, since Jonah had fled from the face of the Lord, had been displeased at Nineveh's repentance, had been rebuked by God, etc.

In the event he did not abide by this commonsense limitation. Almost every detail in the tale is presented as foreshadowing some action of Christ's. Jonah's fleeing from the Lord's face, for example, points to the Son's descent from the heavenly realm, his preaching at Nineveh to Christ's command after his resurrection to preach the gospel to the world. Even his distress at Nineveh's conversion is twisted to signify Christ's weeping over Jerusalem. As a result the original message of the book, and the delicate irony with which the author depicts God as chiding Jonah's narrow religious outlook, are totally lost on Jerome. In working out his solutions he probably relied heavily on Origen; and this is confirmed by his indignant rejection (he was now alerted to the dangers of Origenism) of some of his favourite theses.[43] He was also helped, in expounding the literal sense, by rabbinical exegesis; and from his knowledge of Hebrew and observation of local flora he deduced that the tree which overshadowed Jonah (4, 6) must in fact have been a castor-oil plant. But his identification of the king of Nineveh, who repented last (3, 6), with the philosophically educated, who find it more difficult to accept the gospel than even the rich and high-born, seems a contribution of his own, and illustrates his suspicion and dislike of intellectual speculation.

In trying his hand on Obadiah he wished to offer Pammachius something more mature, more respectful of the historical setting of the

[42] Jerome hints at this in his preface. Gregory of Nazianzus reports (*Or.* 2, 106–9: *PG* 35, 505–8) an interpretation which understands Jonah's experiences in a figurative sense, and expresses sympathy with it.

[43] Cf. his insistence, *On Jon.* 2, 7, that the resurrection body will be identical with the natural one; his rejection, *On Jon.* 4, 10, of Origenist subordinationism in regard to the second person of the Trinity; his repudiation, *On Jon.* 3, 6, of the theory that the Devil will in the end be saved.

prophecy, than his extravagantly allegorical effort of thirty years previously which caused him such embarrassment now.[44] This little book consists mainly of threats of vengeance on Edom, Israel's traditional foe to the south, for its indecent gloating when Jerusalem fell to Nebuchadnezzar in 586 B.C. Jerome attacked it with gusto, completing his study (so he tells Pammachius) in a couple of nights, and basing himself on earlier authorities (Origen for certain), but chiefly on rabbinical exegesis. From this he had learned that the author was the Obadiah who (1 Kings 18) had succoured the Lord's prophets in the evil days of Ahab and Jezebel, i.e. more than two and a half centuries before Jerusalem's sack. Thus through no fault of his own he got the historical framework wrong. Granted this, and some slips of translation, his literal exposition is often to the point, and includes some marvellous descriptions, e.g. of an eagle, invisible to the eye, swooping suddenly on a fish in the sea.[45] But, though claiming to give preference to 'the history', it was the spiritual or 'tropological' meaning which, as usual, he exerted his ingenuity to bring out. The Jews, he protested,[46] were idly dreaming when they identified Edom, threatened by Obadiah with destruction, with the Roman empire. In fact, Edom stood either for the Jews themselves[47] (all the hatred of the early Church for Judaism comes out in his sneers at 'the pride of the Jews'), or for the heretics who divide and scoff at the true Church (he got this from Origen),[48] or for the fleshly desires which seek to dominate the soul but are doomed to subjugation.[49]

The *Commentary on Matthew*, in four books, was written in March 398 to oblige his friend (later to be an unscrupulous ally) Eusebius of Cremona, who, about to set sail for Italy, had begged for a severely historical exposition as reading-matter for the voyage. Jerome dashed it off (by his own account) in two weeks lest Eusebius should miss the favourable winds.[50] This need not be an exaggeration; the breakneck speed at which he worked would explain the presence of several historical slips,[51] as well

[44] Cf. *Comm. on Obadiah* prol. See above pp. 44 f.

[45] *Comm. on Obadiah* 4 (*CCL* 76: 368).

[46] *Comm. on Obadiah* 1 (*CCL* 76: 366).

[47] E.g. *Comm. on Obadiah* 1; 10; 21 (*CCL* 76: 365; 374; 384 f.). For other examples of this hatred cf. his comments on, e.g., Matt. 9, 25; 12, 44 f.

[48] E.g. *Comm. on Obadiah* 1; 2 f.; 6 (*CCL* 76: 365; 368; 371). That Origen was his source is shown by his references to Marcion, Valentinus, the Gnostic theory of aeons, etc., knowledge of which he derived only from him.

[49] E.g. *Comm. on Obadiah* 1; 2; 10 (*CCL* 76: 366; 369; 374). Again the thought is typical of Origen.

[50] For these details see the preface (*CCL* 77: 7–8).

[51] E.g. he makes Herod Antipas the successor of Archelaus, and gives Lyons, not Vienne, as his place of exile (2, 22); places John the Baptist's execution in 'a town of Arabia' instead of the fortress of Machaerus (so Josephus, *Ant.* 18, 5, 2); wrongly explains the half-shekel tax (17, 24) as a government impost; states that Pontius Pilate placed an effigy of Caesar 'in the Temple' (24, 15).

as the very cursory treatment (often the comment is briefer than the text). As regards sources, he gives a catalogue of previous commentators on St Matthew, but alleges that he had studied them 'many years ago' and had not had time to consult them afresh. This last remark must be treated with scepticism, for the ample surviving fragments of Origen's great commentary reveal how freely he plundered it. The learned disquisition in the preface about the apocryphal gospels and the origins of the canonical ones is also taken from Origen. But it is noteworthy that Jerome now was not only careful to steer clear of the master's doctrinal 'errors', but seized every opportunity of pillorying them.[52] The much sparser fragments which remain of the commentaries of Apollinarius and of Theodore of Heraclea (mid-fourth-century: also of the Antiochene School) show that he used them too, though more sparingly.[53]

Jerome was of course not exercised, as scholars have been since the early eighteenth century, by the Synoptic problem, i.e. the relationship of the first three gospels to each other. To him it was clear that St Matthew was the first of the three, and that it was originally written in Hebrew, being intended for Jewish converts to Christianity. Nor was he (surprisingly: Augustine was to write a treatise on the subject two years later) troubled by the discrepancies between the evangelists. Where he noticed them, he generally found easy solutions. Thus he harmonised St Matthew's report (27, 32) that Simon of Cyrene carried the cross with St John's that Jesus carried it himself by suggesting that they referred to different stages on the road to Golgotha; while (on 28, 1) 'the different times at which the women are described in the gospels [as visiting the Empty Tomb] are not, as impious people object, a proof of lying, but of the frequency of their devoted visits'. On the other hand, he had a sharp eye for textual variants, and several of those he noted are instructive. He also recorded a number of readings in an apocryphal gospel which he called 'according to the Hebrews' or 'which the Nazaraeans use'.[54]

The commentary itself is very readable, but disappoints by sometimes skipping one or more verses and by treating others scantily or irrelevantly. Time and again it misses the point of a passage—criticising, for example,

[52] For a few examples out of many, cf. his notes on 6, 10 ('thy will be done on earth as in heaven' refutes Origen's theory of souls sinning in heaven); on 18, 24 (he rejects with scorn Origen's identification of the servant who owed his master 10,000 talents, and had his debt remitted, with the Devil); on 26, 24 ('It would have been better for that man not to have been born' does not imply that his soul pre-existed).

[53] These fragments are printed in J. Reuss, *Matthäus-Kommentare aus der Griechischen Kirche* (*TU* 61: 1957). There is a full list of passages of Origen and other writers who have influenced Jerome, so far as they are discoverable, in the critical edition in *CCL* 77 ('Index fontium et imitationum').

[54] For Jerome's Greek text, which was closely related to that of Codex Sinaiticus, see J. Wordsworth and H. J. White, *N.T. Domini Nostri Iesu Christi* (Oxford, 1889–98) 1, 658 f. For the difficult question of 'the gospel which the Nazarenes use', see above p. 65; also the discussion in R. McL. Wilson (ed.), *New Testament Apocrypha* 1, 126–36, by P. Vielhauer.

John the Baptist's disciples for inquiring why Jesus's disciples did not fast (9, 14) and the young man who asked what he should do to win eternal life (19, 16 ff.), and interpreting the child in 'Whoever humbles himself like this child . . . ' (18, 4) as a reference to Jesus himself. Jerome was not helped by his incorrigible tendency (in spite of Eusebius's wishes) to slip in 'flowers of spiritual understanding'. When Jesus, for example, bade the hungry crowd sit on the ground (14, 19), he was in effect, according to Jerome, commanding them to trample down the fleshly pleasures of the world; when he broke the five loaves, he was breaking up the Law and the Prophets which, unless so fragmented, could yield no sustenance. The story of the Entry into Jerusalem, on Palm Sunday (21, 5–7), with its incongruous picture of Jesus mounted 'on an ass and a colt, the foal of an ass', he explained as symbolising the subjection of both the Synagogue and the Gentile world to him; while the garments the disciples placed on them were really the apostolic teachings they needed to cover their pre-conversion nakedness. The blasted fig-tree (21, 19) was also the Synagogue. The wrapping of Christ's dead body 'in a clean linen shroud' (27, 59) was a reminder to believers that they must receive him with a pure heart, its placing 'in a new tomb' a pointer to 'Mary's virginal womb'.

Like other exegetes of the day, he allegorised most of the parables,[55] often copying out (with expurgations) Origen's imaginative surmises. This of course entailed the bypassing of the challenge of much of Jesus's most characteristic teaching. The same weakening of the gospel message is discernible elsewhere—in the mostly jejune comments on the Beatitudes and the Lord's Prayer, in the watering down of sayings like 'Give to him that asks' (5, 42), 'You cannot serve God and mammon' (6, 24), 'Judge not . . . ' (7, 1), and 'If you have faith . . . nothing will be impossible to you' (17, 20), as well as in incidents like the Agony in the Garden (26, 38 f.; 42), in the preference for an exclusivist interpretation of 25, 40 ('As you did it to one of the least of these my brethren, you did it to me') to a more general one, and in the indefinite postponement of Christ's second coming.[56] On the positive side it is the one Catholic Church founded on Christ which stands at the centre of his exposition, with the gates of hell which will not prevail against it being the perverse teachings of heretics;[57] and everywhere one senses a striving to discover

---

[55] For examples see on 13, 44 (the treasure hidden in a field); on 13, 47 (the kingdom of heaven compared to a fishing-net); on 20, 1 ff. (the labourers in the vineyard); 22, 1 ff. (the marriage feast given by the king).

[56] Cf., e.g., his note on 25, 19; also on 24, 34 (where he takes 'this generation' to refer either to the whole of mankind or to the Jewish people, not to Jesus's contemporaries).

[57] Cf., e.g., his note on 7, 25 f. His exegesis of 16, 18 ('You are Peter, and on this rock . . . ') is that Peter is only figuratively the rock. His theory (if he has one) of the Petrine supremacy is definitely pre-Leonine.

the doctrines of current orthodoxy in the text.[58] But one should not be over-hasty in judging Jerome in these things. The process of reading the Church's understanding of itself out of the gospel was already under way when the evangelist wrote, and Jerome's example was to be followed by generation after generation of later Christians. In compensation the reader lights, here and there, on comments and observations which go to the heart of the saying or incident discussed.[59]

(vi)

One or two glimpses we obtain of Jerome's personal affairs in the late nineties of the fourth century reveal that this was a time of trouble and anxiety for him. First, there was his health. This had never been good, and as far back as 381/2 we recorded the violent pains he suffered in his eyes.[60] In 387/8, when working on his Galatians commentary, he was again the victim of severe eye-trouble as well as general physical prostration.[61] Now early in 398, before starting his *Commentary on Matthew*, he had been gravely ill, confined to bed for three months; when he began writing it, he was with difficulty beginning to walk. He referred to this illness in his letters to Lucinus and Evangelus, stating that it was only in Lent that he began to recover from his high fever; while towards the end of the year, writing to Rufinus of Rome, he spoke of his illness extending over twelve months. The energy with which he had flung himself into his 'neglected studies' (the Matthew commentary) had had a deleterious effect on his feeble bodily condition.[62] We have no means of diagnosing the nature of his ailment, but it may well have been a breakdown aggravated by his extreme nervous sensibility and the tensions excited by the fierce quarrels in which he was engaged.

Then there were growing financial worries. The two religious houses at Bethlehem had depended largely on Paula's boundless charity, but there is reason to suspect that even her vast fortune was being steadily frittered away. She had little business sense, and when she died six years later Jerome was to emphasise that she had left not only not a single penny to her daughter but a crippling load of debts; she had reduced herself to real

---

[58] Cf., e.g., his evasion of the implications of 'God only is good' on 19, 17; his striving to preserve Jesus's omniscience on 24, 36, where he rejects the reading 'nor the Son'; the developed Trinitarianism he reads out of 28, 19.

[59] Cf., e.g., his notes on 5, 22 ('Everyone who is angry with his brother . . . '), where he rejects the reading 'without a cause' (but immediately spoils his interpretation by limiting 'brother' to 'brother-Christian'); on 10, 30 ('All the hairs of your head are numbered'); on 16, 24 ('If any man will come after me . . . '); on 19, 14 ('For of such is the kingdom of heaven': but contrast with this the note on 18, 2 ff., where he identifies the child with Jesus himself).

[60] *Origen's Homilies on Ezekiel* prol. (*GCS* 33, 318). See above p. 76.

[61] *Comm. on Galatians* III prol. (*PL* 26: 485–6).

[62] For this illness see *Comm. on Matthew* prol. (*CCL* 77: 7–8): also *Letters* 71, 5 (to Lucinus); 73, 10 (to Evangelus); 74, 6 (to Rufinus of Rome).

225

poverty.[63] The effects of this magnificently Christian improvidence were already showing themselves. The gift of money which (we recall) Paulinus had sent the communities in 394, although cut down by Vigilantius, seems to have come just in time to save them from starvation;[64] while Jerome's invitation to Lucinus to settle in Bethlehem contained a hardly veiled hint that his 'affluence' would be useful there.[65] Shortly after Easter 398 he felt himself 'compelled' to send his brother Paulinian to faraway Stridon 'to sell up the half-shattered farmsteads which have escaped the barbarians' hands and the lands where our parents are buried'.[66] The money was urgently required to keep the ever-growing establishments at Bethlehem going. As he ruefully confessed, the warning in the gospel (Luke 14, 28) was being only too truly fulfilled in his case, for he had not calculated the cost of the tower he planned to build.

---

[63] *Letter* 108, 30 (his threnody on her).
[64] *Against Vigilantius* 13. See above p. 193.
[65] *Letter* 71, 4.
[66] *Letter* 66, 14. For the date, one year after Rufinus's departure from Palestine, see *Apology* 3, 24.

XX

A Fateful Translation

(i)

When Rufinus sailed for Italy in summer 397, there is little doubt that he and Jerome were resolved to forget past squabbles and be friends. The reconciliation, it is true, did not go very deep. Temperamentally the two men grated on each other, and resentment and distrust still lingered. They were at odds, too, on matters on which each held strong views—the authority of the Septuagint vis-à-vis the Hebrew Old Testament, the propriety of using the pagan classics.[1] Then there was the issue of Origenism. This should never have divided them, for both were agreed in valuing what was sound and rejecting what was dangerous in Origen's writings. But their public stances, as in the recent quarrel stirred up by Epiphanius, differed markedly. Rufinus had persuaded himself (as we shall see) that Origen's 'errors' could not fairly be attributed to him. These apart, his admiration for the master was unbounded, and freely confessed. Jerome had swung from just such an admiration to a much more critical posture. His consistent view, in calmer moments, was that, while as an exegete he was outstanding, as a theologian his pernicious doctrines made him deeply suspect.[2] But in the heat of controversy he could give the impression of regarding him as an out-and-out heretic. Not without reason he had the reputation of being against Origen; and he had all the touchiness of the convert on this score. Thus when they parted, while their professions of mutual esteem were sincere—the reproaches each was later to hurl at the other suffice to prove this[3]—their renewed amity was much more fragile than either of them probably supposed.

Rufinus's motives for uprooting himself from Palestine, after being settled there for a quarter of a century, remain obscure. He had friends in Italy, of course, and his long association with Melania the Elder as well as his personal prestige assured him of a warm welcome there. Thus we find him speedily forming close ties with Melania's niece, Avita, and Avita's

[1] See above pp. 169 f.; We recall that it was probably Rufinus who had put Magnus up to criticising Jerome for his use of the pagan classics: see above p. 213.

[2] Cf., e.g., his letters to Vigilantius (61, 2); Tranquillinus (62, 2); Augustine (see above p. 218); Paulinus (85, 4).

[3] Cavallera made this point: see I, 241, where he cites in n. 1 the relevant passages from their respective *Apologies*.

husband, the senator Turcius Apronianus. About this time, too, he entered into relations with Paulinus of Nola, another relative of Melania's,[4] although we do not know when they met. Perhaps, as he grew older, he was becoming nostalgic for the western world of his upbringing. It would be understandable, too, if, for all his reconciliation with Jerome, he now found the atmosphere of Jerusalem oppressive and felt the need of a complete change. One suggestion we can exclude is that he was planning an intensified campaign for 'Origenism' in Italy.[5] Apart from over-simplifying matters, this rests on a misapprehension of his attitude to Origen, and gains no support from even the bitterest of Jerome's later innuendoes.

The element of truth in it is that he was eager to introduce his hero to the Latin-speaking public, and to convince it that he was by no means the dangerous heretic he was painted. But it was not only Origen he wished to popularise in the west, still relatively poor in Christian literature. In the next few years we find him publishing Latin translations of several other leading Greek theologians—Basil of Caesarea, the two Gregories, Evagrius Ponticus (founder of monastic mysticism and continuator of Origen's spirituality), and others. Among the more interesting of these were the free translation and rearrangement of Basil's monastic Rules which he produced in 397 at the behest of Ursacius, abbot of Pinetum (80 km. down the coast from Rome), and a famous version of *The Sentences of Sextus*, recording the (erroneous) tradition that their author was the martyred Pope Sixtus (or Xystus) II. The preface to the former, with its request to Ursacius to have copies made and distributed to other monasteries, reveals that one of his chief concerns was to ensure that the religious houses now springing up in the west should adopt the pattern which was proving successful in the east.[6] Nevertheless, however varied and uncontroversial his objectives, he soon found himself stirring up an anti-Origenist storm which, made more violent by errors of judgment (to say the least) on his part as well as by the malice of ill-wishers, was to lead inexorably to the rupture of his hard-won truce with Jerome.

---

[4] Cf. Paulinus, *Ep.* 29, 5 (*CSEL* 29, 251). It is not clear whether Paulinus and she were first cousins or cousins by marriage: see F. X. Murphy, 'Rufinus of Aquileia and Paulinus of Nola', *Revue des études augustiniennes* 2 (1956), 79. Possibly Rufinus met Paulinus in June 398, for the latter was accustomed to visit Rome each year for the feast of SS. Peter and Paul: see F. X. Murphy, art. cit., 81.

[5] So J. Brochet, *Saint Jérôme et ses ennemis* (Paris, 1905), chap. 4: followed by Grützmacher III, 27.

[6] Cf. his hope (*Prol. in reg. s. Basil.*: *CCL* 20, 241) that 'all the monasteries of the west' will come to know Basil's rules. For *The Sentences* and the problem of authorship, etc., see the critical edition by H. Chadwick in *Texts and Studies* (NS) 5 (Cambridge, 1959). Rufinus records the tradition of Sextine authorship in the preface to his translation (Chadwick, 9).

(ii)

Rufinus was to describe later how he came to make the translation of Origen which brought the storm about his head. He was driven to it, he reported,[7] by the insistent entreaties of one Macarius to be enlightened about Origen's opinions on the baffling problems of divine providence. This high-born Christian intellectual was apparently struggling to compose a refutation, at a philosophical level, of the fatalism inculcated by astrology—a science which had such a powerful grip on all classes in the early centuries that it engaged the attention of a long line of Christian apologists.[8] As he wrestled with the intractable issues, God had revealed to him in a dream that a ship was crossing the ocean which, when it docked, would provide him with their solution. The arrival of Rufinus, renowned for his knowledge of Origen, the most effective critic of cosmic determinism and champion of free-will, seemed the fulfilment of his dream. After some initial hesitation, Rufinus told Macarius that 'the saintly martyr Pamphilus' had touched on these perplexing questions in his *Vindication of Origen*—a collection of summaries and excerpts setting out Origen's teaching in a favourable light which Pamphilus had put together, with the aid of Eusebius of Caesarea, when they were both in prison for the faith *c.* 308.[9] Then reluctantly, under further pressure from Macarius, he translated the first book of Pamphilus's *Vindication* into Latin.

Rufinus was fully aware of the minefield into which he was stepping. Few, if any, at Rome knew Origen at first hand, but there had been fierce hostility to him there for years—as Jerome had angrily complained in 384.[10] While most people were not interested, he now counted as the arch-heretic in the ascetic circles attached to Jerome, which had followed the recent clashes of Epiphanius with Bishop John with partisan excitement. So Rufinus took two steps to forestall criticism. First, he wrote a preface[11] to his translation in which, while acknowledging that it was bound to cause offence because of its sympathetic presentation of Origen, he begged critics to suspend judgment. He inserted in it a brief profession of faith designed to eliminate doubts as to his own orthodoxy, stressing especially the identity of the glorified resurrection body with the physical body, and

---

[7] *Apol. c. Hier.* 1, 11.

[8] On the whole issue, with a full analysis of the key-texts in Origen, see esp. D. Amand de Mendieta, *Fatalisme et liberté dans l'antiquité grecque* (Louvain, 1943). There are useful summaries in *RAC* 1 (under 'Astrologie') and 7 (under 'Fatum (Heimarmene)').

[9] Pamphilus was imprisoned in 307 in the persecution of Maximin Daia, and remained in prison until his execution in 309 or 310. An enthusiastic admirer of Origen, he wrote his *Vindication* of him in five books with the aid of Eusebius, the church historian and later bishop of Caesarea. After his death Eusebius completed it by adding a sixth book.

[10] *Letter* 33, 5 (see above p. 98).

[11] *Prol. in apol. Pamph. mart. pro Orig.* (*CCL* 20, 233 f.).

ending with a statement that this was the doctrine taught at Jerusalem by Bishop John. Secondly, he appended a short essay, entitled *The Falsification of Origen's Works*,[12] propounding the original thesis that the master's writings had been subjected to large-scale interpolations by unscrupulous heretics. It was this, he argued, that accounted for the presence of unacceptable doctrines in them, and interpolation was confirmed by the numerous orthodox passages in Origen which plainly contradicted the unorthodox ones. In support of his theory he was able to produce a letter of Origen's complaining that a heretic had concocted a falsified report of a debate he had held with him. He also cited several undoubted examples of ecclesiastical documents which had been similarly tampered with—including (pointedly) the case already mentioned in which Jerome, when secretary to Pope Damasus, had been the victim.[13]

Although literary frauds and forgeries were not infrequent in the early Church,[14] there is not the slightest reason to believe that Origen's works suffered from them to more than a minimal degree. The theory does more credit to Rufinus's idealisation of the Alexandrian teacher, whom he sincerely could not believe to have strayed from the orthodox path, than to his critical acumen. But the essay was, as it were, a preparatory study for a vaster, more fateful task he now undertook. This was the translation, again to satisfy Macarius, of Origen's wide-ranging, controversial masterpiece, the *Peri Archōn* or *First Principles*. He finished the first two books at great speed, with Macarius at his side to spur him on, during Lent 398, and the remaining two books at a more leisurely pace, Macarius having now moved to a remote part of the city, in the weeks following Easter.[15] The method he adopted was the one we should expect in the light of his theory of interpolations. In general his version (following the accepted norms of translation) was a free paraphrase which, while allowing numerous abbreviations and expansions (e.g. for the sake of clarity), reproduced the sense of the original with reasonable fidelity. But where he came across passages which clashed with current orthodoxy, he felt free to modify, suppress or replace them in the conviction that they had been inserted by heretical hands. In fact the most thorough corrections concerned doctrines which had been defined, notably the relations of the persons of the Trinity. He was much less drastic, more selective, where Origen's speculations did not touch on the substance of the faith, but on matters still open

---

[12] *De adulteratione librorum Origenis*: PG 17, 615–32, but see also the critical edition by M. Simonetti in *CCL* 20.

[13] See above p. 81.

[14] For an interesting account see G. Bardy, 'Faux et fraudes littéraires dans l'antiquité chrétienne', *RHE* 32 (1936), 5–23; 275–302.

[15] The accepted division into four books, which Rufinus took over, is unlikely to go back to Origen: cf. B. Steidle, 'Neue Untersuchungen zu Origenes' Peri Archon', *ZNTW* 40 (1941), 236–43; M. Harl, 'Recherches sur les περὶ 'Αρχῶν d'Origène', *TU* 78 (1961), 57–67.

to discussion, declaring, for example, that he had abstained from interfering with his treatment of the origin of souls. Where he substituted passages, he claims to have drawn them from other works of Origen.[16]

Rufinus did not disguise this peculiar procedure, but frankly explained it, with references to his *The Falsification of Origen's Works*, in his two prefaces to Books I–II and III–IV respectively. But the most intriguing feature of the former preface is the assertion that, both in undertaking the translation of Origen into Latin and in censoring the doctrinally offensive passages, he was only following in Jerome's steps. True, he nowhere mentions Jerome by name, but nobody could miss the identity of 'my brother and colleague' who, 'when requested by Pope Damasus he had translated two homilies on Song of Songs from Greek into Latin, gave them an introduction so glowing and magnificent as to inspire everyone with an eagerness to read and assiduously study Origen'. He went on to recall Jerome's statement that, while in his other works Origen had surpassed all Christian writers, in this he had surpassed himself, so much so that the inspired words, 'The King has brought me into his chamber' (Song of Songs 1, 4), fittingly applied to him. Indeed, Jerome had promised[16a] to let the Latin-reading public have as many of Origen's works as possible, but subsequently had preferred the nobler role of a creative writer to that of a mere translator. 'Thus I am taking over the project which he began and commended by his example, although it is beyond my capacity to adorn the utterances of this great man with an eloquence matching his.'

After quoting Jerome's dictum that Origen was second only to the Apostles as a teacher of the Church, Rufinus expressed the fear that he himself lacked the literary skill to present him in his true colours. Because of this, he explained, he had until now resisted the pleas of many Christian friends to translate the *First Principles*. If he had finally, against his will, yielded to Macarius's importunity, it was on the strict understanding 'that, in making my version, I should as far as possible follow the method of my predecessors, and especially of that man whom I mentioned above'. In his numerous translations of works by Origen, 'he so modified or corrected whatever in the Greek original is in any degree objectionable

---

[16] The best and fullest discussion of his procedure remains G. Bardy's *Recherches sur l'histoire du texte et des versions latines du De Principiis d'Origène* (Paris, 1923). For an excellent summary see M. Simonetti, *I Princìpi di Origene* (Turin, 1968), 13–17. We can check Rufinus's Latin by (a) the Greek excerpts contained in the *Philocalia*, an anthology of Origen compiled by Gregory of Nazianzus and Basil the Great, (b) some fragments of Jerome's literal translation of the *First Principles* which survive in *Letter* 124 (see below p. 303), (c) the (often tendentious) twenty-four passages sent in 543 by Justinian to the Patriarch Menas, (d) several other passages preserved in Pamphilus's *Vindication*, Photius, etc.

[16a] Rufinus implies that Jerome made his promise in the preface to his version of the three homilies on Song of Songs; in fact he made it in the preface to his version of Origen's homilies on Ezekiel (*GCS* 33, 318). No doubt a slip of memory.

that the Latin reader comes across nothing in them which disagrees with our faith. Thus, although I lack his stylistic brilliance, I am following him at any rate in his rule and method, taking care not to make public any passages found in Origen's writings which diverge from or contradict his authentic views.'[17]

(iii)

Such is Rufinus's account of how he came to make his famous translation of Origen's *First Principles*. We must examine it more closely, and in particular try to fathom his real intention in writing the first preface, if we are to understand his subsequent relations with Jerome.

Although the story has been dismissed as a later invention, there is no solid reason for doubting that it was his meeting with Macarius that started him off. His prefaces, written at the time, confirm that his translation was undertaken under pressure from Macarius. It was also entirely natural that the troubled philosopher should seek ammunition from Origen for his attack on the astrologers. Even Jerome, though jeering[18] at the idea of Rufinus's bringing the key to these dark problems, did not cast doubt on the incident itself. But if Rufinus's only concern was to assist Macarius, it is hard to see why his first act was to produce a translation of Pamphilus's *Vindication of Origen*, still less why he should compose his own *The Falsification of Origen's Works*. The latter, of course, had nothing to do with the issue in hand. The first book of the *Vindication* contains a few passages affirming free-will, but Macarius could not have been greatly helped by them. In any case Origen's really penetrating critique of astrological fatalism was to be found, as Rufinus must have known, neither there nor even in the *First Principles*, but in his *Commentary on Genesis*.[19] The truth seems to be that, while willing enough to aid Macarius, he seized on his approach as a God-given opportunity for carrying out a project closer to his heart, viz. that of presenting Origen to cultivated circles in the west as a great Christian teacher who had been grievously wronged, and thus dissipating the suspicion which surrounded him. Hence his elaborate preparatory moves, including the reference to 'the saintly martyr Pamphilus' (on which Jerome was to pounce) and to the exact agreement of his own faith with that of John of Jerusalem. The one reminded readers that Origen had already been defended by one revered

[17] For the two prefaces see *CCL* 20, 245–8.
[18] *Apology* 1, 3; 2, 15; 3, 24; 29. Cavallera (1, 232 n. 2) was surely wrong in saying that he threw doubt on the veracity of the incident.
[19] The relevant passage is his lengthy, profound exposition of Gen. 1, 14 ('And let them [the stars] be for signs etc.'), which survives as chap. 23 of the *Philocalia* (ed. J. A. Robinson, Cambridge, 1893: 187–210). It has been analysed and discussed by D. Amand de Mendieta, op. cit. 1, 307–18.

for his martyr's crown, the other was a subtle allusion to the Apology John had sent to Theophilus, which (as we noticed)[20] had been given a favourable reception at Rome.

In thus exploiting Macarius's démarche Rufinus was not making propaganda for Origenism, except in so far as he was giving currency to Origen's speculations on several issues which had not been formally defined. He could not have made it more clear that it was Origen, not the dubious dogmas attributed to him, that he was championing. Nor was he, here at any rate, guilty of bad faith towards Jerome. He had never concealed his admiration of Origen, nor had their compact included any agreement to refrain from publishing his works. It is a more delicate question what exactly he had in mind when he dragged Jerome into his first preface, representing him, with such fulsome flattery and such a blaze of publicity, as the enthusiast for Origen whose brilliant precedent he was only, though with feebler talents, continuing. Primarily, no doubt, he reckoned that his attempted rehabilitation of Origen would be all the more successful if he placed it, as it were, under Jerome's patronage. He could honestly do so, it has been argued,[21] without unfairness towards his friend, because the preface did not claim that Jerome was a partner in his enterprise, but merely a predecessor in the translation of Origen's writings whose methods he proposed to follow. Alternatively, according to others,[22] he sincerely believed that Jerome, like himself, regarded the unfortunate quarrel at Jerusalem as a matter of personalities, and now that it was over had reverted to an estimate of Origen closely resembling his own.

What explanations like these overlook is that Rufinus, if anyone, knew that, however ardent Jerome's earlier esteem for Origen, he had drastically qualified it at least since Atarbius's challenge, and that as a result the preface gave a completely misleading picture of his present attitude. True, he was still prepared, when giving a balanced assessment, to acknowledge the good things in Origen, but even allowing for them he now regarded him as a heretic comparable to Tertullian and Apollinarius. His public image, since the rumpus in Jerusalem, was that of an anti-Origenist; and Rufinus had not forgotten how furious he had been when, only a couple of years earlier, Vigilantius had spread it about that he was an Origenist.[23] He must have realised that the language of the preface, without any hint of Jerome's change of heart, and the eulogies of Origen it recalled, were bound to compromise him with his friends and wound him personally. If he was prepared to take that risk, there was more than 'bad taste', or even

[20] See above p. 206.
[21] So Cavallera, I, 241.
[22] So F. X. Murphy, *Rufinus of Aquileia* (Washington, 1945), 99 f.
[23] *Letter* 61. See above p. 206.

'imprudent cunning', involved.[24] As their outbursts in their later *Apologies* painfully reveal, while both wanted at this stage to be friends, both nourished pent-up feelings of grievance and ill-will; and even friends more firmly united than they sometimes yield to the urge to be cruel to each other in order to get their own back. Rufinus had no wish to break with Jerome, and was to be genuinely shocked to discover that the explosion he had set off was more violent than he had calculated. We can only guess what his motives were, but perhaps he judged that this public reminder of his former adulation of Origen would make it more difficult for Jerome to criticise his work—and would throw the anti-Origenists in Rome into disarray. He had also been disgusted by Jerome's volte-face over Origen. Sensing the irony that runs through his preface, one suspects that he felt it would serve Jerome right for the world—and himself—to be reminded of that earlier adulation.

(iv)

Although it did not throw them into disarray, Rufinus's literary activity certainly caused consternation among Jerome's group of friends at Rome —the redoubtable Marcella with her young companion Principia, Pammachius, Oceanus, and others. Already suspect for his support of John of Jerusalem and his stubborn refusal to abjure Origen, he must have aroused their worst fears when he published his rendering of Pamphilus's *Vindication of Origen*. He did not improve matters by attaching to it his ingenious theory that the dangerous errors to be found in Origen's writings were interpolations by heretics. Since they had never read these works but owed their knowledge of them to hearsay, they were in no position to judge his (in fact quite untenable) argument, but any attempt to whitewash such a man seemed to them sinister. The news that he was actually translating the *First Principles*, reputed to be one of Origen's most controversial productions, had already got around by the time he had finished the first two books. In his preface to Books III–IV he remarked to Macarius, 'You will remember how I warned you in my earlier preface that certain people would be filled with indignation when they heard that we had no evil to say about Origen. This, as I think you have observed, has not been long in coming about.' He went on to predict the outcry and partisan excitement which would attend the publication of the remainder of the treatise.

We are fortunately able to trace some of the actions, not altogether creditable to the parties concerned, which they took. Eusebius of Cremona arrived in Rome (refreshed, no doubt, by his study of Jerome's *Com-*

---

[24] The former expression is Cavallera's (1, 240), the latter ('astuzia imprudente') Penna's (250).

mentary on Matthew on the voyage)[25] soon after Easter 398, i.e. when Rufinus was working on the rough draft of his translation. At the start he and Rufinus lived as neighbours, met frequently on friendly terms, worshipped together.[26] But Eusebius was a fanatical anti-Origenist, and also 'one of those subordinates with more zeal than conscience'.[27] When he discovered the work Rufinus had in hand, he did not scruple to possess himself, according to Rufinus[28] by theft, of an unfinished and unrevised copy. This he promptly passed on to Marcella, Pammachius, and the rest of the pro-Jerome clique. Their reaction was one of shock and confusion. They were deeply disturbed by Rufinus's insinuation that he was only completing a work already promised by Jerome, with the implied suggestion that Jerome was of his way of thinking. They were also perplexed because, while they noticed several doubtfully orthodox statements in the treatise, they suspected that the original contained many more of a downright pernicious character which Rufinus had removed with the aim of passing Origen off as an orthodox teacher. So, without consulting Rufinus, much less asking his leave, they despatched the manuscript to Jerome, with a covering letter[29] entreating him both to prepare a literal translation of the *First Principles* which would show up the dangerous errors Rufinus had sought to disguise, and also to defend himself against the suspicions people must inevitably feel in regard to his own position.

Rufinus was later to complain bitterly of the treatment he had received.[30] Before he had put the finishing touches to his translation, his manuscript had been stolen by a man who, to all appearances, was a friend. And he might have expected something better from Pammachius at least, a devout Christian deservedly respected for his good works. If he had found anything offensive in his draft, surely he could have remonstrated with him privately as a fellow-Christian—he lived close by—instead of sending it off by the next post to the east, there 'to set wagging the tongue of that man who never knew how to control it'. He had behaved much more charitably with the indiscretions contained in Jerome's *Against Jovinian*, doing his best to suppress copies of the pamphlet, rebuking people who rushed in to criticise the author, and persuading Jerome to introduce appropriate corrections.

Meanwhile, without waiting for a reply from Jerome, his friends unleashed a violent campaign at Rome against Origenism in general and

---

[25] Jerome had written it to serve as reading-matter on the ship: see above p. 222.

[26] Rufinus, *Apol. c. Hier.* 1, 20. He does not name Eusebius here, but Jerome discloses his identity in *Apology* 3, 20.

[27] This apt description is Cavallera's (1, 234 n. 1).

[28] *Apol. c. Hier.* 2, 44.

[29] *Letter* 83 (from Pammachius and Oceanus to Jerome). It gives the evidence for the reaction described above.

[30] *Apol. c. Hier.* 2, 44.

Rufinus in particular. According to Jerome, Marcella, who had long observed a discreet silence, emerged from her seclusion and took a leading part; while Eusebius, according to Rufinus, went about vilifying him in private houses and monasteries, among pious ladies and good Christian men.[31] Their denunciations met at this stage with a cool reception from the pope and the official clergy, who Jerome alleges were taken in by the heresy. But Rufinus had had enough of it. He had stayed in Rome much longer than he had intended, shattered by his mother's death and reluctant to revisit immediately his home with its painful memories.[32] The atmosphere at Rome, however, was becoming so unpleasant that he travelled north to Aquileia, the city of his baptism, there to enjoy the companionship of trustworthy friends like Bishop Chromatius and to continue his scholarly translations. Before leaving the city, he took the precaution of obtaining 'ecclesiastical letters' from Pope Siricius, who apparently esteemed him highly, attesting his full communion with the Roman Church.[33] He also wrote to Jerome informing him of his move and the reasons for it. The letter has disappeared, but from the latter's reply[34] we gather that, while complaining of the hostile attitude of Jerome's friends, its tone was amicable and implied no break in their friendship.

(v)

It was towards the end of 398 that the letter of Pammachius and Oceanus, along with Rufinus's unfinished draft of the *First Principles*, reached Bethlehem. In the summer or autumn, although scarcely recovered from his long illness and besieged by crowds making all sorts of demands, Jerome had completed (in three days, he reports) translations of Proverbs, Song of Songs, and Ecclesiastes from the Hebrew. He had sent these to Chromatius and Heliodorus with warm thanks for providing the money to pay for his copyists. At the same time he had pointed out to them that Ecclesiasticus and Wisdom, books which were widely believed to be also by Solomon,[35] were not canonical, and therefore could be read for edification but not to support church doctrine.[36] Indefatigable as ever, he

---

[31] Cf. *Letter* 127, 9, which suggests that Marcella took the lead, and that they tried to get Pope Siricius to condemn Rufinus, but in vain, since he 'judged other as guileless as himself'; also Rufinus, *Apol. c. Hier.* 1, 21 for Eusebius's activities.

[32] So we gather from *Letter* 81, 1 (to Rufinus: see below pp. 239 f.).

[33] For these 'ecclesiasticae epistulae' see *Letter* 127, 10, where Jerome represents Rufinus's departure as a flight. See also *Apology* 3, 21; 24.

[34] *Letter* 81.

[35] For contemporary opinion cf., e.g., Augustine, *De doctr. christ.* 2, 12 f.; *Spec.* 21 (*CSEL* 80, 40; 12, 113). While reporting the common view, Augustine does not himself share it, but thinks that these books have been attributed to Solomon because of stylistic similarity with Proverbs, Song of Songs, and Ecclesiastes.

[36] For these items see *Pref. to Solomon's Books* (PL 28, 1241–4). For Jerome's attitude to the Apocrypha see above pp. 160 f.

was busy with a commentary on Daniel, which he had (apparently) promised for Paulinus of Nola,[37] when the package arrived from Rome, but when he grasped its contents he put this at once on one side. He was deeply worried and incensed, and saw that immediate action was called for.

First, he set himself, in the winter months of 398/9, to make the severely literal version of Origen's *First Principles* for which he had been asked. It was not just Pammachius, he was to explain[38] to Paulinus by way of excuse, but practically all his Christian friends in Rome who were clamouring for it. The faith of many there, they had assured him, was being put in jeopardy by Origen's perverse teachings. His action might seem paradoxical. It was in stark contradiction not only to his theory that a good translation should be a free one, but also (as Rufinus was to point out)[39] to his own avowed policy of correcting or excising whatever was dogmatically offensive in Origen. More important, if Rufinus's bowdlerised version was upsetting people's faith, what appalling damage they must sustain from a completely uncensored exposition of his opinions. Jerome's later defence[40] was that his work had a twofold advantage: it showed up the heretical author in his true colours, and convicted the translator [Rufinus] of untrustworthiness. But Pammachius, devout and orthodox-minded, took a very different view. When he read Jerome's unexpurgated version, he was so scandalised that he locked it in his desk for fear that its dissemination would have a disastrous effect.[41] And, as a matter of history, it soon lapsed into oblivion apart from a few important fragments quoted by Jerome in a later letter[42]—but not before providing the anti-Origenists in Rome with the ammunition they needed. From the rare cases where these fragments overlap with surviving fragments of the original Greek, the translation (over which Jerome took great pains) would appear to have been extremely close but not slavish, while subtly highlighting, here and there, some of Origen's objectionable statements.[43]

Parallel with this, Jerome prepared and despatched to Rome a detailed reply[44] to the letter of Pammachius and Oceanus, a reply which he intended for public circulation. Although promising to stick to self-defence, he soon passed to attack; and although professing to avoid personalities, it was clear that in inveighing against Origen's supporters in general he was making Rufinus his real target. The charge, or rather the imagined

---

[37] So we gather from *Letter* 85, 3: see below p. 240.
[38] *Letter* 85, 3.
[39] *Apol. c. Hier.* I, 21 (quoting his remark to Vigilantius in *Letter* 61, 2, that as a result of his policy Latin readers knew what was good in Origen while remaining ignorant of what was bad).
[40] *Apology* I, 7.
[41] So Jerome reports in *Letter* 124, 1.
[42] *Letter* 124 (to Avitus: see below p. 303).
[43] Cf. G. Bardy, op. cit., 182 ff.
[44] *Letter* 84: a 'public letter', according to *Apology* I, 12.

charge, against which he defended himself was that of being an Origenist. This he took to be implied in Rufinus's preface, with its 'insults disguised as compliments'; and it was necessary that he should rebut it because his friends, apparently, were seriously worried where he stood. There were only two passages, he contended[45] with unblushing optimism, in which he had applauded Origen. Even in them it was the exegete, not the teacher of dogma, the man's genius, not his beliefs, that he had praised. For his true judgment on Origen people should examine (again unblushing optimism) his commentaries on Ecclesiastes and Ephesians. There they would find he had always contradicted his characteristic doctrines. In any case what harm was there in studying Origen, as he had studied heretics like Apollinarius and Didymus and as Cyprian had studied Tertullian, or for that matter in emptying his purse to collect Origen's works, so long as he rejected his false teachings—'poisonous teachings', which ran counter to Scripture and had paved the way for Arius?

Such was the gist of the self-defence which he deemed necessary (although in fact, so far from accusing him of accepting Origen's erroneous views, Rufinus had commended him for removing them). Turning to the offensive, Jerome first castigated the unnamed Origenists as heretics who, craftily veiling the real drift of their teaching from the uninitiated, duped them with falsehoods.[46] As an example he fastened on the resurrection of the flesh, protesting that they used ambiguous language about it, refusing to come clean and acknowledge that the resurrection body would be identical with the physical one, with its hands, feet, hair, and other parts. If told that this is the correct doctrine, 'they burst into fits of laughter, jeer that in that case we shall need barbers and doctors . . . and go on to inquire whether we believe that the genitals of both sexes will be raised as they are'. After brandishing other errors of Origen's (the pre-existence of souls, etc.) which they refused to repudiate,[47] Jerome turned on Rufinus himself (anonymously), rebuking him for his impudence in translating the *First Principles*. No other Latin author had 'ever wished to cover himself with infamy with such an infamous work', and Origen himself, had he been alive, would have been shocked. He was certainly a remarkable man who, in his zeal for God, castrated himself, spurned covetousness, knew the Bible by heart, and published commentaries beyond count. But he also erred grievously in the faith, and it was nonsense to pretend that these errors in his writings were interpolations by heretics. As for Pamphilus's *Vindication*, either the book had been

---

[45] *Letter* 84, 2. The passages were the preface to his rendering of Origen's homilies on Song of Songs and the preface to *Hebrew Names* (see above pp. 86 and 153 f.).

[46] *Letter* 84, 1 ('they can't bear being heretics unless I am one too'); 3 (they work on the principle that the pearls of their esoteric teaching should not lightly be fed to swine).

[47] *Letter* 84, 7.

falsely foisted on him, or Pamphilus wrote it before being martyred and effaced the sin of it by the blood of martyrdom.[48]

This was an important letter, carefully constructed so as to allay the suspicions which Rufinus's preface had aroused that Jerome was still a partisan of Origen. Hence its angry tone and often intemperate language (although there is a remarkable lack of the abuse customary in Jerome's diatribes), in spite of the fact that in much of it he was beating his fists against phantoms. Hence, more specifically, its vehement repudiation of Origen's 'errors' and its description of Origen as the precursor of Arius, its dishonest (or did his excitement blur his judgment?) playing-down of his earlier reverence for him, its proud declaration that he would adhere as an old man to the strict Roman faith into which he had been baptised as a youth and would have no truck with novelties.[49] Hence, too, its distasteful branding of Rufinus as a heretic, its ascription to him of an exaggeratedly spiritualising conception of the resurrection body which he never held, its outrage at his having translated the *First Principles,* its complete neglect of his important point that many of Origen's speculations had dealt with matters on which the Church had not yet declared an official view. Jerome professed[50] to believe that he had shown extreme moderation in not naming Rufinus, but if he really imagined that anyone could mistake the reference he was duping himself. The fact was, he was more concerned, in this letter, with restoring his public image than with being fair to Rufinus.

Much about the same time, early in 399, he wrote a second letter,[51] this time a private one to Rufinus, probably intending it to be a foil to the public one to Pammachius and Oceanus. This was in reply to the letter his friend had sent him before leaving Rome for Aquileia. Alluding to Rufinus's complaint about the hostility of his Roman supporters, he called God to witness that since their reconciliation he himself had nursed no feelings of rancour, but had taken every precaution to prevent misunderstandings. Then he went straight to the controversial preface in which 'covertly, or rather openly, I am the person attacked. You best know your intention in writing it, but any fool can see how it is to be understood.'

---

[48] *Letter* 84, 11. Jerome had himself stated in *Famous Men* 75 that Pamphilus had written a *Vindication of Origen*. Lightfoot (*Dict. of Christian Biography* II, 340b) justly remarked, 'Jerome's treatment of this matter is a painful exhibition of disingenuousness, self-contradiction, ill-humour, and spite'; but his persistence from now onwards in denying Pamphilus's authorship suggests that he had worked himself into a state of mind in which he sincerely believed this. It was, of course, awkward for him to concede that so holy a martyr had stood up for such a 'heretic'. Eusebius records (*Hist. eccl.* 6, 33, 4) that Pamphilus and he were joint authors; the general view is that Pamphilus wrote the first five books of the work with Eusebius advising him, and Eusebius the sixth.

[49] *Letter* 84, 9.

[50] *Apology* 1, 12; 3, 37.

[51] *Letter* 81.

Although he could if he had wanted to, he did not propose to imitate Rufinus's technique of insincere flattery, still less to reply to injury with injury. Though Rufinus had wronged him, he preferred to expostulate amicably rather than give public vent to his rage. When he had been reconciled to a friend, his way was to behave loyally, not to offer bread with one hand and fling stones with the other. He added that he had asked his brother Paulinian, whom Rufinus would be meeting in Aquileia, and the rest of his friends in Italy to show him the respect and courtesy he himself felt. It was now up to Rufinus and his friends to show proper restraint and avoid giving offence; they would not always find people so patient as Jerome.

This was a sharp, even stinging note, but the indignation and reproof were kept in tight control. Rufinus's letter had been a sign that he wished to avoid the threatened breakdown of their friendship, and Jerome's reply indicated, in his awkward and grudging way, that he shared this wish. Only, the responsibility for peace, he made clear, now rested with Rufinus. Most unfortunately, when it reached Rome this guardedly eirenic message fell into the hands of Pammachius and others of Jerome's circle, and they decided not to forward it to Rufinus at Aquileia—while widely circulating Jerome's public apologia. Their reason for this chicanery, according to Jerome's later explanation,[52] was their annoyance with Rufinus for the disagreeable things he had been saying about Jerome and his way of life.

(vi)

We have another letter from 399, to Paulinus of Nola, which throws an interesting side-light on Jerome's manoeuvres in the quarrel over Origen. We recall how in 394, with Paulinus deferentially taking the initiative, a correspondence had been started between him and the famous monk of Bethlehem.[53] The correspondence continued, and there is evidence that at least two pairs of letters, now lost, were exchanged between 395 and 399.[54] Paulinus, we may suspect, was the more eager and pressing of the two, but although he managed to extract from Jerome an undertaking to prepare a commentary on Daniel for him, he seems to have been disappointed that the great man did not make his replies longer or take more care over them. He was also anxious about Jerome's delay in producing the promised commentary. The letter[55] which concerns us here shows

[52] *Apology* 1, 12; 3, 38.

[53] See above pp. 162-4.

[54] On this see P. Courcelle, 'Paulin de Nole et saint Jérôme', *Revue des études latines* 25 (1947), 266 f.

[55] *Letter* 85. Its date is probably 399, for Jerome remarks that he has 'recently' translated the *First Principles*.

Jerome deliberately going out of his way both to smooth Paulinus's ruffled feathers and also to clarify his own behaviour and attitude in his eyes.

Paulinus had submitted two problems to him. First, did not God's hardening of Pharaoh's heart, as described in Exodus (4, 21; 7, 13; etc.) and taken up by St Paul in Romans 9, 16–18, undermine the belief in free-will? Secondly, how could St Paul properly call the children of baptised parents holy (1 Cor. 7, 14), since to be saved they surely needed personally to receive and hold fast to God's grace? Short though it was, Jerome's letter was full of effusive compliments—praise for Paulinus's almost Ciceronian style, which he himself could only envy; praise for his knowledge of Greek; praise, too, for his mastery of the Bible. If his own letters struck Paulinus as too brief, this was because he hesitated to expose himself at greater length than necessary to such an accomplished critic; if they seemed unpolished, the explanation did not lie in any intentional carelessness, but in the huge number of letters he was called upon to write all at once whenever the time came for vessels to set sail for the west. But he did not overlook Paulinus's problems. For the second he referred him to Tertullian's *On Monogamy*,[56] adding on his own account that in Scripture 'holy' does not necessarily connote 'justified by grace,' but can be applied more widely (e.g. to inanimate objects). As for the first, he remarked, 'Origen provided a very convincing solution of it in his *First Principles*,' and suggested that Paulinus could borrow a copy of the translation he had recently made from Pammachius, although with his knowledge of Greek he could study the original.

It is ironical that Paulinus's first problem was closely related, though without the reference to astrological fatalism, to the one which had troubled Macarius, and that Jerome had no qualms about directing him, as Rufinus directed Macarius, to Origen. Even more intriguing, however, is the way Jerome seized on the opportunity to justify to Paulinus his translation of the *First Principles* and to impress on him his sensible and balanced estimate of the controversial thinker. The translation, he explained, had been made as a matter of extreme urgency, being demanded by 'almost all our brothers in Rome' because so many there were being taken in by Origen's perverse teachings. It was therefore sheer necessity which had obliged him to translate the treatise, in which he knew there was 'more that was pernicious than good', and to translate it literally. It was this necessity, and his unavoidable preoccupation with the grave crisis, which had forced him to defer yet again his commentary on Daniel.

---

[56] This was a powerful invective against second marriages, written in Tertullian's Montanist period. But Jerome's memory was at fault, for while *De monogamia* revolves around 1 Cor. 7 it nowhere discusses verse 14, which worried Paulinus. It was in *De anima* 39, 4 that Tertullian explained the difficulty along the lines summarised by Jerome.

At the same time he begged Paulinus, as a man of culture and learning, not to imagine that he was an ignorant buffoon who condemned indiscriminately everything Origen had written, as Origen's 'intemperate admirers' (i.e. Rufinus and Melania) were falsely alleging against him. He had certainly not changed his views about Origen all of a sudden (evidently people were saying that he had), and it was only his objectionable dogmas that he repudiated.

The background of these expostulations, as of his flattering approach to Paulinus, is not far to seek. It was the anti-Origenist campaign which Marcella, Pammachius, Eusebius of Cremona, and Jerome's other friends were conducting in Italy with Rufinus as their chief target. Paulinus, the wealthy aristocrat turned monk, was becoming an increasingly respected figure in western ascetic circles. There was a friendship of long standing between him and Eusebius.[57] But he had the regard and confidence of other, very differently oriented, Christian groups; and Rufinus, much more like him in temperament than Jerome, had become his friend too, and their friendship was firmly rooted and was to endure. Moreover, Melania, Rufinus's patroness and collaborator on the Mount of Olives, was a relative of his; and in 399 she was preparing to leave Jerusalem and make her way to Rome. With her powerful connections she was well placed to protect Rufinus; and it was natural that Paulinus should move over to her side.[58] Hitherto Jerome may have underestimated Paulinus and treated him with a certain off-handedness; but he could afford to do so no longer. Even without the advice of his friends in Italy, he must have judged it prudent to reassure him about his position in the debate over Origen, and to do everything possible to retain his confidence and regard.

---

[57] For this friendship, stretching back to 378–81 when Paulinus was governor of Campania and Eusebius a prominent advocate, see P. Courcelle, art. cit., 264–6.
[58] For the relations of Rufinus, Melania, and Paulinus, see P. Brown, *Religion and Society in the Age of Augustine* (London, 1972), 210.

XXI

The Final Break

(i)

So far the squabble between Jerome, supported by his anti-Origenist partisans at Rome, and Rufinus had been a largely personal one. But in 399, and increasingly in 400, events in the Church at large conspired, for a time at any rate, to blow it up into an issue of widespread public interest. At Rome a change of popes suddenly made the ecclesiastical climate there much more propitious to Jerome's party and its crusade against Origenism. Even more decisive, however, was the conversion of Theophilus, the powerful, ambitious, and entirely ruthless patriarch (or 'Pharaoh')[1] of Alexandria, to the same cause.

When we last met him, as mediator between Jerome and John of Jerusalem in 396/7,[2] Theophilus had been, like many cultivated Easterners, an admirer of Origen without professing his 'errors'. So too had been his confidential agent Isidore, the octogenarian he had unsuccessfully intrigued to get elected bishop of Constantinople in an effort to establish his own ascendancy there. He himself had shown marked favour to the Origenist-minded monks living in the desert of Nitria, especially to the four saintly Tall Brothers[3] whom they revered as their leader. But in 399 he executed an astonishing volte-face, his motive being to placate the desert monks, the great majority of whom, simple and uneducated men, conceived of God as corporeal, and had demonstrated violently against his January pastoral castigating such 'anthropomorphism'. More interested in power politics than in dogmatic truth, he at once sensed the importance of having the formidable army of monks as his devoted storm-troopers, and hastened to assure them that he too pictured God as bodily and rejected Origen's intellectualism.[4] About the same time,

---

[1] This title, common applied to him, seems to derive from the statement of Isidore of Pelusium (d. *c.* 450), made with reference to him, that Egypt always perversely preferred a Pharaoh to a Moses (*Ep.* 1, 152: *PG* 78, 285).

[2] See above pp. 204 ff.

[3] These were Ammonius, Dioscorus, Eusebius, and Eutimius. For Theophilus's initial regard for them see Socrates, *Hist. eccl.* 6, 7 (*PG* 67, 685A). He had consecrated Dioscorus, against his will, as bishop of Hermopolis in 390–4 (he was a bishop by 394: see Mansi, *Sacr. concil. coll.* III, 852C).

[4] Socrates, *Hist. eccl.* 6, 7; Sozomen, *Hist. eccl.* 8, 11 (*PG* 67, 684; 1545).

having broken with his old friend Isidore after a squalid wrangle, and with the Tall Brothers, who backed Isidore,[5] he turned his fury on them and their associates, making their attachment to Origen his pretext, and in summer 399 issued letters ordering their expulsion from Nitria.[6]

Thus it came about that in the latter part of 399, when Theophilus's mind was turning against Origen, Jerome at Bethlehem received an unexpected letter from him. He himself had continued to write to the bishop (we recall the admiration he had conceived for him in 396),[7] in a recent letter apparently informing him of the revival of the quarrel over Origen. So far Theophilus had not deigned to reply. In breaking his long silence now he reproved Jerome for welcoming at Bethlehem a fugitive under his ban,[8] and reminded him of the Nicene canons prohibiting such friendly acts to excommunicate persons.[9] He was already preparing, it seems, to make things difficult for refugees from Nitria. Apart from that, the letter was an amicable one and, although it counselled patience in dealing with Origenism, Jerome was delighted at the resumption of relations. His satisfaction comes out in his brief reply,[10] in which, while dutifully accepting Theophilus's rebuke, he assured him that his chief priority was to observe canonical order and cleave fast to 'the Roman faith which the Apostle himself applauded and which the church of Alexandria is proud to share'. Then, becoming bolder (he was probably fully cognisant of recent happenings in Egypt), he warned Theophilus that 'many good Christians' were disappointed by his leniency towards 'the abominable heresy' which was rending the Church's vitals. They were afraid lest, while he hesitated to intervene, the abandoned faction would grow stronger and more audacious.

Shortly after this, exasperated by the ill success of his order of expulsion, his resolution perhaps strengthened by Jerome's hint of what Christians farther afield were expecting of him, Theophilus proceeded to more drastic measures. First, he encouraged the desert hermits not to listen to the teaching of the Tall Brothers that God was incorporeal, for Scripture

---

[5] The most recent discussion of the whole affair is by A. Favale, *Teofilo d'Alessandria* (Turin, 1958), 96 ff.

[6] See Palladius, *Dial.* 6 (Coleman-Norton, 37). A precise dating of these events, as of this phase of the Origenistic controversy generally, is very conjectural. See esp. K. Holl and A. Jülicher, *Die Zeitfolge des ersten Origenistischen Streites* (in K. Holl, *Gesammelte Aufsätze*, vol. 2: Tübingen, 1927–8); E. Schwartz, 'Palladiana' (*ZNTW* 36, 1937, 161–204).

[7] See above p. 208.

[8] Probably the Bishop Paul (otherwise unknown) whom Theophilus had expelled, and whom Jerome had sheltered in his monastery and encouraged to appeal to the emperor against his expulsion: see *Apology* 3, 17.

[9] Canon 5, which prescribed that persons excommunicated by their own bishops should not be received by others: Pitra, *Iuris ecclesiarum Graecarum historia et monumenta* 1, 429.

[10] *Letter* 63: now generally agreed to date from 399, not from the time of the controversy between Jerome and Bishop John. My reconstruction of Theophilus's letter, which has not survived, is derived from it.

clearly testified that 'he has eyes, ears, hands, and feet like men'.[11] Then, confident of their support, he assembled a packed synod at Nitria which anathematised the writings of Origen.[12] Finally, using their sympathies with Origen as a pretext against Isidore and his companions and reinforced by an imperial edict, he made a bloody punitive expedition against them at the beginning of 400 and had them ejected from Egypt.[13] He thereupon wrote to the new pope, Anastasius I (there were traditional ties between the churches of Alexandria and Rome), soliciting his endorsement of his condemnation of Origen. Significantly, he arranged that the bearer of this letter, the monk Theodore, should travel via Bethlehem, stay with Jerome, describe to him as an eye-witness how effectively the monasteries of Nitria had been cleansed of Origenism, and deliver a personal note[14] requesting his help against 'saboteurs of the truth' in Palestine. Meanwhile the unhappy refugees from Nitria had fled to that country, but Theophilus sent his agents, Eubulus and Priscus, to harry them. Jerome was over-joyed, and in an excited letter[15] congratulated him on the success of his energetic policy. His earlier criticisms of his leniency had been mis-judged; Theophilus, he now realised, had only been forbearing so as to strike all the harder when the right moment came. In a postscript he begged the patriarch not to be too hard on John of Jerusalem for having harboured 'a certain individual', for he had received no specific instruc-tions to the contrary, and certainly would neither wish nor dare to injure Theophilus. If (as seems likely)[16] the 'individual' was Palladius, the historian of Egyptian monasticism and hated critic of Theophilus, Jerome was probably passing useful information to his patron and at the same time, while pretending to excuse him, stabbing John in the back.

From now onwards Jerome was to be the Egyptian Pharaoh's eager, uncritical collaborator. Somewhat later, in summer 400, the bishop, evidently dissatisfied with the lukewarm response of leading figures in the

---

[11] Socrates, *Hist. eccl.* 6, 7 (*PG* 67, 688A).

[12] Cf. Theophilus's synodical letter (*Letter* 92, 1 in Jerome). For Palladius's account see *Dial.* 7 (C.N. 38).

[13] For his attack see Socrates, *Hist. eccl.* 6, 7; Cassian, *Coll.* 10, 2 (*PG* 67, 688; *CSEL* 13, 287). Both Jerome (*Apology* 1, 12) and Palladius (*Dial.* 17: C.N. 106) mention or imply an imperial edict ordering the expulsion. No trace of it survives, but it could have followed the pattern of that of 398 forbidding the reading of the books of Montanus and Eunomius (*Codex Theod.* xvi, 5, 34). Pope Anastasius also speaks of an imperial pronouncement prohibiting the reading of Origen in his letter to John of Jerusalem (*Ep.* 1, 5: *PL* 20, 72).

[14] *Letter* 89 in Jerome's correspondence.

[15] *Letter* 86.

[16] K. Holl, *Die Zeitfolge* etc., 327, argues for Isidore, pointing out that Sozomen (*Hist. eccl.* 8, 13) reports that he fled in company with the Tall Brothers; but this is too general. E. Schwartz (*ZNTW* 36, 175) connects Jerome's remark with a passage in Theophilus's synodal (*Letter* 92, 1 in Jerome), in which he speaks of the Tall Brothers journeying to Palestine 'along with certain travellers who were for some time resident in Egypt'. After nine years at Cellia, Palladius spent a spell in Alexandria, and then on doctor's orders went to Palestine.

Holy Land (almost certainly John was one of them), sent him another letter[17] in which, recalling his successful purge of 'the wicked fanatics' at Nitria, he urged him to employ all his eloquence to bring the dupes of Origenism in Palestine to a correct frame of mind. In his reply,[18] while again congratulating Theophilus ecstatically, Jerome promised to exert himself more strenuously than ever against the heretics, even if he should incur 'certain people's wrath' (language suggesting that he had Bishop John in mind). He made the point that he had already written to the west exposing the errors of Origenism, and Theophilus's letter to Anastasius had had the happy effect of confirming his testimony. At the same time he begged Theophilus to forward to him any synodical briefs he had bearing on the subject so that he might, 'fortified by the authority of so great a pontiff', speak out the more freely and confidently on Christ's behalf. This was to prove a mutually advantageous arrangement. Through Jerome's Latin versions of his skilfully argued denunciations of Origen's teaching and of the Origenists in Egypt the patriarch might expect to justify his policies at Rome, while Jerome's circle of friends there would be furnished with useful ammunition for the anti-Origenist campaign.[19]

(ii)

The anti-Origenist storm which Theophilus, largely for political motives, had stirred up in Egypt and was energetically extending far beyond its confines had swift repercussions in the west. On 26 November 399 Pope Siricius died. Suspicious of Jerome, he had placed entire confidence in Rufinus, and had turned a deaf ear to the fanatical anti-Origenist coterie in Rome. His successor, Anastasius I (399–402), looked with a kindlier eye on the strict ascetic movement,[20] and almost immediately found himself under strong pressure from Marcella to have Origen's writings proscribed. Aided and abetted by her devoted protégée Principia, she paraded Christians who had allegedly been corrupted by them, produced evidence of the large numbers so affected, and pointed accusingly at 'the impious volumes of *First Principles* as corrected by the Scorpion's hand' (i.e. by Rufinus).[21] Anastasius must have been thoroughly confused, for, as his later briefs dealing with the 'heresy' make clear, Origen had been till then a mere name to him and he had no grasp whatsoever of the theological issues

---

[17] *Letter* 87 in Jerome's correspondence.

[18] *Letter* 88.

[19] For Jerome's campaign to mobilise sympathy for Theophilus, and for the anti-Origenist cause, see below pp. 260 f.

[20] Cf. E. Caspar, *Geschichte des Papstums* (Tübingen, 1930) I, 285; as an illustration he points to the marked sympathy, in contrast to the coldness of Siricius, which Anastasius showed to Paulinus of Nola.

[21] For her activities see Jerome, *Letter* 127, 10.

involved.[22] When he was trying to make up his mind in spring 400, the monk Theodore, fresh from his colloquies with Jerome, arrived in Rome, and presented him with Theophilus's letter dwelling on the evil caused by reading Origen's works and reporting their recent condemnation in Egypt. Thoroughly horrified by what he read, which confirmed the worst he had heard from Marcella, he convoked a synod which proceeded to anathematise Origen's blasphemies, and wrote to Simplicianus, bishop of Milan (then the imperial residence), inviting his adhesion, and that of the other bishops of north Italy, to the anathema.[23]

This was the moment of triumph for Jerome's friends in Rome; little wonder that he was later to extol Anastasius, whose reign ended in December 402, as too good for this wicked world.[24] Nor were they slow, or unduly scrupulous, in exploiting it. It was Eusebius of Cremona[25] who carried the pope's letter to Milan, and there took place there a confrontation between him and Rufinus, probably at some inquiry before the local bishop.[26] When Eusebius read out a passage from *First Principles* implying the inferiority of the Son to the Father and of the Spirit to the Son, Rufinus indignantly exclaimed that this was not his translation but a garbled travesty of it. All Eusebius could do when interrogated was to mumble that he had obtained the copy from which he was reading from 'a certain lady'—Marcella. The story reveals that they were at least as much interested in convicting Rufinus of heresy as Origen. Nor was this an isolated incident. According to Rufinus,[27] Eusebius travelled up and down Italy stirring up suspicion and poisoning the minds of bishops against him, even pointing to his self-restraint as proof of a guilty conscience. Rufinus firmly believed that this smear-campaign was being conducted on Jerome's express instructions, but Jerome's later denial[28] of the charge should be accepted. This was not the first, or the last, time that his over-zealous admirers carried their animosity against Rufinus further than he himself would have wished.

Clearly Rufinus, reserved man though he was, could not afford to let matters stay as they were. Widely respected, he had powerful friends in Italy, including his aristocratic and greatly admired patroness Melania, who had just returned from Jerusalem.[29] But now that Origenism had

---

[22] Cf. his letters to Simplicianus of Milan (d. 15 Aug., 400: *Letter* 95 in Jerome), and to his successor Venerius (text in *Revue d'histoire et de la littérature religieuse* 4 (1899), 7).

[23] See the letters mentioned above. The one to Venerius mentions the bishops of north Italy.

[24] *Letter* 127, 10.

[25] So Anastasius states (*Letter* 95, 3 in Jerome's correspondence).

[26] Rufinus, *Apol. c. Hier.* 1, 17–20 (esp. 19).

[27] *Apol. c. Hier.* 1, 21.

[28] E.g. *Apology* 3, 5; 35.

[29] She did not, as used to be supposed, return with Rufinus in 397. For the date 400 see E. Schwartz, 'Palladiana', *ZNTW* 36 (1937), 166–8; 176: also F. X. Murphy, *Traditio* 5 (1947),

been officially condemned, these slurs on his orthodoxy were likely to ruin his reputation at Rome if not rebutted. So in autumn or early winter 400 he prepared and sent to Anastasius a short defence of his position and conduct.[30] Years later Jerome was to insinuate[31] that he had been formally cited to Rome to explain himself; but there is no hint of such a summons in the 'apology' itself. With its confident tone and caustic references to his assailants, it leaves the impression of having been written by Rufinus on his own initiative. He could not believe, he began, that the pope had paid any attention to calumnies about a Christian in his absence, a Christian whom he knew to be united to him in the faith and love of God. If he now furnished him with a statement of his beliefs, it was not so much to clear his mind of suspicion as to give him a cudgel with which to drive the baying dogs away.

After this preamble Rufinus insisted that his orthodoxy had been sufficiently proved by his steadfastness under persecution years ago in Egypt. To reassure doubters, however, he inserted a profession which showed that his belief was entirely correct on the Trinity, the incarnation, and, more particularly, the resurrection both of Christ and of Christians. The risen body, though glorified, would be identical with the natural body. Also, there would be a judgment in which the devil and his angels would be consigned to eternal fire. As regards the origin of human souls, he reviewed the various opinions that were currently canvassed, including Origen's that they were all created in the beginning. For his own part, he regarded none of these as certain, being content with the Church's teaching that God is the maker of souls and bodies alike. Finally, the charges brought against him for translating Origen's *First Principles* were the product of sheer malice. He had made the translation only because he had been requested to do so; and if there was anything offensive in it, the original author, not he, should be blamed. True, he had introduced some changes, but only where he suspected that Origen's orthodox text had been tampered with. In any case he was no champion of Origen, nor the first to put his works into Latin. If an order should be issued banning such translations, it should apply to the future, not the past; but if to the past, censure should fall first on those who had taken the first step. As for himself, he had never held, nor ever would hold, any faith other than that proclaimed equally at Rome, Alexandria, Aquileia, and Jerusalem. People who through ill-will stirred up dissensions would have to answer for it at the day of judgment.

55–77. She was probably motivated by the hostile measures taken by Theophilus against the monks she favoured, but also (as Murphy remarks) by concern for her relatives in Italy.

[30] His *Apologia ad Anastasium*: critical edition in *CCL* 20.

[31] *Letter* 127, 10 (date 413).

This spirited, even combative, apologia left Anastasius, still under the influence of Marcella and her coterie, completely unconvinced. Writing in 401 to John of Jerusalem, who was worried about the treatment of his old friend, he made it plain that he had the gravest doubts about Rufinus's motives for translating Origen, indeed could only conclude that he approved his perverse opinions. He had, however, taken Rufinus's hint that his faith was that of the church of Jerusalem, i.e. of Bishop John; he was also aware of the prestige he enjoyed in important circles in Italy. So he informed John that he preferred that Rufinus should make his own peace with God. He himself had no wish to know either where he was or what he was up to.[32]

(iii)

Rufinus's anxiety about his public reputation was more than matched in 399 and 400 by his growing resentment against Jerome. His feelings would have been very different had he received the sharp but basically eirenic note Jerome had despatched to him personally after hearing of his translation of *First Principles*, but (as we observed) Pammachius and Marcella had intercepted and suppressed it.[33] The lack of any response to his own friendly overtures must have worried him as the months slipped by, and worry must have turned to bitterness when his disciple Apronianus sent him a copy of Jerome's public apologia, which Pammachius and Oceanus were broadcasting at Rome. From the moment he read it, with its veiled attacks on himself and its insinuations of heresy and bad faith, he had felt that a full-dress rejoinder was called for. Now the campaign of vilification which Eusebius and others, acting (as he believed) as Jerome's agents, were conducting left him no option. Hence his *Apology against Jerome*,[34] which finally appeared in 401. He toiled two full years over it, and when completed it proved as much an indictment of Jerome and his partisans as a vindication of Rufinus himself.

The slurs which particularly rankled with him were that he was a heretic (he had never impugned Jerome on that score), that in translating *First Principles* he had had the impudence to do what no one before him had dared do, and that like his master Origen he believed in duping unsophisticated Christians with falsehoods. Once again therefore he expounded his creed at length, stressing the Aquileian church's belief in 'the resurrection of *this* flesh', and pointing out that the literalism Jerome demanded

[32] For his letter to John, who had written expressing concern at complaints people were making about the treatment of Rufinus, see *PL* 20, 68–73: also *ACO* t. i, vol. v, 3 f.

[33] The note is *Letter* 81. For its contents and suppression see above pp. 239 f.

[34] Critical edition by M. Simonetti in *CCL* 20. Simonetti has also published (1957) an edition with a valuable introduction, a translation (Italian), and a few notes. Jerome was to sneer (*Apology* 3, 10) that Rufinus took three years over it.

went beyond what the Apostles themselves had required.[35] His translation, he explained, had been undertaken expressly to assist Macarius; if earlier writers had not anticipated him, it was because they had been ignorant of Greek. In his prefaces he had taken every precaution both to safeguard his own orthodoxy and to justify his theory that Origen's interpolated text needed correction.[36] In any case he was no apologist for Origen; while amending contexts he believed to have been altered by heretics, he had never promised that everything in the resulting work would be consonant with sound faith.[37] As for lying to simple folk, he had never read any book of Origen's defending such a practice, which he personally considered abhorrent in a Christian, but he could point to a passage by Jerome which seemed to approve it.[38] Then, taking the offensive, he recounted the story of Eusebius's attempt to incriminate him by tampering with his translation at a crucial point, and bitterly reproached both him and Pammachius (the latter more in grief than anger) for their unbrotherly treatment of him.[39] He proceeded to tear to shreds Jerome's rash boast that he had never had any sympathy with Origen and had only praised him twice, first assembling and minutely scrutinising a host of passages from his *Commentary on Ephesians* (the book he had singled out as innocent of Origenism) in which he had adopted, or reproduced without criticism, speculations of Origen's which he now branded as blasphemous, and later compiling an extensive dossier (it could have been fuller) of places in which he had eulogised Origen, the theologian as well as the exegete.[40] If after acclaiming Origen for thirty years he now denounced him as a heretic, he was surely passing sentence on himself.

With a telling thrust Rufinus pointed out that through Jerome's literal version of *First Principles* Latin-speaking Christians now had access to all that was bad in Origen.[41] At the same time he gave vent to a whole mass of grievances he had been nursing, some of them for years. How could Jerome consistently complain of lying, since he had broken the solemn vow made in his dream never to possess or read the pagan classics, cramming his works with them and even teaching them to children, and since he had circulated the most libellous falsehoods about Christians of every rank?[42] Who was he to accuse Origen of heathen doctrines, having himself surpassed the heathen in impiety by saluting Paula as 'God's

[35] *Apol. c. Hier.* 1, 4–9.

[36] *Apol. c. Hier.* 1, 10–16; 2, 31.

[37] *Apol. c. Hier.* 1, 10; 14; 16.

[38] *Apol. c. Hier.* 2, 1–4. The passage was Jerome's comment on Eph. 4, 25, in which he seemed to suggest that divine truths should be concealed from all except a privileged inner circle.

[39] *Apol. c. Hier.* 1, 18–21; 2, 44.

[40] *Apol. c. Hier.* 1, 22–44; 2, 13–22; 2, 28.

[41] *Apol. c. Hier.* 1, 21.

[42] *Apol. c. Hier.* 2, 4–8.

mother-in-law' when she dedicated Eustochium to Christ, and having boasted that Porphyry, the arch-opponent of Christianity, had been his instructor?[43] Indeed, it was a rare compliment to be denigrated by Jerome, who had torn Ambrose to pieces, cut the saintly Melania out of his *Chronicle*, and dragged one good Christian after another in the mire.[44] Again, what of Jerome's presumption in jettisoning, in obedience to his Jewish mentor Barabbas (so Rufinus twisted his name Baranina), the Septuagint version of Scripture handed down by the Apostles, and in cutting out books (i.e. the Apocrypha) treasured in the churches?[45] In conclusion Rufinus declared that, if a synod of bishops were to condemn the doctrines censured by Jerome, it would have to condemn Jerome's works too, for they contained those very doctrines.

Rufinus's *Apology* had little, if any, of Jerome's dialectical verve, but with its massive, mainly accurate use of documents and its relentless logic it made a formidable polemical pamphlet.[46] Leaving peripheral issues on one side, it was particularly effective in brushing aside the aspersions on Rufinus's orthodoxy and conduct, and in confronting the new anti-Origenist Jerome with Jerome the sometime adulator of Origen. With characteristic caution Rufinus circulated it privately among friends before publishing it, and through leaks Jerome was able to get advance knowledge of much of its contents. His brother Paulinian, who was returning from Italy to Palestine about this time, also supplied him with some excerpts he had memorised.[47] Infuriated by what he heard, Jerome decided not to wait for the original before making his reply, and in 401 dashed off his *Apology against Rufinus*, dedicating it to his chief informants, Pammachius and Marcella. In writing it he took account not only of the reports of Rufinus's *Apology*, but also of his other controversial writings (the prefaces, the *Apology to Anastasius*, etc.), and of criticisms of himself alleged to be current in Italy in Rufinus's circle.

Jerome's *Apology* was in two books, the first taken up largely with self-defence. After taunting Rufinus for his shamelessness in attacking an old friend behind his back, he dealt with the objections he heard were being raised to his literal translation of *First Principles*. It had the aim, and the value, of exposing Origen for the dangerous heretic he was, whereas the unwary reader of Rufinus's dishonest adaptation was beguiled into swallowing his errors.[48] His own earlier translations of Origen, to which Rufinus

[43] *Apol. c. Hier.* 2, 12; 9. For the description of Paula as 'socrus Dei' see *Letter* 22, 20.

[44] *Apol. c. Hier.* 2, 22–6.

[45] *Apol. c. Hier.* 2, 32–7.

[46] M. Simonetti gives a good analysis and critical assessment in the introduction to his edition (see above).

[47] *Apology* 1, 1; 3. For Paulinian see *Apology* 1, 21.

[48] *Apology* 1, 1–7. We now have an exhaustive summary and analysis of the work in I. Opelt, *Hieronymus' Streitschriften* (Heidelberg, 1973), 83–118.

impudently appealed as precedents, were entirely innocuous; Rufinus's one and only translation had justly created scandal. It was useless his attempting to whitewash the heretic by pretending that the martyred Pamphilus had written the *Vindication of Origen*. The real author was Eusebius of Caesarea, the standard-bearer of Arianism, and Rufinus should come clean and acknowledge the fact, especially as both Theophilus and Anastasius had now condemned Origen.[49] Jerome himself had praised Origen as he had praised Eusebius, as a writer and not as a theologian, and he had done so before setting eyes on *First Principles*.[50] Again, why should Rufinus take such offence at Jerome's public apologia? The fulsome, insincere flattery of his prefaces had implied that Jerome was an Origenist; if he had remained silent, he would have been judged guilty. Even so, he had had the decency not to mention Rufinus by name, and had also written a private letter of expostulation (of which he now enclosed a copy since his friends, he explained, had suppressed it in their disgust at Rufinus's behaviour).[51] Jerome then passed in close review the passages from his Ephesians commentary in which Rufinus alleged he had adopted Origen's blasphemous speculations. The charge showed ignorance, for he had made it plain that, like a responsible exegete, he was setting down the views of other commentators without necessarily agreeing with them, and as often as not he had indicated his dissent.[52] Finally, his habit of citing secular authors only showed what a good memory he had for his schoolboy lessons; he could swear he had never studied them since leaving school. In any case, it was preposterous to hold a man to a promise made in a dream.[53]

In his second book Jerome took the offensive, pouncing on Rufinus's *Apology to Anastasius*. Sneeringly he called in question his boast to have suffered for the true faith in Egypt, and challenged him to produce written proof of it. His statement of his beliefs was completely unsatisfactory, riddled with ambiguities. And how could he be ignorant of the origin of souls, a matter on which the Church had sure knowledge?[54] Equally unsatisfactory was the explanation he had given Anastasius of how he had come to translate *First Principles*. Instead of translating it, as requested, he had inserted unasked-for corrections, even so leaving unaltered a mass of Origen's most outrageous statements. His plea that he was justified in

[49] *Apology* 1, 8–10.
[50] *Apology* 1, 11 and 14.
[51] *Apology* 1, 11–12.
[52] *Apology* 1, 15–16; 21–9.
[53] *Apology* 1, 30 f.
[54] *Apology* 2, 3 (Rufinus's sufferings queried); 2, 4–10 (Rufinus's beliefs). Jerome's statement (2, 10 ad fin.) that 'the churches of Christ claim sure knowledge' about the origin of souls was mere bluster. His own later correspondence (see below pp. 304 and 321) was to show that he was in the same perplexity as Rufinus, 'but less ingenuous in confessing it' (W. H. Fremantle, *Nicene and Post-Nicene Fathers* iii, 506).

amending Origen because he had treated the same issues in a Catholic sense elsewhere was nonsense.[55] His argument that any blame for translating Origen should fall on those who took the first step was a malicious stab at Jerome. Yet his real fault lay not in translating Origen, but in translating this infamous work of his. It was for this that Anastasius had wisely censured him in his letter to Bishop John (of which he subjoined a copy:[56] Rufinus was apparently unaware of its existence). His disclaimer to be a defender of Origen was refuted by his own theory of the interpolation of his writings by heretics, an untenable theory which, if accepted, would enable one to acquit any heretic of one's fancy. After much more in this strain, Jerome bluntly accused Rufinus of having forged a letter which, according to Eusebius of Cremona, was being handed round in Africa and which purported to be an expression of regret by Jerome for having, under Jewish influence, translated the Old Testament from the Hebrew.[57] He then laboured to prove, with extensive quotations from his prefaces, that, contrary to Rufinus's allegations, he had always respected the Septuagint and used it as the basis of exegesis, and that Rufinus himself, and every serious scholar, as well as the Lord and his Apostles, had recognised the value of the Hebrew original.

Jerome rounded off his pamphlet with the bitter remark that it was easier to guard against a professed enemy than an enemy masquerading as a friend. But a rapid summary of its contents conveys little idea of its ferocious tone and polemical brilliance. Written with a passion that is all the more effective because controlled, it abounds in coarse abuse and contemptuous sneers, in wounding caricatures of Rufinus's stupidity, self-indulgence, and avarice—even of his wrinkled forehead, knitted eyebrows, and ponderous gait—in mockery of his clumsy Latinity and pretentious learning. It contains probing passages which, confronting Rufinus with dilemmas as unacceptable as unreal, read like the brutal interrogation of a prosecuting counsel. Throughout Jerome is revealed as an unscrupulous, relentlessly mordant satirist in the finest Roman tradition. So far as the argument went, Jerome was sometimes right, as in his defence of his resort to 'the Hebrew verity', sometimes wrong, as in his tireless efforts to attribute Pamphilus's *Vindication of Origen* to Eusebius or to portray Rufinus as a heretic—but no more wrong than Rufinus in his fanciful theory of the interpolation of Origen's works. On the main issue, so petty in itself but so important to the two parties, Rufinus had little difficulty (though he sometimes overplayed his hand)[58] in exposing

[55] *Apology* 2, 11–13.
[56] *Apology* 2, 14.
[57] *Apology* 2, 24.
[58] E.g. in arguing that Jerome had incorporated Origen's heretical views in his Ephesians commentary, he failed to acknowledge that in several of the passages adduced he had clearly stated that he was citing another exegete's opinions without necessarily sharing them: cf. esp.

Jerome's earlier sympathies with Origen and in brushing off the aspersions on his own orthodoxy; but he nowhere satisfactorily explained, much less justified, his deplorable gaffe in publishing his translation of *First Principles* under the uninvited patronage of Jerome, at a time when he knew full well that his friend had become an anti-Origenist of the school of Epiphanius. Yet it was precisely this gaffe, and the great public embarrassment resulting from it, which aroused Jerome's unbridled wrath.

(iv)

In spring or early summer 401 a merchant ship from the east docked in the great harbour of Aquileia, and its captain delivered Jerome's *Apology* to Rufinus. His indignation as he read it can be imagined, but Bishop Chromatius intervened. The affectionate, trusted friend of both men, he was appalled by the widening breach in their friendship, and determined that it should not become irreparable. He therefore urged Rufinus to refrain from making a public rejoinder, and at the same time wrote to Jerome counselling peace.[59]

So Rufinus contented himself with a private letter. The text is unfortunately lost, but something of its drift can be recovered from Jerome's admittedly tendentious citations from and resumés of it. It was evidently a fierce letter combining angry expostulation with positive menaces. Among other things Rufinus denied having shown his *Apology* to more than a few friends who had felt themselves injured by Jerome's slurs; denounced afresh Eusebius's unscrupulousness in stealing and falsifying his unfinished manuscripts; jeered at Jerome's new-found friendship with Theophilus; expressed disbelief in the genuineness of Anastasius's letter censuring him and even of Jerome's placatory letter to himself (the one Jerome's friends had suppressed); and bitterly reproached Jerome for having proved unfaithful after the restoration of their friendship.[60] He also threatened that, unless he shut up once for all, he would make public the discreditable circumstances of Jerome's enforced withdrawal from Rome in 385, and would reveal certain disgraceful misdeeds Jerome had confided to him when they were intimate friends. He even talked of dragging him before the law-courts on what Jerome implied would be a capital charge. At the same time he despatched to Jerome an authentic copy of his own *Apology*, with the sneering comment that he was letting

---

Jerome's defence in *Apology* 1, 22 of his exegesis of Eph. 1, 4, where he had expressly refuted Origen's interpretation.

[59] For these facts see Jerome, *Apology* 3, 10 (the ship from the east); 3, 2 (Chromatius's intervention).

[60] Jerome picks out these points in *Apology* 3, 3; 4; 17; 20; 38; 37.

him have it free of charge so as to save him from having to bribe his secretary.[61]

Jerome made Rufinus's menaces a pretext for disregarding Chromatius's plea for restraint, and in the following year (402) added a third book to his *Apology*. In much of it he went over the same ground, reiterating and reinforcing his charges of falsehood and double-faced flattery, of implication in Origen's heresies, of insulting Pamphilus by representing him as Origen's defender, of upsetting Roman Christians by his scandalous translation of *First Principles*, and so on.[62] But he also dealt with fresh points raised in Rufinus's letter. For example, while dissociating himself from Eusebius's attacks (he disapproved of one Christian accusing another), he dismissed as libellous the insinuations that Eusebius had falsified Rufinus's manuscripts and that he himself had obtained copies of them by bribery. Rather it was Rufinus, with his Croesus-like wealth, who was guilty of the latter conduct. It was no good Rufinus appealing to Siricius's testimony to his orthodoxy; Siricius was dead, but Anastasius was alive, and he would find that his letter of censure was absolutely genuine. He spurned Rufinus's oath that he was not the author of the retractation, purporting to be by Jerome, circulating in Africa; its inimitable style proved him a liar. It was not Jerome who had betrayed their restored friendship, but Rufinus, who had traduced his friend in his prefaces. As for his hints that he could tell a discreditable story about Jerome's departure from Rome, let him produce a single incriminating document if he could. In bringing accusations of immorality against his opponent, Rufinus was doing something which had been characteristic of heretics in religious controversy, but never of good Christians. If Rufinus was out to destroy Jerome, he would be better advised to hire a thug to kill him than resort to such unworthy measures. In any case Jerome would not be cowed by his threats into acquiescing in heresy.[62a]

If anything, this third book was even more insulting and violent than its predecessors. While announcing[63] that he at any rate would avoid abuse ('Let him speak filth who can behave filthily') and observe the Apostle's dictum (Rom. 12, 19 f.) that a Christian should not seek to avenge himself, he filled it with attacks on Rufinus's wealth, mendacity, pedantry, literary incompetence, etc. It abounded in sallies[64] like, 'Old

---

[61] *Apology* 3, 1–2 (threats of death); 3, 8 (law-courts); 3, 21 (threats to tell the true story of Jerome's exit from Rome); 3, 41 (threats of exposure); 3, 4 (despatch of *Apology*).

[62] *Apology* 3, 1; 13; 34 f. (falsehood etc.); 3, 14 f., 20 f.; 33–7 (Origenism); 3, 12 (Pamphilus); 3, 34–6 (effects of his translation).

[62a] *Apology* 3, 5 (Rufinus's insinuations against Eusebius false); 3, 20 f. (Siricius and Anastasius); 3, 25 (the alleged retractation); 3, 24; 33–5 (Rufinus betrayed the friendship); 3, 22 (Jerome's departure from Rome); 3, 41 f. (Rufinus's charges of immorality: let him hire a 'percussor').

[63] *Apology* 3, 1.

[64] *Apology* 3, 3 and 42.

man as you are, you concoct such calumnies against another old man as a murderer would not bring against a gangster, a whore against a prostitute, a buffoon against a clown'; and, 'You distil from the dunghill of your breast at once the scent of roses and the stench of rotting corpses . . . So great is your purity that the devils sniff noisily at your vests and under-pants.' Yet it was typical of Jerome that from time to time, when his vituperation had reached its height, a nostalgia for reconciliation kept breaking in. Did not the Apostles, he recalled, have their acrimonious quarrels, and yet remain friends? Or again, 'How can people be edified by two old men coming to blows about heretics? . . . Let us join hands and hearts . . . As young men we both made mistakes, let us put things right now that we are old . . . Forgive me for having praised Origen's Scriptural learning in my youth, before I fully grasped his heresy, and I shall pardon you for having defended his works when your head was grey.'[65] But the book ended with a string of texts from Proverbs denouncing malevolent slanderers like (so Jerome claimed) Rufinus, and from the Psalms proclaiming the damnation in store for them. He himself, he strangely added, had disdained retaliation, but feared that his restraint would meet with no response. His last words were coldly uncompromising: 'If you really want peace, lay down your arms. I can be reconciled with one who shows kindness, but I have no fear of threats. Let us be united in faith, and peace will follow immediately.'

It was to be peace, that is to say, on Jerome's terms, and Rufinus could not accept that. His angry letter and Jerome's vitriolic rejoinder signalled the end of their lifelong, but in recent years increasingly fragile, friendship. Whether prompted by Chromatius or by his own good sense, Rufinus made no further response, although he continued to criticise Jerome in private.[66] Withdrawing from all controversy, he spent the remaining eight years of his life indefatigably translating Greek theological and historical works and occasionally producing an original one. In 407, with the death of Chromatius and the worsening situation in the north, he left Aquileia for Rome and Pinetum, but next year had become a fugitive before Alaric's advancing hordes. For him the quarrel over Origen was an episode that was best forgotten; he only once alluded to it in his subsequent writings.[67] Many of these, we should note, were translations of homilies and commentaries by Origen. The fact that he could publish these, so soon after Origen's official condemnation, without arousing a breath of protest, demonstrates how artificially the Origenistic

---

[65] *Apology* 3, 2 and 9.

[66] Jerome was occasionally to complain of this criticism: e.g. *Letter* 119, 11 (date 406)—'Why do my enemies tear me to pieces, and the gross swine, silent though I am, *grunt* against me?; *Comm. on Isaiah* x prol. (date 408)—'the Scorpion, that dumb and poisonous beast who will perish in his own *pus*', is criticising a passage in Jerome's *Comm. on Daniel*.

[67] In the 'peroration' to his translation of Origen's *Commentary on Romans* (PG 14, 1293–4).

issue had been blown up in the west. But in his quiet way Rufinus took his revenge on Jerome. When he translated Eusebius's *Ecclesiastical History* and added two books of his own, carrying the story down to the death of Theodosius I (395), he included in them accounts of the leading Christian personalities of east and west, but made no mention of his famous friend. As Jerome was in the habit of doing with his *bêtes noires*,[68] he simply consigned him to oblivion.

Jerome's behaviour was very different. If Rufinus could maintain silence at any rate in public, Jerome certainly could not, and for the rest of Rufinus's life, and even beyond the grave, he continued to pursue him with contempt and insults. In preface after preface, letter after letter, without directly naming him, he abusively denounced 'the Scorpion' or 'Grunting Pig' ('Grunnius': such were his preferred nicknames), the charlatan who turned good Greek into wretched Latin and who could not recognise a forgery when he saw one.[69] Early in 411, when utterly shattered by the news of the deaths of Pammachius and Marcella and of the sack of Rome, he could not conceal his satisfaction at Rufinus's death: 'The Scorpion lies under the soil of Sicily . . . The many-headed Sea-serpent has at last ceased to hiss against me.' Several months later, when giving ascetic advice to a monk, he delivered himself of the high-minded sentiment, 'Never speak evil of anyone, never imagine you make yourself better by tearing someone else to pieces', and immediately proceeded to give a cruel caricature of Rufinus: 'When Grunting Pig was about to speak, he would advance at a snail's pace and pronounce a few words at such long intervals that one thought he was gasping for breath, not conversing. Yet when he had placed his desk in position and piled his books on it, he would knit his brow, draw in his nostrils, wrinkle his forehead, and snap his fingers as a sign to command his pupils' attention. He would then pour out a flood of nonsense and declaim against one writer after another. You would suppose he was a critic like Longinus, an authorised censor of Latin style who could pass sentence on whom he willed and ban him from the senate of the learned. Having bags of money, he made himself more popular by giving banquets. Little wonder, since he stuffed so many bellies, that when he walked abroad he was surrounded by a chattering throng. He was a Nero in private, but in public a Cato. Formed of various and contradictory elements, he presented different faces. You could say that he was a unique and novel monstrosity, like the beast described by the poet[70] as "in front a lion, behind a dragon, around

---

[68] E.g. in his *Famous Men* (see above p. 177). Cf. also his excision of Melania from his *Chronicle*.

[69] For a fairly complete list of abusive passages see Cavallera II, Note S. His outburst on Rufinus's death comes from his *Comm. on Ezekiel* I prol. The caricature which follows is taken from *Letter* 125, 18 to the monk Rusticus (date probably 412).

[70] Lucretius, *De nat. rer.* 5, 905.

the middle a goat". Men like him you should not see or associate with.'

It was left to Augustine, to whom Jerome had sent his *Apology* but who had not seen Rufinus's, to express the shock and grief which he and other serious Christians felt at the collapse of their friendship. Writing in 404,[71] he informed Jerome that nowhere in Africa had he come across any alleged retractation of his; the story of one, which had added to Jerome's exasperation, had evidently been an unscrupulous canard invented by Eusebius of Cremona. He went on: 'After reading your *Apology*, I confess I was keenly distressed that such a tragic discord should have arisen between friends so loving and intimate, united by bonds of affection well known to almost all the churches . . . Here we see fulfilled the prophecy of him who is the truth, "Since wickedness has multiplied, the love of many will grow cold." For what trusting hearts can now risk baring themselves to each other? Into whose breast can confiding love now pour itself without reserve? In short, where is the friend who is not to be feared as a future foe, now that this lamentable breach has yawned between Jerome and Rufinus?' What grieved him particularly, he added, was that 'this disastrous bitterness' should have come between them at a time when, mature men who had abandoned worldly cares, they were following the Lord, living together in that land which his feet had trodden and in which he had proclaimed, 'My peace I give you.' If only Augustine could meet them both, he would fall at their feet and implore them, for their own sakes and for the sake of the weak for whom Christ had died, to refrain from writing harsh words about each other—words which, once written, were likely to prevent a reconciliation, and which, if they should be reconciled, they would be afraid to read lest they should start quarrelling afresh.

Inevitably, this noble plea came too late. But if it had come earlier, we may doubt that it would have fallen on receptive ears.

[71] Augustine, *Ep.* 73, 6 (= *Letter* 110 in Jerome's correspondence).

XXII

Theophilus, Chrysostom, Augustine

(i)

Throughout the first five years of the fifth century, both during and after the cessation of his private pamphlet war with Rufinus, Jerome was energetically collaborating in the field of church politics with his new-found patron, Theophilus of Alexandria. As we saw in the previous chapter,[1] the bishop had astutely enlisted his support when planning his violent measures against Isidore and the Tall Brothers, and Jerome was overjoyed to place himself at the service of so prominent and outspoken a convert to the anti-Origenist cause. Theophilus valued Jerome, partly for the practical help he could give him in Palestine, but even more because, by getting him to put his official pronouncements into Latin and transmit them to his influential friends in Rome, he was able to present his policies there in the most favourable light. This was important not only because of the exceptional position of the Roman see, but also because of the close traditional ties linking Alexandria with Rome. In his blind admiration Jerome seems to have been oblivious of the fact that Theophilus's hostility to Origenism was a guise temporarily assumed for political ends, and that the unscrupulous prelate was manipulating him as a tool.

Theophilus's immediate objective was to make life impossible in Palestine for the refugees from Nitria, while at the same time convincing the world that the actions he had taken against them were entirely justified. Jerome did everything in his power to ensure that none of them was given hospitality, and even seems to have required visitors to Bethlehem to sign a list of anathemas condemning characteristically Origenistic propositions.[2] He also translated and sent to Rome the important synodical letter[3] which Theophilus addressed to the bishops of Palestine assembled in Jerusalem for the Dedication Festival of 400 (14–21 September). This reported the condemnation of Origen at Nitria, listed and refuted a

[1] See above pp. 244–6.
[2] See E. Schwartz, 'Palladiana', ZNTW 36 (1937), 171 f. He refers to an 'abbreviatio fidei catholicae exposita de fide a sancto Hieronymo' containing such a list which is found in the Collectio Palatina (in ACO t. 1, vol. v, 4 f.).
[3] Letter 92 in Jerome's correspondence.

selection of his errors, and gave a colourful, shamelessly partisan account of the wickedness of the Origenist monks, Isidore in particular. As these had now moved to Palestine, Theophilus exhorted the bishops to shield their flocks from their pernicious teachings. Jerome also translated other related documents. One was the bishops' diplomatically cautious response,[4] assuring Theophilus that they abhorred Origen's blasphemies, but that Palestine was entirely free of them, and promising to exclude persons he had excommunicated from their churches. Another was a letter[5] which the bishop of Lydda (Lod), Dionysius, who found this collective reply too tepid for his taste, wrote to Theophilus, congratulating him on the benefits he had conferred on the world 'by throwing out the criminal disciples of blasphemous Origen', and entreating him to persevere in the good work.

As a result the Tall Brothers and their companion monks soon found their position in Palestine desperate. Their only hope, it seemed to them, was John (later to be called Chrysostom, or 'Golden-tongued'), patriarch of Constantinople, and so (October 400) they set sail for some port on the south coast of Asia Minor. Theophilus immediately sent a copy of his recent synodal to the Palestinian bishops to the bishops of Cyprus, writing at the same time personally to Epiphanius.[6] The immense prestige of that experienced heretic-hunter could be invaluable to him, and so he pressed him to convoke a council to condemn Origenism, and transmit its decisions at once to John of Constantinople as well as to himself; also to acquaint the bishops of the provinces through which the fugitives would be travelling with the full facts about them (as seen by Theophilus). Epiphanius at once wrote[7] to Jerome enclosing copies of Theophilus's letters, and expressing his delight that in his old age the cause for which he had struggled all his life had found so doughty a champion. He also held a council, as requested, which banned Origen's books, and tried to persuade Bishop John to follow suit.[8] Meanwhile, in spite of all attempts to stop them, or to ensure that if they got there they would meet with a hostile reception, the Tall Brothers managed to reach Constantinople. There Bishop John provided them with shelter and arranged for their support, but was careful (he was fully alive to the awkward position in which their presence in his city placed him) not to admit them to formal communion. Soon they were pouring their complaints about their outrageous treatment at Theophilus's hands not only into his ears but into the ears of the empress, Eudoxia, and the court.

Throughout Jerome was doing his best to swing public opinion in Rome behind his hero. He translated and sent there the documents

[4] *Letter* 93 in Jerome's correspondence.
[5] *Letter* 94 in Jerome's correspondence.
[6] *Letter* 90 in Jerome's correspondence.
[7] *Letter* 91 in Jerome's correspondence.
[8] Socrates, *Hist. eccl.* 6, 10.

mentioned above, and in addition Theophilus's Easter pastorals[9] for 401 and 402. Both were magnificently eloquent in their indictment of Origenism, although the theses selected were often absurdly distorted, and were not in the least likely to represent the views of the Tall Brothers and their companions. The latter indignantly trounced these for haunting the palaces of the rich and tearing their former bishop's reputation to pieces in the capital. Jerome's own accompanying note to Pammachius and Marcella, while exulting that through Theophilus's efforts Origen was now outlawed everywhere, likewise attacked[10] them for 'rabidly denigrating Christ's illustrious pontiff' on the shores of the Bosphorus. He had reason for apprehension for, Bishop John's attempts to mediate with Theophilus having met with an ignominious rebuff, the Tall Brothers had turned to the government as a last resort. The petitions they had prepared setting out their grievances against Theophilus and his agents made a favourable impression on the empress, and in summer 402 an imperial order went out summoning the patriarch to Constantinople to answer for his conduct before a synod presided over by John Chrysostom.

(ii)

Theophilus's position must now have seemed to most people dangerous in the extreme, but he himself treated the summons as a challenge not only to extricate himself from immediate difficulties, but to pull off a masterly political coup. He had been intriguing against John since 398,[11] furious at his having been chosen bishop of the imperial city in preference to his own nominee Isidore (then his friend and confidant). A true Alexandrian, he bitterly resented the promotion of the see of Constantinople, by the council held there in 381, to a precedence in Christendom second only to Rome. Nothing could satisfy him more than at a single blow to compass the ruin of the one, and the humiliation and weakening of the other. That was what, by playing his hand with consummate skill and by exploiting the weaknesses of his saintly but intransigent rival, he in fact achieved. Arriving in the capital in summer 403 (Epiphanius had been there earlier to prepare the ground), he swiftly turned the tables on John, becoming his prosecuting judge instead of (as had been intended) a defendant before him, and at the synod of the Oak (a palace at Chalcedon, now Kadiköy, on the Asiatic shore opposite Constantinople) had him tried and deposed.

[9] *Letters* 96 and 98 in his correspondence. For the rebuke to the Tall Brothers (not named) see *Letter* 98, 22. It is interesting that this letter also censured Origen (par. 10) for substituting allegory for 'the truth of Scripture'.

[10] *Letter* 97, 2. Jerome was more explicit in *Apology* 3, 18, denouncing those who, 'themselves condemned, haunt the royal palace, and in serried ranks persecute the faith of Christ in the person of a single man'.

[11] See Socrates, *Hist. eccl.* 6, 5.

The proceedings were so irregular that John should have been able to retrieve the situation without difficulty; indeed he was temporarily reinstated. But his violent, astonishingly tactless diatribes had alienated the court, and in 404 he was finally driven into exile.

Meanwhile Theophilus, to strengthen his position, had reconciled himself with the Tall Brothers.[12] Origenism had become a secondary issue, and his Easter pastoral for 404 (also Latinised by Jerome)[13] contained only a fleeting, almost perfunctory censure of it. More significant was the prayer he inserted 'for our religious emperors': he desired the court to administer the *coup de grâce* to John. In fact, Theophilus soon returned to the selective reading of the theologian he had castigated so savagely. The historian Socrates reports[14] that, on getting home to Alexandria from his triumph, 'he resumed studying Origen's books without restriction. When asked why he was again enjoying works he had banned, he answered, "Origen's writings are like a meadow full of flowers of every sort. When I light on an admirable specimen, I cut it; but when something with thorns turns up, I pass it by so as to escape being pricked".'

Jerome was no idle spectator of the drama taking place at Constantinople. His letter to Pammachius and Marcella of early spring 402 had ended with an urgent appeal to the Roman see to range itself on Theophilus's side in the crisis then brewing for him.[15] There was no love lost between him and John, whom he must have known (even if he did not meet him) during his sojourn at Antioch as a devoted disciple of Meletius, the bishop he regarded as a heretic and usurper, and who had been ordained in 386 by Meletius's successor, Flavian. Although he must have been aware of his distinction as a preacher, he had dismissed him with a disparagingly curt entry in *Famous Men*.[16] He rejoiced, we may be sure, at John's downfall, in spite of the fact that his trusted friend Chromatius came out strongly in his support and wrote to the western emperor, Honorius, on his behalf.[17] He must have been appalled when the new

---

[12] The sources differ as to the moment of the reconciliation (Dioscorus was already dead), but Sozomen (*Hist. eccl.* 8, 17: PG 67, 1560) is probably correct in placing it before John's deposition, perhaps even before the synod. See A. Favale, *Teofilo d'Alessandria* (Turin, 1958), 133–5.

[13] *Letter* 100 in his correspondence. Chiefly concerned with fasting, penitence, and moral admonition, it touched on Origen's errors only in pars. 12–14. Sozomen reports (loc. cit.) that at the synod Theophilus had not raised the question of Origen at all. For the prayer 'pro piissimis imperatoribus' see par. 16.

[14] *Hist. eccl.* 6, 17.

[15] *Letter* 97, 4, where he exhorts them to pray that the chair of St Peter will back up that of St Mark (i.e. Alexandria).

[16] *Famous Men* 129.

[17] According to Palladius, Chromatius was one of the western bishops to whom Chrysostom wrote complaining of the terrible events attending his deposition; he in return sent Chrysostom a letter of brotherly sympathy (*Dial.* 3; 4: C.N. 16; 22). In 406 the latter responded with a letter of grateful appreciation (*Ep.* 155: PG 52, 702 f.).

pope, Innocent I (402–17), in autumn 404 recognised the justice of John's cause, and finally broke off relations with Theophilus and the rest of his persecutors.[18] Even so, staunch Roman though he professed to be, he continued to back the Egyptian Pharaoh blindly. Late in 404, made all the more implacable by the pope's support of John, Theophilus composed an invective of hysterical violence, denouncing the exiled patriarch as a foul murderer, an enemy of the human race, a godless priest who made sacrilegious offerings, a blasphemer of Christ who would share the fate of Judas.[19] There was much more abuse of this kind in 'the monstrous document' by which, as its horrified sixth-century preserver noted, Theophilus hoped to show the western world exactly what kind of man John was; and it was Jerome who made this possible by putting it into Latin. Even the death of the tragic patriarch in exile (407) did not still Jerome's rancour, for years later (in 413) he was to characterise him as one who had been led astray by the Origenists as Barnabas had been by the Judaisers in the apostolic Church (Gal. 2, 13), and who had been guilty of murder, not in deed, but in intention.[20]

(iii)

While Jerome was thus playing the political game, from the side-lines but with a supporter's blind enthusiasm, he was also occupied, off and on, with what should have been a dryly intellectual debate with Augustine. In the event, through the mischances of the post but even more his own irascible refusal to be drawn into discussion, it remained for two years a sterile but remarkably revealing exchange.

The two great men, we recall, had begun corresponding in the mid-nineties of the fourth century.[21] In 394/5 Augustine, eager for closer

---

[18] Sozomen (*Hist. eccl.* 8, 26) reproduces the two letters he sent, one to John asserting his innocence and exhorting him to bear his sufferings with resignation, and the other to the clergy and people of Constantinople expressing sympathy and calling for the canons of Nicaea to be observed. For his breach with Theophilus see A. Favale, op. cit., 158 f., where the evidence is set out.

[19] Facundus of Hermiane (sixth century) has preserved a summary of this 'innormis liber' in his *Defence of the Three Chapters* 6, 5 (*PL* 67, 676–8), and C. Baur showed (*RB* 23, 1906, 430–6) that Jerome's *Letter* 113 is almost certainly a fragment of it. Scholars have sometimes tried to argue that Theophilus was not the author, nor Jerome the translator, of such a frightful libel, but they have been convincingly refuted: see esp. C. Baur, art. cit.; also his *John Chrysostom and his Times* (ET London, 1960), II, 328–30.

[20] *Letter* 127, 11. The man veiledly referred to as Barnabas is not named, but I agree with Tillemont (*Mémoires pour servir à l'histoire eccl. des six premiers siècles*, vol. xii, art. 105: Paris, 1707) that he must be John. The smear is reminiscent of the absurd charges brought against him at the Oak.

[21] See above pp. 217 ff. For Jerome's controversial exegesis of Gal. 2, 11–14 see above p. 148. The whole correspondence is conveniently assembled in *Florilegium Patristicum* xxii (Bonn, 1930) by J. Schmid, who provides an admirable introduction and notes. See also D. de Bruyne, 'La correspondance échangée entre Augustin et Jérôme', *ZNTW* 31 (1932),

relations with his famous contemporary, had written to Jerome (Letter 28A) criticising his preference for the Hebrew original of the Old Testament, and taking strong exception to his view that the rebuke St Paul claims (Gal. 2, 11–14) to have administered to St Peter at Antioch had been merely simulated. When this letter had stopped dead, he had written again c. 398 (Letter 40A), enlarging on these latter objections and calling upon Jerome to 'sing a palinode' like Stesichorus, i.e. to recant. The exchange had then lapsed for several years. Most unfortunately Letter 40A got held up in Rome, where, through carelessness or malice, its contents were leaked. Jerome being a controversial figure, it was soon being eagerly devoured throughout Italy and even further afield, and must have brought equal satisfaction to his enemies and dismay to his supporters. A friend of Jerome's, the deacon Sisinnius, came across a copy, correctly addressed but without the conventional autograph greeting at the end, on an island in the Adriatic, and when he arrived in Bethlehem delivered it to him.[22]

Morbidly suspicious and ready to take offence, it was easy for Jerome to conclude that this letter, which had been seen by so many eyes before his own, had all along been intended for public consumption, and that in writing it Augustine had been seeking to deflate his reputation and boost his own.[23] Hence when Augustine learned in 402 that Jerome had at last received Letter 40A (he had been impatiently awaiting a reply for years), he also learned, to his distress, that gossipy tongues at Bethlehem were accusing him of being the author of a book against Jerome, which he had allegedly sent to Rome. At once he wrote[24] to his friend expressing surprise that he had not answered Letter 40A, and calling God to witness that the rumour was totally false. In setting down views different from Jerome's, he had never intended to attack him, but only to make his own position clear. For his part, he was eager to listen humbly to any strictures Jerome had to make on his works; indeed, he begged him to criticise them. Augustine clearly sensed Jerome's irritation, and was anxious to soothe it. He concluded with an affectionate prayer that, since they could not live together or even be neighbours, Jerome would take pains to keep their

---

233–48. The best examination of the respective positions of the two men is by P. Auvray, 'Saint Jérôme et saint Augustin: La controverse au sujet de l'incident d'Antioche', *Recherches de science religieuse* 29 (1939), 594–610.

[22] *Letters* 102, 1; 105, 1. In the latter passage, written 403/4, Jerome says Sisinnius had found it 'some five years ago', i.e. in 398/9. We have no clue as to when he delivered it to Jerome, but it was probably not long after he had found it.

[23] This emerges from Jerome, *Letters* 102, 2; 105, 4: also Augustine, *Ep.* 67, 2 (see next sentence).

[24] *Ep.* 67 (= *Letter* 101 in Jerome's correspondence). It must date from after 401, for Augustine sends regards to Jerome's brother Paulinian, who returned from Stridon to Bethlehem in that year, and probably belongs to late 402 or early 403, since Jerome wrote *Letter* 102 immediately on receiving it.

correspondence alive, and would not disdain to answer letters from time to time.

For once this letter (Letter 67A) reached its destination without mishap, and as a subdeacon (Asterius) was on the point of setting out for north Africa Jerome was able to despatch his rejoinder[25] immediately. Formally polite and even affectionate in places ('Would that I could deserve your embrace, and that by friendly interchanges we could teach, and learn from, each other'), Letter 102J did not conceal his deep resentment and suspicion. He had obviously been stung by Augustine's critique of his exegesis, and was understandably outraged that the letter containing it had been broadcast at Rome and elsewhere before he had even set eyes on it. So he refused to discuss it, declaring that since it lacked an autograph subscription he could not properly assume it was genuine. If it was, Augustine should admit the fact frankly, or else send a more accurate copy. He had certainly no wish to pick holes in Augustine's writings, and Augustine could judge how sincerely he loved him from the fact that he declined to believe him the author of what he would severely censure in another. It was a sign of youthful arrogance, he remarked ominously, to try to build up a reputation by assailing 'prominent figures'. It ill became a young man (Augustine was in fact nearing fifty) to challenge a veteran in the field of Scripture. If he did, he should recall (here he capped Augustine's reference to Stesichorus in Letter 40A with one from Vergil) how the elderly Entellus had triumphantly outboxed youthful Dares;[26] also the proverb, 'It's the tired ox that treads more firmly.' Finally, with a contemptuous cut at Rufinus, he said he was enclosing a copy of his *Apology* against him. Probably this was to be an object-lesson to Augustine of what he might expect if he insisted on controversy.[27]

It is scarcely credible that Jerome really questioned the authenticity of the letter Sisinnius had given him.[27a] The superscription bore Augustine's name, 'its style and method of argument' (he admitted) were his, it was taken for granted at Bethlehem that he was the author (hence the ugly rumour). If he had ever had doubts, they must have been dissipated when he received Letter 67A, which began, 'I hear that my letter has reached you.' It seems more likely that he assumed an affectation of uncertainty because he had been shaken by the case Augustine had argued against his interpretation of Galatians 2, 11–14, but could not bring himself to avow

---

[25] *Letter* 102 (= *Ep.* 68 in Augustine's correspondence). Again the date must be 402/3, since Jerome enclosed his *Apology* 3, which belongs to the middle of 402.

[26] For the story see Vergil, *Aeneid* 5, 362–484. The seemingly unequal contest took place at the games which Aeneas held in Sicily to honour the anniversary of his father Anchises's death. Dares was a young Trojan, Entellus a retired Sicilian champion.

[27] So J. Schmid, op. cit., 4. This seems to have been his second *Apology*, i.e. book 3 of the *Apology*, written mid-402.

[27a] On this see D. de Bruyne, art. cit., 237 f.

publicly that he had been wrong. His stalling suggests that he wished the subject dropped altogether. But Augustine could not let that happen. The issues under discussion were important to him; he deemed it essential to have the truth established. Further, he had at last learned of the mishaps which had caused his Letter 40 to be held up in Rome, and published there, and which explained both the rumours of his having sent a book attacking Jerome to the capital and Jerome's hitherto inexplicable silence. It was now 403, and he seems to have sent off two letters to him separated by a short interval. The first is lost, but we can infer its existence from the fact that in his next letter (Letter 105) Jerome refers to information about the fates of Letters 28A and 40A which he had received from Augustine, but which is found in none of his surviving letters.[28]

The second of these letters (Letter 71A)[29] was apparently drafted before the arrival of Jerome's polite, but unmistakably suspicious, warning Letter 102 summarised above; this correspondence was even more bedevilled by letters crossing than by letters failing to reach their destination. For once, Augustine began, he had found an absolutely reliable courier, Cyprian, and since he was persuasive as well, he could expect a reply from Jerome with reasonable certainty. Just in case his letters had gone astray, he appended copies.[30] Since the clash between St Paul and St Peter had been fully treated in these, he proceeded to make some fresh points about Jerome's Old Testament translations. First, he had heard that he had produced a fresh version of Job, based on the Hebrew, but found it strange that he had not furnished this, as he had his earlier version based on the Septuagint, with critical signs indicating discrepancies between the Hebrew and Greek texts. Secondly, as an additional reason for sticking to the Septuagint, he pointed out that, if Jerome's rendering from the Hebrew were to gain general acceptance, it could open a split between eastern and western Christendom, since Greek-speaking Christians would continue using the Septuagint. Thirdly, he described the tumult which had broken out at Oea (Tripoli, in Libya) when the local bishop, who had adopted Jerome's version, read out from a key-passage of Jonah a word which was unfamiliar to the congregation instead of the traditional one.[31] When consulted, some resident Jews, 'through malice or ignorance', pronounced in favour of the Septuagint. He ended by complimenting Jerome on his revision of the Latin Gospels, and asked him to explain the frequent differences between the Hebrew and Greek texts of the Old Testament—

[28] *Letter* 105, 1. For the lost letter see J. Schmid, op. cit., 4; D. de Bruyne, art. cit., 238 f.

[29] *Ep.* 71 = *Letter* 104 in Jerome's correspondence: date 403.

[30] It is not clear which letters these were. They may have been either *Epp.* 28 and 40, or *Epp.* 28, 40, and either 67 or the lost one. See D. de Bruyne, art. cit., 239.

[31] Although Augustine does not mention it, the passage was Jonah 4, 6 where Jerome had substituted 'ivy' for 'gourd'. See above p. 221. Jerome makes this plain in *Letters* 112, 22; 115, 1.

especially as the latter was so authoritative and, on his own admission,[32] had been used by the Apostles.

Before receiving this (again a case of letters crossing), Jerome wrote a second time to Augustine (Letter 105J).[33] He now had before him the latter's lost letter telling him what had happened to Letters 28A and 40A, Letter 67A, and Letter 40A itself, whose genuineness he still professed to doubt. Brushing Augustine's explanations aside with incredulity, he expressed amazement that the damaging Letter 40A should have been seen by everyone in Italy before himself, to whom alone it was addressed. Excellent Christians at Jerusalem were suggesting that, in demanding an answer, Augustine was trying to become famous at his expense, demonstrating that he alone could muzzle his garrulity. In fact he had kept silence because he could not believe the letter was by Augustine; also he had no wish to censure a Catholic bishop, especially as he had found it tainted with heresy. As he had said before, Augustine should either send him a signed copy, or cease badgering an old monk in his cell. If he wanted to show off, there were plenty of clever young men at Rome he could cross swords with. He equally refused to accept Augustine's solemn assurance (in Letter 67A) that he had not written a book attacking him. Had he not seen it with his own eyes? Did not Italy possess copies? (He seems to have forgotten that this was Letter 40A, which he declined to accept as Augustine's.) He had no objection to differences of opinion, but Augustine's challenge to 'sing a palinode' (this had evidently got under his skin) violated the laws of friendship. He had no wish to quarrel with him, still less to criticise his writings, which he had never studied carefully. Rather he wanted to love Augustine. But if Augustine had to confess that 'the book' (so he still called Letter 40A) was by him, he would have only himself to blame if Jerome felt obliged to hit back.

Despite occasional flashes of affection, even of common-sense ('Let not the world see us quarrelling like children'), Letter 105J surpassed Letter 102J in hostile insinuations, distrust, cantankerousness. A halt in the friendly interchanges between the two men seemed inevitable, perhaps even a final rupture in their relations analogous to that between Jerome and Rufinus. But before it reached him, Augustine had despatched in 404 a marvellously self-effacing, conciliatory reply to Letter 102J, one of his most deeply felt and beautiful compositions (Letter 73).[34] He did not hide his disappointment at Jerome's surly tone: 'How can we discuss these matters if you are resolved to injure me?' But he did not press this point,

---

[32] Augustine had failed to observe that this had been prior to his conversion to 'the Hebrew verity'. For his mature view see *Preface to Chronicles* (Vulgate) (PL 28, 1325 f.); *Apology* 2, 34.

[33] This appears as *Ep.* 72 in Augustine's correspondence.

[34] *Letter* 110 in Jerome's correspondence. Parts of the section deploring the rupture between Jerome and Rufinus have been quoted above, p. 258.

declaring that he would not dream of taking it amiss if Jerome could prove his exegesis of Galatians 2, 11–14 to be correct. Indeed, Jerome (he was convinced) was not the man to have adopted such a hostile attitude had not he himself been to blame. So he begged him, by the mercy of Christ, to forgive him any wrong he might inadvertently have done him. Treating Jerome's reference to Entellus and the aged ox as 'genial pleasantry rather than angry threatening', he welcomed any blows he might shower upon him; they would be salutary medicine. More than anything else he longed to sit at Jerome's feet and learn of him; he could never hope to equal him in Scripture knowledge. More than once he wistfully quoted Jerome's prayer, 'Would that I could deserve your embrace, etc.' He also dwelt, sorrowfully and at great length, on the tragic break between friends so trusting and intimate as Jerome and Rufinus. That sad example of the fragility of human ties made him tremble for his own relations with the man he loved. So he entreated Jerome that they should desist from further discussions unless they could freely criticise each other without taking or giving offence.

Augustine took the precaution of sending this letter to Praesidius,[35] now a bishop, with the request that he would forward it to Jerome, and himself put in a good word on his behalf. He asked him to warn him if he thought its contents in any respect unsuitable, so that he might personally apologise. To fill in the background he enclosed his own Letter 40 and Jerome's Letter 102, so that Praesidius might see 'both the moderate tone I thought it proper to observe, and the vehemence on his part which has, not unreasonably, made me afraid'. By now he was becoming aware what a prickly person Jerome was, and how carefully he needed to be handled.

(iv)

It seems extraordinary that, although half a dozen letters had passed between Bethlehem and Hippo in two years, Jerome had nowhere discussed the issues raised by Augustine's Letter 40, originally written *c*. 398. He had made his justifiable indignation at its having been leaked, and his much more questionable doubts about its genuineness, the pretext for postponing the awkward debate, best of all pushing it under the carpet. Late in 404, however, the deacon Cyprian, proving as reliable as Augus-

---

[35] Augustine, *Ep.* 74 (= *Letter* 111 in Jerome's correspondence). The text assumes that this Praesidius is identical with the deacon of that name whom Jerome recommended to Augustine in *Letter* 103 (see above p. 220). It must be appreciated, however, that this identification is impossible if *Letter* 103 dates from 402 (see above p. 220, n. 39). In any case this Praesidius should probably be identified with the Numidian bishop who in 410 was a member of the delegation led by Possidius to the court at Ravenna (Mansi, *Sacr. concil. coll.* III, 810D; IV, 504A), and who in 416 took part in the synod of Milevum (Mansi IV, 335A; Augustine, *Ep.* 176). His connection with the Praesidius to whom Jerome wrote about the paschal candle (see above p. 111) is conjectural. For see details see *PW* XXII 2, 1565 f.

tine had predicted, brought him the bishop's Letter 71A, which freely acknowledged authorship, and along with it authenticated copies of Letters 28A and 40A. The correspondence was probably exciting wide-spread interest, and a formal response, Jerome must have realised, could no longer be deferred without loss of face. So he composed and despatched a veritable short treatise (Letter 112J) covering most of the disputed points. He described it as an improvisation, thrown together in three days while Cyprian impatiently waited to set out on his return-journey. In fact it was 'a chef d'oeuvre of style and erudition', carefully planned with an eye to wider publication.[36]

The bulk of the letter was a defence of his view that St Peter and St Paul had both been acting parts at Antioch, the one in seeming to revert to Jewish food-laws, the other in apparently admonishing him for it. First, he claimed that this interpretation was not his own; it had been proposed by Origen, and a long line of leading Greek commentators, specifically to silence Porphyry, who had made capital out of the alleged quarrel of the Apostles. Then, with a mass of New Testament citations, he sought to show that St Peter had been just as fully convinced as St Paul of the supersession of the Law, but that both had on numerous occasions pre-tended to observe it out of fear for the Jews. This should not be construed as lying (Jerome was no champion of falsehood), but as the exercise of legitimate prudence. Finally, he castigated as heresy[37] Augustine's theory that, as Jews, the Apostles were entitled to observe the Law, provided they did not regard it as mediating salvation. Earlier he had misrepresen-ted it ('You assert . . . that Jews who come to believe are still subject to the Law'); now he professed not to understand the all-important proviso, contending that obedience to the Law could not be a matter of indifference but was clearly pernicious, as much for converted Jews as for Gentiles. To be consistent Augustine (again he caricatured his position) should, as bishop, allow converts from Judaism to go on keeping the Sabbath, circumcising their children, and the like.

He dealt much more briefly, but no less sharply, with Augustine's other queries. The correct title of his biographical work (Letter 40A), as Augus-tine's good sense and literary training ought to have told him, was *Famous Men*. (Yet, oddly enough, after this brusque explanation he

---

[36] *Letter* 112 (= *Ep.* 75 in Augustine's correspondence). Its date must be late 404 because (a) it makes no allusion to Paula's death in January of that year, and (b) refers in par. 6 to John Chrysostom, deposed in June 404, as 'who used to govern the church of Constantinople'. That it was intended for a wider readership is shown not only by the careful style and construction, but by the tell-tale 'These citations should not be tedious to the readers' (see D. de Bruyne, art. cit., 240).

[37] Thus in *Letter* 112, 13 and 16 he warns him that he is falling into the heresy of Judaising Christians who falsely believed that the Mosaic Law was still binding on Christians: a typical but unworthy controversial ploy.

himself seemed not at all sure.) As for his new translation of Old Testament books, Augustine clearly did not understand what he was asking if he regretted (Letter 71A) the absence of asterisks and obeli. His earlier translation had been from Origen's amended, or rather corrupted,[38] Septuagint, where these signs served a purpose; his new one was based on 'the Hebrew verity'. In making it he had not been moved by a passion for innovation (had he not translated the corrected Greek text into Latin?), but by the desire to let the public know what the Hebrew original contained before the Seventy had tampered with it. In any case no one was obliged to read it.

There was more like this, including some effective raillery at Augustine's naive idea (Letter 28, 2) that after the Seventy there was no room for more work on the Old Testament; Augustine himself had been able to make some fresh comments on the Psalms, although a host of commentators had preceded him. Throughout Jerome's language was condescending; here and there he contrasted, with mock humility, the monk in his wretched cell with the bishop on his throne, or inserted a cutting sneer like, 'If you write to me, Italy and Rome are sure to get the letter before it finds its way to me.' At the beginning he had brushed aside Augustine's courteous greeting and the compliments 'by which you attempt to take the edge off your censure'. He closed with an abrupt request to Augustine to leave him alone in his monastery and confine himself to teaching his flock. Shortly afterwards, when he had received and digested Augustine's magnanimously conciliatory Letter 73, Jerome rushed off a short note[39] greeting him with effusive affection. There had been nothing personal, he assured him, in his recent sharp rejoinder; after all, it was Augustine who had provoked it. He begged him to blame Rufinus, not himself, for their quarrel, and prayed that in future they should exchange letters of love, not contention. 'If you would like it, let us disport ourselves in the field of Scripture without wounding each other.' The fiery old man had been bowled over by Augustine's generous, self-effacing appeal, and in his clumsy way he was making amends.

When Augustine next wrote, he had this friendly note before him, as well as Jerome's harsh Letter 105 and his brilliant set-piece justifying his position (Letter 112J). His own rejoinder (Letter 82A)[40] was even longer than this last, and though inferior in dialectical verve was more measured in tone. It was largely a restatement, with clarifications and fresh arguments, of his view that the clash between the Apostles at Antioch had

---

[38] Here Jerome criticises Origen's hexaplaric text of the Septuagint as diverging from the pure original, since he had filled in missing passages with excerpts from Theodotion's (Jewish) version. Elsewhere (e.g. *Letter* 106, 2 ad fin.) he gives it high praise.

[39] *Letter* 115 (= *Ep.* 81 in Augustine's correspondence). Date: late 404 or early 405.

[40] *Letter* 116 in Jerome's correspondence.

been a real one, and that when on various occasions they had observed the Law they had been exercising an option which was open to them as Jews with the object of winning over Jews. He rejected Jerome's charge that this was heresy, stressing the points that they enjoyed this liberty only because of their firm conviction that the Law did not convey salvation, and that it was a temporary liberty limited to the apostolic age. Once again he set his guiding principle in the foreground: 'You say it is incredible that Paul censured in Peter what he had done himself. I am not now inquiring what he did, but what he wrote.' It was essential that what he wrote should be true if the truth of Scripture itself was to be upheld. As for the Greek authorities to whom Jerome had appealed, he insisted that several of them (e.g. Origen) had been heretical, and so might well have been mistaken. In support of his interpretation he could cite Cyprian and Ambrose—and St Paul himself, who had declared (Gal. 1, 20), 'In what I am writing, before God, I do not lie.' After disposing of this issue, he confessed that he had been persuaded of the usefulness of Jerome's translation of the Old Testament from the Hebrew, but he preferred that it should not be read publicly lest the faithful, accustomed as they were to the Septuagint, should be upset. He also begged Jerome to send him a copy of his translation of the Septuagint; he had not heard that it had been published.

While quite unyielding on the main issue of the Apostles' behaviour at Antioch, Augustine's letter was throughout couched in terms of great courtesy, even deference. He asked forgiveness for any wrong he had done Jerome, tried to set his references to Stesichorus's palinode in perspective, promised to ensure that future letters did not fall into other people's hands before reaching him. There was not a word which could reasonably be taken as intended to hurt. Even the disquiet he felt, a little pompously, at Jerome's unfortunate phrase about 'disporting them-selves' in the field of Scripture studies was expressed with delicate tact. And in both the opening and the closing sections he laboured the point that Christian friends, engaged as they were in the search for the truth, should surely be able to criticise each other's writings with complete frankness without arousing irritation or incurring suspicion of un-worthy motives. What he yearned for in their relationship, he insisted emphatically, was not simply mutual love, but that freedom of speech without which true friendship is impossible. It is obvious that he was taken aback by Jerome's hypersensitivity and readiness to take offence, and found them deeply disturbing.

This was the last letter, to the best of our knowledge, in this main chapter of their correspondence. To modern students it seems plain that, if Jerome showed the true scholar's instinct in preferring the Hebrew Old Testament to the Septuagint, Augustine was broadly correct in his assessment of the confrontation between the two Apostles. Some have felt that Jerome's defence of his rather artificial interpretation, while spirited, lacked conviction. The fact is, once he had read Letter 40A, he was sharp-witted enough to realise that it destroyed the traditional Greek exegesis of Galatians 2, 11–14; but he was not big enough to avow his mistaken preference, and instead stalled and tried every device to get the discussion dropped.[41] But the overriding interest of these letters, the reason too for submitting them to such a detailed analysis, is the revealing light they throw on the characters of both men, particularly for our purposes of Jerome. We have to remember, of course, in fairness to him, that Augustine was much the younger man, still at the beginning of what was to be an increasingly splendid career. Jerome could not be expected to view him as the towering figure to which later generations, with the hind-sight of history, look back. Nevertheless in these letters, so different in literary style and controversial tactics, both men spring startlingly to life, and the lineaments of each, his personal traits and foibles, his greatnesses and weaknesses, become more sharply etched by comparison with the other.

---

[41] So D. de Bruyne, art. cit., 238 and 247 f. He points out that Jerome seems to have changed his mind about the dispute of the two Apostles in 402 (*Apology* 3, 2) and, still more clearly, in 415 (*Dialogue against the Pelagians* 1, 22).

XXIII

The Death of Paula

(i)

In 401 or thereabouts, when the storms of the Origenist controversy and Jerome's quarrel with Rufinus were at their height, joyful news arrived at Bethlehem. After a series of miscarriages Laeta, Paula's aristocratic and devoutly Christian daughter-in-law, had at last given birth at Rome to a daughter, and she had named her Paula after her grandmother. While still in her womb, Laeta had vowed the infant, when she was born, to the religious life; her husband, Toxotius, was a Christian too. Now, along with Marcella, she wrote to Jerome for advice on how she should be educated.

This was a request to which he could respond with enthusiasm. According to his thinking, marriage and child-bearing were excusable provided their fruits were consecrated virgins. So he set to with gusto, sending Laeta a short treatise in the guise of a letter.[1] This opens with an expression of confident hope that, surrounded as he is by so many keenly Christian relatives, Laeta's still pagan father, Publilius Caeionius Caecina Albinus,[2] will be finally converted by his new grand-daughter chanting alleluias in his arms. It then sketches the principles which should govern not only the child's elementary and literary studies, but also her general upbringing. Finally, giving voice to doubts which he is sure her mother must be already feeling, Jerome suggests that it will not be practicable to carry out his austere curriculum in Rome, with its bustling crowds. Let Laeta send her little girl as soon as she is weaned to Bethlehem, where Eustochium will be her companion and model, Paula her experienced instructress in chastity, Jerome himself (like Aristotle to Alexander the Great) her foster-father and tutor, carrying her about on his shoulders.

The letter has often been admired as unveiling an altogether new Jerome, sensitive in his feeling for children and engagingly ready to meet

---

[1] *Letter* 107. It must pre-date the long illness of Paula in 402–4, and was probably written in 401 or early 402 since it speaks of the temple of Marnas at Gaza as shut and 'dreading destruction at any moment' (par. 2). It was in 401 that Porphyry, bishop of Gaza, obtained an order for its destruction, and in May 402 that this was carried out. See *PW* xiv (2), 1904.

[2] For his career etc. see *PLRE* i, 34 f. (under 'Albinus' 8). The identification is very probable but not quite certain. Jerome speaks of him a 'pontifex'. There is no evidence that his hope for his ultimate conversion was fulfilled.

them on their own level.[3] It certainly contains attractive passages, replete with paedogogic insight and good sense. Learning the alphabet should be turned into a game, the techniques of writing made easier by ingenious devices. Competition should be stimulated by prizes, scolding should be avoided and lessons made enjoyable. A distaste for study acquired in youth, he wisely observes, will persist into adult years. Jerome has assuredly adopted these ideas, and has moulded them into his scheme; but they are not really his own. The passages containing them (others too) are straight paraphrases from Quintilian's (first century) humane counsels about childhood education.[4] Jerome's original contribution shows much less understanding of the normal child's nature. It is directed rather, such is his zeal for ascetic perfection, at suppressing anything, however innocent ordinary people might judge it, which might interfere with advancement towards this.

Thus little Paula, as we should expect, must make an early start with Greek. This was in keeping with the conservative tradition of aristocratic Roman families even at this late date.[5] But her reading must be confined to the Bible and the orthodox Fathers; those of doubtful orthodoxy she should study critically. Beginning with the Psalms, Proverbs, Ecclesiastes, and Job, she should pass on to the Gospels, Acts, and the Epistles. Then back to the Prophets and other Old Testament books. Only when well grounded in all these may she look into Song of Songs; if she tackled it too soon, she might jump to the mistaken, damaging conclusion that its theme is physical love. She must of course steer clear of the Apocrypha; pagan literature, too, is excluded.

Boys, wanton creatures as they are, must be kept at a distance. Her girl companions and maids should have no worldly associates. Feminine adornment, whether of dress, ear-rings, or cosmetics, is completely banned (in this purple passage Jerome the satirist lashes, unmercifully and brilliantly, the vanities of fashionable women). When she gets older, she should not dine with her parents in case tasty dishes should whet her appetite. While young, she may bathe occasionally, and take a little wine and meat; but when full-grown, she should shun baths altogether (they only add fuel to sexual desire, and she should be ashamed to see herself naked), and eat much more sparingly, without however fasting immoderately. She should never appear in public without her mother, never be present at weddings of family slaves or noisy household games. No smart young man must be allowed to smile at her, and her female companions

---

[3] Cf. Cavallera's (I, 292) oft-quoted remark, 'Jérôme s'y fait petit avec les petits'.

[4] *Letter* 107, 4: compare with Quintilian, *Inst. orat.* I, I, 24–9. For other borrowings from Quintilian in the letter see H. Hagendahl, *Latin Fathers and the Classics* (Göteborg, 1958), 199–201.

[5] See H. I. Marrou, *Histoire de l'éducation dans l'antiquité* (6 ed., Paris, 1965), 384. The passage (par. 9) is borrowed from Quintilian.

should not be fashionably dressed or pretty, but pale, shabbily clad, with sad looks. Her occupations should be spinning coarse wool and reciting psalms at midnight, early morning, the third, sixth, and ninth hours, and in the evening.

This educational scheme was plainly not one for general application. Jerome himself did not employ it for the education of the Latin-speaking lads whom he tutored at Bethlehem, and whom he initiated without compunction into the pagan classics. Both the programme and the method bear certain resemblances to those laid down a generation earlier by Basil the Great for the children brought by their parents, at their most tender years, to his monasteries.[6] But Basil's indoctrination was less fanatical, depending more on suggestion and persuasion than on compulsion. Little Paula was to be forcibly trained up as a nun, never forgetful of the Bridegroom for whom she was destined, always vigilant to keep her virginity intact for him. So Bible-reading followed by prayer, prayer alternating with Bible-reading, was to be the pattern of her days.

(ii)

Not that the religious houses at Bethlehem were invariably the models of ascetic perfection which Jerome and Paula wanted them to be. A famous letter of his[7] survives which, if accepted at its face value, discloses that very human passions could sometimes find an outlet in them. We are wholly in the dark as to its date, but it may be fittingly mentioned here as portraying a very different side of monastic seclusion from that idealistically presented in the letter to Laeta.

In form a fatherly summons to repentance, this letter tells the dramatic but scandalous story of the young man, a deacon called Sabinian, to whom it is addressed. He had turned up one day at Jerome's monastery, declaring that he wished to be a monk, and as he was armed with excellent references from his bishop he was taken in. No one knew that his previous life in Italy had been a continuous round of sexual exploits, culminating in adultery with the wife of a formidable barbarian, probably a Gothic general. His flight to the Holy Land had been to escape from her outraged husband, descending 'like a new Hannibal from the Alps'. Once installed as a monk, however, he soon resumed his licentious habits, and found an all too complaisant victim in a girl from the convent. He left love-letters for her in (of all places) the grotto of the Nativity, while she secreted to him a lock of her hair, handkerchiefs, a girdle. As he sang in the choir, the two would exchange conspiratorial glances; at night he would spend

---

[6] Cf. his *Reg. fus. tract.* 15 (PG 31, 952–7). The comparison is made by H. I. Marrou, op. cit. 473.
[7] *Letter* 147.

course, blown the story up larger than life, and has laid the colours on rich and thick. As he meant the piece to be read by a large, predominantly western public, he naturally inserted explanatory details which would have been superfluous in a private communication. But there is nothing implausible in the incident itself, and we need not doubt its substantial truth. Read in this light, the letter shows us a Jerome who is understandably indignant, but also surprisingly moderate, deeply concerned for the young man's repentance and reform.

(iii)

Little Paula, Laeta's daughter, was eventually to come to Palestine as Jerome had hoped,[10] but she was never to set eyes on her grandmother. In Letter 102, dictated probably in the second half of 402, Jerome had spoken feelingly to Augustine of Paula's 'protracted illness'. Having to sit for long hours at her sick-bed, he explained, had put his friend's letter out of his mind. It was evidently a serious illness, for in justification of his forgetfulness he quoted the text 'A tale told at the wrong time is like music in mourning'.[11] It dragged on for months, indeed throughout the whole of 403. Her constitution, it seems, had never been strong, for Jerome was to speak[12] of 'her sicknesses and frequent indisposition'. She had further enfeebled it, he added with a note of implied criticism, by the excessively severe regimen to which she submitted herself, especially in food and drink and work. By the end of the year her life was ebbing away, and Jerome's vivid brush depicts a distracted Eustochium nursing her mother, personally attending to all her needs, but still finding time to slip away to the cave of the Nativity to pray. He himself was with her at the end. His account of this is largely stereotyped, but there is an authentic ring in his reminiscence that, when he anxiously asked why she did not answer and whether she felt pain, she whispered in Greek that she had no suffering, that everything looked calm and peaceful.

When Paula died on 26 January 404, she was fifty-six years, eight months, and twenty-one days old. Bishop John of Jerusalem and several other bishops were present. With their own hands they carried the dead woman on a bier into the Church of the Nativity, while others held torches and candles, and still others directed choirs. There she rested, Jerome reports,[13] three days, and then 'the whole population of the cities of Palestine assembled for her funeral'. She was buried 'underneath the church,

[10] She was with him in 416, when he wrote *Letter* 134 to Augustine: see below p. 321.

[11] Ecclesiasticus 22, 6. Augustine's *Letter* 40 was, apparently, an 'importuna narratio'.

[12] *Letter* 108, 19. Penna (289) seems mistaken in describing her as enjoying 'enviably good health'. For her fastings etc. see *Letter* 108, 17; 21. The other touches in this paragraph come from this letter (Jerome's threnody for her).

[13] *Letter* 108, 29, where her burial is described.

close to the Lord's cave'. The actual spot was in a deep grotto under the east end of the north aisle of the church, linked by a subterranean passage with the Saviour's birth-place, and there the visitor today is shown the altar which marks her cenotaph.[14] Jerome composed two sets of somewhat stilted hexameters, the only verses of his that survive, and caused one (extolling her lineage, and her claim to be the first Roman aristocrat to embrace Christ's poverty and come to Bethlehem) to be carved on the tomb itself, the other (linking her resting-place with Christ's crib) on the doors of the grotto.

Jerome was absolutely shattered by Paula's death. For almost twenty years their lives had been closely intertwined, each depending on the other far more than, in all probability, either of them guessed. For some months he could undertake no literary work. It was only with difficulty and after long delay, he confessed[15] to Theophilus, that he could summon the strength to put the bishop's Easter pastoral for 404 into Latin. Not only was he nervously prostrated, but his health too gave way, and he fell sick with a raging fever. The loss of one of the very few people in the world, perhaps the only one,[16] for whom he felt real tenderness and affection was taking its physical toll. 'All of a sudden,' he blurted out pathetically to Theophilus, 'I have lost her who was my consolation.' In saying this, he hastily added, he had been thinking of what she had done, not for himself, but 'for the relief and refreshment of the Christian folk whom she devotedly served'. But in the first half of the sentence we can glimpse the immense gap which had yawned in his personal life. As the months slipped by, however, he pulled himself together, and set himself to compose, with care and deliberation, his memorial to her. This was the great threnody[17] in which, in the form of a consolatory letter to Eustochium, he painted the glittering portrait of his heroine.

Fortunately for posterity, the portrait is in the main biographical. Jerome expatiates on Paula's ancestry (while insisting that such matters are unimportant for Christians), her splendid marriage, her conversion to the service of Christ's poor and to asceticism after her husband's death, the hospitality she offered bishops Epiphanius and Paulinus in 382/3, and then, in picturesque detail, her journey to the east, her pilgrimage through the Holy Land and down to Nitria, her eventual settlement in Bethlehem. Only at this point does he bring himself into the narrative; the reader would never suspect that she had known him at Rome or that her de-

[14] For details see R. W. Hamilton, *The Church of the Nativity, Bethlehem* (Jerusalem, 1947), 90; B. Bagatti, *Gli antichi edifici sacri di Betlemme* (Jerusalem, 1952), 135 f. The latter contains useful plans. The normal approach is by a staircase from the Franciscan monastery to the north of the Church of the Nativity.

[15] *Letter* 99, 1.

[16] So, correctly as I think, D. S. Wiesen, *St Jerome as a Satirist* (Ithaca, New York, 1964), 142.

[17] *Letter* 108.

parture from the capital had had anything to do with him—indeed, he cunningly leaves the impression that it was somehow connected with the bishops' return home. The routine of her convent and her supervision of its inmates are carefully set down, while the paragraphs assigned to her last illness, her death, and her funeral are richly coloured and full of pathos. At the same time he dwells on her virtues—her wonderful humility, her charity to all and sundry, her extraordinary mortifications, her passionate devotion to Scripture, her zeal for orthodoxy (a long section recalls the sinister attempts of an unnamed Origenist to deflect her from it), her sublime faith in illness and suffering. More than once he highlights her boundless generosity, as a result of which she used up all, indeed more than all, her vast fortune, leaving not a penny to Eustochium, but on the contrary a crippling burden of debts. From time to time the story is interspersed with the traditional themes of Christian consolation. If her friends grieve, he emphasises, it is not for her, for she is at last with Christ. Once she wore sackcloth, but now white raiment. She has won the crown of martyrdom, for a life like hers is made up of daily martyrdoms. Her faith and works unite her with Christ, and standing in his presence she can the more readily obtain her petitions.

This great piece is the longest, and perhaps the most splendid, of Jerome's 'epitaphia'. With a conventional affectation of modesty, he confesses that he worked only two nights on it, apologising for the resulting 'rudeness of diction, devoid of elegance and stylistic charm'. In fact it is a work of consummate art, as much in its prose as in its general design. Sentence after sentence dazzles the reader with its careful construction, its euphonious cadences. All the devices of rhetoric are deployed with studied effect, and one admires the skilful use of abundant and aptly chosen quotations from Scripture, occasionally ones from Vergil and other classical authors too. Satire and invective are from time to time brought in, adding a mordant quality—as when Jerome, extolling Paula's virtues, lashes out against the vanities and self-indulgence of lesser women. The eulogy is often extravagant (e.g. 'Whenever I have tried to move my stylus to accomplish my promised task, my fingers have stiffened, my hand has gone limp, all feeling in it has become numb'). Nevertheless the artificial forms prescribed by the genre[18] cannot conceal the intense regard and genuine emotion pervading the panegyric. Jerome was fully conscious of his achievement, for towards the end he addressed Paula directly, borrowing famous words from Horace: 'As you see, I have built you a monument more enduring than bronze, which no passage of time will be able to destroy.'[19]

[18] For this see Ch. Favez, La consolation latine chrétienne (Paris, 1937).
[19] Cf. Horace, Carm. 3, 30, 1 for the words 'Exegi monumentum aere perennius'.

(iv)

Paula's death, in itself a blow which left her inconsolable,[20] imposed a two-fold responsibility on Eustochium, now in her late thirties. Somehow or other she had to take her mother's place with Jerome, nearing his middle seventies, desperately lonely and in need of affection and support. His last letters,[21] written years later and shortly after her death, hint that she had filled this gap. And the superintendence of the convent, on which Paula had exhausted her physical and nervous energies, inevitably now devolved on her. Fortunately she had plenty of experience, having always taken her full share of even the most menial tasks of the community. If exemplary in modesty, she was also, though small in stature, a woman of decision and character.[22] But she was to need all the courage, resolution, and practical flair she could summon. With Paula's fortune now completely dissipated and the growing demands made on their charity, both her convent and Jerome's, with the hospice they administered, were in desperate straits financially.

As it happened, help came to them in this hour of need from an unexpected quarter. Some time in 404, when both were still overwhelmed with grief for Paula's loss, a priest named Silvanus sent Jerome copies of certain fundamental writings of Pachomius, the reputed founder (c. 320) of the communal form of monasticism in Egypt, and of his disciples, with the request that he would translate them into Latin. Numerous Latin-speaking monks, apparently, were joining monasteries run on Pachomian lines in the Thebaid, in Upper Egypt, and at Canopus, to the north-east of Alexandria, and understood neither Coptic nor Greek. Jerome yielded to the pressing entreaties of Leontius, Silvanus's emissary, and his companions, and dictated to a secretary a Latin rendering of the Greek translation of the original Coptic with which they provided him. The works so Latinised comprised not only the so-called Rule of Pachomius and eleven of his letters, but also the extremely important *Doctrina de institutione monachorum* of his second successor Horsiesi (d. c. 380), and certain associated texts.[23]

Pachomius's Rule (the earliest of the kind extant) was a compilation of

[20] Cf. Jerome's remark to Theophilus in *Letter* 99, 2: 'quae nullam pro matris absentia recipit consolationem'.

[21] *Letters* 151, 2; 153, 1; 154, 2.

[22] For her modesty see Palladius, *Hist. Laus.* 41; for the other traits mentioned Jerome, *Letters* 54, 13 ('in parvulo corpore ingentes animos'—probably of her, not Paula); 66, 3 (decision); 66, 13 (menial tasks).

[23] For the above see the preface to his translation (A. Boon, *Pachomiana Latina*, Louvain, 1932, 3–5). Both Cavallera (I, 295) and, following him, Penna (292) suppose that Silvanus's envoys acted as interpreters, translating the Coptic into Greek there and then while Jerome immediately rendered their Greek into Latin. But Jerome's language ('ut erant de aegyptiaca in graecam linguam versa'), as well as his earlier reference to 'books' and statement that the precepts of Pachomius and his disciples were available in Greek and Coptic but not in Latin, make it plain that he was furnished with a Greek text.

instructions which, worked out in the light of accumulating experience, he had put together, 'little by little and groping his way', over many years.[24] It covered all the various aspects of the monastic life, such as the organisation of the houses under superiors, morning and evening worship, the daily conduct of monks, the care of the sick, arrangements for the reception of guests, etc. A great deal of space is assigned to the agricultural tasks or the numerous trades in which the monks were engaged, for everyone was to be allocated work in proportion to his strength. Thus Pachomius's communities were provided with a solid economic foundation from the beginning. It was precisely this that had been lacking to Jerome's and Paula's houses, with their amateurish arrangements (as we may suspect) and their inevitable, but as events were all too painfully proving hopelessly improvident, reliance on their patroness's originally boundless wealth. As Jerome translated Pachomius's and Horsiesi's down-to-earth, practical regulations, all drafted with an eye to self-sufficiency and good order, we may fairly conjecture that he realised their relevance to the organisational and economic needs of the communities at Bethlehem. At any rate he remarked in his preface that in breaking his long silence one of his objects was to provide Eustochium with something she might pass on to her sisters to put into practice, and to enable his own brothers to imitate the pattern of life of the Egyptian monks.

As we noted,[25] Rufinus had published a Latin adaptation of Basil the Great's monastic Rules only a few years previously. These were very different in provenance and inspiration from Pachomius's; they also reflected a more advanced stage of cenobitism. In any case, quite apart from Silvanus's specific request, Basil, the supporter of Meletius of Antioch against Paulinus and of the 'three hypostases' theology, was not a figure to whom Jerome was likely to look for advice. It is nevertheless ironical that, deadly enemies as they had now become, Rufinus and Jerome were now in effect collaborating, albeit along separate lines, in mediating to the west the rich and varied experience in monastic communal living which the east had accumulated. The influence of Jerome's translations has often been greatly exaggerated. It seems certain, for example, that Cassian of Marseilles (c. 360–c. 433), who transmitted and interpreted the Egyptian ascetic ideal to western Europe, never set eyes on them (although he probably made some slight use of Rufinus's adaptation of Basil's Rules).[26]

---

[24] So L. Th. Lefort, *Oeuvres de s. Pachôme et de ses disciples* (Louvain, 1956) I, xiii. In his view it is extremely unlikely that Pachomius's followers, Theodore and Horsiesi, added to or tried to improve on his Rule.

[25] See above p. 228.

[26] See H. Leclercq, art. 'Cénobitisme' in *DACL* II, 3108 f.; C. De Clercq, 'L'influence de la règle de saint Pachôme en occident' (*Mélanges Louis Halphen*, Paris, 1951), 174; O. Chadwick, *John Cassian* (2 ed., Cambridge, 1968), 55–60. For Cassian's use of Basil see O. Chadwick, op. cit., 60–5.

Nevertheless his contemporary Vigilius, when he drew up (probably in Gaul, in the 420s) his Eastern Rule,[27] embodied in it, along with much that was original, substantial borrowings from Jerome's Pachomius. His choice of material for inclusion and omission was dictated by its suitability for a western milieu. Further, in the centuries immediately following a shortened recension of Jerome's version—shortened again on the principle of excising elements inappropriate to western conditions—had a wide diffusion in Italy at any rate. As thus edited and adapted the Rule of Pachomius, in Jerome's rendering, was able to make a contribution, much more modest than has sometimes been supposed but none the less discernible, to the enormously influential Rule of St Benedict in the sixth century.[28]

[27] For his *Regula orientalis* see *PL* 50, 373–80. For an analysis of Vigilius's borrowings see C. De Clercq, art. cit., 173 f.

[28] For the manuscript tradition of the shorter recension see A. Boon, *Pachomiana Latina*, Introduction. There is a full discussion of the impact of Jerome's version of the Rule in C. De Clercq's article cited above.

XXIV

Scripture: Polemics: Exegesis

(i)

Late in 404, more probably in 405, Jerome set the seal on the most ambitious and successful of his literary enterprises, the translation or revision of the Old Testament on the basis of the Hebrew. As long ago as 398 the goal had been in sight. Writing in that year to the wealthy Spaniard Lucinus, he informed him that only the Octateuch (i.e. the five books attributed to Moses, Joshua, Judges with Ruth, Esther) was still outstanding, and he was already at work on it.[1] Once the Origenistic controversy, however, with its excitements and distractions intervened, the project seems to have faltered and progress to have become spasmodic. It was only several months after Paula's death that he bestirred himself to resume and finish the interrupted task.

First he tackled the Pentateuch, being pressed to do so by his friend Desiderius.[2] Actually he had got some way with it (how far we cannot guess) well before 401. At any rate he was able in that year to include the Preface, in which he trounced objectors to his preference for the Hebrew original and poured scorn on the fable that the Seventy were inspired men who, enclosed in separate cells, had produced an identical Greek version, in his *Apology* against Rufinus.[3] Just possibly Desiderius stayed with him in Bethlehem in 398,[4] and took away with him the first instalments of the translation along with the Preface. But this selfsame Preface, with its request for the help of Desiderius's prayers in putting the books into Latin, makes it plain that a great deal still remained to be done. On the other hand, the Preface[5] to Joshua, which speaks of Paula's death as an event of the past, opens with what sounds like a sigh of relief, 'Having at last completed Moses's Pentateuch, I feel like a man released from a crippling load of debt.' It is therefore reasonable to infer that he had laid

---

[1] *Letter* 71, 5. See above p. 213.

[2] Cf. the preface (*PL* 28, 147–52). Desiderius was probably the person to whom he had written *Letter* 47 (see above p. 180) in 393, for in both the letter and the preface he compares him, in almost identical language, with the prophet Daniel because of the significance of his name (= 'desideriorum vir').

[3] *Apology* 2, 25.

[4] *Letter* 72, 5 mentions a Desiderius as carrying it to Vitalis, thus suggesting that he had been in Bethlehem.

[5] *PL* 28, 461–4.

some of the books at any rate aside for a spell of years, and finally got down to them only in 404/5.

The remaining three books (four by our computation) he dedicated, Paula being now dead, to Eustochium. Again the Preface is chiefly taken up with vindicating his translation from the Hebrew. Those who disliked it, he pointed out, were not obliged to read it; his prime object in making it was to assist Christians in controversy with Jews. The Church had never given its final sanction to the Septuagint, but read Daniel in Theodotion's version. It was high time, he snarled, that the Scorpion (i.e. Rufinus) ceased wounding him personally and attacking a holy work with his poisonous tongue.[6] Yet here again Jerome seems to have accomplished his task by stages, for Esther has a quite separate Preface[7] addressed to Paula and Eustochium jointly, implying that the former was still alive when the version was begun. The whole enterprise must have been brought to completion in 405/6, for in the Preface to Joshua Jerome declares himself resolved to devote himself henceforth to the task, abandoned for several years, of expounding the prophets, and we know that he resumed publishing commentaries on these late in 406.

Thus Jerome had taken some fourteen years, from *c*. 391 to 405, to carry out his famous Vulgate version of the Old Testament. Throughout he had stuck loyally to the Hebrew canon, never deigning to touch the so-called Apocrypha or deuterocanonical books. But now (perhaps earlier)[8] he found himself, to his chagrin, compelled to break his rule and translate Tobit and Judith. In the case of the former, almost certainly of the latter too, the compulsion took the form of the request, rather the importunate demand (as he was quick to emphasise), of his close friends Chromatius and Heliodorus.[9] Both, we should note, gave him regular, substantial financial subsidies, and this probably swayed his decision. But he made it plain that it went against the grain to translate books which, in his view, lacked the authority of the Hebrew canon. So far as Judith was concerned, he eased his conscience with the reflection that the

---

[6] PL 28, 463.

[7] PL 28, 1433–6. This Paula cannot be the younger Paula, for she did not come to Palestine till much later and in any case was too young to be a Hebrew scholar, as the Paula of the dedication is presupposed to be. For a discussion of the dates of the translations see L. H. Cottineau, 'Chronologie des versions bibliques de saint Jerome', *Miscellanea Geronimiana* (Rome, 1920), 55–68.

[8] All we really know is that they must have been produced before 407, the year of Heliodorus's death. I cannot agree with Cavallera (1, 291, n. 3) that they 'are presupposed by *Letter* 71, 5, which mentions only the Octateuch' as outstanding, for that letter speaks specifically of the 'Hebrew canon'.

[9] Cf. *Preface to Tobit* (PL 29, 23–6), which is addressed to them. The *Preface to Judith* (PL 29, 37–40) contains no names, but (a) uses the plural 'vestrae', (b) employs the identical expression 'your exaction', (c) stresses that *men* may use Judith with profit. It is inconceivable that Eustochium, or Paula and Eustochium, knowing Jerome's views on the Apocrypha, should have requested a translation. The facts in this paragraph are derived from these prefaces.

council of Nicaea (we have no other evidence of this) was alleged to have reckoned it Holy Scripture; its heroine, too, had been a paragon of chastity, one who could be profitably imitated by men as well as women. He had access only to Aramaic ('Chaldaean') texts, and as he was unfamiliar with this language he employed for Tobit (for Judith too, we may conjecture) an interpreter who knew both it and Hebrew. He worked very rapidly, devoting (so he claims) a single night's labour to the one, a single day's to the other. Both translations were closely dependent on the existing Old Latin version, and Jerome on his own admission treated the Aramaic pretty freely. His rendering of Tobit, for example, contains a certain amount of additional matter found in no other text. This includes, significantly, the suggestion that the newly wed should abstain from intercourse and devote themselves to prayer for the first three nights of their marriage. Although we may be sure that Jerome heartily approved this advice, it would be hazardous to assume that these expansions and re-writings represent contributions of his own.[10]

(ii)

Jerome's translation of the Old Testament was now completed, but we have fascinating evidence of his abiding interest in the text of the Psalter at any rate (a book to which he was continually returning) in a curious item of his correspondence dating from between 404 and 410. This is Letter 106, an inordinately long and, to most people, aridly fatiguing composition addressed to two Goths, Sunnia and Fretela, commonly held to be clerics resident at Constantinople.[11]

Keen students of Scripture, these had been puzzled by the numerous discrepancies between Jerome's Gallican Psalter based on Origen's Hexapla[12] and the Greek text (the Septuagint) they knew in the capital, and had submitted to him 178 of these, drawn from 83 psalms. What particularly thrilled Jerome was their eagerness to know what the Hebrew original had to say, and in his reply he lyrically congratulated them on their keen-sighted appreciation, conspicuously lacking among educated Greeks, of its authority. He then embarked on an exhaustive critical examination

[10] On these Vulgate editions see M. M. Schumpp, *Das Buch Tobias* (Münster in Westf., 1933), xxxii f.; 143–8. For the 'Tobias nights' see Tob. 6, 18–22; 8, 4 f. (Vulgate). These texts have had a considerable influence on the advice given to the newly married in the Roman Catholic church till quite recently.

[11] The main argument for this is the reference in pars. 2 and 86 to 'my devout son Avitus', who is taken to be the Avitus of Constantinople who persuaded Jerome to write to Salvina (*Letter* 79: see above p. 216). Most of the Goths were Arians, but there were orthodox ones in the capital, and John Chrysostom (cf., e.g., *Hom.* 8: *PG* 63, 499 ff.) set aside a church where they could celebrate the liturgy in their own language. The date of the letter is uncertain, but for a persuasive argument that it must be after 404 and before 410 see B. Altaner, *VC* 4 (1950), 246–8.

[12] For this see above p. 135.

of all the points raised. As a result the letter contains a thoroughgoing correction of his Gallican Psalter, but also one or two ploys of his own which can scarcely have meant much to the Goths (e.g. a veiled attack on Augustine's revision of the Latin psalter). For this reason, and also because the whole discussion is so specialised, so exclusively directed at Latin-speaking readers, it has been suspected that the letter is a literary fiction, and Sunnia and Fretela creatures of Jerome's imagination. But this hypothesis, as well as being belied by concrete personal allusions (to Avitus, and in par. 46 to the presbyter Firmus), overlooks the fact that Jerome's letters often soared above his immediate correspondents' heads, being deliberately aimed at a much wider audience. As it stands, Letter 106, with its mass of textual material, is one of the most precious sources for the study of the Latin psalter. It also reveals that, in this book at any rate, obviously because of its regular use in the liturgy, Jerome was some-times prepared to prefer a reading consecrated by tradition and church usage to the one required by the Hebrew. Had the considerations urged by Augustine, even by Rufinus, persuaded him to make this concession?[13]

(iii)

In the second half of 404, when he was beginning to revive his neglected Scripture studies, Jerome received a disturbing letter from faraway Gaul.[14] Its author was a learned priest of Aquitaine, Riparius by name, who had written to inform him that Vigilantius was attacking the cult of relics and the practice of keeping vigils by night in south-west Gaul. This was that same Vigilantius who, supported by letters of introduction from Paulinus of Nola, had called on Jerome in 395, had cut short his stay on discovering that his host was excommunicate, and on returning to the west had spread embarrassing rumours of Jerome's sympathy for Origenism.[15] Jerome retained the most unflattering recollections of the man and his visit, but for the moment he contented himself with a short riposte, though rich in scurrilous abuse (e.g. 'Vigilantius [i.e. Wideawake], more correctly called Sleepyhead, is again opening his fetid lips to vomit out a torrent of filth against the holy martyrs' relics'; or again, 'The doctors should cut his tongue out, or treat him for insanity'). He expressed

[13] For the hypothesis that *Letter* 106 is fictional see the able article by D. de Bruyne, 'La lettre de Jérôme à Sunnia et Fretela sur le Psautier', *ZNTW* 28 (1929), 1–13. For rejoinders see J. Zeiller, 'La lettre de saint Jérôme aux Goths Sunnia et Fretela', *Comptes rendus de l'Academie des Inscriptions et Belles Lettres* (1934), 338–50; A. Allgeier, 'Der Brief an Sunnia und Fretela und seine Bedeutung fur die Textherstellung der Vulgata', *Biblica* 11 (1930), 80–107. See also A. Allgeier, *Studien zur Geschichte und Kultur des Altertums* 22, Heft 3 (1940), 63 ff.

[14] For this paragraph see *Letter* 109, which is Jerome's reply to Riparius's disturbing letter. It must date from the second half of 404, for in *Against Vigilantius* 9 (autumn 406) he says that he wrote his letter to Riparius 'about two years ago'.

[15] See above pp. 193; 202; 206.

shock that Vigilantius's bishop, instead of peremptorily silencing him, appeared to acquiesce in his follies, made the theological point that Christians did not in the strict sense worship martyrs' relics but rather honoured them in order to adore him for whom they had died, and assembled texts in support of vigils (e.g. Matt. 26, 40 f.: 'Could you not watch with me etc?'; 2 Cor. 11, 27: 'in watchings often'). Nevertheless he offered to prepare a full-dress refutation if Riparius would send him actual copies of Vigilantius's treatises ('his nonsensical dronings').

Jerome had to wait two full years before he had the evidence he wanted. They were years crowded not only with translation work on the Old Testament, but (as we have seen)[16] with the final phases of his dispute with Augustine and his collaboration with Theophilus of Alexandria in his campaign to blacken John Chrysostom's reputation. In 405 he also completed (so we learn from Letter 114) a particularly careful translation of a treatise by Theophilus dealing with the eucharist and the reverence due both to the sacrament itself and to the sacred chalices, veils, and other ornaments used in its celebration. These, Theophilus had argued with Jerome's enthusiastic approval (approval all the more interesting in view of the stance he was adopting against Vigilantius), were not commonplace objects devoid of all holiness, but 'because of their association with the Lord's body and blood deserve to be reverenced with the same awe as they'. This same letter, however, paints a graphic picture of painful trials which afflicted Jerome at this time. His work on the treatise had been interrupted by the sudden invasion of marauding Isaurians (an untamed tribe settled on the north face of the Taurus range), who had spread devastation in 405 along the coast of Phoenicia and throughout Galilee.[17] In the resulting panic the defences of Jerusalem had to be hurriedly repaired. Then the winter of 405/6 had been inordinately severe, and there had been a terrible famine which had imposed grievous burdens on the brothers of the monastery. On top of all this Jerome himself had been dangerously ill in Lent 406: 'I was brought to the threshold of death.' Then at last, in the autumn of that year, the monk Sisinnius arrived from Aquitaine bringing Jerome both copies of Vigilantius's writings from Riparius and Desiderius, and also substantial gifts of money for his monastery (for the monks of Nitria, in Egypt, too) from Exsuperius, bishop of Toulouse.[18]

Vigilantius's writings have disappeared, and our entire knowledge of

[16] See above chap. xxii.

[17] The period 404–8 was marked by violent, wide-ranging attacks by the Isaurians. For the coast of Syria see Theodoret, *Hist. rel.* 10; for east Anatolia see Chrysostom, *Epp.* 13; 14; 15; for Phoenicia Sozomen, *Hist. eccl.* 8, 25; for Syria Philostorgius, *Hist. eccl.* 11, 8.

[18] Sisinnius is probably the deacon of that name who came across Augustine's *Letter* 40 on an island in the Adriatic (see above p. 264). For his bringing Vigilantius's writings see *Against Vigilantius* 3. For Exsuperius's gifts see *Comm. on Zechariah* i, prol.; ii, prol.

his position derives from the short, vulgarly abusive pamphlet Jerome now prepared in order to demolish him. Fortunately this pinpoints his principal theses, even preserving a few sentences extracted from his books, and so we have a reasonably clear idea of what he stood for. First, he branded as superstitious the devotion paid to the remains of martyrs and other holy persons, particularly the practice of carrying them round ceremonially in gold vessels covered with silken veils—'Why do you kiss adoringly a fragment of dust wrapped in a cloth?' Equally he condemned the offering of prayers to saints and martyrs, since they were at rest with God; criticised, as smacking of resurgent paganism, the lighting of numerous candles by daylight in their shrines; and questioned the miracles alleged to be performed there. Secondly, he denounced the observance of frequent all-night vigils, with the chanting of alleluias all the year round and not just at Easter. Besides opening the door to misbehaviour under cover of darkness, this was an illegitimate extension of the traditional vigil of Easter Even. Thirdly, he protested against the ascetic ideals of fasting, monastic withdrawal, and virginity. It was an excellent thing, he argued, for the clergy to be married; and if everyone were to remain a virgin, the human race would come to an end, just as if everyone became a monk, there would be no ordinary Christians to preach Christ's gospel to the world. Finally (and this must have been the last straw to Jerome), he called a halt to the sending of alms to Jerusalem for the support of the idle army of monks there. More generally, he deplored the fashion of divesting oneself of all one's property at one fell swoop. It would be far better for each diocese to reserve its resources for its own poor, and for a man of means to keep what he had, distributing the income little by little among the really needy.

Vigilantius's polemic, even as seen through Jerome's distorting glass, provides a fascinating picture of the exotic forms Christian piety was assuming, in the far west as well as in the east, in the fourth and early fifth centuries. He was not inviting, as has often been claimed, a return to primitive simplicity. From its early days the Church had taken for granted the veneration of martyrs' relics, the invocation of their prayers,[19] asceticism in various forms. Nevertheless in the fourth century, with the acceptance of the Church in society, there had been a vast proliferation and elaboration of these practices, an ever more enthusiastic pushing of ascetic ideals. Rather he seems to have been led by the abuses to which they could give rise (even Jerome warned little Laeta not to move a nail's breadth from her mother's side at a vigil)[20] to call in question the validity

---

[19] For relics cf., e.g., *Martyrium Polycarpi* 18 (date 155/6); *Martyrium Perp. et Felic.* 21, 3 (date 203); for invocation see G. Dix, *The Shape of the Liturgy* (London, 1943), 345 f. (with references to the graffiti in the early Roman catacombs, Origen, *De orat.* 11 and 14, etc.).
[20] *Letter* 107, 9 ('. . . ne transversum quidem unguem a matre discedat').

of the whole conception of Christianity implied. It is significant that several bishops, including Jerome's friend and benefactor Exsuperius, not only sympathised with his views but acted upon them.

Not that this inclined Jerome to soften his counter-attack—rather the contrary. Rarely mealy-mouthed in controversy, he surpassed himself in his *Against Vigilantius* in sheer coarseness and personal insinuation. The poor man's name is twisted ad nauseam to 'Sleepyhead', and his prose style is lampooned.[21] He himself is saluted as a resurrected Jovinian, while his objection to excessive austerities is interpreted as a sign of gluttony and drunkenness, his plea for married clergy as 'giving the rein to sexual lust'. A great deal of crude fun is made of his being the son of an inn-keeper. Short though the pamphlet is, space is found for a laughable though scarcely relevant description of how he had panicked years before during an earthquake at Bethlehem. 'You, the most prudent and wisest of mortals, began praying naked as you were. You reminded us of Adam and Eve in Paradise. Only, they blushed when their eyes were opened and they saw that they were naked. They covered their private parts with leaves, whereas you, stripped alike of your shirt and your trust in God, overcome with sudden terror and with the fumes of the previous night's debauch still hanging round you, began exposing the shameful region of your body to the eyes of decent Christian people as evidence of your prudence.'

The treatise is interesting for the specimens it provides of Jerome's satiric technique of blowing up an opponent by grossly caricaturing his position. Is Vigilantius worried that the immoral will exploit vigils? Then even the Easter vigil should be abandoned, for passions must be at bursting-point after the frustrations of Lent. Does he advocate married clergy? Presumably no one should be ordained unless his wife is pregnant and has a howling infant in her arms. And so on. But there is a serious vein of argument running through it too. Jerome restates the distinction, suggested in his letter to Riparius, between the respect paid to martyrs and the worship due to God alone. He appeals to tradition and authority. The pope offers mass on the tombs of St Peter and St Paul, while the emperor Constantius II surely committed no sacrilege in transferring the bonesof other Apostles to Constantinople. He justifies invoking the martyrs on the ground that, although dead, they are really alive with Christ. If so, can their prayers be less effective now than when they walked on earth? The lighting of candles in their shrines is no vain attempt to cheat the daylight, but an understandable piety. In criticising it Vigilantius is showing the same insensitivity as the disciples did when (Matt. 26, 6–13) they were annoyed with the woman who emptied her jar of expensive ointment on Jesus's head. As for sending alms to Jerusalem, Jerome

[21] Gennadius (*De vir. ill.* 36) commends his polished prose style.

agrees that we should strive to help all poor people without distinction, but recalls that St Paul had repeatedly singled out poor Christians in Jerusalem for special treatment. He also agrees that not every Christian is called upon to abandon all material possessions, but points out that this was the ideal Jesus had held up to anyone aiming at perfection. On virginity he does not argue; admittedly few aspire to it, but it would be wonderful if all did. As for monastic withdrawal, his defence of it is the negative one ('I admit my own weakness') that a man is only safe if he is removed from the world's temptations.

By his own account this unpleasant fly-sheet was the product of a single night's work. He had nothing but contempt for Vigilantius's 'mournful whinings', but apart from that he was obliged to hurry. He had been expecting Sisinnius to stay in Bethlehem until Epiphany 407, but the news of famine in Libya, of a disastrous short-fall of water in the Nile, and of the distress from which the Egyptian monasteries were suffering as a result, forced the deacon to speed his departure.[22] Had he been gifted with foresight, Jerome would have had the satisfaction of knowing that the practices and austere disciplines he was defending, so far from being checked by Vigilantius's critique, were to become the accepted norm of western Catholicism, and were to be officially justified by substantially the same apologetic as he was sketching out. Yet Vigilantius himself does not seem to have been seriously discredited by the abusive attack to which he had been subjected. Although he disappears from history, Gennadius of Marseilles, who characterised some of his views as heretical but commended his prose style and his religious zeal, reports that he had charge of a congregation in the diocese of Barcelona, just across the Pyrenees from Toulouse.[23] Perhaps the bishops who sympathised with his protests declined to surrender him to the wolves.

(iv)

The *Against Vigilantius* was by no means the only work Sisinnius carried away with him in his baggage. As we noted,[24] in his preface to Joshua Jerome had promised, once his translation of the Old Testament was off his hands, to resume commenting on the prophets. He now kept his word, tackling first, in that order, Zechariah, Malachi, Hosea, Joel, and Amos— the last after a further debilitating illness. Thus at long last he set the keystone on his exposition of the twelve Minor Prophets, begun some fourteen years earlier. One's first impression is that he squeezed these five massive studies into the closing months of 406, between Sisinnius's arrival

---

[22] *Against Vigilantius* 17; *Letter* 119, 1.
[23] *De vir. ill.* 36.
[24] See above p. 284.

and departure. There are hints, however, that he had been engaged on them, perhaps preparing initial drafts, for some years. In his Zechariah, for example, he suggests that his work on the Minor Prophets was approaching its conclusion when Sisinnius arrived; while elsewhere he states that he had promised his Hosea, Joel, Amos, and Zechariah to Paula when she was still alive.[25]

The Zechariah commentary, in three books, was much the longest, and he dedicated it to Exsuperius of Toulouse. It was a thank-offering for the lavish, desperately needed financial subsidies which the bishop had sent by Sisinnius for the Bethlehem monasteries. He apologised for having been obliged, because of Sisinnius's impatience to be on the road, to complete it in a hurry, without adding the final polish.[26] The commentary on Malachi he presented to two scripturally curious monks, Minervius and Alexander, also from Toulouse, the ones on Hosea, Joel, and Amos to Pammachius, Paula's son-in-law and spiritual heir. It was he who had prodded him into writing on the prophets, and to whom he now looked for help in warding off the Scorpion's venomous attacks.[27] In addition, however, he despatched to Minervius and Alexander a prolix, ill-digested letter attempting to explain two knotty passages (1 Cor. 15, 51 and 1 Thess. 4, 15–17) which had puzzled them (they had submitted many other problem texts, but he had to postpone his solutions). In both St Paul graphically describes Christ's Second Coming, implying that it will take place in his lifetime. Jerome's exposition is chiefly remarkable for the strenuous efforts he makes to evade this obvious interpretation, with its unpalatable corollary that the Apostle had been mistaken.[28]

In plan the five commentaries followed the earlier ones on the Minor Prophets. For each verse or group of verses a double translation was (generally) provided, from the Hebrew and from the Septuagint. Then came a 'historical' or literal exposition based on the former, a 'spiritual' one based on the latter. The relative space assigned to each varied remarkably, the determining factor being apparently the subject-matter (e.g. Zechariah's apocalyptic visions invited exuberant allegorising). The prophets themselves differed widely in situation and message—Zechariah,

[25] Cf. *Comm. on Zechariah* prol. (*CCL* 76A: 775–8). In all three prefaces to this commentary he speaks of the speed at which he had been obliged to work, but he seems to be referring to his lack of opportunity for correcting what his copyists had produced. See also *Comm. on Joel* prol.; *Comm. on Amos* 1, 1 (*CCL* 76: 167–8; 224) for his original intention to dedicate the books to Paula.

[26] Cf. the three prologues (*CCL* 76A: 775–8; 825–6; 881–2).

[27] *Comm. on Hosea* prol.; II prol.; *Comm. on Joel* prol.; *Comm. on Amos* III prol. (*CCL* 76: xxii; 52; 167–8; 309).

[28] *Letter* 119. For 1 Cor. 15, 51 ('We shall not all sleep, but we shall all be changed') he prefers the reading 'We shall all sleep, but we shall not all be changed'. These and other mistaken variants found in western (and other) codices are attempts to get round St Paul's apparently unfulfilled prophecy. If the received, in fact correct, text is accepted, he insists that it be interpreted metaphorically. So too 1 Thess. 4, 15–17 should be taken in a 'spiritual sense'.

like Haggai, concerned in 520–518 B.C. with the rebuilding of the Temple; the anonymous Malachi (= 'my messenger') denouncing, possibly *c.* 460 B.C., perfunctory worship, mixed marriages and divorce, and announcing the Lord's coming to sift his people; Hosea (eighth century B.C.) poignantly illustrating God's love for Israel by his own relationship with his adulterous wife; Joel (early fourth century B.C.) interpreting a disastrous plague of locusts as heralding the divine judgment; Amos (760–750 B.C.) warning that the Day of the Lord, to which people looked forward with ill-founded optimism, would be a day of destruction and doom because of the blatant immorality and social injustice in which they were sunk. Modern criticism recognises that all these books embody later, sometimes substantial, accretions (e.g. Zech. 9–14), but Jerome naturally treated them as unities. He also attributed them to the authors whose names they seem to bear. Following Jewish traditions, he mistakenly identified Malachi as Ezra the Scribe, and made Joel a contemporary with Hosea.[29]

His sources were, as usual, contemporary rabbinical exegesis and earlier Christian commentators. The former he generally used for his 'historical' exposition, drawing on it lavishly (especially for Malachi) and for the most part without critical comment. But he was quick to reject, to give one obvious example, specifically Jewish hopes of a splendidly restored Jerusalem dominating the rest of the world.[30] For Hosea, Zechariah, and Malachi he claims to have used, among others, Origen, Hippolytus, Didymus of Alexandria, and Apollinarius. He had clearly studied previous commentators for Amos and Joel, but does not name them.[31] Almost all these commentaries have disappeared, but the fortunate discovery in 1941, at Toura in Egypt (south of Cairo), of Didymus's vast, five-book commentary on Zechariah lays bare the enormous extent of Jerome's indebtedness to him (he claims that Didymus had dictated it at his request when he was staying in Egypt).[32] In countless passages, while drastically abbreviating, he has taken over the master's allegorical and moral explanations; and even where he disagrees with him, he makes his comments his own starting-point. His dependence on the others, especially Origen,

---

[29] *Comm. on Malachi* prol.; *Comm. on Joel* 1, 1 (*CCL* 76A: 939–41; 76: 169).

[30] *Comm. on Joel* 3, 12–17 (*CCL* 76: 213 f.). In *Comm. on Zechariah* 6, 9 f. (*CCL* 76A: 827) he states his resolve 'to introduce to Latin readers the mysteries of Hebrew scholarship and the learning of their synagogue masters'.

[31] Cf. *Comm. on Hosea* prol.; *Comm. on Zechariah* prol.; *Comm. on Malachi* prol. (*CCL* 76: xxii; 76A: 777–8; 941–2). For Joel and Amos see his references to 'others': *Comm. on Joel* 2, 28; *Comm. on Amos* 3, 3 (*CCL* 76: 202; 253). He must have used a commentary by Origen, of which a few fragments survive to attest his borrowings: see R. Reitzenstein, *ZNTW* 20 (1921), 90–3, where he edits Pap. Oxyr. 1601.

[32] *Comm. on Zechariah* prol. (*CCL* 76A: 777–8). L. Doutreleau has published the commentary, with admirable introduction, translation, and notes: *Didyme l'Aveugle: sur Zacharie* (3 vols., Paris, 1962). In vol. 1, 129–37 he has carefully analysed Jerome's use of and dependence on this diffuse work.

was undoubtedly equally close. It is interesting that, while criticising Origen's neglect of 'the history', he hardly anywhere takes exception to his characteristic 'errors'.[33] On the other hand, he occasionally adopts Origen's spiritualising conceptions, emphasising, for example, that God is incorporeal, and that neither anger nor swearing nor hatred should properly be attributed to him.[34]

These prophets offer difficulties which even modern scholarship finds baffling. With the much more modest, pre-critical equipment at his disposal Jerome could not be expected to unravel them, but in his 'historical' exposition he made valiant, occasionally successful efforts to do so. Everywhere his vast knowledge of the Old Testament impresses the reader. His real concern, however, was not primarily with the prophets' message for their own day, but with their significance for Christians. Quite a number of oracles were obvious enough, for they had already been fulfilled—and certified as fulfilled by the New Testament writers or the Lord himself—in the events of the Christian dispensation.[35] Jesus, for example, had taken (Matt. 26, 31) Zechariah 13, 7 as predicting the scattering of the disciples after his arrest; while Hosea's (6, 2) 'On the third day he will raise us up' unquestionably points to the resurrection. Joel's prophecy (2, 28–32), 'I will pour out my Spirit on all flesh', had been fulfilled, as St Peter had confirmed (Acts 2, 14 ff.), in the descent of the Spirit at Pentecost. In Mark 1, 2 we have inspired authority for understanding Malachi's (3, 1), 'Behold, I shall send my messenger before my face', as spoken in advance by Christ of John the Baptist and his own earthly coming.[36]

Apart from passages like these Jerome had recourse, as usual, to 'tropology' or allegory. Hosea, for example, and 'the wife of harlotry' God commanded him to take in fact symbolise, he contends,[37] Christ and the Church, which was enslaved to idols before he called it. The man whom Zechariah saw 'riding upon a red horse' is (here he follows

---

[33] Of Origen's commentary on Malachi he remarks (*CCL* 76A: 941–2), 'he almost wholly neglected the history, and in characteristic fashion concerned himself exclusively with allegorical exposition'. This passage contains the only clear case of doctrinal criticism: he rejects Origen's suggestion that Malachi was an angel because it seems to imply the pre-cosmic fall of souls. The theory that the two olive trees in Zech. 4, 11 f. signify the Son and the Spirit, which he castigates as blasphemy, he had come across in Didymus, who attributes it to 'a teacher who once ruled the Catholic Church' (probably Athanasius, who may have got it from Origen): see Doutreleau, op. cit. 1, 342 and 374, with notes.

[34] *Comm. on Amos* 6, 7–11; 8, 7 f.; *Comm. on Zechariah* 1, 2; *Comm. on Malachi* 1, 2–5 (*CCL* 76: 316; 339; 76A: 780; 946).

[35] So he remarks (*Comm. on Zechariah* 11, 4 f.: *CCL* 76A: 884), 'Where a prophecy is quite obvious and the correct sequence of history is reported figuratively, a tropological explanation is superfluous'. Cf. *Comm. on Malachi* 1, 11 (*CCL* 76A: 952).

[36] *Comm. on Zechariah* 13, 7; *Comm. on Hosea* 6, 2; *Comm. on Joel* 2, 28 ff.; *Comm. on Malachi* 3, 1 (*CCL* 76A: 910 f.; 76: 61 f.; 201; 76A: 969–71).

[37] *Comm. on Hosea* 1, 2 (*CCL* 76: 4 f.).

Didymus) Christ made flesh; and when Malachi rails against the polluted food the priests offer, he is really rebuking Christian clergy and laity who communicate unworthily.[38] Joel's plague of locusts, which Jerome refuses to accept as a historical event, figuratively refers to the four passions— grief, joy, hope, fear—which, according to Stoic doctrine, throw men's souls into turmoil. He probably got this idea from Origen, but it was also suggested to him by Cicero's *Tusculan Disputations* iv, 11—a passage which must have been much in his thoughts at the time, for he had already identified the four horns of Zechariah 1, 18 f., which 'scattered Judah, Israel, and Jerusalem', as the same four passions.[39] This instance alone— countless others could be cited—shows how arbitrary, indeed fantastic, this kind of exegesis could be. Jerome, it is true, sometimes speaks of 'rules of tropology', meaning, for example, the long-standing tradition that, in elucidating the Old Testament, Israel should be understood as denoting heretics, Judah the Church.[40] He found it impossible, however, to observe this consistently, and had to admit, for example, that when Amos (3, 1) said to Israel, 'You only have I known of all the families of the earth,' he was in fact addressing all the twelve tribes.[41] Thus even this rule left the door wide open for subjectivity.

(v)

Prolix and densely packed, these commentaries make heavy going. Jerome himself warns the reader that flowers of rhetoric and stylistic richness are not to be looked for in the exposition of Scripture.[42] In fact his prose maintains its customary fine quality. Classical quotations and references to classical authors are unevenly distributed among the five, being numerous in the Hosea and Amos commentaries but (why, one cannot guess) non-existent in his Malachi.[43] Here and there the forbiddingly monochrome façade is broken by a brilliant flash of colour, as when he vividly describes the serried ranks of locusts which quite recently had darkened Judaea until the wind arose and swept them away to the Dead Sea and the Mediterranean, or the havoc wrought by barbarians ranging throughout Illyria, Thrace, Macedonia, the whole vast region from the Bosphorus to the Julian Alps.[44] Again, there is a purple passage

[38] *Comm. on Zechariah* 1, 8; *Comm. on Malachi* 1, 7 (*CCL* 76A: 785; 948 f.).
[39] *Comm. on Joel* 1, 4; *Comm. on Zechariah* 1, 18 f. (*CCL* 76: 171 f.; 76A: 791 f.). At the end of the Joel passage he again cribs from Cicero, *Tusc. disput.* iii, 7; iv, 10, without acknowledgement. For details see H. Hagendahl, *Latin Fathers and the Classics* (Göteborg, 1958), 331–46.
[40] For 'leges tropologiae' see *Comm. on Amos* 3, 9 f. (*CCL* 76: 257). For Israel and Judah see *Comm. on Hosea* 1, 6 f.; 4, 15 f;, 11, 12; *Comm. on Amos* 7, 10 ff. (*CCL* 76: 9; 44; 132; 332).
[41] *Comm. on Amos* 3, 1 (*CCL* 76: 251).
[42] *Comm. on Hosea* 2, 16 f.; 10, 13; *Comm. on Amos* III prol. (*CCL* 76: 25; 118; 309).
[43] For particulars see H. Hagendahl, op. cit., 215–24.
[44] *Comm. on Joel* 2, 1 ff.; *Comm. on Hosea* 4, 3 (*CCL* 76: 186 and 195; 35).

in which, closely copying Didymus, he conjures up the age of the great persecution, when every island, prison, and salt-mine was crowded with Christian captives in chains, and contrasts with it the present era when (such are the seemingly impossible transformations worked by God in his goodness) the selfsame imperial government which used to make a bonfire of Christian sacred books has them adorned sumptuously with gold, purple, and precious stones, and, instead of razing church buildings to the ground, pays for the construction of magnificent basilicas with gilded ceilings and marble-encrusted walls.[45]

In one eloquent paragraph[46] Jerome paints what must surely (even allowing for the exaggerations of conventional rhetoric) be a portrait of himself, now in his middle seventies and ruefully conscious of his years—a portrait, moreover, which for a moment lays bare his guilt-ridden psychology. Old age, he muses, brings with it both blessings and misfortunes. It is to be welcomed because it liberates one from the dominance of shameful pleasures, sets bounds to gluttony, breaks the onset of lust, bestows enhanced wisdom, a more mature good sense. As the bodily organism grows chill, one is glad to leave sensual enjoyments to younger people. On the debit side, however, must be set frequent illnesses, disgusting phlegm, fading eyesight, digestive acidity, trembling hands, gums receding from the teeth, and the teeth themselves dropping out as one eats. On top of all this one is the victim of griping stomach pains, gout in the feet and arthritis in the hands, so that holding a pen to write and walking on one's own feet are well-nigh impossible. Whole parts of one's body seem already dead. Then, after this terrifying catalogue, he adds with relief: 'In spite of all this, in making my choice of misfortunes I shall the more readily put up with illnesses provided I am released from that uniquely burdensome tyrant, sexual desire. Admittedly even old age is exposed at times to the incitements of passion. No one, as the holy martyr Cyprian expressed it, can remain safe for long while he is close to danger. But it is one thing to be titillated by carnal pleasures, quite another to succumb to them. It is youth, aware of the urgent needs of the burgeoning body, which cries with the Apostle, "It's not the good act I want to perform that I do, but the bad act I detest . . . Wretch that I am, who will rescue me from this doomed body?" When one is old, the spark now and then glows among the burnt out ashes and tries to come to life, but it cannot get the blaze going.'

---

[45] *Comm. on Zechariah* 8, 6 (*CCL* 76A: 841). For his source see Didymus, *In Zach.* ad loc. (Doutreleau, op. cit. ii, 562: also 563, n. 3).

[46] *Comm. on Amos* II prol. (*CCL* 76: 263–4). Most biographers cite the passage in this connection (e.g. Grützmacher III, 113 f.; Cavallera I, 309 f.; Penna, 314).

XXV

Gathering Gloom

(i)

The first decade of the fifth century was marked by mounting alarm, confusion, and catastrophe in the west. So far the Rhine frontier at least had been firmly held; and although the Visigoths settled as 'federates' south of the Danube in 382 had asserted their independence in 395 and, under their vigorous young king Alaric, had threatened Constantinople and ravaged Macedonia and most of Greece,[1] Italy had remained untouched. In 401, however, and again in 403 Alaric, exploiting the friction between the two halves of the empire, invaded it. On both occasions he was defeated and forced to withdraw by Stilicho, the half-Vandal whom Theodosius I had promoted and who was now Honorius's commander-in-chief and all-powerful minister. Then, late in 405, a horde of Germans, mainly Ostrogoths, crossed the Alps and, led by their savage chieftain Radagaisus,[2] hurled themselves on Italy. Again it was Stilicho who, enlisting even provincials and slaves, destroyed them in August 406. Soon after, on 31 December 406, enormous masses of Vandals, Sueves, and Alans swarmed over the inadequately defended Rhine into Gaul, sacking its chief cities and spreading havoc and terror. Finally Alaric re-emerged, at first nominally in the service of the western government; in 407 the Senate was persuaded by Stilicho to pay him a huge sum of gold as blackmail. Relations deteriorated, however, when Stilicho was executed in August 408 and an anti-barbarian party took power in Rome. Twice he blockaded the capital, being bought off with bribes, but, exasperated by his failure to reach agreement with Honorius, he besieged it a third time in August 410, seized it (the citizens were on the verge of starvation), and pillaged it for three days.

In distant Bethlehem Jerome was watching the terrifying drama; his shocked awareness of it colours his correspondence.[3] In 407, when urging a wealthy Dalmatian, Julian, who had suffered tragic family bereavements, to strip himself of all he possessed and embrace Christ-like poverty, he

---

[1] Cf. *Letter* 60, 16. See above p. 215.

[2] Orosius describes him (*Hist. adv. pag.* 7, 37: *CSEL* 5, 538) as 'far and away the most savage of all [Rome's] past and present foes'.

[3] For his attitude see J. R. Palanque, 'St Jerome and the Barbarians', in F. X. Murphy, *A Monument to St Jerome* (New York, 1952).

recalled[4] that the unhappy man had seen his entire province laid waste by barbarian enemies, his private property ruined, his flocks and herds driven off, his slaves either taken captive or butchered. About the same time he was exhorting[5] Rusticus, a devout Christian in Gaul who had made a vow with his wife, Artemia, to abstain from sexual intercourse but had failed to live up to it, to do penance by joining her at Bethlehem. But he reinforced his appeal by conjuring up the appalling situation in which Rusticus was now placed, with friends being slaughtered and towns and country mansions overrun. Better abandon a homeland that was a homeland no more, and seek peace in the spots hallowed by the Saviour's cradle and cross. Two years later (409), seeking to deflect a young widow in Gaul, Geruchia, from marrying again (there is no evidence that she was in danger of slipping), he invoked the breakdown of civilisation there as a fresh and clinching argument. How could she think of a second marriage at a time when everything pointed to the approach of Antichrist and the end of the world. The whole country between the Alps and the Pyrenees, between the Rhine and the Atlantic, had been devastated by ferocious barbarians. Noble cities like Mainz, Rheims, and Strasbourg had succumbed to famine and the sword. Rome itself was having to fight within its own frontiers, not for glory but for bare life. Indeed, so far from fighting, she was reduced to buying the right to exist by bribing her foes.[6]

The same despairing note, in the background but none the less ominous, can be overheard in two other letters dated 412 and 413 respectively. The former[7] is an elaborately composed manual on monasticism for a young man from Toulouse, Rusticus, who after an expensive education had decided to adopt it, possibly as a prelude to joining the regular clergy. Fascinating for its personal reminiscences, the graphic contrast it draws between a good and a bad monk, and its famous caricature of Rufinus,[8] the letter warns Rusticus against mixing with girls, baths, excessive fasting, etc., and is remarkable for its reasoned argument in favour of the communal form of monasticism (with plenty of manual work) as against the solitary. But it closes with the prayer that the world-renunciation and poverty we embrace may, 'amidst our present miseries, with the sword wreaking havoc around us', be voluntary, not imposed by the conqueror. The second[9]

---

[4] *Letter* 118, 2. Since Paulinus of Nola is called a presbyter in par. 5, it must be prior to his consecration as bishop in 409. The reference may be to Radagaisus's invasions.

[5] *Letter* 122. For the date see Cavallera II, 52.

[6] *Letter* 123, 15–17 (the reference is to the Senate's lavish subsidy to Alaric: see above).

[7] *Letter* 125. This Rusticus is not the recipient of *Letter* 122 (see above), but is probably the one who later became bishop of Narbonne and to whom Leo the Great addressed his *Ep.* 92.

[8] See above p. 257.

[9] *Letter* 128. Following Grützmacher (III, 251), many hold that this letter shows Jerome prepared to modify his rigorous programme. That is based on a misunderstanding of par. 2, where he certainly presents the case for relaxing the rules in infancy, only however to refute it in par. 3.

gives advice for the upbringing of Pacatula, a little girl whom her father Gaudentius had dedicated to virginity from birth. Closely similar to the longer, more celebrated letter to Laeta,[10] it lays down the same harsh rules (no association with boys, exclusively scriptural studies, total confinement to her room, etc.), and states the case for relaxing them in infancy only in order to refute it. But the backcloth to this austere programme is the picture of the world collapsing in ruins, Rome, its capital, enveloped in flames, and yet sin flourishing everywhere unchecked. 'Such are the times in which Pacatula is born . . . destined to know tears before laughter, and to feel grief before joy.'

Politically Jerome's reaction to these disasters often seems naive. The blame for the blackmail Alaric had extorted from the Senate, he shrilly exclaimed,[11] should not be laid 'on our emperors [the effete Honorius and Arcadius], who are devoutly religious men, but on the wickedness of the half-barbarian traitor (Stilicho) who has used our wealth to arm our enemies against us'. Soon he was to hail Stilicho's execution as God's deserved retribution.[12] Yet in fairness we should recall that, justly or unjustly, Stilicho was widely execrated, blamed in circles more cognisant of affairs than Jerome for delivering the empire to the barbarians. Thousands shared his disgust that 'in our civil wars, and our wars against other nations, we are forced to depend on the help of alien barbarian tribes'.[13] It remains true, however, that for all the anguish he felt as a proud Roman at the collapse of the empire, he showed no understanding (any more than other contemporary intellectuals) of the forces contributing to it. As a Christian he preferred to interpret it as God's vengeance on a rotten society. 'It is because of our sins,' he had written in 386, 'that the barbarians are strong, because of our vices that the Roman army is defeated.' The havoc unleashed throughout the Roman world by hitherto unknown, savage tribes was a sign of God's anger at its neglect of him.[14] As a moralist and spiritual guide, too, it was natural for Jerome to exploit the instability and sheer frightfulness of life as a crowning motive for escaping from it into world-renouncing asceticism.

(ii)

Actually, he was far more at home in exegesis than in politics. In 407, having put the Minor Prophets behind him, he published at last the commentary on Daniel which he had promised years ago to Paulinus of

---

[10] *Letter* 107: see above pp. 273–5.
[11] *Letter* 123, 16.
[12] *Comm. on Isaiah* xi prol. (*CCL* 73: 451–2).
[13] *Comm. on Daniel* 2, 40 (*CCL* 75A: 634).
[14] *Letter* 60, 17; *Comm. on Isaiah* 7, 22 (*CCL* 73: 115).

Nola.[15] Having been criticised for excessive prolixity,[16] he made it much shorter than usual, contenting himself (for the most part) with terse notes on specially obscure passages and curbing his penchant for allegory. Nor did he provide, as hitherto, a double translation, his reason being that the Greek version used in the churches was not the Septuagint but Theodotion's, which agreed closely with the Hebrew or Aramaic original.[17] He did, however, perhaps for the sake of completeness, include notes on the Song of the Three Children and on the stories about Susanna and about Bel and the Dragon, additions which are not found in the Hebrew and which he regarded as uncanonical.[18] The section on chapters 11, 20–12, 13, which Christians took as a prediction of Antichrist and where his exposition becomes continuous and diffuse, gives the impression of being a separate treatise which he had prepared earlier and now incorporated, embellished with fresh material.[19] The finished work he dedicated, not to Paulinus of Nola (his name nowhere appears), but to Pammachius and Marcella. He could still recommend Paulinus as a model of asceticism, but he knew that he now belonged to the opposing camp. The relative and admirer of Melania, Paulinus had become the affectionate friend of Rufinus, whom he looked up to as 'a genuine Christian, devoutly learned', and whom he was now consulting on Scriptural matters.[20]

Next Jerome plunged into Isaiah, and at intervals between 408 and 410[21] composed the most voluminous of all his commentaries, a vast sprawling work in eighteen books. He was interrupted by frequent illnesses which disappeared as suddenly as they came. They were divinely sent reminders, he mused,[22] of his age and approaching death, which was perhaps only being deferred until his exposition of the prophets was complete. There were other hold-ups, caused by physical weakness, the shortage of professional stenographers, etc.;[23] and the prefaces are full of

[15] For the date see Cavallera II, 52. For the promise to Paulinus see *Letter* 85, 3 (date 399); also above p. 240.

[16] Cf. *Comm. on Isaiah* XI prol. (*CCL* 73: 451–2).

[17] *Comm. on Daniel* prol.; 4, 5 (*CCL* 75A: 619–20; 646).

[18] See above pp. 160 f. In the English Bible they appear in the Apocrypha, in the Vulgate as Dan. 3, 24–90, 13, and 14 respectively.

[19] F. Glorie, *CCL* 75A, 757 f. makes out a good case for this section's having originally been a separate treatise. But I see no evidence for his claim that Jerome put it together and sent it to Paulinus in 399/400 to fulfil his promise.

[20] See esp. P. Courcelle, *Revue des études latines* 25 (1947), 274–9. Cf. Jerome, *Letter* 118, 5 (praise for Paulinus); Paulinus, *Ep.* 28, 5 (his regard and affection for Rufinus).

[21] He began it after finishing *Comm. on Daniel*, i.e. probably in 408, and completed it before the sack of Rome in August 410 (*Comm. on Isaiah* I prol.; *Comm. on Ezekiel* prol.: *CCL* 73: 1–2; *CCL* 75: 1–2).

[22] *Comm. on Isaiah* XIV prol. (*CCL* 73A: 577–8).

[23] *Comm. on Isaiah* X prol. (*CCL* 73: 417–18). For his other complaints cf. ibid. and *Comm. on Isaiah* IX prol.; XI prol.; XII prol. ('Luscius Lanvinus', i.e. Rufinus); XIV prol.; XV prol. (he challenges critics of 'the Hebrew verity'); XVIII prol. (*CCL* 73: 369–70; 451–2; 73A: 493–4; 577–8; 625–6; 769–70).

murmurings against real or imagined enemies, particularly Rufinus ('the Scorpion, that dumb but poisonous animal . . . destined to perish in his own pus'), who had dared criticise his Daniel commentary. As the fifth book he inserted the strictly 'historical' explanation of the ten Visions (more correctly, Oracles) forming Isaiah 13–23 which he had reluctantly produced in 397 to satisfy Bishop Amabilis,[24] dedicating the sixth and seventh books to a lavishly allegorical interpretation of them. These sections apart, Jerome followed his normal practice of alternating literal and 'spiritual' exegesis, although to avoid excessive length he reproduced the Septuagint version only where it diverged significantly from the Hebrew.[25]

The *Commentary on Daniel* has exceptional interest. This collection of stories and apocalyptic visions purports to have been written in the sixth century B.C., and to foretell God's judgment on successive heathen empires that would oppress the Jews. The last persecution would be particularly harrowing, but God would destroy the sacrilegious tyrant, vindicate his faithful people, and inaugurate his everlasting kingdom. For contemporary Jews it seemed to point to the overthrow of their nation by the Romans in A.D. 70, and its eventual restoration by a Messiah yet to come. Christians read the book as a manifest prophecy of Christ, of his triumph over Antichrist at the end of the world, and of the general resurrection. In fact, though dressed out as prophecy, Daniel can be shown to be a tract for the times, written between 167 and 164 B.C. to encourage the Jews suffering under the terrifying pogrom of the Seleucid monarch Antiochus IV Epiphanes, and to assure them that the time of their tribulation would be short.

This correct interpretation had been worked out, with remarkable critical insight and learning, by the Neoplatonist Porphyry (third century), who had incorporated it in his anti-Christian polemic.[26] Jerome knew his work, almost certainly not at first hand, but through the attempts of Eusebius of Caesarea and others to refute it.[27] As we should expect, he rejected it with contempt, holding that 'none of the prophets had spoken so openly of Christ' as Daniel, and everywhere found the Christian revelation foreshadowed in the book. Typical was his suggestion that 'the stone . . . cut from a mountain by no human hand' (Dan. 2, 45), which the

---

[24] See above p. 220; also the prologue (*CCL* 73: 168).

[25] For the double exegesis cf. *Comm. on Isaiah* VII prol.; VIII prol.; for his use of the LXX *Comm. on Isaiah* prol. ad fin. (*CCL* 73: 277–8; 327–8; 5–6).

[26] In book xii of *Against the Christians* (now largely lost). Cf. *Comm. on Daniel* prol. (*CCL* 75A: 617–18), where Jerome summarises Porphyry's position. For a valuable discussion see J. Lataix, *Revue d'histoire et de littérature religieuses* 11 (1897), 164–73; 268–77.

[27] Cf. P. Courcelle, *Late Latin Writers and their Greek Sources* (ET, Cambridge, Mass., 1969), 75, who points out that Porphyry's works were almost certainly not available to Jerome, having been banned by Constantine I.

author had meant to signify the eschatological kingdom which God alone would set up, was none other than the Saviour conceived without human intercourse.[28] Yet, for all his sparring, he found himself forced to concede that Porphyry had been right in identifying the final onslaught with Antiochus and his reign of terror. The solution he proposed was that, while the sixth-century prophet (as he thought him) had accurately foreseen historical figures and events, these were but shadows and partial types which would be fully realised in the clash between Antichrist and the Lord's saints at the end of the world.[29] His failure to grasp the critical problem, in spite of Porphyry's having supplied the key, was understandable, perhaps inevitable. But it is ironical that the sharp-witted pagan critic of Christianity should have outmanoeuvred him as a biblical scholar.

In dealing with Isaiah Jerome was unavoidably hampered by the assumption (almost universal till the rise of modern criticism)[30] that the entire book was the work of one man, the late eighth-century prophet whose name it bears, and not an amalgam dating from widely separated periods. It remains, however, the most successful and instructive example of his eclectic exegetical method.[31] He wanted to 'show that Isaiah was not only a prophet, but an evangelist and an apostle'.[32] So in his exposition the pattern of this richly variegated poetic tapestry is revealed as anticipating Christ, his incarnation, passion and resurrection, and the Church. In keeping with this he insisted, with a good deal of special pleading, that the Septuagint for once was right in reading 'A virgin shall conceive' at Isaiah 7, 14, as against 'A young woman shall conceive' of the other versions. The commentary breathes an even fiercer animosity than usual against the Jews, not only rejecting their characteristic exegesis, but upbraiding their blindness, immorality, and greed, and exulting in their present humiliation, which (he judged) would last until the world's end.[33] But Jerome castigated abuses in the Church too—the influence women exert in ecclesiastical appointments, the diversion of the Church's wealth

[28] This exegesis was not original, but was widely current among the earlier commentators whom he plundered.

[29] See esp. *Comm. on Daniel* 11, 21 (*CCL* 75A: 711).

[30] According to R. H. Pfeiffer (*Introduction to the Old Testament*, London, 1952: 415 n.), Ibn Ezra (d. 1167) was the first to express, in carefully guarded language, some doubts about Isaiah's authorship of Isa. 40–66.

[31] Cf. the remarks of F. M. Abel, 'Le commentaire de saint Jérôme sur Isaïe', *RB* 3 (1916), 200: echoed by A. Penna, 318, and S. Gozzo, 'De s. Hieronymi commentario in Isaiae librum', *Antonianum* 35 (1960), 169.

[32] *Comm. on Isaiah* prol. (*CCL* 73: 3–4).

[33] E.g. *Comm. on Isaiah* 1, 30; 27, 12; 42, 18 f.—their ignorance of Scripture, and blindness (*CCL* 73: 29; 368; 73A: 514); 2, 7; 3, 3—their avarice (*CCL* 73: 36; 52); 45, 19; 66, 17—their pride and immoralities (*CCL* 73A: 543; 815 f.); 1, 12; 59, 16 f.—the Temple will remain desolate for ever; when they conquered the Jews, the Romans were God's agents (*CCL* 73: 21; 73A: 711).

from the poor, for whom it had been contributed, to private pleasure and advantage, etc.[34] Further, the commentary abounds in interesting textual notes and in discussions of the different Greek versions.

Both commentaries, needless to say, were largely compilations from earlier Christian exegetes. They included, too, a mass of contemporary Jewish exegesis, generally with the object of refuting it; that on Isaiah records a few Jewish Christian (Nazaraean) interpretations.[35] Origen was Jerome's principal source, but there were many more; his acknowledgments were fuller than usual.[36] Where a check is possible, as with Eusebius's commentary on Isaiah,[37] his borrowings can be shown to be far-reaching and, on occasion, word for word. In one remarkable section, being completely baffled by the mysterious 'seventy weeks of years' of Daniel 9, 24–7 (as well he might be, since the author meant the 'weeks' to culminate in the ending of Antiochus's persecution, whereas for Christians they ushered in Christ's second coming), he simply transcribed the opinions of several predecessors without venturing a decision between them. But if he was sometimes frank, at other times he could not resist the temptation to dazzle his readers with a parade of learning he simply did not possess. Thus he solemnly warned them that for understanding the closing chapters of Daniel an extensive familiarity with Greek historians was indispensable. He then reeled off a string of names, adding that 'Porphyry too admits he followed them'. Yet it is certain that whatever knowledge he had of these, or at any rate most of these, writers had been derived from none other than Porphyry himself (probably via Eusebius).[38]

(iii)

Jerome's large-scale dependence on Origen in these commentaries was no more than the continuation of his life-long practice. But it is noticeable that his use of the master had become markedly more critical. He did not hesitate now to stigmatise his objectionable views, generally without naming him. Origen, for example, had taken Nebuchadnezzar as a type of the Devil, and his conversion (LXX Dan. 3, 95 f.) as proof that even the Devil would eventually be saved and preach repentance. This Jerome branded as mischievous exegesis.[39] Similarly he more than once repudiated

---

[34] E.g. *Comm. on Isaiah* 3, 12 and 15 (*CCL* 73: 57; 59).

[35] For references to the *Evangelium Nazaraeorum* (see above p. 65) cf. *Comm. on Isaiah* 8, 11–15; 19–22; 9, 1 f.; 11, 1–3; xviii prol. (*CCL* 73: 122; 128; 156; 73A: 769–70).

[36] Cf., e.g., his mention of Origen, Eusebius of Caesarea, Didymus, and Apollinarius, as well as Victorinus of Pettau, his only Latin source, in *Comm. on Isaiah* prol.

[37] A. Mohle showed that it survives almost entire on the margin of the Florentine MS *Bibl. Laur. Plut.* xi, 4 (*ZNTW* 33, 1934, 87–9).

[38] *Comm. on Daniel* prol. (75A: 621–2). For his lack of direct knowledge of these historians see P. Courcelle, op. cit., 75.

[39] *Comm. on Daniel* 3, 95 f. (*CCL* 75A: 644).

Origen's theory that heaven and earth, the stars and the underworld, are rational beings endowed with souls. He also dismissed as impious the suggestion, which years earlier, when translating Origen's homilies, he had accepted with a cautionary editorial note, that the two Seraphim of Isaiah's vision (Isa. 6, 2) represent the Son and the Holy Spirit.[40] And when Isaiah prophesies (Isa. 27, 1) that the Lord will finally slay 'the dragon that is in the sea', he scornfully challenged Origenists to reconcile this with their notion of the Devil's ultimate repentance and restoration.[41]

As it happened, Jerome's obsession with Origen's errors, never dormant for long since the great controversy, was stirred into fresh life by a letter he received when he was still struggling with his Isaiah commentary. This was from a friend named Avitus, probably a priest from Braga in Spain, who asked for an accurate copy of his rigorously literal translation of Origen's *First Principles*.[42] Apparently a hasty, garbled version of the work, which had originally been intended for Pammachius's private eye, had got into circulation through someone's misdirected zeal and dishonesty.[43] Jerome complied with Avitus's request, and in a covering letter[44] supplied a short analytical summary of Origen's treatise, interspersing it with frequent citations of sentences or longer excerpts from his translation (which itself has disappeared). Strongly, even violently worded, this letter lays bare the fanatical hostility Jerome now felt for Origen. When condensing his ideas in his own words, he almost invariably distorts them or presents them in an unfavourable light. For example, where Origen had canvassed alternative solutions (e.g. on the nature of the resurrection body), without coming down on one side or the other, Jerome depicts him as dogmatically defending the more unpalatable option.[45] On the other hand, the direct citations from his own version (although even they need to be used with caution, since that version was apparently not so absolutely literal as Jerome claimed) are precious as

[40] *Comm. on Isaiah* 1, 2; 5, 14; 13, 13; 45, 12 (*CCL* 73: 11; 79; 242; 73A: 539). For the Seraphim, *Comm. on Isaiah* 6, 2 (*CCL* 73: 92). Rufinus reminded him (*Apol. c. Hier.* 2, 27) that, when translating a homily of Origen's on Isaiah (see above pp. 76 f.: text in *GCS* 33, 244), he had reproduced faithfully his dangerous interpretation but had inserted a warning note that the equality of the persons of the Trinity must be upheld.

[41] *Comm. on Isaiah* 27, 1 (*CCL* 73: 361).

[42] Probably not the Avitus who instigated Jerome to write *Letter* 79 to Salvina in 400 (so Vallarsi and others: see above p. 216 for the letter), for he lived in Constantinople. The Avitus mentioned by Gennadius, *De vir. ill.* 48, seems a more plausible candidate. He was in Jerusalem in Dec. 415 when the relics of St Stephen were translated and persuaded the discoverer, Lucian, to write an account of the events which he himself then translated into Latin. For Jerome's literal translation of *First Principles* see above p. 237.

[43] So Jerome, *Letter* 124, 1.

[44] *Letter* 124. The date must be 409/10, for he states (par. 1) that he had made his translation of Origen's *First Principles* 'about ten years ago'.

[45] Cf. the comments of M. Simonetti, *I Princtpi di Origene* (Turin, 1968), 20 f. As a glaring example he points to the way in which Jerome (pars. 4 and 7) misrepresents Origen's discussion of the transmigration of souls, a doctrine which he denied.

providing in many cases the only surviving rendering of the original text
that is at all trustworthy.

(iv)

It was Jerome's intention, once his commentary on Isaiah was out of the
way, to produce one on Ezekiel and thereby 'make good the promise' he
'had so often given to his zealous readers'.[46] Hardly had he taken this
fresh task in hand, however, when terrible, heart-rending news reached
him: Rome had been seized and pillaged by Alaric. The disaster sent a
shudder of horror through the Roman world, but its impact on Jerome
was particularly cruel. By the same post, or shortly after, he learned that
Pammachius and Marcella, as well as many other Christian friends, were
dead. So benumbed was he that he had to suspend all work. 'For days
and nights I could think of nothing but the universal safety; when my
friends were captured, I could only imagine myself a captive too . . .
When the brightest light of the world was extinguished, when the very
head of the Roman empire was severed, the entire world perished in a
single city.'[47] 'Who could believe,' he was to write,[48] 'that after being
raised up by victories over the whole world Rome should come crashing
down, and become at once the mother and the grave of her peoples?'
He wrote in 411 in a similar strain to two correspondents, Flavius
Marcellinus and his wife Anapsychia, who had consulted him on the
vexed question of the origin of the soul. After referring them to his
Apology against Rufinus and, since they wrote from Africa, to Augustine
(who could personally explain to them his and Jerome's views on the
subject), he confessed that he had been so shattered by the devastation of
the western provinces, and especially of Rome, that he almost forgot his
own name. For a long spell he had been obliged to abandon Ezekiel and
remain silent, 'knowing this was a time for tears'.[49]

We may feel sure that, anguished as he was by the humiliation of the
proud western capital, his grief for the passing of his lifelong friends,
confidants, and supporters was even more poignant. No account of
Pammachius's death has come down, but Jerome allows us a glimpse of
Marcella's in the dignified, unusually restrained epitaphium[50] he dedicated

---

[46] *Letter* 126, 2 (date 411: see Cavallera II, 53 f.).

[47] *Comm. on Ezekiel* prol. (*CCL* 75 : 3–4).

[48] *Comm. on Ezekiel* III prol. (*CCL* 75 : 79–80).

[49] *Letter* 126, 2. The reference was to *Apology* 2, 10. For Marcellinus see *PW* XIV (2), 1445 f.
He was a high-ranking official ('tribunus et notarius') who was sent to Africa in 411 to settle the
Donatist controversy. A Christian with strong theological interests, he corresponded with
Augustine, who dedicated his *City of God* to him. He got involved in the revolt of Heraclianus
and was executed in Sept. 413.

[50] *Letter* 127: addressed to Principia.

to her memory in 413. His two years' silence, he brusquely explained to her much younger protégée Principia (who had been impatiently demanding the tribute), was not the result of negligence, as she wrongly supposed, but of his overwhelming sorrow. Relatively short and pervaded with intense respect for the remarkable woman, the threnody dwells on her resolute devotion to chaste widowhood, her immunity from the least breath of scandal even in a gossipy city like Rome, and her delight in the Bible, extolls her as the first Roman matron of rank to take up the monastic vocation, and expatiates on her strength of character and severe but commonsense asceticism. In an important section, not devoid of scurrilous abuse of Rufinus, Jerome describes the unyielding stand she had made against Origenism in Rome when even Pope Siricius allowed himself to be imposed upon; indeed it was she who had personally exposed the heretics and ensured 'the glorious victory'.

Finally, amidst the horrors of the sack of Rome, she had remained superbly cool and intrepid. When blood-stained barbarians broke into her mansion and she failed to convince them that she had already stripped herself of her riches, she had endured a brutal beating-up without any apparent sensation of pain. Her overriding concern had been to shield Principia from the lusts of the soldiers, and by her insistent pleadings she had prevailed on them to allow herself and her young friend a safe refuge in St Paul's basilica. But the excitement, violence, and strain had evidently been too much for the indomitable old lady. A few months later, though apparently active and in good health, she had died peacefully in Principia's arms—'While you wept, she was smiling, conscious of having lived a good life, and confident of her future reward.'

(v)

At last, in the autumn or winter of 411, Jerome felt able to resume his exposition of Ezekiel. Eustochium was continually pressing him, his 'great wound' was gradually healing, the scorpion Rufinus was safely under ground in Sicily (he could not repress his glee), and so he could concentrate on Scripture rather than on rebutting heretics.[51]

Even so, the work was repeatedly held up. First, there were crowds of refugees, men and women, once rich but now reduced to abject beggary, who swarmed to the Holy Land from the disasters in the west. Desperate for shelter, lacking food and clothing, they obliged Jerome to drop his biblical studies in order to minister to their needs.[52] Then, when he had

---

[51] *Comm. on Ezekiel* prol. (*CCL* 75: 3–4). Rufinus fled from Aquileia to Rome before the Gothic invasions in 407, then to Paulinus's monastery at Pinetum, and finally with Melania the Younger (grand-daughter of Melania the Elder) and her husband Pinianus to Sicily. He died there in 410.

[52] *Comm. on Ezekiel* III prol.; VII prol. (*CCL* 75: 79–80; 239–40).

305

got to the end of the third book, an invading horde, possibly of pillaging Arabs from the south, 'overran like a torrent the frontiers of Egypt, Palestine, Phoenicia, and Syria'.[53] It was only by Christ's mercy, he claimed, that he and his companions escaped their violence. Amid alarms like these scholarly labour, which demands peace, plenty of books, and industrious secretaries, was out of the question (he neatly quoted Cicero in support). We know that he was occupied with the ninth book towards the end of 413, for in it he glances at the 'recent' revolt and downfall of Heraclianus, the military commander of Africa and consul for that year.[54] But when he approached Ezekiel's vision of the restored Temple (chaps. 40–8), yet further delays were imposed on him, this time by his own lack of confidence in his ability to expound it. He was overwhelmed with doubts, he confessed, whether he should tackle this difficult theme or frankly avow his ignorance. It was only in 414, after the fresh interruption of having to write his letter to Demetrias, that he completed the task.[55]

Like that on Isaiah, the commentary on Ezekiel is a diffuse, unwieldy work, fourteen books in all. It resembles its predecessor in lay-out, too, basing itself almost exclusively on the Hebrew original. Scorning the 'howling' of the Rufinus faction, Jerome criticised the Septuagint for its many omissions,[56] and sought to undermine its authority, at any rate for Ezekiel and the prophets, by pointing out that, according to Aristeas, Josephus, and other learned Jews, the Seventy had translated only the five books of Moses.[57] To make sense of the (notoriously corrupt) Hebrew text he made frequent recourse to the other Greek versions. He nowhere names the Greek and Latin sources from which he drew his exegesis, but it is certain that they included Origen, whose commentary on Ezekiel he had listed in Letter 34 and fourteen of whose homilies on the prophet he had put into Latin years before. For example, while the book abounds in sharp attacks on what are clearly Origen's heterodox interpretations,[58] there are other passages where fragments of Origen's exegesis survive and where he can be shown to have copied him almost word for word. But there were others too; he speaks of having 'commentaries by Greeks' read

---

[53] *Letter* 126, 2. We hear of this raid, which must have taken place in 411, from no other source. Jerome likens the raiders to Vergil's 'wide-ranging Barcae' from Cyrenaica (*Aen.* 4, 42 f.) and to Ishmael, whom Josephus calls 'founder of the race of the Arabs' (*Ant.* 1, 12, 2).

[54] *Comm. on Ezekiel* 28, 1–10 (*CCL* 75: 329). For Heraclianus's condemnation on 3 August 413 see *Cod. Theod.* xv, 14, 13. In *Comm. on Ezekiel* vii prol. (see also *Letter* 130, 7) Jerome deplored the brutality and greed with which Heraclianus fleeced the hapless refugees passing through Africa.

[55] *Comm. on Ezekiel* xi prol.; xii prol.; xiii prol. (*CCL* 75: 405–6; 462; 505–6). For *Letter* 130 to Demetrias see below pp. 312 f. According to par. 2, he was engaged on Ezek. 41 when the request to write to Demetrias arrived.

[56] *Comm. on Ezekiel* 1, 22 ff.; 16, 13d (omitted, Jerome alleges, in case it gave offence to Ptolemy); 33, 23 (sneer at the 'Grunnianae factionis heredes') (*CCL* 75: 19; 159; 401).

[57] *Comm. on Ezekiel* 5, 12; 16, 13d (*CCL* 75: 53; 159).

[58] E.g. *Comm. on Ezekiel* 16, 1–3; 26, 19–21; 40, 44–9 (*CCL* 75: 143; 302–3; 492).

to him.[59] His sources also included the Jewish exegetical tradition, although he used it much more sparingly here than in his commentary on Isaiah.

Even if its substantial unity is accepted, Ezekiel confronts the exegete with exceptional difficulties. The work of a priest deported to Babylon in 597 B.C., it comprises oracles, theophanies, and apocalyptic visions, some prior to and some later than the fall and destruction of Jerusalem in 587. It culminates in a prophecy of Israel's resurrection and the detailed portrayal of the new Temple which will replace the old. For the first thirty-seven chapters Jerome stuck much more closely than was his habit to straightforward, literal exposition—extracting from it, however, wherever the opportunity presented itself, edifying moral, spiritual, or ecclesiastical lessons. But when he tackled the invasion of Gog (the leader of the forces which would launch a final, unsuccessful assault on the people of God) in chapters 38 f. and the idealised description of the restored Temple in chapters 40-8, he gave free rein to his (rather, perhaps, his authorities') imaginative fantasy. Rejecting the views that Gog represented the Devil warring with God in the heavenly Jerusalem (Origen), or the Scythians sweeping across the Caucasus or the Goths ravaging the Christian world (Ambrose), he argued, on the basis of a far-fetched etymology, that the name designated the arrogant pseudo-knowledge that sets itself up against the truth—in a word, the arch-heretics.[60] As for the Temple, all its details and furnishings, all its measurements so lovingly described by the prophet, seemed to him so many veiled pointers to the manifold mysteries of the Christian revelation. A fascinating example is his discussion of 44, 2, which states that the eastern gate 'shall remain shut; it shall not be opened, and no one shall enter by it; for the Lord, the God of Israel, has entered by it'. This gate, he declared, signifies the Law and the Prophets, the knowledge of Scripture, which was a closed book before Christ's coming; or even (Jerome approves this highly, as did others at the time) the Virgin Mary, through whom the Lord God passed, and 'who remained a virgin both before giving birth and after giving birth'.[61]

This huge compilation shows no signs of declining vigour. Despite advancing years Jerome was at the height of his powers, writing with undiminished force and clarity, and embellishing his exposition with skilfully chosen quotations from the classics, especially his beloved Cicero and Vergil (some thirty lines).[62] Here and there we may perhaps overhear the first rumbling of renewed hostility to John of Jerusalem, for

[59] *Comm. on Ezekiel* VII prol. (*CCL* 75: 239-40).
[60] *Comm. on Ezekiel* 38 1 ff. (*CCL* 75: 444-8).
[61] *Comm. on Ezekiel* 44, 2 (*CCL* 75: 538). Note that Jerome still does not teach the virginity of Mary 'in partu': see above p. 106.
[62] Cf. the detailed analysis by H. Hagendahl, op. cit., 236-44.

in at least two passages he lashes out against clerics who lord it as pontiffs in spite of having compromised the faith in the past. The graphic picture of bishops lolling on their thrones, tasteless in their outpourings, rich and delicately living, seems to fit his conception of his old adversary, with whom he was soon to clash afresh.[63] But there are vivid touches about himself and his difficulties too. So preoccupied is he with the needs of the wretched refugees by day that he can only snatch time to work by night. His eyesight, he complains, is growing increasingly dim so that he cannot read his Hebrew books by lamp-light. Even by the light of day the small-ness of the letters prevents him from deciphering them. As for the Greek commentators, he confesses, he has to rely on brothers in the monastery to read them aloud to him. This he finds profoundly unsatisfactory, 'for everyone knows that food which has been chewed first by someone else's teeth nauseates the man who has to eat it'. But his unremitting toil brings him at least one consolation. His work by night provides some compensa-tion for the miseries of the day, and while he studies the sacred books his mind forgets the calamities of the age, which seem to portend the approaching end of the world.[64]

---

[63] *Comm. on Ezekiel* 44, 9 ff.; 48, 10 (*CCL* 75: 545; 606). After noticing these passages (also 34, 1 ff.: *CCL* 75: 410), I was glad to find my interpretation confirmed by Y. M. Duval, 'Sur les insinuations de Jérôme contre Jean de Jérusalem', *RHE* 65 (1970), 371–4.
[64] *Comm. on Ezekiel* VII prol.; VIII prol. (*CCL* 75: 239–40; 283–4).

XXVI

The Last Controversy

(i)

While Jerome was still wrestling with Ezekiel, a fresh stimulus to exasperation and controversy entered his life. This was the arrival in Palestine of the famous moralist-theologian Pelagius, a man deeply respected for his personal sanctity, but before long to be excommunicated as a pernicious heretic. Some twenty years earlier, when settled in Rome, Pelagius had incurred Jerome's ire by inveighing against his disparagement of marriage.[1] Since then he had grown greatly in reputation and influence as a teacher and counsellor, enjoying the friendship of leading Christians like Paulinus of Nola and the patronage of powerful families, including the most glittering of them all, the *gens Anicia*.[2] He was the author of a remarkable commentary on St Paul's Epistles, in which he had ventilated his characteristic ideas. In 409/10, however, accompanied by his nobly born, more combative disciple Caelestius, he had joined the flood of refugees from the threatened capital. In spring 411 the two landed at Hippo, in north Africa; then moved to Carthage, where Pelagius and Augustine once or twice glimpsed each other, but exchanged no words. Before many months, leaving Caelestius behind, Pelagius re-embarked and sailed eastwards, eventually reaching the Holy Land.[3]

Pelagius had no wish to be anything but strictly orthodox, strictly traditional. Appalled by the easy-going standards of conventional Christianity, he sought to impress on people what being an authentic Christian involves; every baptised person, he was sure, was called to total commitment. He rejected as Manichaean, as well as stultifying to endeavour, the notion that human nature has been corrupted by original sin transmitted from Adam, and can raise itself only by God's help. Although a habit of sinning has set in, a man is always free to shake it off, and by the exercise of his will to choose either right or wrong. Indeed, so far from there being

[1] See above pp. 187 f.
[2] Cf. P. Brown's perceptive articles 'Pelagius and his Supporters' and 'The Patrons of Pelagius' (*JTS* 19, 1968, 93–114; 21, 1970, 56–72): reprinted, with additions, in *Religion and Society in the Age of Saint Augustine* (London, 1972).
[3] For most of these details see Augustine, *De gest. Pel.* 22, 46. We do not know precisely when Pelagius arrived in Palestine; Augustine simply notes that 'he hastened away ... ad transmarina'.

any necessity of sinning, a man is in principle able to live without sin. Regarding sin as a voluntary act, he denied that new-born babies, who have no choice, can be guilty of it, yet he upheld the traditional practice of having them baptised. Assuredly men always need God's grace; but Pelagius defined grace, not as an inner power transforming them, but as their original endowment with rational will, the divine forgiveness they obtain through baptism, and the illumination provided by the law of Moses and the teaching and example of Christ.[4]

Pelagius's optimistic view of human nature, and his drastic narrowing down of God's supernatural help, were soon to be criticised, and were eventually rejected. So far, however, no suspicion of heresy touched him personally. It was the more headstrong, argumentative Caelestius who provoked a storm, calling in question the transmission of sin from Adam and the need of infants to be cleansed of it by baptism. In Africa at any rate these ideas were taken for granted, and when he was condemned at a synod at Carthage, probably late in 411,[5] he quitted the country. But this was by no means the end of the matter. The 'Pelagian' theses were being widely canvassed and were meeting with support. In 412 Augustine felt obliged to intervene, and began striking at them in letters, treatises, and sermons. His critique envisaged the views of Pelagius's disciples as well as of Pelagius himself, and until 415 he professed himself unable to believe that so good a Christian could hold them. Nevertheless, for all his tactful avoidance of confrontation, his awareness of Pelagius's responsibility is obvious, and comes out in the coolly polite note[6] he sent him in 412/13. Regard for Pelagius's exalted patrons, as well as respect for his person, may have made him hesitate to drag him into the debate at this stage.[7]

Meanwhile Pelagius was in Jerusalem, basking in the friendship of Jerome's *bête-noire*, Bishop John,[8] and making successful propaganda for his doctrines. Eastern theology, which traditionally stressed the importance of free will, was inclined to be more receptive of them than north Africa, and he found appreciative audiences which included many women.[9] At Bethlehem Jerome must have known of his presence in the Holy City,

---

[4] The best summary of Pelagius's teaching available in English is by R. F. Evans in *Pelagius: Inquiries and Reappraisals* (London, 1968), chap. 6.

[5] For the date see F. Refoulé, 'Datation du premier concile de Carthage contre les Pélagiens et du *Libellus fidei* de Rufin' (*Rev. études August.* 9, 1963, 41–9); he argues that the synod must have taken place after September 411.

[6] Augustine, *Ep.* 146. Cf. the unmistakable hint in the request that Pelagius should *pray* for him, that *the Lord may make him* the kind of person he (i.e. Pelagius) supposes him to be. I cannot agree with R. F. Evans (op. cit., 76) that the letter contains no 'double meanings'.

[7] So P. Brown, *Religion and Society in the Age of Saint Augustine*, 217.

[8] Augustine, writing in 416 (*Ep.* 179, 1), remarks that he hears that John is 'extremely fond' of Pelagius, and warns him not to be taken in by him.

[9] For his female supporters see Jerome, *Letter* 133, 4 and 11; *Dial. against the Pelagians* 1, 25; *Comm. on Jeremiah* 16, 1–4 (*CCL* 74: 951).

and received reports of his teaching, from the moment of his arrival. And from that very moment the old animosity between the two men seems to have flared up. We can sense it in Jerome's complaint,[10] penned as early as 412, that although the sea-serpent (i.e. Rufinus) had been blasted by God's hand, his progeny continue to rage against him. The reference is almost certainly to Pelagius, whom Jerome (as we shall discover) regarded as a disciple and spokesman of Rufinus. For the next three years his writings were to be full of vulgar abuse of Pelagius, sneers at his success with women (his 'Amazons'), caricatures of his figure and appearance, and the like.[11]

The bickering was certainly not one-sided. It is indeed evident that during these years Jerome was irritated and disturbed by the running fire Pelagius was directing at him. To be more precise, he was apparently reproaching Jerome, the notorious censor of Origen's errors, with having shamelessly cribbed from Origen in his *Commentary on Ephesians*. This may have been an astute tactic in self-defence, for Jerome persistently castigated him as an Origenist. In addition Pelagius was once again deploring Jerome's depreciation of marriage in his *Against Jovinian*.[12] His motive for reviving this hoary criticism is more obscure, but it is conceivable that the two men had clashed on the question of the remarriage of widows; in reply to the slur that he was a new Jovinian, Pelagius may have riposted that Jerome's views on marriage did not bear examination. In any case these were both stale charges, Jerome expostulated, which he had long ago satisfactorily disposed of. It was infamous that this 'dolt weighed down with Scots porridge', this 'big, bloated Alpine dog, able to rage more effectively with his heels than his teeth', should be regurgitating them as if they were his own.[13] Nevertheless, although he referred[14] Pelagius indignantly to his refutation of the former aspersion in his *Apology* and of the latter in Letter 49 to Pammachius, 'which Rome received with delight many years ago', his unease that they should be brought to public notice once again is painfully obvious.

(ii)

This was personal wrangling, but it reflected a serious disagreement on the theological level. From the start Jerome found certain features of Pelagius's programme objectionable, particularly his exaltation of free

[10] *Comm. on Ezekiel* VI prol. (*CCL* 75 : 197–8).

[11] For his women admirers see n. 9 above; for Pelagius's appearance see next paragraph.

[12] For the former charge see *Comm. on Jeremiah* prol.; 22, 24–7 (*CCL* 74: 835–6; 994); for the latter *Comm. on Jeremiah* prol.; 16, 1–4 (*CCL* 74: 835–6; 951). There is an excellent discussion, to which I am indebted, in R. F. Evans, op. cit., esp. 20 and 27 f.

[13] *Comm. on Jeremiah* prol.; III prol.; IV prol. (*CCL* 74: 835–6; 925–6; 967–8).

[14] *Comm. on Jeremiah* prol. (*CCL* 74: 835–6). For *Letter* 49 see above pp. 188 f.

will and his doctrine of the possibility of living without sin in this life. We may surmise that he kept himself informed of Pelagius's teaching at Jerusalem, and he seems to have been acquainted with the letters[15] in which he set it out. Two important documents, both dating from 414, show him joining issue with the British monk.

The first, Letter 130 to Demetrias, is one of his most impressive literary productions, and while glancing marginally though pointedly at Pelagius's ideas, merits examination in its own right. A teenage girl of the illustrious Anician family, Demetrias with her mother and grandmother (her father was already dead) had fled to north Africa in 410 after the sack of Rome. Here she fell under the influence of Augustine and Alypius and in 413, when preparations had been made for a splendid marriage, astonished the world—and her family, to which such a renunciation was a novelty—by dedicating herself to virginity and receiving the veil from Bishop Aurelius of Carthage. Whatever their real feelings in the matter, her mother and grandmother were resolved that the young nun should not lack proper guidance, and requested the foremost masters of the spiritual life, Pelagius (a trusted family friend) and Jerome (the renowned ascetic) to supply it.[16] Pelagius responded with alacrity, despatching an exhortation which was also a powerful exposition of his theology; he was making the most of this golden opportunity to present it in the best possible light in Carthage. Jerome, too, was flattered by the invitation. When it arrived, he was struggling to explain Ezekiel's description of the holy of holies and the altar of incense in the Temple.[17] He was overjoyed, he exclaimed with unctuous flattery, to turn aside for a moment from that altar to another altar, on which he might consecrate Demetrias, a living sacrifice without blemish, to eternal chastity.

Much of the letter is in the same fulsome, even for Jerome, extravagant vein. The struggle Demetrias had with herself in reaching her great resolve, and the exultation of her family once the decision was taken, are dramatically described. All the churches of Africa, Jerome claims, danced for joy, Italy put off her mourning, the calamities of the Gothic invasion seemed reversed. Even he, however, suspected that his adulation of the noble heiress and her family might be misinterpreted, for he defensively interjected,[18] 'My monkish cell, wretched food and foul clothing, my advanced age and the short portion remaining to me, exempt me from any charge of toadying.' When he at last came to practical advice, it

[15] *Dial. against the Pelagians* 2, 12; 3, 14.

[16] For this request cf. *Letter* 130, 1 (her grandmother and mother 'command', 'request', 'insistently require'); Pelagius, *Ad Dem.* 1 ('I write at the request, indeed at the command, of her mother . . . she insistently requires it of me . . . ') (*PL* 30, 16).

[17] So *Letter* 130, 2. The reference is to Ezek. 41, where Jerome (see his comments *ad loc.*) mistakenly took the 'altar of wood' (41, 22) to be the altar of incense.

[18] *Letter* 130, 7.

followed his stock pattern—constant study of Scripture, regular though moderate fasting, obedience to her mother and grandmother, avoidance of loose talk, laughter ('leave laughter to worldlings'), and the company of young men and married women, plenty of manual work, etc. When her mother died and she gained control of her fortune, she should not, like many rich Christians, spend it on building or decorating churches, but on helping the poor, the sick, the hungry, but especially (here he hinted at the needs of his monasteries at Bethlehem, in dire financial straits) communities of monks and nuns, 'servants of God . . . who while on earth reproduce the life of angels'.

Though often compared with Letter 22 to Eustochium, this famous piece (the last of its kind to come from Jerome's pen) is more temperate in its ascetic teaching, but also more artificial; for all his graphic descriptions, the writer knew Demetrias only by hearsay. One or two of its expressions, it is interesting to note, echo turns of phrase used by Pelagius in his parallel letter,[19] which Jerome had evidently read. More significantly, he went out of his way to put Demetrias on her guard against Origen's errors.[20] Pope Anastasius, he reminded her, had crushed the hissing sea-serpent, but rumour had it that its poisonous offshoots were still alive and active in certain quarters. Origenism was no menace at this time in Africa; he was thinking of Pelagius, the disciple (so he reckoned) of Origen and Rufinus. She must not listen to this impious teaching, however wise and ingenious it may be made to appear (a reference, we may guess, to Pelagius's persuasive letter). If she cared, he would gladly send her another work in which, with God's help, he was refuting it.[21]

Naturally Jerome did not mention Pelagius by name; he was well aware that the powerful Anicii were his protectors. But elsewhere in the letter his criticism was less oblique. 'Where there is grace,' he remarked,[22] 'this is not a reward for works done but the free gift of the giver, so that the Apostle's saying (Rom. 9, 16) is fulfilled, "It depends not on man's will or exertion, but on God's mercy." Certainly it belongs to us either to will or not to will. Nevertheless this liberty of ours is ours only by God's mercy.' Although Pelagius could have accepted this, it seems intended as a correction of his reiterated insistence[23] to Demetrias that the achievement of perfection rested entirely with her own decision.

---

[19] E.g. Jerome takes up Pelagius's 'Novum aliquid et inusitatum requirit, praecipuum ac singulare quoddam flagitat' (Ad Dem. 1: PL 30, 16), and re-writes it as, 'Neque enim ut novum quiddam et praecipuum a me flagitant . . .'.

[20] Letter 130, 16 ('I had almost omitted what is particularly important . . .').

[21] This 'other work' is often taken to be Letter 124, which is, however, a heavily biassed presentation of Origen's doctrines rather than a refutation of them. The reference is probably to Letter 133 to Ctesiphon, written about the same time or shortly before.

[22] Letter 130, 12.

[23] Cf. his Ad Dem. 3; 8; 11 (PL 30, 17 f.; 22 f.; 26 f.).

By contrast the second document, Letter 133 to Ctesiphon (written about the same time, or even shortly before),[24] was a direct attack on ideas Pelagius was propagating (the more sinister of them to esoteric groups, Jerome alleges)[25] at Jerusalem. Again Pelagius's name is deliberately avoided, but several times the 'esteemed professor', the 'teacher of perverse doctrines', is challenged to come into the open and defend his errors if he can.[26] We have no certain clue to Ctesiphon's identity, but Jerome's jibes at his 'religious, illustrious house' where the 'heretic' holds forth, and at people who supply him with money, suggest that he was one of Pelagius's wealthy lay supporters.[27] He had taken the initiative in writing to Jerome on Pelagius's behalf, apparently with the object of starting an amicable debate between the two men. But Jerome was in no mood for that. His reply was designed, as he freely admitted, to sting Pelagius into openly committing himself to positions which would compromise him.[28]

Letter 133 does not touch on original sin and the resulting need of infants for baptism. News of Caelestius's condemnation and of Augustine's early anti-Pelagian treatises had not yet percolated to Bethlehem, and Jerome does not seem at this stage to have been shocked by Pelagius's attitude to these issues. The two points on which he concentrated his fire were Pelagius's claim that a man, if he so wills, can live without sin, and his restrictive definition of grace. The former, he argued, was blasphemous since it implied man's equality with God; was confuted by the lives of the saints, none of whom was faultless, as well as by the unvarying teaching of Scripture (e.g. Rom. 3, 23: 'All have sinned etc.'); and was a shameless re-hash of the ultimately pagan theory of 'apathy', or the soul's ability to rise superior to the passions which normally disturb it. In its Christianised form this perverse notion, he pointed out, was traceable to Origen and had been developed by his disciple Evagrius Ponticus (made even worse in Jerome's eyes by his friendship with Rufinus's patroness, Melania the Elder, 'whose name attests the blackness of her perfidy'), whose works had been Latinised by none other than Rufinus.[29]

Orosius spoke of it as 'recent' at the Jerusalem conference in July 415; a date somewhere in 414 seems reasonable.
[25] Cf. *Letter* 133, 11 ('Preach publicly what you tell your disciples in secret. Your private apartments hear one doctrine, the ordinary crowd of Christians another'; etc.).
[26] For this challenge and these sneering titles see *Letter* 133, 11 and 12.
[27] *Letter* 133, 13. Cf. G. de Plinval, *Pélage: ses écrits, sa vie, et sa réforme* (Lausanne, 1943), 213: he plausibly identifies him with the 'Lentulus' of *Letter* 138 and the 'patronus et consors' of Pelagius of *Letter* 151, 1; also with 'the armour-bearer' who, according to Orosius (*Lib. apol.* 2, 5; 24, 3), does not himself fight but supports his 'Goliath' with his money.
[28] *Letter* 133, 11.
[29] *Letter* 133, 3. Evagrius (d. 399), born at Ibora in Pontus, lived for many years in the desert and was the founder of monastic mysticism. His ideas exerted a profound influence in both east and west (e.g. on John Cassian). He was condemned in 553 as an Origenist.

Furthermore, the presumptuous claim to sinlessness stemmed from the Pythagorean philosopher Xystus, whose collection of maxims Rufinus again had had the impudence not only to translate but to attribute to Sixtus II, the martyr bishop of Rome. It also had strong affinities with Jovinian's second proposition, viz. that 'those who with full faith have been born again in baptism cannot be overthrown by the Devil'.[30]

Turning to grace, Jerome brushed aside the Pelagians' plea that they made full allowance for it by pointing out that for them it denoted no more than free will itself and God's revealed law, and exposed the contradiction (as he saw it) in their claim on the one hand that man by his own efforts can be sinless, on the other that he can do nothing without grace.[31] Their doctrine, he protested, made nonsense of prayer, of fasting too and continence, since it implied that man needs no external supernatural aid.[32] This whole discussion is remarkable for its minute marshalling of Pelagian arguments, including fascinating specimens of the intricate dialectic they were deploying at Jerusalem.

Jerome promised a more detailed exposure of the heresy in a fuller subsequent work. Within its limits, however, Letter 133 is an effective controversial piece. Jerome, we should note, was crossing swords with Pelagius personally at least a year before Augustine was to do so.[33] Some of his allegations about Pelagius's intellectual ancestry were recklessly wide of the mark. There was no kinship, for example, between him and Manichaeism or Gnosticism,[34] but rather sharp antipathy. He was at fault, too, in equating Pelagius's doctrine of sinlessness ('impeccantia') with the Greek notion of 'apatheia'.[35] Nevertheless he was entirely right in detecting the influence of Origen, as mediated by Rufinus, in Pelagius's thinking. When preparing his *Expositions* of St Paul's Epistles (c. 405), Pelagius had drawn heavily on Rufinus's abbreviated paraphrase of Origen's *Commentary on Romans*, taking from it a whole range of what have come to be regarded as his distinctive ideas (e.g. the power of choice implanted by the Creator conceived of as grace, the paralysing effect of evil custom, the possibility of living without sin).[36] Jerome was also correct in pointing to the *Sentences of Sextus* as one of Pelagius's sources, although he was in error in contending that, in the form Pelagius knew it, this was a pagan

[30] See above pp. 181; 184.
[31] *Letter* 133, 5–8.
[32] *Letter* 133, 5.
[33] Augustine's first treatise directed specifically against Pelagius was his *De natura et gratia* of 415.
[34] As he asserts in *Letter* 133, 3.
[35] Pelagius showed that there was nothing in common between his doctrine of 'sinlessness' and the eastern notion of *apatheia*, since no sin attaches to evil thoughts that arise in the mind so long as the will rejects them (*Ep. ad Dem.* 26 f.; *Ad Cel.* 56).
[36] See the full discussion in T. Bohlin, *Die Theologie des Pelagius und ihre Genesis* (Uppsala-Wiesbaden, 1957), esp. 87–103.

Pythagorean work. In fact its author was a (probably) second-century thinker who adapted earlier pagan material but was himself a Christian.[37] More questionable is his branding of Pelagius as a disciple of Jovinian. In part this was a groundless slur, probably reflecting Jerome's outrage at being criticised for his denigration of marriage. In part, however, it sprang from his mistaken view that Pelagius's teaching on the possibility of being without sin was the equivalent of Jovinian's second proposition. It is in fact most unlikely that Pelagius would have felt any sympathy for that proposition, since it would seem to him to entail that the Christian man was incapable of sinning.[38]

(iii)

The letters to Demetrias and Ctesiphon were written while Jerome was immersed in his *Commentary on Ezekiel*. He was impatient, before he died, to tackle Jeremiah, the one prophet still outstanding.[39] He seems to have started work on him at the end of 414 or the beginning of 415.[40]

This last commentary presents certain interesting features. First, Jerome carried still further the tendency, noted in the commentaries on Isaiah and Ezekiel, to focus attention primarily on the Hebrew text. The Septuagint, he declared,[41] not only included matter which did not properly belong to the prophet (the Book of Baruch and the Epistle of Jeremy—in the English Bible placed among the Apocrypha), but its text had been corrupted by copyists, sometimes tendentiously.[42] Secondly, his denunciation of Origen, 'the insane allegorist',[43] is more open and fiercer than in any other commentary, and seems to extend beyond his 'errors' to his proficiency as a commentator (this reflects his detestation of the Pelagians, his supposed disciples). Thirdly, his exegesis has become predominantly historical; allegory and tropology take second place except where (e.g. at Jer. 11, 19 ff.: 'I was like a gentle lamb led to the slaughter . . . ') the Church's tradition demanded a Christological interpretation. This is to be explained, not by a revolution in his exegetical principles, but in part by the character of the material commented on, in part by the fact that he was

---

[37] On this see H. Chadwick, *The Sentences of Sextus*, Texts and Studies NS v (Cambridge, 1959). There is a useful summary and discussion in R. F. Evans, op. cit., chap. 4.

[38] See R. F. Evans's discussion, op. cit., 28–30. Cf. Pelagius's repudiation of Jovinian in his *Libellus fidei* 12 f. (sent to Pope Innocent in 417: *PL* 45, 1716–18).

[39] See his remarks in *Comm. on Ezekiel* xiv prol. (*CCL* 75: 561–2).

[40] When he wrote the preface to book iv of his *Comm. on Jeremiah*, he had not begun the *Dialogue against the Pelagians*, which (see below p. 319) we know he composed between summer 415 and the end of the year. See Cavallera ii, 55.

[41] *Comm. on Jeremiah* prol. (*CCL* 74: 833–4).

[42] E.g. at Jerem. 17, 1–4, which he alleges the LXX omitted out of consideration for the feelings of the Jews (*CCL* 74: 956–7).

[43] For this expression (or its like) see *Comm. on Jeremiah* 24, 1–10; 25, 26; 27, 9–11; 28, 12–14 (*CCL* 74: 1012; 1020; 1033; 1039).

writing for his ambiguous friend Eusebius of Cremona, who preferred literal exegesis.[44] Finally, the commentary is remarkable for the continuous, remorseless polemic it wages against Pelagius and his allies. Time and again Jerome reiterates that their new heresy is only a revival of the heresies of Origen, Jovinian, and Rufinus (it is 'the dung of Grunnius's family'). As in Letter 133, it is their exaltation of free will at the expense of God's grace, and their arrogant claim that perfection is attainable in this life, that he singles out for attack.[45]

Jerome was destined never to complete this last commentary. From the outset he could work on it only in the intervals snatched from ministering to refugees and supervising his monastery.[46] But an increasingly serious cause of interruption was his involvement with the Pelagian affair.

(iv)

His involvement became intensified when, in spring or early summer 415, a Spanish priest, Paul Orosius, arrived from north Africa and took up residence in his monastery. This talented, opinionated, narrowly orthodox, impetuous young man had been staying with Augustine at Hippo, battering him with theological conundrums, and the bishop had advised him to seek a solution from Jerome.[47] He brought two letters for Jerome, each virtually a small treatise.[48] In one Augustine confessed his perplexity about the origin of the soul: is each man's soul created by God at his conception, or is it transmitted from his parents and so, ultimately, from Adam? He understood that Jerome was inclined to the former view (creationism):[49] but how was it to be reconciled with original sin and the need of children for baptism—tenets 'believed by the entire Church'? In the second he sought Jerome's views on the text (James 2, 10), 'Whoever keeps the whole law but fails in one point has become guilty of all of it.'

Neither letter so much as breathed Pelagius's name, but both raised issues which the Pelagian debates had brought into the limelight. It was urgently necessary, in view of Pelagius's dismissal of original sin, to have a

[44] He refers to this preference in the Prologue, expressing the hope that, since he has supplied only 'the warp and woof', Eusebius will himself weave it into 'a resplendent garment', i.e. will work out the higher spiritual meanings. Cf. the sensible remarks of A. Penna, *Principi e carattere dell'esegesi di S. Gerolamo* (Rome, 1950), 38 f.

[45] For 'Grunnianae familiae stercora' see *Comm. on Jeremiah* 29, 14–20 (*CCL* 74: 1047). R. F. Evans (op. cit., 126 n. 9) has conveniently listed twenty-two passages (the number could be increased) from the body of the commentary in which points of Pelagian teaching are attacked.

[46] Cf. *Comm. on Jeremiah* iv prol. (*CCL* 74: 965–6).

[47] Orosius, *Lib. apol.* 3, 2; Augustine, *Letter* 166, 2.

[48] *Letters* 166 and 167 in Augustine's collection, *Letters* 131 and 132 in Jerome's.

[49] Jerome shows himself decidedly creationist in *Comm. on Ecclesiastes* 12, 7; in *Apology* 2, 8–10 and *Letter* 126, 1 he does not come down clearly on either side.

doctrine of the soul's origin which was consistent with it. Pelagius, again, was emphasising that all God's commandments must be observed without exception, citing James 2, 10 as his authority.[50] It was tempting, though a grave error, to equate this (as Augustine does in the letter) with the Stoic notion of the equality of sins. Augustine's sending of Orosius 'to sit at Jerome's feet' was thus a deliberate move in the controversy; we need not doubt that he was anxious to alert the church at Jerusalem, where Pelagius was being hospitably entertained, and Jerome in particular to the dangers of the new movement. Orosius's baggage, it seems clear, contained copies of Augustine's anti-Pelagian treatises to date[51] (including *On Nature and Grace*, completed early in 415 and aimed specifically at Pelagius). The courier himself was only too eager to give a circumstantial account of Caelestius's condemnation and of the dismay which the Pelagian ideas were causing in Africa.

Aggressive and tactless (we need not take literally his claim[52] to have 'lain in obscurity at Bethlehem, an unknown, penniless stranger'), Orosius soon had Jerusalem in a fever of excitement. Bishop John deemed it advisable to hold an informal conference on 28 July, with both Orosius and Pelagius present, to investigate the matter. Orosius recounted what had happened in Africa and asserted that Pelagius's theses had been refuted by Augustine, and also by Jerome both in his Letter to Ctesiphon and in a treatise he was currently preparing.[53] Pelagius, however, skilfully turned the tables on his accuser, and although the meeting reached no decision was effectively vindicated. Towards the end of December, a formal charge having been lodged against him, he was summoned before a synod of fourteen bishops, presided over by the metropolitan of Palestine, at Diospolis (Lydda, now Lod), and once again was able to clear himself, though only by producing judicious explanations of his position and making certain real concessions. The synod pronounced him to be in full communion with the Catholic Church.[54] Jerome was not present at either gathering, but with Orosius as his guest could not fail to be a deeply concerned spectator. Little wonder that (as he confessed to Augustine early in 416)[55] he found this 'an extremely trying time, when it was better for me to keep silence than to speak, so much so that serious

---

[50] Cf. *Dialogue against the Pelagians* 1, 19: also Pelagius, *De virg.* 7 (*CSEL* 1, 232 f.); *Expos. in Gal.* 3, 10 (Souter, 319). What Pelagius really meant was that, while sins differ in heinousness, one should be as much on one's guard against committing a slight one as a serious one (see his *Ep. ad Cel.* 6: *CSEL* 56, 334).

[51] He himself reports (*Lib. apol.* 3) that he had brought Augustine's letter to Hilary of Syracuse (*Letter* 157). It was probably he who furnished Jerome with copies of *De pecc. merit. et remiss. peccat.*, *De sp. et litt.*, and *De nat. et grat.* (see *Dial. against Pelag.* 3, 19).

[52] *Lib. apol.* 3, 2.

[53] *Lib. apol.* 4.

[54] Augustine, *De gest. Pel.* 20, 44.

[55] *Letter* 134, 1 (the letter which Orosius carried back to Hippo).

study had to cease and speech degenerated (in Appius's phrase) into the snarling of dogs'.

These excitements apart, Jerome was occupied with his *Dialogue against the Pelagians* (the fuller treatise which he had promised in the Letter to Ctesiphon, and to which Orosius had referred at the Jerusalem conference) from at any rate early summer 415 till the close of the year.[56] As its title implies, this takes the form of a quasi-Socratic dialogue between Atticus, the exponent of the orthodox (i.e. Jerome's) standpoint, and the Pelagian Critobulus, the object being to set the opposed cases out fairly.[57] Though aggressive in tone and replete with blustering rhetoric and exaggeration, the treatise is relatively temperate by Jerome's controversial standards. Not that this prevented him from caricaturing Pelagius's heavy build, his (quite imaginary) smugness at being free from sin, and the hold he had over women through specious flattery.[58] Nor did he stick slavishly to the dialogue form; most of Book II, for example, consists of a massive string of texts assembled by Atticus to demonstrate the universality of sin. Even so, Critobulus is no paper disputant, but comes out with spirited answers and questions which, in the great majority of cases, accurately reproduce Pelagian positions—and which deserve something better than the cavalier treatment they all too often receive. The treatise has the subsidiary value of incorporating copious excerpts of a book in which Pelagius buttressed his theses with quotations from Scripture.[59]

In substance the *Dialogue* falls short of being 'the spiritual bludgeon' with which Jerome meant to clobber the British monk.[60] In the prologue he repeats his fallacious equation of the Pelagian ideal of sinlessness with the Stoic/Origenistic 'apathy', or detachment from the passions. In the first two books he is chiefly concerned with the Pelagians' conception of grace, their claim that a man can live without sin, and the critical analysis of statements extracted from the book just mentioned. The discussion of grace is superficial and inconclusive; Atticus does little more than affirm the need for divine help in every action. Although Critobulus protests that the perfection the Pelagians envisage is a relative one adapted to the human condition, Atticus brushes this aside and credits them, quite unfairly, with postulating an absolute perfection which would make man the equal of God. The proposition 'Men are governed by their own free

---

[56] Orosius (*Lib. apol.* 4) supplies the former date, Jerome the latter in *Letter* 134, 1 (where he states that he 'recently published' the *Dialogue*).

[57] Cf. *Dialogue* prol. 1, 1.

[58] *Dialogue* 1, 28; 3, 16 (heavy shoulders; tortoise-like gait); 1, 28; 2, 24 f. (thinks himself sinless, immune from temptation); 1, 25; 2, 24; 3, 14 and 16 (his 'Amazons'; his blasphemous flattery of Juliana).

[59] Cf. *Dialogue* 1, 25-32 in great part. The lost work is the *Testimoniorum seu eclogarum liber*. Cf. Gennadius, *De script. eccl.* 42 (*PL* 58, 1083).

[60] *Comm. on Jeremiah* III prol. (*CCL* 74: 925–6): 'spiritali percutiendus est clava'.

will' is slickly refuted by texts like 'I came not to do my own will but the will of him who sent me', and 'One can easily fulfil God's commandments if one so wills' by the sheer impossibility of finding a man who has actually kept God's law perfectly.[61] Scripture is emphatic, Atticus maintains with the support of an avalanche of texts, that all men are prone to sin, and that all the saints of the old and new dispensations were without exception marred by some fault. In his zeal to prove this Jerome contends that even Jesus's will was defective; he had need of God's help, said one thing and did another, and showed irresolution.[62] Pelagius was later to get his own back by pouncing on these rash admissions.[63]

In the third book Jerome raises issues which Letter 133 had either not touched on or merely glanced at. Thus the Pelagians set great store by the release from sin conferred by baptism and the resulting possibility of a completely new start. Atticus objected that this was simply to revive Jovinian's second proposition,[64] referred Critobulus to that heretic's official condemnation, and bluntly asserted that while baptism washes away past sins, it cannot guarantee good behaviour in the future—thereby missing the point, since Critobulus had not insisted that it did. The question of predestination then cropped up. Atticus's emphasis on the need for divine help in everything a man does seemed to Critobulus to abolish free will and make God responsible. Atticus responded that, while God foreknows whatever men will do, his foreknowledge in no way determines their actions; rather he leaves them free to act by the exercise of their free will.[65] Finally, Jerome came to grips with an aspect of Pelagian teaching which he had neglected hitherto, the need of infants to be baptised. It was Orosius, armed with Augustine's treatises, who had thrust this problem on his attention. When Critobulus protested, 'What sin are they guilty of?', Atticus replied that all men without exception, even children who have not willed a sinful act, are implicated in the guilt of Adam. This was a novel departure for Jerome, for while he had always been certain of the universality of human sinning, he had never regarded it as a direct inheritance of Adam's transgression; indeed such an idea was excluded by his belief that each man's soul is created at his birth. It was Augustine who had converted him to the strict doctrine of original sin. Very fittingly, therefore, he abstained from elaborating a theme for which he was ill prepared, and through Atticus referred his readers to the

[61] *Dialogue* 1, 27; 32 ff.
[62] *Dialogue* 2, 14; 16; 17.
[63] Cf. e.g. his *Libellus fidei* 10 and 11 (PL 45, 1718), where he castigates the notions that God's commands are impossible of fulfilment by men, and that the Son of God lied and was unable to accomplish what he wished.
[64] See above p. 181 and p. 315. He had merely mentioned this in *Letter* 133, 3, without developing the point.
[65] *Dialogue* 3, 5 f. For the same teaching see *Comm. on Jeremiah* 26, 1–3 (*CCL* 74: 1025).

treatises in which Augustine, 'that holy and eloquent bishop', had expounded it, and which he had recently received from Orosius.[66]

(v)

Jerome had scarcely completed the *Dialogue* when the synod of Diospolis met and, taken in by his astute though doubtfully honest manoeuvres, pronounced Pelagius orthodox. For a few months the sun was to shine on the heretic. Orosius must have found the atmosphere at Jerusalem distinctly uncongenial, and so went back to Africa as soon as the sea-routes re-opened in 416. He carried with him a short letter from Jerome to Augustine.[67]

This letter is a most revealing one. The first to be despatched by Jerome to Augustine since their unhappy wrangle a dozen years back, it glows with the immense respect and affection the aged monk had come to feel for the now commanding champion of orthodoxy. The frictions of the past have been laid aside and forgotten: 'It is my resolve to love you, look up to you, reverence and admire you, defend your words as if they were my own.' The letter has an additional personal interest in that we learn from it that Jerome and Eustochium are no longer alone. Paula, the daughter of Laeta and grand-daughter of the elder Paula, a girl of around sixteen, is now with them in Bethlehem and joins in sending greetings. We are nowhere told when she had arrived, but it is a plausible conjecture that, like so many other wealthy aristocrats, she had left Italy after the sack of the capital in 410 and had found her way by stages to her aunt's convent in the Holy Land.

Jerome's chief object in writing was to explain his failure to reply to Augustine's two searching letters inviting his views on the soul's origin and the correct interpretation of James 2, 10. He excused himself by the distractions of the Pelagian debate in Palestine ever since Orosius's arrival there. But the real reason lay elsewhere: partly (one suspects) in the sheer difficulty he found in treating speculative theological issues on which the Church had given no clear ruling, partly in the fear (we can detect this, reading between the lines) that he and Augustine might find themselves adopting different solutions, e.g. on the origin of souls. The heretics, he remarked, would be sure to make capital out of any divergence of opinion between them. Finally, after mentioning his recently published *Dialogue* and its complimentary references to Augustine, Jerome denounced the evasive double-talk of the Pelagians, by which alone (as shown at Diaspolis) they managed to maintain their platform in the Church.

Jerome's direct involvement in the Pelagian affair was now at an end.

[66] *Dialogue* 3, 19.
[67] *Letter* 134 (*Letter* 172 in Augustine's collection).

But before very long, used as he was to pamphlet warfare in which no quarter was given, he found himself exposed without warning to physical attack. At some unknown date in 416 a mob of hooligans set upon the Latin monasteries at Bethlehem; their buildings were destroyed by fire, their male and female inmates were brutally assaulted, a deacon was murdered. Jerome himself, presumably with Eustochium and the younger Paula, was able to escape only by fleeing to a fortified tower built as a refuge from Bedouin raids.[68] We have no certain knowledge who the marauders were. Pope Innocent expressly states that, when the two noble ladies wrote to him deploring the incident, they refrained from mentioning the guilty parties or their motives. Jerome, too, to the pope's disappointment, was equally unforthcoming.[69] But suspicion was quick to fall on Pelagius; the rabble were his supporters, and the murderous foray was their vengeance for Jerome's persistent hostility to his teaching. It is unconceivable that Pelagius himself should have been implicated; such a dastardly act was totally out of keeping with his character and style. But it would be quite understandable that fanatical, undisciplined partisans of his, scenting blood after his triumph at Diospolis, should resort to mob violence against the cantankerous, unpopular old monk who had so mercilessly lambasted their leader with his pen and his tongue.[70]

The news sent a shudder of horror through the west. Jerome was now revered as a luminary of Latin Christianity, while Eustochium and Paula were closely linked with the greatest patrician families at Rome. When it reached Augustine at Hippo, he immediately penned a furious paragraph noting that 'the gang of ruffians' were alleged to be backers of Pelagius, and calling for their summary punishment by the bishops on the spot or in the vicinity.[71] Pope Innocent, who had been informed both by Aurelius of Carthage (whom Jerome had requested to get into touch with him) and directly by Eustochium and Paula, was quick to exploit the welcome opportunity for asserting the papal supremacy in the east.[72] To Jerome he wrote expressing shocked sympathy and assuring him that he had set 'the authority of the holy see' in motion to crush the evil. If Jerome would only come out with specific accusations against particular individuals, he would take whatever judicial, or even more drastic, action was necessary. About the same time, as he informed Jerome, he despatched a blistering rebuke to his 'greatly esteemed brother', John of Jerusalem, who (although Innocent

[68] For the events see Augustine, *De gest. Pel.* 66 (written shortly afterwards).

[69] Cf. Innocent's letters to John of Jerusalem and to Jerome (137 and 136 in Jerome's collection).

[70] G. de Plinval's playing down of the 'bagarre' (op. cit., 306–8: 'il y avait plus de peur que de mal') and of the implication of Pelagius's supporters in it is hard to understand.

[71] *De gest. Pel.* 66. He had just completed the book with a summary of the synod of Diospolis, and added this as a postscript.

[72] *Letters* 136 and 137 in Jerome's collection.

could not be aware of the fact) was already probably dead. The identity of the culprit, he declared, was no mystery to anyone, but John should have taken more efficient precautions for the safety of his flock instead of by his negligence encouraging evil-doers to make havoc of it. He stood condemned as a bishop that such an atrocity should have been perpetrated in his diocese, and as a pastor that he should have been so behindhand in providing help and consolation to the noble victims. He had better bestir himself to correct and repress the barbarities that had been reported, or he might find himself called upon to account for his failure to act.

Certain pointers suggest that the menacing atmosphere continued for some time after the raid itself. According to the pope in his letter to John, Eustochium and Paula were complaining that their present fears were even greater than the sufferings they had already had to bear. Then Jerome and Eustochium, for a period at any rate, were obliged to leave their monasteries, and this not simply because the fabric was devastated but because they were confronted with an unacceptable choice. 'For myself,' he was to write in 417 to his friend Riparius, 'I have thought it better to change my locality than the truth of the faith, and to lose my pleasant home and residence rather than be polluted by intercourse with people to whom I should have to make concessions—or else fight it out with them with the sword.' In much the same language he was to record that Eustochium had preferred to abandon her possessions and abode rather than associate with heretics.[73] The obvious implication of this is that pressure had been put upon them, possibly by the provincial authorities,[74] either to desist from controversy or to get out. Although no charge was brought against Pelagius, similar pressure seems to have been put upon him. At any rate Jerome had the satisfaction of being able to report to Riparius, in the same letter, that the heretic had been driven not only out of Jerusalem but out of Palestine itself; the only pity was that allies and abettors of his still lingered at Jaffa.

There are obscurities, both about the raid on the monasteries and about its aftermath, which have so far not been convincingly cleared up. But it must have gladdened Jerome's heart to know that Pope Innocent was firmly on his side and had been moved to deliver a shattering admonition to Bishop John.

[73] *Letters* 138; 154, 2.
[74] So G. de Plinval, op. cit., 308.

XXVII

The Curtain Falls

(i)

The two or three remaining years of Jerome's life are hidden behind a wall of silence which is broken only by a handful of short, fortunately revealing letters. Although these do not disclose where he and his monastic companions lived for much of this period, they make it clear that they were back at Bethlehem, possibly in reconstructed parts of the monasteries, at any rate by early 419.[1] One assured fact, however, which stands out from all of them is Jerome's unceasing, obsessional preoccupation with the menace of Pelagianism. He took no active part in the controversy personally, but from the sidelines was watching with mounting concern the fluctuating fortunes of the Pelagian party.

The pendulum was certainly swinging dramatically to and fro for it. At Diospolis Pelagius had out-manoeuvred his accusers and emerged vindicated. Before a year was out the African episcopate, consternated by what they took to be a slap in the face after their censure of Caelestius, closed ranks and condemned his and his aggressive disciple's teaching as an abominable error.[2] They simultaneously appealed to Pope Innocent I to add the anathema of the holy see to theirs. This Innocent did on 27 January 417, pronouncing the two leaders, and anyone agreeing with them, excommunicate until they should discard their pernicious opinions.[3] Within a few weeks, however, he was dead, and the new pope, Zosimus (March 417–December 418), for a time turned his predecessor's policy upside down. Impressed by Caelestius personally, impressed too by the profession of faith Pelagius had submitted and by a glowing testimonial in his favour furnished by Praylius, the new bishop of Jerusalem, he recognised Pelagius's entire orthodoxy at a Roman synod in mid-September 417, and wrote sharply to the African bishops rebuking them for their precipitancy.[4] Finally, after a winter of anguish but furious activity for

---

[1] Cf. *Letter* 143, 2: 'has litterulas de sancta Bethleem . . .'. Written after Eustochium's death, it must date from spring or summer 419 (see Cavallera II, 50).

[2] For the synods of Carthage and Milevum see Augustine, *Epp.* 175 and 176, which refer the matter to the pope.

[3] *Ep.* 182, 6 in Augustine's correspondence. See also *Epp.* 181 and 183.

[4] Cf. his two letters, *Magnum pondus* and *Postquam a nobis*, to Aurelian and the African bishops respectively (*PL* 45, 1719–23).

Augustine and his friends, the situation was once again reversed. In spring and early summer 418 the Pelagian leaders found themselves and their teaching proscribed by the government,[5] and anathematised not only by an African plenary council but, after a remarkable volte-face, by Zosimus.[6]

Just occasionally we catch a glimpse of Jerome's reaction to these exciting events. Late in 417, when congratulating his friend Riparius (with whom he was exchanging letters on an annual basis) on the fight he was putting up for the Catholic faith, he notes anxiously that 'the winds are contrary', and that 'people who ought to have been the world's champions are backing the cause of perdition'—an allusion to the indulgence being shown by Pope Zosimus and others at Rome to the heretics.[7] In Palestine, he reports with satisfaction, Pelagius has been forced to leave not only Jerusalem but the entire province, although regrettably many of his fellow-conspirators still linger at Jaffa. He himself has chosen to leave his home rather than make any compromise.[8] Early next year (418) we find him ecstatically applauding[9] Augustine's resolute opposition to current moves to rehabilitate Pelagius; again Zosimus is the unnamed culprit. 'Well done! Your fame resounds throughout the world. Catholics venerate you as the restorer of their ancient faith . . . while (a token of even greater glory) the heretics to a man detest you.' Not to be left out himself, he continues, 'Me too they are pursuing with identical hatred, seeking to destroy me with their prayers since they cannot kill me with their swords' (a reference to the abortive attack on his monastery).

We have a second letter to Augustine from 418, written a little later when Zosimus had published his *Epistula tractoria* outlawing Pelagianism and the cause dear to Jerome's heart had officially triumphed. It is a mere fragment[10] which shows him grumbling against people 'who are lame in both feet and refuse to bow their heads even when their necks are broken, who cling to their old errors even when they have lost the freedom to proclaim them'. In elaboration of this enigmatic statement he adds that 'captive Jerusalem is in the hands of Nebuchadrezzar, and refuses to listen to Jeremiah's advice'. The most plausible interpretation of this is that Jerome, who casts himself in the role of the prophet, is complaining of the attitude of his near neighbour Praylius, bishop of Jerusalem (416–25) in

---

[5] For the two exceptionally severe constitutions see *PL* 48, 379–86 and 392–4.

[6] In his *Epistula tractoria*, now largely lost. See Marius Mercator, *Common.* 1, 5; 3, 1 (*PL* 48, 77–83; 90–5).

[7] *Letter* 138. Riparius is probably the man of that name to whom Jerome sent *Letter* 109 (see above pp. 286 f.) in 404 and his *Against Vigilantius* in 406. For this identification see Cavallera 1, 333 n. 2. For his annual exchange of letters with Jerome see *Letter* 151, 2 ('per singulos annos').

[8] G. de Plinval (*Pélage*, Lausanne, 1943, 308) is probably right in detecting here a reference to the events following the raid on the monasteries: see above p. 323.

[9] *Letter* 141. Note the expression 'contra flantes ventos', almost identical with 'ventos . . . contrarios' of *Letter* 138.

[10] *Letter* 142. Jerome's reference is to Jeremiah 43.

succession to John, for long an active supporter of Pelagius, although he
was eventually to abandon him.[11]

Even after the full weight of Church and state had moved against
Pelagianism, Jerome was to continue suspicious and vigilant, bitterly
hostile to any compromise with the heretics. The fact was that, though
struck down, the movement was far from dead. In many regions in the
west it had sympathisers who found the doctrines of original sin and grace
as defined by Zosimus and the African episcopate novel and unpalatable,
and a group of eighteen Italian bishops, brilliantly led by Julian, the able
young bishop of Eclanum (in Apulia), at once leapt to its defence. Thus
late in 418, writing to Apronius,[12] Jerome voiced his distress that a noble
house had gone over to the Pelagian side. What made it worse, the people
involved were friends, and he himself deserved God's wrath for harbour-
ing his foes. He advised his correspondent to come to Palestine, especially
to the Holy Places. Here at least everything was quiet, and though the
heretics were still as poisonous as ever they dared not open their mouths.
About the same time he wrote again,[13] somewhat overconfidently perhaps,
to Riparius, bidding him not to be too greatly worried by Julian, Pelagius,
Caelestius, and the bishops who had declared themselves for the heresy.
He had not read their writings (they were men lacking intelligence,
literary gifts, and knowledge of Scripture), but if they should come into his
hands he would demolish their laborious efforts (he was a match for the
drivel they wrote) with a single short pamphlet. Riparius was pressing
him to produce a full-size polemical treatise. This, he pleaded, was too
heavy a burden for an old war-horse like himself. 'My intellectual sharpness and my physical vigour have all but deserted me, worn down as I
am by continuous illnesses.'

(ii)

Meanwhile the *Commentary on Jeremiah*,[14] which was to be the coping-
stone of Jerome's exposition of the prophets, had come to a complete

[11] Praylius finally turned against Pelagius when the latter had been condemned and banished
from the Holy Places by a synod presided over by Bishop Theodotus of Antioch (Marius
Mercator, *Common.* 3, 5 : PL 48, 100 f.; Mansi, *Sacr. concil. coll.* IV, 475 f.). Its date is unknown.
Cf. De Plinval, op. cit., 329 n. 1.

[12] *Letter* 139. The date seems broadly fixed because the letter falls between the official pro-
scription of Pelagianism and Eustochium's death. Some conjecture that the 'noble house' (cf.
the parallel expression in *Letter* 133, 13) may be that of Ctesiphon (see above p. 314).

[13] *Letter* 152. Notice the identical phrase 'fidei calore ferventem' in both letters. D. de
Bruyne, who discovered this letter (RB 27, 1910, 1–11), dated it to the summer of 419, making
it contemporary with *Letter* 153 (to Pope Boniface). But Cavallera (II, 61) rightly pointed out
that by that date Jerome could not have been ignorant (cf. '... eorum scriptis, quae ignoro ...')
of the writings of Julian and his allies. Nor, it may be added, is it likely that he would then have
treated them in such a cavalier manner.

[14] See above pp. 316 f.

stop. From the start his work on it had been interrupted by distractions of different kinds, but it must have been brought to a halt by the assault on the monastery. We can only speculate why it was never resumed. His temporary quarters may not have lent themselves to study and composition; the atmosphere of persecution and harrying in which he lived for a year or two cannot have helped. It is more than likely, too, that his richly stocked library, on which he inevitably relied, went up in flames with the buildings in which it was housed. When more stable conditions returned, he was rapidly ageing, subject to serious illness, and the sustained effort required for concentrated work may have been too much for him.[15] It is significant that, while his letters during these years sparkle with the old vigour and pungency, they are all brief notes, hardly more than a paragraph long. Whatever the cause, the commentary that has come down is a torso, covering only thirty-two of Jeremiah's fifty-two chapters, with Lamentations (which he had intended[16] it to embrace) completely untouched. The loss is regrettable, for with its predominantly historical treatment and avoidance of allegorical extravagances this promised to be (by modern standards at any rate) one of Jerome's most satisfying exegetical achievements.

The letters breathe no word about the commentary. Most fortunately, however, they yield two precious glimpses of the personal affairs of Jerome and his devoted circle (that the community had remained intact is clear from his references[17] to 'the brothers who are with me'). First, there arrived in Jerusalem, probably around 417, Melania the Younger, her husband Pinianus, and her mother Albina. This Melania was the granddaughter of Melania the Elder, the aristocratic, strong-minded lady who had been Rufinus's close friend and patroness, thereby earning not only Jerome's dislike and enmity but the lash of his spiteful tongue.[18] As a girl of fourteen the younger Melania had been obliged to marry her cousin Valerius Pinianus, but after the death of their two infant children the couple had decided to live together in perfect chastity and, flouting the shocked disapproval of high society, to dispose of their enormous fortune. Before the siege of Rome, along with her mother, they had accompanied Rufinus, fleeing from Italy before the advancing barbarians, and had been with him when he died in Sicily in 410. For seven years[19] they had stayed

[15] Cf. his remarks in *Letter* 152 (quoted above) about a full-size work being too heavy a burden for an old man, and about the fading of his intellectual powers.

[16] Cf. *Comm. on Ezekiel* prol. (*CCL* 75 : 3–4).

[17] *Letters* 138; 151, 3.

[18] For her relations with Rufinus see above pp. 121; 200. We recall that Jerome spitefully expunged his complimentary references to her from his *Chronicle* (see above p. 251), and had recently insulted her in *Letter* 133, 3 (see above p. 314).

[19] For this seven years' stay, so important for the dating of their moves, see *Vit. Mel.* 34 (Greek text: ed. D. Gorce, 190).

in Africa, gladly accepting Augustine and Alypius as their spiritual mentors and continuing their lavish charitable works. Then, like so many others, they journeyed on to the Holy Land, where for the rest of their lives, apart from visits to the desert monks in Egypt and to Constantinople, they made Jerusalem their home.

One would not have expected much love to be lost between Jerome and this earnestly eccentric group. Not only did they belong to a circle in which Rufinus had been honoured and loved, but in 404 they had hospitably put up the eastern delegation which had come to Rome to enlist support for John Chrysostom.[20] Their family and they also counted amongst Pelagius's patrons and sympathisers, and in 418, when the sentence of excommunication descended upon him, Melania, Pinianus, and Albina were discussing the situation with him in Jerusalem, trying to persuade him to renounce the doctrines attributed to him, and in fact extracting important admissions from him (which, however, did not satisfy Augustine).[21] It is remarkable, however, that they seem to have cherished no ill feelings for Jerome, nor he (this is perhaps more surprising) for them. When he wrote to Augustine and Alypius in 419, they were staying with him, apparently in complete amity, at Bethlehem, and he joined their greetings with his own.[22]

The other glimpse the letters afford us of Jerome's personal affairs is, by contrast, a poignant one. Towards the end of 418 or the beginning of 419 Eustochium died. She can hardly have been much more than fifty, and her death was sudden. For Jerome it was a crushing blow. She had been his spiritual daughter *par excellence*, the virgin whose piety, studies, and consecrated life he had lovingly directed ever since those far-off days in Rome in the 380s. Since her mother Paula's death in 404 she had been his closest companion, the mainstay both of himself and of the convent for women. In every letter from now onwards there is a mention of her, direct or indirect; he makes no attempt to conceal his grief. 'I have been saddened beyond measure,' he exclaimed to Riparius,[23] 'by Eustochium's unexpected passing; it has virtually altered the whole tenor of my existence.' To Alypius and Augustine he wrote,[24] 'Forlorn and wretched, your daughter Paula begs you to remember her': a sentence which mirrors the desolation of the entire bereaved community, in which the teenage girl would now have to shoulder responsibilities beyond her years. Yet pride was mingled with his sorrow when he recalled Eustochium's heroism in the period of harassment since the raid on his monastery: 'She died in the

---

[20] Palladius, *Hist. Laus.* 61. Cf. the interesting remarks of P. Brown, *Religion and Society in the Age of Augustine* (London, 1972), 214–16.

[21] Cf. his *De gratia Christi et de pecc. orig.* 1, 2.

[22] *Letter* 143, 2.

[23] *Letter* 151, 2 (this is the sole source from which we learn that her death was 'repentina').

[24] *Letter* 143, 2.

very act of joyfully witnessing to Christ, for she preferred to abandon both her patrimony and her home and to undergo honourable exile rather than be polluted by intercourse with heretics.'

(iii)

After Eustochium's death Jerome continued his correspondence with the west for several months. Letters have come down addressed to his friend Riparius, to Alypius and Augustine, to Pope Boniface, and to Donatus (otherwise unknown). Each uncovers some facet of his changing moods, some detail of his life and interests.

The first[25] shows him depressed and worried. Depressed not only by his bereavement, which his language suggests is recent, but also by the burden of years: 'I just cannot do many things I want to do, for the feebleness of old age undermines my mental energies.' Worried too because, although he knows Riparius has struggled bravely and successfully against them, the Pelagians are still influential in Gaul, in Italy, in Jerusalem itself. In the warm, affectionate letter[26] to Alypius and Augustine he is more cheerful: through their efforts the heresy of Caelestius has been finally silenced. They had inquired whether he has prepared a rejoinder to a pamphlet which Annianus, the Pelagian translator of Chrysostom's homilies, had recently published attacking his Letter to Ctesiphon. Jerome admits that he has been sent a copy in loose sheets by Eusebius of Cremona (never behindhand in supplying documents of the sort) but, upset as he has been by illness and grief, has judged it contemptible stuff. However, if God grants him life and he can muster enough stenographers, he will rush off a refutation of his 'nonsensical puerilities' in next to no time. But Augustine would do the job better than he could. Here for the first time we observe the indomitable fighter hinting that he would prefer to pass the burden to another.

The third[27] is a reply to a letter from the new pope, Boniface (December 418–September 422), announcing his election. On Zosimus's death in December 418 two popes, Boniface and Eulalius, had been separately elected, and disputed the papal throne for some months. After intervention by the government Boniface's title was eventually recognised, and he made his formal entry into Rome on 10 April 419. He and Jerome, the letter implies, had known each other, though not intimately, long ago;

---

[25] *Letter* 151. I should date this to the first half of 419. Cf. D. de Bruyne's remark (*RB* 17, 1910, 7) that in it 'la douleur semble la plus vive ...'.
[26] *Letter* 143. This again belongs to 419, for Jerome's grief for Eustochium is still fresh. It may have been written in spring and carried by the same presbyter Innocentius who bore *Letter* 153 (see below) to Pope Boniface, and who seems to have travelled via Africa.
[27] *Letter* 153. As Boniface would scarcely have formally announced his election before its official ratification, this probably dates from spring or early summer 419.

his connexion with Eustochium and her family had evidently been much closer and warmer. It was natural that, once his position was assured, he should hasten to inform these friends of his at Bethlehem, the more so as they formed an important outpost of Latin Christianity in the east; but his writing to Jerome was also significant as a token of the prestige he now enjoyed in Rome. In his reply, while congratulating the pope, Jerome describes how overjoyed Eustochium would have been had she lived to know that her spiritual father had been promoted to the apostolic see. With a pathetic touch he adds that he alone is now responsible for young Paula, whom Boniface had known in her infancy: only the Lord knows whether he will be able to shoulder the burden. Then, in a postscript of extraordinary vivacity, he urges the new pontiff to exert himself energetically against the Pelagians. 'Let the heretics know you as a foe to their perfidy, and let them hate you.' He must be ruthless against the bishops who had come out in support of Pelagius.

The letter to Donatus[28] ends with personal greetings to Marius Mercator, a disciple of Augustine and one of Pelagius's most determined critics; even so Jerome exhorts him to show utter loathing for the heresy. It also contains greetings to five otherwise unknown persons who had narrowly escaped being ensnared by it. Until this note was discovered,[29] no one suspected that Jerome so much as knew Mercator, much less was on such cordial terms with him as his language suggests. His mention of the five others, his 'comrades in the Lord' (as he calls them), is eloquent of the extent and variety of his friendships right to the end—eloquent, too, of the yawning gaps in our knowledge of him. But the real interest of the letter lies elsewhere. Donatus was apparently worried by Pope Boniface's indecisiveness and leniency towards the Pelagians; he was afraid that any change of heart they might affect was not sincere. Jerome expresses full agreement on this point; he himself is resolved never to trust their recantations, for he knows that their hearts can never be cleansed. He seeks to reassure Donatus about the pope's attitude. If at the start of his reign he has taken a soft line, this is through his charitable desire to save the misguided wretches. Jerome is convinced, however, that 'he will destroy them root and branch by the spirit of Christ'. Then he spells out his own policy uncompromisingly: 'With these heretics we should put into practice that programme laid down by David, "I spent the mornings destroying all the

[28] *Letter* 154. It is unlikely that Donatus wrote to Jerome voicing his anxiety about Boniface's leniency until the pope had been formally in office for some weeks at least. Thus the letter is likely to be somewhat later than *Letter* 153; at earliest it belongs to autumn 419, and it might be as late as early 420. Cavallera's argument (II, 58 f.) that they are contemporary, Boniface's postscript being an afterthought instigated by Donatus's warning, seems forced. This letter (see below) is a key one for dating Jerome's death. If the argument that it is posterior to *Letter* 153 is accepted, Jerome is unlikely to have died (as Cavallera wished to show) on 30 Sept. 419.

[29] Cf. D. de Bruyne, 'Quelques lettres inédits de saint Jérôme', RB 27 (1910), 1–11.

sinners of the land.'[30] They must be wiped out and spiritually slaughtered. They must be cut to pieces with Christ's sword, for neither plasters nor soothing medicaments can enable them to recover sound health.'

(iv)

With this ferocious but characteristic outburst of fanatical intolerance Jerome disappears from our view. He may have written further letters, but if so they have been lost; and no other record of him survives. The correspondence we have been studying portrays him as an ageing and broken man, still vigilant for what he considered to be the true faith, still able to pen a trenchant sentence or paragraph, but prostrated by repeated illnesses and conscious of diminishing physical and mental powers. In his *Chronicle* Prosper of Aquitaine records[31] that he died on 30 September 420 'in the ninety-first year of his age'. Prosper was frequently inaccurate, and plainly slipped up in this estimate of Jerome's age. If the *Chronicle* was correct in placing his birth in 331 (before 30 September), he was in fact in his ninetieth year when he died.[32] A biography compiled, not by a contemporary (such as Prosper was), but by an unknown writer somewhere between the sixth and the eighth centuries agrees about the 30 September, but fixes his death a year earlier, in 419.[33] Some modern students have preferred this. Their chief ground is the long interval, a year or more, which, if Prosper's dating is accepted, they infer must have elapsed between Jerome's last letters and his death, an interval which they find inexplicable since, for all his complaints of age and sickness, these last letters radiate verve and pungency.[34] But the gap need not have been inordinately long. The letter to Donatus, which they make contemporary with that to Pope Boniface, is much more naturally placed after it,[35] possibly quite late in 419 or even early in 420. Further, even if we assume that Jerome wrote nothing more (an assumption which needs to be justified), there is nothing improbable or extraordinary in an old man stricken with sickness and growing enfeeblement lingering on for a protracted period.

While certainty is out of the question, there seems no solid reason for discarding the date 420. When Augustine died at Hippo almost exactly

[30] Ps. 101, 8. Jerome follows the LXX 'I was destroying' rather than the Hebrew 'I shall destroy'.

[31] *Epitoma chronicon* 1274 (MGH *auct. ant.* ix, 469).

[32] We note (see below p. 337. n. 1) that P. Hamblenne has made a valiant attempt (*Latomus* 28, 1969, 1113) to eliminate Prosper's apparent slip by arguing, on the basis of the reading of one of the MSS, that he really placed Jerome's birth in 330.

[33] *Hieronymus noster* (PL 22, 184). For a discussion of the date of this life see Cavallera II, 137–40.

[34] See esp. Cavallera II, 63.

[35] See note 28 above.

ten years later, his friend and future biographer, Possidius, was in his monastery, and later prepared an impressive eye-witness account of the closing scene of his life;[36] but no one performed a like service for Jerome. Legend was soon to weave picturesque, edifying stories around his last hours, but we are in fact completely ignorant of the circumstances of his death. He was buried, as he had himself arranged, in one of the underground grottoes beneath the north aisle of the Church of the Nativity, close to the two women, Paula and Eustochium, whose lives had been so strangely intertwined with his.[37] Only a few yards away, directly connected by a subterranean passage, was the larger grotto in which the infant Jesus, the object of his and their intense devotion, was believed to have been born. An Italian pilgrim who visited Bethlehem a century and a half later noted[38] that 'at the very entrance of the cave the priest Jerome had an inscription carved on the natural rock and made for himself the tomb in which he is laid'.

[36] *Vita Augustini* 29–31.

[37] For the position of his grave see R. W. Hamilton, *The Church of the Nativity, Bethlehem* (Jerusalem, 1947), 90; B. Bagatti, *Gli antichi edifici sacri di Betlemme* (Jerusalem, 1952), 137; also the detailed plans in both volumes.

[38] *Antonini Placentini itinerarium* 29 (in the older recension provided by codices G and R) (*CCL* 175, 143). The author of this itinerary from Milan to the Holy Land is not, as the title suggests, the early fourth-century martyr Antoninus of Piacenza, but an anonymous member of a party of pilgrims from that city who made the journey *c.* 570 (see esp. the edition of J. Gildmeister, Berlin, 1889).

XXVIII

Epilogue

For most of his adult life Jerome had been the focus of bitter controversy, as passionately detested in some circles as loved and admired in others. By the time he died the suspicion and hostility he aroused had begun to die down, and for the next thousand years and more a crescendo of adulation was to surround him.

Apocryphal lives extolling his sanctity, even his miracles, were quick to appear, and in the eighth century he was to be acclaimed, along with Ambrose, Augustine, and Gregory the Great, as one of the four Doctors of the Church.[1] In the middle ages his works were eagerly copied, read, and pillaged; while towards the end of the thirteenth century the clergy of Santa Maria Maggiore, at Rome, were to persuade the public, perhaps themselves too, that his remains had been transported from Bethlehem to Italy, and could be venerated close to certain presumed fragments of the Saviour's crib.[2] At the renaissance the elegance of his style, his seemingly encyclopaedic learning, and his success at putting classical culture to the service of Christianity, were to captivate humanist scholars. Erasmus in particular was to fall under the spell of the Christian Cicero, finding him more congenial than Augustine, and was to publish the first collected edition of his writings.[3] He was also, from the thirteenth to the eighteenth centuries, to inspire the brushes of great artists as no other early Christian figure. These portraits, presenting him (often accompanied by a docile lion)[4] as a cardinal in red hat and mantle, as an emaciated penitent in the

---

[1] This was formally ratified by Pope Boniface VIII on 20 Sept. 1295: see *Corpus iuris canonici* II, 1059 (ed. E. Friedburg, Leipzig, 1879–81). The original number four (the list was later to be greatly expanded) was chosen so that the Doctors could match the Evangelists.

[2] The story of their alleged translation, in response to a visionary appearance of Jerome himself, is set out by J. Stilting in *Acta Sanctorum* XLVI, Sept. VIII, 636 (Antwerp, 1762); it is reprinted in *PL* 22, 237–40. Stilting also provides a discussion of its date, veracity, etc. on pp. 635–49.

[3] In nine volumes (Basle, 1516). For Erasmus's great admiration for Jerome see the prefaces to these as well as the *Epistula nuncupatoria*: also *Letters* 138 and 141 (Allen). For his preference for him to Augustine cf. *Letter* 844 (to John Eck: 1518). But the influence of Augustine on Erasmus should not be underrated: see Ch. Béné, *Érasme et saint Augustin* (Geneva, 1969).

[4] The story of how he healed a lion by removing a thorn from its paw, and how it thereafter became his faithful companion, appears first in the anonymous *Vita* 'Plerosque nimirum' (after 570: *PL* 22, 209–12). Many (cf. J. Stilting, op. cit., 661 f.) suspect that it is a borrowing from the legend of St Gerasimus of Palestine (cf. John Moschus, *Pratum spirituale* 107). Cavallera's criticism of the theory (II, 141 f.) is not wholly convincing.

desert, as a scholar in his study, as a dying man receiving last communion, are as numerous as they are varied in motif.[5]

In differing degrees these posthumous tributes distort the reality. Jerome was of course never a cardinal; the representation of him as one was an absurd, and anachronistic,[6] blowing up of his brief secretarial service with Pope Damasus. His sojourn in the desert of Chalcis, such a favourite theme of artists, was a short, highly untypical episode in a mainly bookish career. A talkative man with a craving for company (especially where his influence was accepted), he was much more at home in Evagrius's mansion, in the salons of rich, devout ladies, in his monastery dictating to stenographers, supervising assistance to pilgrims or refugees, or giving addresses to the local congregation. Never was a soubriquet less fitly chosen than 'the solitary of Bethlehem'. Even the description of him as a Doctor of the Church needs qualification. Insofar as it suggests a creative theologian grappling with, and seeking to elucidate, the problems of Christian belief, it was wide of the mark. In contrast to Augustine, Jerome had neither the aptitude nor the inclination for adventurous thinking.[7] Suspicious of novelties and abhorring heresies, he preferred the straight and narrow path marked out by authority, best of all by the see of Rome. Where he abundantly deserved the title was, first, as the articulate spokesman and pugnacious defender of popular Catholicism, and, secondly, as a translator and expositor of Scripture. Although his exegesis was largely derivative and biased in favour of an allegorism which is now unfashionable, his Vulgate Bible and his great series of commentaries rendered an incalculable service to western Christendom.[8]

There can be no gainsaying Jerome's learning; he was the best equipped Christian scholar of his day, and for centuries to come. It is a pity that his vanity made him claim to be even more widely read than he was, and that his tendency to rush work made him slipshod and careless. But when it came to the crunch, as in his decision to go back to 'the Hebrew verity',

[5] See *Bibliotheca sanctorum* (Rome, 1965) VI, 1132–7 for a useful survey of his iconography.

[6] While the title 'cardinal' became current during the barbarian invasions of western Europe, especially in the sixth century, and designated a bishop whose see had been overwhelmed and who had been translated to a vacant see, it was only in the eleventh century that the Sacred College at Rome took institutional form, the Roman cardinals becoming the principal counsellors and assistants of the popes and (from 1059) papal electors. Cf. esp. H. W. Klewitz, 'Die Entstehung des Kardinalkollegiums', *Zeitschrift der Savigny-Stiftung für Rechtsgeschichte* 25 (1936), 115–21; also M. Andrieu, 'L'origine du titre de cardinal dans l'église romaine', *Miscellanea G. Mercati* V, 113–44, esp. 114–23 (*Studi e Testi* 125).

[7] Cf. A Harnack's remark (*Lehrbuch der Dogmengeschichte*, 3rd ed., 1897: III, 27) that 'man in einer Dogmengeschichte doch von ihm schweigen kann'. He added that the ascription of the title to Jerome might be a compliment to the man, but scarcely to his church.

[8] Described by the Council of Trent as 'doctor maximus in sacris scripturis explanandis', he has been consistently held up in the Roman Catholic church as a model to exegetes: cf., e.g., the encyclicals *Spiritus Paraclitus* (Benedict XV: 15 Sept. 1920) and *Divino afflante Spiritu* (Pius XII: 30 Sept. 1943).

his scholarly instinct triumphed, at no little cost to himself. Nor should we underrate his contribution to the establishment of monasticism as a major expression of Christian life and culture in Europe. From the institutional angle younger contemporaries, like Augustine and John Cassian, played a more constructive role; but Jerome's impact through his personal example, his letters of advice, his ferocious attacks on critics of the movement, his translation of the Egyptian rules, was impressive. Along with this his influence on Latin asceticism, as on the Mariology of the western church, was far-reaching. At the heart of his teaching lay the conviction that chastity was the quintessence of the gospel message, and that its supreme exemplification and proof was Mary, the virgin mother of the virgin Saviour. This complex of beliefs was to remain a central bastion of Catholic spirituality in the west, and Jerome was one of its chief architects. Perhaps this in part explains why Catholic students have in the past tended to overlook or play down the personal shortcomings and extravagances of so doughty a champion.

It would be a mistake, however, to assess Jerome's significance in exclusively ecclesiastical terms. As well as a churchman he was a man of letters, and his literary achievement was one which even those least sympathetic to his interpretation of Christianity could not begrudge him. It was all the more remarkable because he was for years painfully embarrassed by what he took to be the incompatibility between his ascetic ideals and the pagan culture on which he had been nurtured, and never succeeded in entirely resolving the conflict. Nevertheless the fact stands out that, at a time when the western empire was crumbling, he emerged as one of the greatest of Latin stylists, trained in the rhetoric of the schools but adapting it to Christian purposes. As a translator, whether of the Greek theological writings with which he enriched the west or of the Bible, he was a master *sans pareil*. Whatever genre he took in hand—satire, letter-writing, polemical pamphlets, romantic lives of desert heroes, even Scripture commentaries—he was supreme as a literary craftsman, deploying the Latin language with an expertise and a flexibility, and a sense of colour and cadence, which recalled, and sometimes surpassed, the giants of the classical era. The renaissance humanists were quick to recognise this, but since their day until quite recently scant justice has been done to him in this regard.

As a man Jerome presents a fascinating puzzle. None of the famous figures of Christian antiquity known to us had such a complex, curiously ambivalent personality. Far cleverer and more versatile than Rufinus, more learned and acute than Augustine, he lacked the balance and solidity of the one, the nobility and generosity of the other. His affection for his friends, while they were his friends, was unstinted though possessive; once they ceased to be his friends, he could pursue them with a rancour and spitefulness which still dismay.[9] Warm-hearted, kind to the poor and the distressed, easily reduced to tears by their sufferings,[10] he was also inordinately vain and petty, jealous of rivals, morbidly sensitive and irascible, hag-ridden by imaginary fears. There can be no doubt of the reality of his conversion, or of his passionate devotion to Christ and the world-renouncing asceticism he believed to be inculcated by the gospel; but if this burning commitment was the driving-force of his life, the forms in which it found an outlet were often strange, sometimes repellent. Some of these contradictions may have had their roots in the ill-health which dogged him, or in his troubled awareness of his sensual nature; others we should probably trace to more fundamental flaws of character which we can only surmise. The deeper springs of his psychology elude us, and for all his readiness to talk about himself there is an unsolved enigma about the real Jerome.[11]

---

[9] One recalls the oft-quoted comment of Le Nain de Tillemont, *Mémoires pour servir a l'histoire ecclésiastique des six premiers siècles* (Paris, 1707), t. xii, 2: 'Quiconque l'a eu pour adversaire a presque toujours esté le dernier des hommes.'

[10] For an example cf. his deeply felt, anguished descriptions of the refugees flocking to the Holy Land after the sack of Rome in *Comm. on Ezekiel* iii prol.; vii prol. (*CCL* 75: 79–80; 239–40).

[11] For one of the most suggestive and penetrating studies of Jerome's personality, based on his self-disclosures in his iii prefaces, see Ch. Favez, 'Saint Jérôme peint par lui-même', *Latomus* 16 (1957), 655–71; 17 (1958), 81–96; 303–16.

APPENDIX

The Date of Jerome's Birth

Prosper of Aquitaine records that Jerome was born in the consulship of Bassus and Ablavius, i.e. in 331. He later notes that he died in 420, remarking (with a curious slip) that he was in the ninety-first year of his age.[1] Early tradition agreed that he was 'about ninety' when he died.[2] In harmony with this Augustine, writing just after his death, speaks of him as having lived 'to decrepit old age', while in 419 Jerome himself laments that he has been 'worn out by protracted age'.[3]

The birth-date proposed by Prosper receives support from at least three directions. First, the correspondence which Jerome and Augustine, who was born in 354, were to exchange in later life presupposes that they were widely separated in age, indeed belonged to different generations. Augustine, for example, when sixty-one and already (as he confesses) an old man, salutes Jerome as 'greatly senior to myself'. Jerome, similarly, compares his relationship to Augustine to that of a father to a son, or an elderly veteran to a young man.[4] Secondly, Jerome's description of himself as 'an old man' ('senex' and equivalents) dates, with one exception which can be easily explained, from 396, when, on Prosper's reckoning, he was in his middle sixties. This accords with his normal usage of these terms in contexts unrelated to himself. After 400 he employs progressively stronger language ('extreme old age', 'well-nigh decrepit', etc.) which would most naturally fit a man in his seventies or eighties.[5] Thirdly, one or two historical happenings which the elderly Jerome records as having occurred in his 'infancy' seem to date from the 330s or early 340s, the most striking of these being the meeting in Alexandria in 338 of

[1] *Epitoma chronicon* (MGH *auct. ant.* ix, 451 and 469). P. Hamblenne (art. cit. below, 1113) seeks to eliminate the inconsistency by arguing, on the basis of the reading of V, the most ancient of the MSS, that Prosper in fact dated Jerome's birth in 330.

[2] Gennadius, *De vir. ill.* prol.; Marcellinus, *Chron.* 5 (MGH *auct. ant.* xi, 63). According to Th. Mommsen (ad loc.), the latter is an expansion of Gennadius.

[3] Augustine, *C. Iul. Pel.* 1, 34; Jerome, *Letter* 154, 3.

[4] Augustine, *Ep.* 166, 1 (date 415); Jerome, *Letters* 105, 5; 122, 2.

[5] For an analysis both of Jerome's general use of 'senex' etc. and of his application of these terms to himself, see P. Hamblenne, 'La longévité de Jérôme', *Latomus* 28 (1969), 1087–91; 1096–1111. In his *Life of Malchus* 10, written in 386/7 when he was fifty-five or so, Jerome speaks of himself as 'senex', but that was to make a rhetorical contrast.

Athanasius, Antony, the reputed founder of Egyptian anchoritism, and the blind biblical scholar Didymus.[6]

In spite of this convergent testimony the great majority of scholars this century have rejected Prosper's dating.[7] What has chiefly aroused their scepticism is the impossibility of reconciling it with another, even more celebrated reminiscence of Jerome's, viz. that when he was 'still a boy' at his grammar school the totally unexpected death of Julian the Apostate was suddenly announced, and a pagan bystander exclaimed that this showed that, so far from being long-suffering, the Christians' God was an exceedingly swift avenger.[8] As Julian died of wounds in June 363, Jerome must on Prosper's computation have been thirty-two—and still a schoolboy! Their doubts have been reinforced by Jerome's habit of describing himself as having been 'a young man' ('adolescens', 'iuvenis', etc.) at times when, assuming he was born in 331, he was in his thirties, forties, or even fifties. On the same reckoning his younger brother Paulinian, whom we know to have been about 30 in 394, must have been some thirty-three years his junior. These incongruities would be smoothed out, in particular Jerome could plausibly have been still at school in 363, if only he were a dozen or more years younger than Prosper suggests. Hence there has been almost unanimous agreement to place his birth in the 340s, preferably in 347, which would make him just sixteen in 363. Prosper, it has been argued, frequently made mistakes about dates,[9] and the wide discrepancy of age implied by the Jerome-Augustine correspondence can be discounted. After all, the two men never set eyes on each other. Jerome, moreover, both was morbidly preoccupied with his age, and had a controversial interest in impressing on Augustine that he was greatly his senior and therefore entitled to deference.

Despite the support it has attracted, this artificially constructed chronology is unconvincing. The debate is complex, but it is sufficient to single out two salient points. First, the unmistakable implications of the letters exchanged by Jerome and Augustine cannot be brushed aside. While Augustine never met Jerome, he had received a full and lifelike description of him from his friend Alypius, who had stayed with Jerome before the correspondence began.[10] Jerome was in any case a renowned figure at the time, visited by scores of people; his age must have been common

---

[6] *Letter* 68, 2. Cavallera (II, 4) dates this meeting to 355. P. Hamblenne (art. cit., 1103 f.) effectively criticises this date, but himself gives either between 335 and 337 or between 339 and 346. For the date August 338, see E. Schwartz, *Gesammelte Schriften* (Berlin, 1959) 3, 286 f. This visit of Antony to Alexandria is the one described by Athanasius in *Vita Ant.* 69–71.

[7] So, e.g., Grützmacher I, 45–50, and (esp.) Cavallera II, 3–12.

[8] *Comm. on Habbakuk* 3, 14 (*CCL* 76A: 660).

[9] For a lengthy list of mistakes by Prosper see L. Valentin, *Saint Prosper d'Aquitaine* (Toulouse, 1900), 430–5. Cf. also Th. Mommsen's remarks in MGH *auct. ant.* ix, 348; 351.

[10] Augustine, *Ep.* 28, 1 (*Letter* 56, 1 in Jerome's correspondence: date 394/5).

knowledge. Secondly, a rigorous analysis of Jerome's use of the terms denoting the successive stages of life reveals that, while (leaving out references to himself) he consistently restricted 'old man' and equivalent expressions to people of sixty or over, he was surprisingly flexible, by modern standards, in his employment of 'young man' and its equivalents. For example, while he could use 'adolescens' ('young man') and its cognates in a strict sense to designate a man of thirty-three or less, he could on occasion use them as synonymous with 'iuvenis', in effect covering the whole span from boyhood to old age. In the light of this analysis Jerome's application of 'young man' to himself, no less than of 'old man', accords much better with his birth in 331 than in 347.

Indeed, with one single exception, all the evidence bearing on the question strongly favours Prosper's date, and much of it (especially his references to himself as an 'old man') would be reduced to nonsense by the acceptance of the revised date.[11] That single exception, of course, is Jerome's reminiscence of the news-flash of Julian's death. If taken at its face value, it certainly presents an awkward obstacle to the traditional date, but the fact that it stands alone makes one wonder whether it is as reliable as it looks. It is possible that Jerome, looking back when he was about sixty, mistakenly attributed to his schooldays an incident which in fact occurred in his early manhood. Alternatively, since his object in recording it was to highlight the pagan's comment, he may have sought to give it an enhanced authenticity by suggesting that he had been present when it was made.[12] Whatever the explanation, however, the reminiscence cannot by itself warrant our abandoning the date indicated by Prosper and supported by the bulk of the evidence at our disposal.

---

[11] Thus he speaks of himself as having been white-haired in 386 (*Letter* 84, 3), and as being a 'senex' about the same time (*Life of Malchus* 10), when according to Cavallera and others he was scarcely forty. For an exhaustive and convincing discussion, to which I am much indebted, see P. Hamblenne's article.

[12] For similar discussions of this difficult text see P. Peeters, *Anal. Boll.* 42 (1924), 183 f. (in a review of Cavallera's book); P. Hamblenne, art. cit., 1099 f.

Index

341

Index

INDEX

INDEX